Soviet Communism
and the Socialist Vision

NEW POLITICS BOOKS INCLUDE:

NP1 Soviet Communism & the Socialist Vision
NP2 Autocracy and Insurgency in Organized Labor

Series Editor: Julius Jacobson

Soviet Communism and the Socialist Vision

edited by

Julius Jacobson

transaction books
New Brunswick, New Jersey
Distributed by E.P. Dutton & Co.

Contents

Introduction

Julius Jacobson

In the more than 120 years since Marx and Engels heralded the death throes of capitalism, history has provided but two instances of successful proletarian revolts: the Paris Commune of 1871 and the Russian Revolution of October 1917. The Commune survived but a matter of months, coming to final rest on the blood-spattered Murs des Federees. The Russian workers' state had a longevity of several years before it came to its final rest in the dungeons of the Lubyanka and the slave labor camps that cemented the Stalinist system with the mortar of terror and death. While the Commune collapsed largely under the weight of armed counterrevolution, the Russian Revolution was overwhelmed less directly by military resistance than by internal decay born of a host of disadvantageous circumstances. Russia was technologically backward to begin with and this liability for the new Soviet power was aggravated by three years of war preceding the Revolution and an economy further ravaged by three years of civil war after the Revolution. Even more devastating for Russian socialism than its shattered economy was that the anticipated revolution in the West, on which the fate of the Russian Revolution always hinged, was, by 1921, clearly no longer on the order of the day. These major historical factors devitalized the Revolution, depleting it of economic, physical and moral reserves. As the socialist character of the Russian state was eroded, the void that would otherwise have been left by an exhausted and demoralized proletariat was being filled by an emerging, new counterrevolutionary class, which consolidated its power in the wake of a famine (for which it was largely responsible) and through an all-pervasive terror.

There are a number of significant differences between the defeat of the Communards and the collapse of the Russian Revolution. In terms of human suffering, the cruelty evinced by Thiers and his legions was immense; but the barbarism with which Stalin destroyed millions was without precedent. In social terms, the consequences of the two defeats were qualitatively more pronounced in their dissimilarity. The most relevant difference is that following the fall of the Commune, socialism proved its recuperative powers in France and throughout Europe in the nearly 50 years from the fall of the Commune to the Soviet conquest of power. The aftermath of the Russian defeat was altogether different and totally tragic. In the 50 years between the destruction of proletarian democracy in Russia and today, revolutionary socialism (i.e., Marxism) has been unable to establish itself as a significant organized force; not in Russia or in Eastern Europe, not in Western Europe or in the Western hemisphere. This near vacuum is the terrible legacy of Stalinism and the counterrevolution which destroyed a revolution in the name of its victims. The greater the tempo of its repression of socialism, the more tightly Stalinism wrapped itself in the garments of socialist ideology. Democracy was denied in the name of "democratic centralism," Lenin's collaborators liquidated in the name of Leninism, weaker nations overrun in the name of self-determination, a modus vivendi with Nazis arrived at under the banner of internationalism, as totalitarian terror became "socialist legality." Thus was socialism destroyed in its own name. And effectively so, organizationally and ideologically.

Organizationally, the retrospective judgment can be fairly made that by the middle twenties not a single Communist party retained, in any basic sense, committed to the ideological passions that moved a Marx, a Luxemburg or a Lenin. Before the end of that decade until the death of Stalin, every Communist party functioned as an arm of Russia's ruling class. *Ideologically*, the Russian rulers succeeded in convincing their own followers and the world at large that Russia was a socialist state (or at least embodied some form of socialism) and that Stalinist dogma was socialist thought (or at least a variant of socialist doctrine). As a result, workers moved by radical impulses, particularly in Western Europe, often looked to Russia as a fraternal land of socialism still led by the party of Lenin. The bourgeoisie was only too pleased to promote the myth of Stalinism as socialism since it became

Stalinism also proved attractive to many intellectuals partly because it was a power, an *anticapitalist* power that spoke in the name of socialism. They, in turn, served to debase further the meaning of socialism by lending their skills to rationalizing and justifying Stalinist terror. Indeed, the bulk of material turned out by American and European Communist party and fellow-travelling intellectuals was little more than overt homage to Stalin and glorification of the purges. Those on the socialist left who maintained their allegiance to elementary socialist notions of freedom and democracy and understood the reactionary content of Stalinism were reduced to a small, embattled group looked upon as starry-eyed idealists by some and as fascist mad dogs by others.

But, it might be said — and is — that this is all in the past: Stalin is no longer revered even in the Communist world, everyone knows that the Moscow Trials were frameups and so forth. All true perhaps, but the legacy of Stalinism survives.

Shortly after Stalin's death the East German workers revolted. The fissures that always existed in Communist Russia gradually opened and widened with Khrushchev's revelations at the Twentieth Congress. There were massive upheavals in Poland in 1956, and later that year the entire Hungarian people rose up in an effort to cast off the yoke of Russian imperialism and create a free socialist nation. Disarray and revolt within Russia and within its empire during these three tumultuous years encouraged the view that the Soviet system was in its final death agony. It was a tragically mistaken forecast. But even though Stalinism survived these trials in Eastern Europe and Russia, it seemed that Communism as an ideological force would be irreparably damaged in the Western world. Surely, when Stalin's barbarism was laid bare by Khrushchev, and Khrushchev's "socialism" stripped of all pretenses by the Hungarian Revolution, the conditions were ripe for a socialist renaissance. But again, our optimism proved premature.

At the very least, many American socialists found some comfort in the thought that any new radical movement that might emerge from the ferment among the young, already visible in the late 1950s, would be free of illusions about the nature of Stalinist countries.[1]

Born when the hydrogen bomb was being perfected, reaching adolescence when black children were murdered in their own churches and coming of age in the shadow of America's criminal war in Vietnam, young people today display a marvelously low level of tolerance for the absurdities, the hypocrisy, the violence of "the American way." They cannot be mollified or seduced by patriotic clichés or the promise of affluence. Their anger and hostility toward the establishment is a deeply rooted cultural and social phenomenon expressed in antiwar demonstrations, long hair, passive resistance, confrontations, communes and drugs. There is, on the whole, far more to admire than to decry in the attitudes of the young.

1. In these brief introductory remarks as well as in many of the following essays, the terms Stalinist and Communist are used interchangeably. Admittedly, this can be misleading unless it is understood that the term Stalinism is intended to define a social category and not necessarily a degree of terror paralleling the terror of Stalin. Modern Russia, the countries of Eastern Europe, Cuba, North Korea, North Vietnam, Yugoslavia, Albania and China are all Stalinist countries; not in the sense that they match Stalin's total terror (though this may have been the case, at least episodically, in China) but because they share in common certain basic totalitarian characteristics with each other and with Stalin's Russia: the ownership and control of the means of production by a state which in turn is controlled by a single ruling party, and whose power is dependent on their ability to prevent the emergence of democratic institutions. Understood as such, Stalinism did not retreat with Stalin's death but in varied forms has extended its authority over the lives of millions of new victims.

Yet, things are said — and not said — by them that do give one pause. We need mention only one: their relative silence — with few exceptions — about the injustices and inhumanity of the Communist world. Among the articulate spokesmen of the militant young, this writer does not know of one who has taken a strong and uncompromising position against all forms of totalitarianism. When Russian tanks rolled into Prague in 1968 with the immediate blessings of Fidel Castro and Ho Chi Minh there was merely a token protest in this country instead of the mass demonstrations that should have been organized in front of every Russian Embassy and Consulate. For the struggle of the Czech youth and America's alienated young is inseparable: for freedom, for democracy, for social justice. When, only yesterday, Polish workers fought their Party bosses there was not even the dim protest of 1968. And today, when Russian dissidents young and old display such moving courage in their quest for freedom, only to suffer confinement to lunatic asylums, and corrective labor camps, or when the Russian government reveals itself as the most anti-Semitic of any contemporary regime, "the movement" hardly utters an audible protest.

This silence does not stem, as some would have us believe, from the fact that Poland and Czechoslovakia are distant lands whose fate does not impinge on American life. That, at best, is a rationalization. Instead, many young activists feel that "the enemy of my enemy is my friend" — or, at least, he is not my enemy. Hence, since American imperialism is my enemy and Communist regimes are the enemy of American imperialism, these regimes are not my enemy. It is a naive, illogical and dangerous notion. A reasonable extension of such faulty logic would make intimates of George Wallace and Eldridge Cleaver, since both are opponents of Nixon, and give credence to the idea that Hitler and Trotsky may have been in league, after all, since both were enemies of Stalin. Yet, the failing is more than a matter of faulty logic. It is also a failure of consciousness and understanding, a failure which is one of the persisting historic liabilities of Stalinism. The concept and vision of socialism have been so thoroughly abused and corrupted by Stalinism that the illusion continues

— after the Twentieth Congress, after Hungary, Poland, Czechloslovakia — that Stalinism remains a form of socialism. Thus we have the sad spectacle of young radicals applauding Mao and memorizing passages from that incredible melange of reactionary clichés, *The Little Red Book*, in part because of ignorance and in part because of indifference to the atrocities committed by the "Cultural Revolution." No less disturbing is the sight of young protesters demonstrating against American militarism and calling for "Power to the People" at the same time as they reverentially repeat Castro's odious dictum "Power comes from the barrel of a gun," apparently indifferent to the utter powerlessness of the Cuban masses.

Antitotalitarianism must be an essential feature of any political movement in this country if it is to earn the support of the American people. Not the anti-Communism of a Nixon or a Johnson, nor the anti-Communism of a politically reactionary labor leadership, and not the anti-Communism of sophisticated ex-radicals whose anti-Stalinist credentials are compromised by their pro-Western apologetics. Instead, the anti-Communism that is necessary flows ineluctably from the uncompromising and fundamental democratic aspirations of Marxism, and is imbued with opposition to capitalism and to those Communist societies that are anathema to socialism.

It is our hope that the essays in this book prove of interest and value to historians, scholars and students. No less important, we hope they serve to heighten and deepen the socialist consciousness of the radical young.

June 1971

Soviet Intellectual Opposition

Jacob S. Dreyer

Only during the past several years has the dissent movement in the Soviet Union begun to attract a significant amount of attention. Yet organized dissent in the USSR has existed since the end of World War II. The early postwar period was characterized by unrest among the population of annexed Western territories.[1] In order to subdue the militant nationalists of the western Ukraine and the Baltic states, the Kremlin occasionally had to engage its military units in large-scale operations against the Ukrainian or Latvian guerillas. A subsequent period of political purges coincided with the proliferation of short-lived opposition groups in urban centers and remote labor camp areas. From the scarce evidence available, one can infer that the opposition groups of this period belonged to opposite ends of the ideological spectrum. In the labor camps these groups were formed mainly by imprisoned members of different religious sects. In the large cities the founders of various opposition groups were frustrated Communists advocating a return to Leninist legality. Some of these ephemeral organizations, like "The

---

1. The following is based on "Samizdat 1. La voix de l'Opposition Communiste en U.R.S.S." (Paris, 1969).

Truth of Lenin's Work," "Workers' Opposition" and the "Lenin Group," even managed to issue political programs. However, the years 1945-1953 were hardly propitious for the development of a thriving opposition movement in Soviet Russia.

Three years before Khrushchev made his historic speech to the Twentieth Party Congress, the first of the inmates of the vast Stalinist prison system left the camps—as a result of an amnesty proclaimed by the new rulers three weeks after the tyrant's death.

Although only special categories of prisoners could benefit from the amnesty, it contained a clause which turned out to be of subsequent importance. The amnesty stipulated that the convictions of its beneficiaries be stricken from the criminal records and consequently allowed them to return to their homes. Many of them returned to large cities and began talking about the horrors of Stalinist camps, singing camp ballads, telling antiregime jokes. Though they did these things cautiously and within small circles of relatives and friends, the truth spread, revealing the bestialities perpetrated by the system. The army of released labor camp inmates was greatly increased in 1955, when tens of thousands of former Soviet servicemen were set free. (In 1945, 10 years at hard labor was a standard sentence for Soviet POWs, whom Stalin considered traitors, and who were therefore transferred from Nazi to Soviet concentration camps.)

At the same time the first signs of liberalization in the arts and letters became visible. Ilya Ehrenburg's "The Thaw" and Vera Panova's "The Seasons" were published and young Leningrad artists semi-openly exhibited their modernistic paintings. Even more important, the overwhelming feeling of fear was slowly vanishing. Then came the Twentieth Congress and dissemination of Khrushchev's revelations among Party and Komsomol members, reconciliation with Tito, mass rehabilitations, publication of Dudincev's novel, *Not by Bread Alone*, and Pasternak's poem, "The Dawn" (included later in *Dr. Zhivago)*, the Polish October and the Hungarian uprising. All these events had a profound impact on many segments of the Soviet population and rapidly radicalized groups of students, young artists and scientists in large Soviet cities. The late fifties witnessed the emergence of a new counterculture, easily attracting increasingly large numbers of adherents among the educated strata of Soviet youth. Several political-literary groups were formed, of which the best known is the "World Alliance of Supporters of Universal Disarmament."[2] Some of these groups were connected with underground journals. Several independent literary revues were also published in those years. The editors were young people who several years later became heroes and martyrs of the Soviet dissent movement: Alexander Ginzburg, who published *Syntaxis 1959*, Vladimir Osipov (Osipov was one of the founders of the "World Alliance"; he recently joined the neo-Slavophiles — a group whose *Weltanschaung* is colored by the ideas of Russian messianism), who was the editor of *Spiral 1960*, and later, together with Yuri Galanskov, published *Phoenix 1961*. All of them eventually ended up with severe sentences in labor camps.

At the beginning the groups were as a rule isolated from each other. It is very possible that the authorities' attempts at silencing the rebellious students led to the forging of links between various groups which suddenly became aware of their common goal and, especially, of their common fate. The authorities succeeded in driving student dissent even deeper underground; they did not succeed in eradicating it. The number of antiregime leaflets in clandestine circulation steadily increased. It was probably during the years 1957-1963 that the dissent movement broadened its social base and matured politically. New groups sprang up and were soon crushed by the KGB. Such was the plight of General Piotr Grigorenko's "Society for the Restoration of Leninism," disbanded in 1963, and the "Leningrad Communards" suppressed in 1965.

In September 1965, two young writers, Andrei Sinyavsky and Yuli Daniel, were arrested and charged with "agitation or propaganda carried out with the purpose of subverting or weakening the Soviet State." Sinyavsky's and Daniel's

2. *Russkaya Mysl* (Paris, April 20, 1968).

writings reached the West, where they were published under
the pseudonyms Abram Tertz and Nicolai Arzhak. In February 1966, the two writers were tried, found guilty as charged
and sentenced to seven and five years respectively at hard
labor. This date, February 1966, may be considered the beginning of the contemporary dissent movement in the Soviet
Union.

EMERGENCE OF THE DISSENT MOVEMENT

In early 1966 some of the conditions necessary for the
emergence of a dissent movement already existed. The trial
itself sparked a wave of protest against what the protesters
considered the rebirth of Stalinism. The crime with which the
two writers were charged, the wording of the verdict, the
conduct of the accused during and after the trial which was
held virtually *in camera* — all were reminiscent of the purges
of the early thirties. The initial protest against the Sinyavsky and Daniel trial generated a dissent movement over the
next several years, encompassing mainly students and young
intelligentsia, yet, as will be shown, attracting people of
various ages and diversified backgrounds. That young Soviet
intellectuals constitute the backbone of the dissent movement
in Russia cannot simply be explained by the "rebellious age"
factor. First, the young people found it impossible to identify
themselves intellectually, emotionally or morally with the
goals promoted by the Party bureaucracy. The youthful
spontaneity and enthusiasm of the twenties was a thing of
the past. Second, and more important, young people felt
aversion to the moral standards of the Party leaders and, for
that matter, to the standards of all those who were too cowardly to speak out against the criminal acts of the Stalin era,
even if they did not actively participate in them. Alienated
from their elders and unable to espouse the regime's cause,
some of those segments of the young generation who were
searching for intellectual fulfillment turned to an entirely
different culture — the culture of dissent.

It is very difficult to define what the dissent movement in
the USSR is. It is certainly not a structured illegal or semilegal political party, although over the last several years
organizations which may be properly called political parties

in embryonic stages have existed. The "All Russian Social-Christian Union for the Liberation of the People,"[3] disbanded in 1967, is an example. However, in most cases, these small groups remain isolated from each other unless they share more than just an overall opposition to the regime. If one assumes that a necessary attribute of a movement is the adoption, by the organizations or individuals comprising it, of an ideological platform, then it becomes possible to exclude from the present analysis those factions which are marginal or alien in relation to the mainstream of the Soviet dissent movement. An example of such a faction has already been mentioned: the "All Russian Social-Christian Union." An even more extreme example is the group of neo-fascists headed by the economist Fetisov.

As is clear from their socio-ideological treatise, *Slovo Natsii (The Word of the Nation),* Fetisov and his followers are admirers of strong rulers (especially Stalin), blindly nationalistic and, of course, fanatically anti-Semitic. Fetisov himself renounced his Party membership because of his disapproval of the Politburo's reluctance to accelerate re-Stalinization. Recent émigrés from Russia maintain that Fetisov has a number of supporters among the Central Committee members, and though he was harassed by the authorities several years ago, today he feels absolutely safe and is convinced of his rising influence among the top Party brass. The rift in ideology between people of Fetisov's persuasion, who oppose the regime from a fascist position, and the liberal mainstream of the dissent movement is obvious.

Less obvious is the classification of those groups which, although sharing the essential goals of this mainstream, such as achievement of more personal freedom, have political programs scarcely compatible ideologically with the position of those considered the spokesmen for the mainstream of Soviet dissent. The "Democrats of Russia, the Ukraine and the Baltic States" serve as an illustration. This group has to date issued three documents of a programmatic nature in which its position is made abundantly clear. These documents

---

3. *Posev,* First Special Issue (Frankfort-on-Main, 1969), p. 12.

contain statements and suggestions pertaining to civil liberties to which every liberal, East and West, could subscribe without hesitation. But in their enthusiastic eulogy of the capitalist system, carried to the extreme of declaring that "the struggle against capitalism is criminal and pointless,"[4] they most certainly remain at odds with the ideological preferences expressed by many prominent liberal dissidents, neo-Marxists and Christians alike.[5] There is no doubt, however, that the "Democrats" and lesser known groups of similar ideological inclination are potent allies of the mainstream of the Soviet dissent movement.

The problem of classification within the dissent movement of such fellow-travelers as the militant national or religious minorities is also complex. Usually the demands of these minorities are restricted to one specific issue. Crimean Tatars, for example, challenge the legality of the government's ban on their resettlement in the Crimea; the Baptists demand the authorities' compliance with the constitutional guarantee of freedom of faith; the Ukrainians demand the extension of their cultural autonomy and so forth. True, all such demands for the resolution of the specific demands of minority groups ultimately amount to the demand for stricter adherence to the principles of socialist legality and respect for human rights. In this respect the goals of Russian dissenters and minority militants coincide. Yet, the difference between the two groups in terms of the scope of demands is of crucial significance for our analysis. For instance, the militant Jews want to go to Israel and let the Soviet Union build its Communist future; the Russian dissidents' main concern is precisely the kind of environment in which this Communist

---

4. Programma Demokraticheskogo Dvizhenya Sovetskogo Soyuza (Program of the Democratic Movement of the Soviet Union) (Amsterdam, 1970).

5. Liberal Marxists' opposition to such a posture is obvious. There exists within the Soviet dissent movement a very strong current of Christian thought. Its eminent speakers (e.g., Levitin-Krasnov, priest Zheludkov) clearly state their preference, on ethical grounds, for a system in which private property of the means of production is abolished. The *Chronicle* disassociated itself from the "Democrats" program, very probably because of its wholesale denunciation of the socialist system as such.

future will be built; i.e., in an atmosphere of respect or contempt for human rights. Despite these differences, there is little doubt that the opposition of militant national or religious minorities to the regime's arbitrariness and inhumanity amplified the Soviet protest movement as a whole.

Our last attempt at narrowing the definition of the dissent movement will be the exclusion of intra-Party factions opposed to the present rulers, conspiratorial cliques, if any, within the government or Party apparatus of the various republics, interest groups composed of the highest ranking military or any other group of people which might have direct designs on power and would, under propitious circumstances, attempt to replace the present leadership.

We shall define the Soviet dissent (or protest) movement as an ideologically heterogeneous, loosely knit coalition of persons opposed to various aspects of Soviet domestic and, to a lesser extent, foreign policy. Despite its heterogeneity the movement forms a group in the sociological sense; it possesses "group self-consciousness, ascribed group status and a set of shared values."[6] The dissent movement's activities extend into areas of traditionally (though not necessarily legally) illegitimate or semilegitimate political activity. The demands of the various individuals who comprise the movement have a definite common denominator: more personal freedom and the rule of law. As to approval of the regime's stated long-term objective — establishment of Communist society — the movement lacks a common platform.

PROMULGATION OF *SAMIZDAT*

The Soviet dissent movement, being nonviolent, uses the written word as its main weapon. The dissidents have produced an impressive amount of material which has been typed and reproduced illegally in the Soviet Union. These manuscripts are circulated within small circles of students and among the creative and scientific intelligentsia, mainly in big cities and settlements around research centers and universities. This form of publication is called *samizdat* (roughly: self-publishing). *Samizdat* publications are charac-

6. Milton Lodge, "Groupism in the Soviet Union," in Frederic J. Fleron (ed.), *Communist Studies and the Social Sciences* (Chicago, 1969).

terized by an extreme variety of types and forms. They include at least three periodicals, of which the most remarkable and vital is the *Khronika tekushchikh sobytii (Chronicle of Current Events)* — a real organ of the dissent movement. We are obliged to the dissidents themselves for almost all we know about the protest activities in the Soviet Union. Against tremendous odds, they have been able effectively to spread word about their cause and their struggle.

In distinguishing the main currents within the movement and the issues they emphasize our analysis is based on accessible *samizdat* writings, from which various ideological positions can be inferred. Roughly speaking, within the Soviet dissent movement as we defined it, two basic approaches prevail: pragmatic and moralistic.[7] If dissent can be viewed as a form of "interest articulation with a normative content,"[8] the two schools of dissent can be classified according to their orientations in two broad areas: the Party's monopoly of power, and man versus the state. Both schools of dissent share in their rejection of the Party's claim to *de facto* unlimited power in the first area and the officially imposed principle of the Soviet citizen's unconditional obligation to authority in the second area. However, the two currents of dissent differ from each other as much as do the philosophical backgrounds, social bases and psychological motivations of their representatives.

The social base of the pragmatic school consists predominantly of natural scientists and members of the technical intelligentsia whose most outspoken representative is the academician, Andrei Sakharov, credited with a decisive contribution in the development of the Soviet H-bomb. This section of the Soviet scientific community became frustrated

---

7. Quite different taxonomies have been adopted by A. Amalrik, "Will the USSR Survive Until 1984?" *Survey* (Autumn, 1969), and by D. Pospielovsky, "The Monk. A New Samizdat Manuscript," *Radio Liberty Dispatch* (January 22, 1970). Similar classification to mine has been proposed by R. Tökés, "Authority and Dissent in Soviet Politics," Paper delivered at the 1971 Annual Meeting of the American Association for the Advancement of Slavic Studies, and by L. Feuer, "Intelligentsia in Opposition," *Problems of Communism* (November-December, 1970).

8. Tökés *op. cit.*

with the Party's persistence in promoting orthodox Marxism-Leninism as a panacea for the country's proliferating economic and social ills. They argue that the Soviet Union has attained a stage of development where the regime's totalitarian practices constitute stumbling blocks to further economic progress. In a letter to the ruling trio — Brezhnev, Kosygin and Podgorny — Sakharov and two of his colleagues — Roy Medvedev and Valerii Turchin — write:[9]

> What awaits our country if the course is not set toward democracy? A growing lag in relation to the capitalist countries.... increasing economic difficulties; a worsening relationship between the Party and the Government apparatus and the intelligentsia; the danger of lurches to the right and to the left....
>
> A shift to the right, i.e., the victory of trends toward harsh administration, the tightening of the screws...will aggravate these problems to the extreme and will lead the country into a tragic cul-de-sac....In a few years, perhaps, it will already be too late.

Sakharov and his friends formulate a number of specific demands:

> Organization of integrated production combines with a high degree of interdependence between production planning, technological progress, marketing and supplies....Scientific determination, after careful research, of the forms and extent of state control.
>
> Gradual implementation of the principle of allowing several candidates to stand for one post in elections for party and governmental bodies at all levels.
>
> Extension of the rights of Soviet (governmental) bodies [as opposed to Party Committees — JSD].

Sakharov leads the "reformist faction" of the pragmatic school, that is, basically he relies on the Soviet ruling elite's ultimate ability to think and behave rationally on the basis of long-term political considerations. This "faction" certainly does not find it advisable to replace the socialist economic and social system with a Western-type democracy. Thus, from a traditional point of view Sakharov and his friends should be classified as neo-Marxists. The emphasis on problems of the economy and technological progress also makes their approach toward the second issue — man versus state

9. *Radio Liberty Register* No. 360, (Munich, 1970).

— rationalistic rather than ethical in character. This did not prevent them from making proposals based on social and moral criteria. Their defense of oppressed national minorities in the USSR or their condemnation of the occupation of Czechoslovakia may serve as examples.

Sakharov's apprehensions and, to some extent, his proposed remedies are no doubt shared by some industrial managers. Some of these people regard liberalization solely as a practical economic imperative and they show even less concern than Sakharov for problems in the category of man versus state. Their attention is concentrated on the allocation and exercise of power. The best available example of a programmatic document emanating from the representatives of the Soviet managerial class is a pamphlet written by two Leningrad technocrats, Zorin and Alekseyev.[10] It deserves special consideration for its lucid analysis of the Soviet power structure. First, they talk, along Djilas' lines, about the New Class — the *nomenclatura* officials:

> The separation (of the Party bureaucracy from all other strata of the population) has found its expression in the concept of *nomenclatura*, in the establishment of lists of persons who have been screened, in whom the Party places the highest trust and who are entitled to responsible positions in the Party and State apparatus. It may happen that some responsible official is removed for transgressing the law or for mismanagement, but if we follow his further career, we inevitably find that he has been transferred to another job at about the same level....
>
> In other words, *nomenclatura* is as *inalienable** as capital in a bourgeois society. It serves as the legal basis for our system in much the same manner as does the law of private property under capitalism.

Then Zorin and Alekseyev say that the nomenclatured officials

> ...*collectively dispose, each according to his rank*...of all budgetary sums and the total surplus value created by the labor of the people. Here, *nomenclatura* emerges as a form of property. It is basically a single state-monopoly trust in which rank and post are equivalent to the ownership of an appropriate number of shares.

10. S. Zorin and N. Alekseyev, "Vremya ne zhdet" (Time Will Not Wait), *Posev*, (Frankfort-on-Main, 1970).

*   Emphasis here and in the following quotations is the author's own.

...under a system of state-owned economy, democratization would mean that the ruling *nomenclatura* is deprived of its property, which is transferred to the people.

Isn't Sakharov's more cautious "determination of the extent of state control" simply a euphemistic rephrasing of Zorin's and Alekseyev's statement? Yet they go much further in their demands than Sakharov's "faction." They contend that

> ...the State bureaucracy should not enjoy absolute power. We need: [implementation of the principles of] electivity and replaceability [of civil servants], [the right to] criticize governmental decisions....But this is possible only when there is political opposition, freedom [to form] parties and organizations, freedom of speech...these are the rudiments of any democracy, whereas the one-party system is a synonym for fascism.

Zorin and Alekseyev are also more categorical than Sakharov in their bleak predictions of the future, should things remain unchanged:

> ...censorship and concentration camps, economic chaos, stealing out of the workers' pockets, the threat of war and [the reign of] terror — *all this will remain so long as a voluntarist system of governing the country permits the leadership to proceed successfully toward its main goal — worldwide military supremacy.*

However, the authors do not assume that things *must* remain unchanged:

> What is capable of stopping them [the rulers]? Only consciousness, which is not yet present. What can influence them? Only fear for their own power. Once they encounter the threatening might of the people's indignation, they will abandon their insane course....
>
> Everyone must feel personal responsibility for his own country....Only passivity and gullibility are fatal, for they give the rulers the feeling of total impunity.
>
> Much more depends on ourselves than is apparent.

In Zorin and Alekseyev's pamphlet, the stress upon ethical aspects of the Soviet system is at best implicit, as it is in several other documents ascribed to the spokesmen of the Soviet technical intelligentsia. There are, however, technocrats for whom the set of problems of the man versus state type is more than just an addition to the criteria of developmental rationality. They judge the ethics of contemporary Soviet society on its own merits. Such a stand is adopted by a group of Estonian engineers in a reply [11] to Sakharov's earlier memorandum, "Progress, Coexistence & Intellectual Freedom." [12] They even criticize Sakharov for paying too much attention to the problems of economics and political structure, although they essentially agree with his assertion that the oppressiveness of the regime impedes further development. Still, for them, freedom is a moral category and as such has priority in their considerations. The Estonians are very much worried by the moral debasement of Soviet society.

> The new materialist ideology has been unable to substitute... the old [moral] values. A moral vacuum has been created, which has resulted in moral schizophrenia [permeating the] society. On the one hand, there is an ostentatious, superficial and hypocritical collectivist morality; on the other, a morality which is concealed, internal, basically greedy and egoistic. This has given birth to a society endowed with a superficial, mechanical solidarity, [which is] in reality erected on an individual who is alienated from this society, afraid of his neighbor and who feels insignificant and alone when faced with the huge machinery of State.

As to the antidote, it is interesting to note that even though the Estonian engineers reached essentially the same conclusions as Zorin and Alekseyev, they approached the social and political problems in quite a different way. In their judgement

> ...only a rise in the moral standards of our society, conscious civic activity, the awakening of the feeling of personal responsibility can offer resistance...to a bloody bacchanal....Our society must find...a new moral and philosophical doctrine.

The authors of this letter are obviously less convinced than Sakharov *et al.* of the leadership's willingness and ability to carry out any meaningful democratization process. Consequently, they prefer to appeal "to the foremost minds in our society: Create new social and moral values....Give us a program of action in case our pleas and hopes should prove to be in vain!"

PRAGMATIC DISSENTERS AND MORALISTIC DISSENTERS

As has already been said, the pragmatic school of Soviet dissent recruits its adherents mostly from the ranks of the

11. *Posev* (No. 1, 1969).

12. New York, 1968.

scientific and technical intelligentsia. The moralist trend finds its supporters among the young creative *(tvorcheskaya)* intelligentsia. Such a pattern seems logical in view of the differences in the professional training of the two groups and, as a result of this, the thinking habits, the techniques of analysis mastered, psychological motivations and, perhaps, unequal levels of sensitivity. Yet, exceptions to this pattern are numerous. Of the two schools of dissent, the moralist school, as a whole, has been more outspoken, more visible, more prolific in writing and has probably also attracted a larger number of active participants. This school's material is almost entirely confined to the problems of man versus state. The lip service it has been paying to the need for economic pragmatism is intended only as a tactical ruse to indicate commitment to the Party's developmental objectives. Recently, however, the "moralists" have apparently realized that their failure to pay due attention to the problems of economic progress and/or their inability to formulate appropriate demands in professionally meaningful and acceptable terms, virtually precludes them from ever influencing the leadership's political intentions. This realization, along with the pragmatists' slow shift toward moral issues, as exemplified by the Estonians' letter, has resulted in an acceleration of the convergence of the two schools.

The man versus state category, with which the moralist school has been traditionally concerned, encompasses the problems of socialist legality (with the closely related topic of the "cult of personality") and the complex area of human rights in a Communist society (to which a number of specific topics are again related, such as freedom of speech, artistic activity, religion, etc.). The emphasis on human rights is manifested in the inscription at the top of the title page of every issue of the *Chronicle of Current Events:* "The movement in defense of human rights in the Soviet Union continues." Thus, the Movement in Defense of Human Rights has become a synonym for the mainstream of the Soviet dissent movement. As was mentioned earlier, the upsurge of this movement was triggered by the Sinyavsky and Daniel trial in 1966. In the eyes of the originally small group of young intellectuals and students, the authorities' handling of the case was legally unjustified and morally reprehensible. This predetermined the two areas of the dissidents' challenge to the authorities: socialist legality and moral norms.

The dissidents' demands for strict compliance to Soviet laws were generated by the political trials of the mid-sixties, which gave rise to the fear of re-Stalinization, and, in particular, of the return to the practices of Stalinist "justice." In the trials of 1967-1968, veterans of the protest movement, Ginzburg, Galanskov, Khaustov, Kushev, Delone, Bukovsky, Brodsky and others, took the risks of even harsher sentences by openly challenging the legality of the court procedure and, even more, the legitimacy of the interpretation of the law which made such trials possible. Commenting on the Sinyavsky and Daniel trial, the editor and writer, Lydia Chukovskaya, in an open letter to Mikhail Sholokhov (who denounced the two condemned writers), said: "Literature does not come under the jurisdiction of criminal courts. Ideas should be combatted with ideas, not with labor camps and prisons." [13] In his final statement at his trial in 1967, Vladimir Bukovsky, charged with violation of public order for his participation in a small demonstration in defense of his imprisoned friends, challenged the very legitimacy of prosecuting him.

> I have here before me the text of the Soviet Constitution which says: "In accordance with the interest of the workers and with the aim of strengthening the socialist system, citizens of the USSR are guaranteed by law...the right of street demonstrations and processions."...it is not necessary to include such an article for demonstrations that are organized by the government; it is clear that no one will disperse these demonstrations. We need no freedom 'pro' if there is no freedom 'anti.' We know that protest demonstrations...are an inalienable right in all democratic states. [14]

What Bukovsky was indignant about was, of course, not only the authorities' intolerance of unauthorized demonstrations. In fact, he attacked the regime's tenet of "democracy — yes, but directed by the Party and the State," and pointed out

13. *The New York Times* (November 19, 1969).

14. Document No. 2, "In Quest of Justice", A. Brumberg, ed. (New York, 1970), p. 83.

that the leadership's refusal to permit the active participation of Soviet citizens in political life, as opposed to docile acquies- cence, is contradictory to Soviet law.

In the aftermath of Galenskov, Ginzburg et al. trial, Pavel Litvinov and Larissa Bogoraz-Daniel appealed to "everyone in whom conscience is alive and who have sufficient courage":

> This trial is a stain on the honor of our state and on the con- science of every one of us. You yourselves elected this court and these judges — demand that they be deprived of the posts that they have abused. Today it is not only the fate of the three ac- cused that is at stake — their trial is no better than the celebrat- ed trials of the 1930s, which involved us in so much shame and so much bloodshed that we still have not recovered from them. [15]

Addressing the members of the Politburo in connection with the same trial, General Pyotr Grigorenko fused different facets of the problem:

> This unwise venture has inflicted the gravest injury on the motherland. Apart from the moral-ethical, political, and juri- dical aspects of the case, I wish to point out, as a military special- ist, that it is difficult even to estimate, on the one hand, the great number of allies lost by our country and, on the other hand, the number of potential supporters acquired by our probable ene- mies during this trial. Not even the fiercest of our enemies could have done us more harm . . ." [16]

By prosecuting the dissenters, especially by employing such procedures as *in camera* trials, the State violates not only their political rights as guaranteed by the constitution but also their human rights as guaranteed by specific Soviet laws and international conventions ratified by the Soviet Union. The arguments of Bukovsky and others fell on fertile soil, and in 1968-1970, the movement for the defense of hu- man rights steadily gained momentum. In April 1968, the first issue of the *Chronicle* appeared. [17] Article 19 of the United Nations Declaration on Human Rights was used as an epigraph and, in juxtaposition to the reports of ruthless suppression of free speech which followed, became in itself a sort of platform for the movement. A year later, the Initia-

15. Document No. 7, *Ibid.*, p. 104.

16. Document No. 24, *Ibid.*, p. 153.

17. *Posev*, 1st Special Issue (1969):

tive Group for the Defense of Human Rights was formed, and
on May 20 it issued its first document, a letter to the United
Nations Human Rights Committee, signed by the 15 founding
members with the signatures of an additional 39 supporters.[18]
At about the same time a brochure by A. Antipov appeared in
samizdat, called *From Fermentation of Minds to an Intellectual Movement.* [19] The author predicted that the dissent
movement and its uncensored "press" — *samizdat* — will
greatly affect the attitude of Soviet people, turning them
into critical individuals struggling for the freedom of ideas
and their unhindered dissemination. The authorities must
have been of quite the same opinion since they then unleashed
a wave of legal and extralegal persecutions of the dissidents.
Eight of the 15 founders of the Initiative Group were arrested; five imprisoned or exiled, the other three confined to a
mental asylum. Equally harsh treatment awaited the supporters of the Group and other dissidents not directly connected with it. The authorities' increasing reliance on con-
fining the dissidents in psychiatric clinics, as a means of
avoiding embarrassing legal procedures to obtain convictions,
produced indignation on the part of the Soviet and foreign
scientific community. When in May 1970 the KGB made the
mistake of committing the prominent Soviet biologist,
Zhores Medvedev, to a psychiatric institution, the leadership
was immediately faced with a strong collective protest
action instigated by top Soviet scientists, including Piotr
Kapitza and Igor Tamm. The pressure was so strong that the
authorities were soon compelled to release Medvedev. This
incident, along with the conviction of the brilliant mathematician, Revolt Pimenov, and the harassment of several other
nonconformist intellectuals made clear to members of the
scientific community that although their privileged position
in the society and their vital importance for the regime make
them slightly less vulnerable than the young writers, by no
means are they guaranteed immunity from arrest and per-

18. *Radio Liberty Register* No. 126, (Munich, 1969).

19. "Ot brozhenya umov k umstvennomu dvizhenyu", *Vestnik RSKhD* No.
     93, (Paris, 1969).

secution. Once more the dreaded ghost of Stalinism has become tangible.

In November 1970, a small group of illustrious scientists headed by Andrei Sakharov and Valeryi Chalidze founded the Committee on Human Rights. They disclosed its very restrictive status and equally limited aims which include studying different aspects of Soviet law and advising the authorities on implementation, should they solicit such advice. The Committee enlisted the support of some well-known Soviet personalities, Solzhenitsyn among others, and vowed to act strictly within the framework permitted by existing laws. Although it was recently learned that the security organs interrogated Chalidze and searched his apartment, the authorities apparently cannot afford to crack down on the Committee. Thus, in the struggle for human rights, the natural scientists (pragmatists by inclination and earlier association with one another) took up the baton from the embattled Initiative Group which was dominated by the members of the creative intelligentsia. The next step toward a complete merging of previously scattered forces of the dissent movement was made.

Samizdat writers concerned with the origin, causes and consequences of the socio-ethical perversion of their society and/or connected questions of the Soviet citizen's rectitude have produced a number of works of great sophistication during the past several years. These writings range from several pages to several volumes; their form varies from pamphlet to fundamental scientific inquiry; their ideology, from Christian Orthodoxy to Marxism; their authors, from workers to philosophers. This essay presents cursorily some of their common features. First, many of the authors try to define contemporary Soviet ethical culture in historical perspective. From the times of the Tatar yoke to the present, "Russian science, technology, education were growing and growing, merging with the growth of Russian slavery." [20] This allegedly resulted in the gradual acquisition by the Russian masses of serfs' psychology to the point where they equate freedom

20. Grossman, "Vsyo techet" (Everything Flows By) (Frankfort-on-Main, 1970, p. 179).

with disorder. [21] There seems to be a quasiconsensus among *samizdat* authors that the regime's spiritual and moral mutilation of the masses has been greatly facilitated by the peculiarities of Russia's historical development. From this consensus the tendency has evolved toward national self-criticism evident in a great number of *samizdat* writings. The second common feature is the unambiguous rejection of the myth of Russian messianism by both the moralist and the pragmatic schools. Third, the great majority of dissident writers display indifference and even hostility to Marxism as an ethical system. In the mid-sixties several sociophilosophical works written from Marxist positions were published in *samizdat* [22] but in recent years the drift away from the ethical foundations of Marxism has become conspicuous. This hardly needs explanation: a half-century of distortion of Marxian ethics by Soviet ideological hawks was bound to produce the described backlash. And last, the authors display a striking similarity of views on the intelligentsia's role in the process of Russian revival. According to one of *samizdat's* most original thinkers, Grigorii Pomerantz, the intelligentsia has a natural inclination toward redefining society's spiritual interests. [23] And since, as another *samizdat* writer, Volnyi, has it, "peoples are subject to education," it follows that "only in the hands of the intelligentsia lies the historical fate of society." [24] All these writings evince the rising self-consciousness of the Soviet intelligentsia as a social class, Sakharov's contention that the intelligentsia "is, in essence, a part of the working class" [25] notwithstanding. (It is not clear

21. Cf. Amalrik, *op. cit.*, and K. Volnyi, "Intellegentsia i demokra ticheskoye dvizhenye" (Intelligentsia and the Democratic Movement), *Radio Liberty Register*, No. 607, (Munich, 1971).

22. E.g., Roy Medvedev, "Before the Court of History" (not available in the West); Yurii Budka, "The Decline of Capital" (The program of "New-type Marxist Party"); and to some extent Zhores Medvedev, "Rise and Fall of Lysenko" (New York, 1969).

23. G. Pomerantz, "Chelovek bez prilagatelnogo" (A Man Without An Adjective), *Grani* (Frankfort-on-Main, No. 77, 1970).

24. Volnyi, *op. cit.*

25. Sakharov, *op. cit.*

whether this blatantly incorrect statement reflects Sakharov's desire to court the working class or was simply used by him as a tactical device to prevent possible accusations of elitism.)

To summarize briefly, the position of the mainstream of the dissent movement, as mirrored in the accessible writing of its representatives, is as follows: liberalization of the regime is both a functional and a moral necessity. It must be carried out by nonviolent means on many levels simultaneously. Liberalization must be accompanied by the spiritual revival of society which is to be initiated by politically aware and morally sensitive segments of the intelligentsia. If these parallel processes of political liberalization and spiritual revival do not occur within the next few years, the country is likely to end up in chaos.

DISSIDENTS' SELF-IMAGE

In our discussion concerning the roots of the Soviet dissent movement we only hinted at the fact that the spread of oppositionist attitudes was, to a significant degree, the result of accumulation of unresolved economic, political and social conflicts and dilemmas. The Party's leadership has often had to admit the existence of unresolved problems, thus giving the members of the functional elite an opportunity to formulate suggestions of how the existing difficulties can be alleviated or future conflicts avoided. In order to be listened to by the Party at all, it is important for the dissidents to take a clearcut position on the regime's societal goals. They can argue with the Party on the ways of achieving the desired results only on the basis of involvement in a common endeavor — creation of a Communist society. Fortified by the awareness of their crucial importance to the country, the dissenters view themselves as the Party's political and moral irreproachable associates in this endeavor, therefore having a claim to superiority over the present rulers, many of whom have an objectionable Stalinist past. This claim is translated into rejection of the doctrine of the Party's infallibility and quite naturally leads to open questioning of the leadership's wisdom, skill and integrity in managing the country. As we have seen, the dissidents assert that the Party leaders' nearsight-

edness will "lead the country into a blind alley." But there is
much more to their challenge than just questioning the
soundness of the leadership's competence on developmental
criteria. In effect, they deny their allegiance to the regime's
proclaimed values and norms. They proclaim their own criteria of evaluation of interpersonal relations, legal systems,
political legitimacy or artistic quality, criteria which are not
subject to voluntary alteration on the grounds of political
expediency, criteria with which democratic and liberal forces
all over the world identify themselves. The defiance of established and, whenever possible, enforced ideological, moral or
artistic standards is tantamount to the adoption of a different
culture by the dissidents and their followers. The Party leaders are perfectly aware both of the attractive force of this
different culture, especially among the young, and of the
potential threat its dissemination presents to their own
political survival. Like every monopolist whose privileged
position is attacked by a rival, the ruling elite employs the
whole panoply of weapons in its possession — from courtship
to repression — in order to silence the proselytizers of the
new faith.

PROSPECTS FOR THE MOVEMENT

In view of the Party's determination to preserve its
unique position as the master of the bodies and souls of
Soviet citizens, what are the prospects for the Soviet dissent
movement in the future? Its fate is evidently closely dependent on the future development of the internal and international situation. Although detailed forecasting of the
future is beyond the scope of this article, one can venture to
say that the dissent movement in the Soviet Union may go
through periods of strain and even decline, but it is essentially
indestructible. Short of re-introduction of Stalinist methods
of all-out, indiscriminate terror which, according to the views
of most knowledgeable scholars in the field, would be a prelude to the doom of the Soviet regime, the government seems
to be limited in its possibilities of containing the spread of
libertarian ideals. It will, no doubt, continue to exhort, to
bribe, to threaten, to persecute, to jail, if not necessarily the
most persistent, then the most vulnerable of the dissidents.

Such methods would be adequate if the authorities had to deal with an isolated conspiratorial group. They are utterly inadequate to eradicate a spreading intellectual and social movement, having many actual and incomparably more potential supporters among restive national and religious minorities in the USSR and enjoying the sympathy (though unfortunately insufficient support) of progressive elements in the West. And the ruling elite cherishes no illusions about the adequacy of these methods.

One would expect that a rational decision-maker who knows he does not have the means to impose his will as he would like to, would opt for compromise rather than for Pyrrhic victory. Whether the Party's ruling elite is, as a whole, a rational decision-making body is a subject for a separate inquiry but it probably is comprised of people who came to the conclusion that an agreement on some sort of *modus vivendi* with the dissenting scientific elites is unavoidable. The qualification "scientific" is of importance in analyzing the possibilities of the dissidents' potential influence on the policy-making process. Although there is some indirect evidence that the dissidents identified with the liberal mainstream, both pragmatists and moralists, may have some sympathizers among high-ranking officials of the party apparatus or even the KGB,[26] it would appear that only scientists have any chances of asserting themselves as the Party's junior partners in running the society. Apart from their established positions as experts in economic and scientific matters and, stemming from that, developmental indispensability, the dissident scientists are very prudent in formulating their demands so that they remain within the realm of legality. In effect, they have already successfully challenged the Party's monopoly on decision-making. The fact that scientists succeeded in obtaining the release of Zhores Medvedev was one such spectacular victory in their opposition

26. Most quoted examples are the apparent lack of determination on the part of the KGB to stop the clandestine circulation of *samizdat* manuscripts, the engineering of the appearance of Khrushchev memoirs in the West (whatever one may think of their authenticity) and, in general, the authorities' ambivalent position in handling the dissent movement.

to regime-sponsored lawlessness. They have also achieved certain successes in wringing concessions from the regime in its policy on science, basic and applied research. These are just the first swallows of Spring, but in comparison with the not-so-remote past when *apparatchiki* used to impose some scientific theories and ban others, the progress is significant. The scientists are likely to be able to widen the field of their prerogatives in determining the directions of scientific research and may even reach an understanding with the ruling elite on their participation in policy-making in other areas of social life as well. In the process of bargaining they may be forced to yield on some of their demands which, with all due caution, they have never presented in "take-it-or-leave-it" form. They may be asked to pledge their political loyalty or to promise not to interfere in certain areas of politics or ideology.

With the Damoclean sword of the Brezhnev doctrine suspended over the liberal elements in the Eastern European countries, the Soviet dissent movement remains the only hope for the rehabilitation of the socialist system as a viable alternative to capitalism.

July 1971

NOTES ON DISSIDENTS QUOTED IN THIS ESSAY

Amalrik, Andrei A., b. 1938

Historian. Author of "Will the USSR Survive Until 1984," "Involuntary Journey to Siberia" and numerous essays. In 1965 he was sentenced to 2½ years in Siberian exile. Arrested in 1970; sentenced to three years at hard labor.

Bukovsky, Vladimir K., b. 1942

Poet and journalist. Arrested in 1963; confined to a special purpose mental institution. Released in 1964. Second arrest in 1965; eight months in a mental institution. Third arrest in January 1967; sentenced to three years at hard labor. Released in January 1970. Fourth arrest in May 1971.

Chalidze, Valeri N.

Physicist. *Samizdat* author and editor. Co-founder of the Committee on Human Rights. Author of numerous essays on Soviet legal doctrine and its applications. Editor of the collection *Social Problems.*

Chukovskaya, Lydia
 Writer and translator. Defended arrested young writers. Wrote
 open letters opposing re-Stalinization and harassment of Solzhenitsyn.

Daniel, Yuli M., b. 1925
 Writer and translator of foreign literature. Under the pseudonym of Nikolai Arzhak published a number of works, of which
 the best known are "Moscow Speaking" and "The Man from
 MINAP." Arrested in 1965; sentenced to five years at hard
 labor. While in the camps and in prison kept writing poems and
 protest letters. Released in 1970.

Delone, Vadim N., b. 1947
 Poet and worker. Arrested in 1967; sentenced to one year at
 hard labor. Released on parole. Arrested again in 1968; sentenced
 to two years and 10 months at hard labor.

Fetisov, A.
 Economist, critic of the regime from extremist totalitarian
 positions. Renounced his Party membership in protest against
 de-Stalinization. Arrested in 1968; released after a short stay in
 a psychiatric hospital.

Galanskov, Yuri T., b. 1939
 Writer and journalist, editor of literary-political journal *Phoe-
 nix-66*. Arrested in 1967. Sentenced to seven years at hard labor.

Ginzburg, Alexander T., b. 1936
 Poet and essayist. Arrested in 1960; sentenced to two years in a
 labor camp. Arrested in 1967; sentenced to five years at hard
 labor.

Grigorenko, Piotr G., b. 1907
 Major general, historian. In 1964 arrested and held for a year in
 a mental asylum. In May 1969, arrested again and confined to a
 special purpose mental institution.

Kapitza, Piotr L., b. 1894
 Physicist; full member of the Academy of Sciences of the USSR;
 Director of the Academy's Institute of Physical Problems —
 honorary member of American and many foreign Academies of
 Science; hero of Socialist Labor and recipient of many other
 Soviet and foreign medals and awards.

Khaustov, Victor A., b. 1938
Poet; worked as craftsman. Arrested in 1967; sentenced to three years at hard labor.

Kushev, Yevgenii Y., b. 1947
Poet. Arrested in 1967; sentenced to one year at hard labor. Released on parole.

Medvedev, Roy A., b. 1925
Mathematician and historian. Member of the CPSU from 1956 to 1969. Author of "Before the Court of History" (a three-volume historiographic analysis of Stalinism) and many *samizdat* writings.

Medvedev, Zhores A., b. 1925
Brother of Roy. Biologist. Author of "The Rise and Fall of Lysenko," "International Cooperation of Scientists and National Frontiers," "The Biological Science and Cult of Personality" and of numerous scientific works. Arrested on May 29, 1970; held in a psychiatric hospital; released on June 17, 1970.

Osipov, Vladimir N., b. 1939
University student, poet, editor of *samizdat* revues: *Boomerang* in 1960, *Phoenix* in 1961, *Veche* in 1970. Arrested in 1961; sentenced to seven years at hard labor. Released in 1968.

Sakharov, Andrei D., b. 1921
Nuclear physicist; full member of the Academy of Science of the USSR. In 1950 proposed use of electrical discharge in plasma located in a magnetic field to obtain controlled thermonuclear reaction. Author of numerous scientific volumes.

Sinyavsky, Andrei D., b. 1925
Writer and literary critic. Under the pseudonym of Abram Tertz wrote a number of publicistic and literary works.

Tamm, Igor Y., b. 1895; died 1971
Physicist; full member of the Academy of Science of the USSR; honorary member of American Academy of Arts; Nobel Prize winner in 1958; member of the Soviet delegation at Seventh Pugwash Conference. Protested against the rebirth of Stalinism.

Turchin, Valeri F.
Physicist and mathematician. Published a great number of scientific papers. Wrote also on philosophy and sociology of

science. Co-authored, with Sakharov and R. Medvedev, an open letter to Brezhnev, Kosygin and Podgorny.

Tverdokhlebov, Andrei N.
Nuclear physicist. Published a number of scientific articles. Author of several *samizdat* writings. Co-founder of Committee on Human Rights. Signed several letters of protest.

Anti-Semitism as a Policy Tool in the Soviet Bloc

Maurice Friedberg

The use of anti-Semitism in fostering government policy objectives has a notoriously long tradition in Eastern Europe —one that reaches back to the massacres of the Ukraine's Jews in seventeenth-century Poland, and even beyond. More recently, anti-Semitism was used at the turn of this century by czarist Russia's reactionary authorities in a vain effort to prop their crumbling regime. At that time, a number of Russia's leading writers and public figures, including Tolstoy, Korolenko, Chekhov and Gorki, denounced the state-condoned, if not indeed state-inspired, pogroms as an outrage against humanity and a blot on Russia's national honor. Lenin, a man far less susceptible to moral considerations, denounced anti-Semitism promarily as a ploy invented by the capitalists to distract workers and peasants from class struggle.

END OF STALIN ERA

Opinions differ regarding the exact stage at which anti-Semitism was first used in the USSR as a policy tool; but most students of Soviet history agree that, by the end of World War II, the Jews had become convenient scapegoats for a variety of failures of the Soviet regime. In other words, Lenin's successors have availed themselves of an instrument that the founder of their state found despicable. In the mid-1940s and early 1950s, i.e., during the last decade of Stalin's life, abundant use was made of anti-Semitism, most of it overt and virulent, in the USSR proper, as well as in the newly established Soviet satellite states of Eastern Europe. The Soviet "anti-cosmopolitan" campaigns of the late 1940s, which culminated in the abortive 1953 trial of a group of Jewish physicians accused of having plotted, in cooperation with Jewish organizations in the West, the mass medical murder of Soviet leaders, are often viewed as aberrations of the diseased mind of an aging dictator. This they no doubt were, but they were also the circuses offered by the Soviet caesars to their subjects in lieu of the bread and freedom they had hoped to obtain after victory over Nazism.

Similarly, in Eastern Europe, the nationalist frustrations generated by a failure to regain true national independence and by the replacement of Nazi occupation armies and Quisling governments with Soviet Russian armies and their local puppets often led to anti-Semitic excesses. This solution, encouraged as an outlet, was facilitated by the all-too-visible fact that Communists of Jewish extraction were quite prominent in the hated Soviet-imposed regimes. There is strong evidence to support the contention that the 1946 Kielce pogrom in Poland, in which several scores of survivors of the Nazi holocaust were killed only a year after the defeat of Nazi Germany, was instigated by Soviet agents in the hope that this would "ease" nationalist tensions and, incidentally, manufacture another excuse for the Soviet military presence in Poland. Similar objectives may well have been behind the shrill anti-Semitic atmosphere of the November 1952 Prague trial of Rudolf Slansky, a former head of Czechoslovakia's Communist party who was of Jewish origin.

In the aftermath of Stalin's death in 1953, there was a revulsion against many of the dictator's policies, including his state-fostered anti-Semitism. Indeed, attitudes toward anti-Semitism in time became a litmus test separating Stalinist conservatives from their foes, the relatively liberal reformers in the Communist parties of Eastern Europe and Russia. The Stalinists denied that anti-Semitism was an issue worth discussing, while their opponents pointed to it as one of the most reprehensible features of Stalin's heritage. Some use of anti-Semitism was made in the struggle between the two factions, but not too much. In the popular mind, "official" anti-Semitism was too closely associated with the other wounds of Stalinism, then still very fresh. Nevertheless, there were some exceptions. Thus, in 1956, *Pravda* cited Hungary's Jewish-born Communist boss Matyas Rakosi as an example of an "antipatriotic" party chieftain in what was an obvious attempt to channel anti-Soviet sentiments in the direction of anti-Semitism.

KHRUSHCHEV REGIME

It was under Nikita Khrushchev that state-instigated anti-Semitism reappeared in the USSR on a large scale. Again, it is our contention that, while his personal anti-Semitic sentiments might have been a contributing factor, Khrushchev, probably the most pragmatic politician so far produced by the Soviet system, must have had some practical considerations in mind. The one that most readily suggests itself is that anti-Semitism might serve as a lightning rod in the threatening storm of discontent over the country's serious economic ills which now could no longer be blamed solely on the consequences of Nazi occupation and general wartime devastation. Appetites for a more abundant life were whetted only lately by Khrushchev himself. On the other hand, economic grievances played an important part in the recent dangerous disturbances among East German and Polish workers, and were a leading factor in the Hungarian revolution of 1956, second only to nationalist and political factors.

All these considerations probably contributed to the Soviet decision to introduce, in 1961, the death penalty for such economic offenses as embezzlement, theft, graft and black marketeering. It should be noted that no precedent is known to exist anywhere for such draconic punishment for economic crimes committed in peacetime, i.e., when they could not directly threaten or adversely affect a country's survival. However, there was reason to believe that the stamping out of such crimes could help the survival of

Khrushchev as the master of the Soviet state. Also, a crusade against such offenses had the added attraction of making it possible to give the campaign an anti-Semitic flavor, which was impossible in other campaigns (e.g., the never-ceasing attempts to rid the Soviet state of the burdensome problem of alcoholism). For in the popular image, one partly borne out by fact, Russia's Jews have traditionally been attracted to such "economic" occupations as minor managerial jobs, accounting, etc. Of course, the fallacy lay in the fact that, while the number of accountants and petty managers among Soviet Russia's Jews may have been high, the percentage of Jews in the country's total population was such that they constituted a miniscule part of all managers and accountants. Nevertheless, of the more than 100 persons executed for economic crimes in 1961-1962, the large majority were Jews, and their trials had strongly anti-Semitic overtones. The obvious insinuation therefore was that shortages of consumer goods and their shabby quality were not to be blamed on the country's leadership or on the Soviet economic system, but on a handful of Jewish black marketeers and corrupt petty officials. In time, the number of trials fell off or, if nothing more, they were given less publicity, at least in part because of the uproar they stirred abroad. Nevertheless, such trials continued well into the mid 1960s.

Anti-Semitism was occasionally resorted to in the skirmishes between the Stalinists and the reformists within the Soviet bloc throughout the 1960s. It was generally used by the conservatives who were fond of hinting that "revisionism" was a Jewish invention and the "true" Russians (or "true" Poles, Hungarians, Czechs, etc.) should not be deceived by its alien heresies. But the true explosion of state-sponsored anti-Semitism in the USSR and the Soviet allies in Eastern Europe, and its sudden escalation into a prime policy tool began in June 1967, immediately after Israel's lightning victory in the Six Day War.

AFTERMATH OF THE SIX DAY WAR

The diplomatic position taken by the USSR and its neighbors was one of unequivocal support of the Arab cause, and consequent hostility toward Israel. The exception was Rumania which, alone among members of the Warsaw Pact, refused to sever relations with Israel. By contrast, Tito's Yugoslavia, otherwise independent in its foreign policy, re-entered the ranks of Soviet satellites on this particular issue, at least partly because of Tito's fears caused by the recent disintegration of the "neutralist bloc," and his long personal friendship with Nasser.

That opposition to Israel, however bitter, did not necessarily imply an espousal of anti-Semitic policies at home has been demonstrated since the war by several East European Communist countries. Understandably, there has been no upsurge of anti-Semitism in Rumania. In Yugoslavia a series of newspaper articles at first attempted to establish a link between Israel's "aggression" and the "perfidious" teachings of Judaism. However, this was soon squashed on the ground that it actually constituted a disservice to the Arab cause, and no major evidence of anti-Semitism was found in the Yugoslav press thereafter. (In fact, a year later it repeatedly denounced the anti-Semitic campaign then in full swing in Poland, rejecting the official Polish disclaimers that only "Zionism" was under attack.) Similarly, while Bulgaria's attacks on Israel at the United Nations were often more poisonous than those of the Arabs themselves, the country's Prime Minister Todor Zhivkov told the General Assembly that "the Bulgarian people have never been and never will be against the Jewish people,"[1] and in the last three years there has been no significant use of anti-Semitism in Bulgaria to complement the strongly anti-Israeli tone of its press. Still more emphatic was the stance of the Hungarian government. Soon after the cease-fire in the Middle East Gyula Kallai, speaker of the Hungarian parliament, denounced "certain people who try to exploit the Arab-Israeli conflict for anti-Semitic incitement," while Zoltan Komocsin, a politboro member, declared in a television appearance that "we dis-

---

1. Quoted in William Korey, "Anti-Israel Policies Split Communist World," *Hadassah Magazine* (May, 1968), p. 13. It is worth pointing out that Bulgaria's record of saving Jews threatened by deportation to Nazi death camps is unrivaled by any European country, with the sole exception of Denmark.

associate ourselves from any symptom of anti-Semitism in our country and shall, as always, fight against it with all our might."[2] Again, there has been no indication of any large-scale use of anti-Semitism in that country since these assurances were given.

The countries of the Soviet bloc where, in the post-1967 period, anti-Semitism emerged as a conscious tool of foreign and domestic policy were Poland, Czechoslovakia and East Germany, as well as the USSR. While a study of possible contributing historical factors is outside the scope of this survey, it is worth pointing out that, paradoxically, both East Germany and Czechoslovakia, i.e., the countries with the most and least intense anti-Semitic traditions in East Central Europe, respectively, "imported" post-1967 anti-Semitism from the Soviet Union. In Poland on the other hand, much of the anti-Semitic campaign was spontaneous and of domestic origin, largely manufactured by Poland's own Communist party. Apparently it only was manipulated by the Soviet Union which at first found it useful but ultimately became aware of the inherent dangers of nationalist frenzy of any sort in an East European satellite.

POLISH ANTI-SEMITISM

The now notorious wave of anti-Semitism in Poland, which has resulted in the virtual disappearance of organized Jewish life in that country and the emigration of all but some 10,000 of its Jews, began in the wake of the Six Day War. At that time Israel's victory was widely hailed in traditionally anti-Russian Poland as the triumph of "our Polish Jews" over "their" (the Russians') Arabs. On June 19 Wladyslaw Gomulka, the head of the Polish Communist Party, warned "Polish citizens of Jewish nationality" against such jubilation. Poland's authorities, Gomulka emphasized, "cannot remain indifferent toward people who . . . come out in favor of the aggressors." Intentionally disregarding popular glee over the humiliation of the Soviet Union and its friends, Gomulka pretended that those disagreeing with Poland's official backing of the Arabs were not "true" Poles. He implied that they were only Zionist Jews.

2. *Ibid.*

At the time Gomulka threatened the Jews, his own rule was being challenged by General Mieczyslaw Moczar, the secret police boss, standard-bearer of a nationalist group within the Communist party and head of the Union of Fighters for Freedom and Democracy (ZBOWiD), a veterans' organization. Gomulka's position was made even more precarious by the country's economic difficulties and, with the whittling away of the democratic freedoms attained during the Polish October 1956 anti-Stalinist and anti-Soviet revolt that swept Gomulka into power, he also by and large lost the support of the liberal segments of the population.

In the months following, anti-Semitism was to become a political football. The use of the "Zionist" bogey became more attractive after a stage adaptation of a Polish classic poem, Adam Mickiewicz's *Forefathers Eve*, was closed in January of 1968 (the play's anti-Russian lines were demonstratively applauded). This incident later resulted in large-scale student demonstrations, some of whose leaders, as it turned out, were Jewish.[3] From now on, each side — Gomulka's "moderates" and Moczar's "nationalists" — tried to outbid the other in blaming the country's foreign and domestic ills on the "Zionists." As suggested before, there was every indication that the Soviet authorities at first were only too pleased to see a potentially anti-Russian explosion channeled in the direction of anti-Semitism in a wave of nationalism and chauvinism that represented no threat to them — at least for the time being.

Until then, anti-Semitic attacks were directed, in the main, on such writers as Jerzy Kosinski and Jean Francois Steiner, whose books on the Nazi holocaust — all published in the West — suggested that, during World War II, many Poles were active or passive Nazi accomplices in the extermination of Poland's Jews. Such attacks were as useful as the constant reminders of the danger of a resurgence of Nazism in West Germany: they were likely to strike a re-

3. Of the eight student leaders named by the Communist party's central newspaper *Trybuna Ludu* on March 10, 1968, five were Jews. On March 19, Gomulka declared that the demonstrations were the work of "over a dozen people, mainly students of Jewish origin."

sponsive chord in every Pole, no matter what his political views. Similar objectives were now pursued by attacks on Jews still living in Poland, some 25,000 in 1967. Thus, attacks on Poland's now pitifully small Jewish community as the main source of the country's many misfortunes were, gruesomely and paradoxically, among the very few slogans that could rally and unite the otherwise hopelessly divided nation.

The anti-Jewish campaign grew in intensity and shrillness with lightning speed. On March 12, 1968, *Slowo Powszechne*, organ of a pseudo-Catholic puppet organization directed by Boleslaw Piasecki, a prominent member of the pre-war Polish fascist party, carried an appeal "To the Students at Warsaw University." It cautioned Polish students that they were being led astray by a Szlajfer, a Werfel, a Blumsztajn and a Rubinsztajn. The danger was then spelled out: "The formost aim of the Zionists in Poland was to influence intellectuals and young people to oppose the national interests of People's Poland."

On the same day, *Trybuna Ludu*, official organ of Poland's Communist party, warned that "we will not allow ourselves to be blackmailed by the bogey of anti-Semitism" and, furthermore, "we will not allow the Zionists to seek protection in accusing others of anti-semitism." This blunt statement, in effect, amounted to a proclamation of an open season on the Jews.

On the following day, March 13, the same top authoritative paper accused Jewish students of a nasty provocation. The students themselves, it claimed, smeared some buildings with swastikas, and then pointed to these daubings as evidence of anti-Semitism. *Trybuna Ludu* then described how a mob was given an anti-Semitic pep-talk before marching to break up a student demonstration: "This morning, when our comrades were mobilized to take part in the operation, they had certain doubts and inhibitions. They had to be told who the instigators were, and with whom they were linked. Then all of the comrades went into action."

Two days later, the same newspaper informed its readers that the Zionists coerce Jews, wherever they may live, to give Israel "economic aid, political assistance (defense of its policies, particularly in the press), supplying of intelligence information etc." *Glos Pracy*, a trade union newspaper, provided a more exhaustive list on March 18:

> In its struggle against Communism, Zionism resorts to a variety of methods. These include provocation, blackmail, subversion, the sowing of unrest and, until recently, the red herring of anti-Semitism. The Zionists are very adept in resorting to the latter device.

On March 19 Gomulka addressed some 3,000 Communist party activists; his speech was relayed by radio and television. Gomulka's questions "Are there in Poland any Jewish nationalists? Are there any supporters of Zionist ideology?" elicited roars of approval that sounded familiar to those who remembered Hitler's speeches. There is some evidence that Gomulka was already beginning to have second thoughts about the wisdom of using anti-Semitism for political purposes, but it was too late. Anti-Semitic hysteria raged throughout the country.

On March 23, 1968, Radio Warsaw broadcast a speech by General Tadeusz Pistrazak, local head of ZBOWiD, the veterans' organization that was General Moczar's center of power. General Pistrazak's speech typically tried to link the "Zionists" with both the hated Stalinist past and present-day troublemakers. Before 1956, said the general, the "Zionists" were in charge of Poland's dreaded secret police, and now they clamored for "democracy": "They [the "Zionists"] simply want the kind of democracy and freedom under which die-hard Jewish nationalists and reactionaries of all kinds can implement anti-Polish and antinational plans that serve the interests of international Zionism and imperialism."

On April 1, 1968, *Sztandar Mlodych*, a youth newspaper, announced that the Joint (American Jewish Joint Distribution Committee) was ordered to cease operating in Poland because its charitable activities were really a cover for espionage. The announcement had an ominous ring: at one time or another, most of Poland's Jews, left destitute after the war, had obtained some form of assistance from JDC and thus could be considered suspect of espionage. The announcement also bore sinister similarity to one made in the USSR when preparations for the trials of those accused of alleged participation in the notorious "doctor's plot" were under way.[4]

On April 5, 1968, General Moczar made yet another attempt to link the "Zionists" to the hated Stalinist regime, if not indeed to shift to them the blame for Poland's postwar status as a Soviet colony. In a television appearance, the general declared that the culprits actually responsible for present troubles were the "politicians" who arrived in Poland in 1944 with the victorious Soviet armies. Of the nine persons cited, eight were Jews and the ninth, a non-Jew, had a Jewish wife.[5]

As the campaign gained momentum, it turned with increasing frequency to familiar themes of pre-war Polish, predominantly nonpolitical, anti-Semitism which was xenophobic, racist and economic in nature. Thus, the April 15-31 issue of the Silesian bi-weekly *Naodrze*, published in Jelenia Gora, brought the sinister news that the Jewish Social and Cultural Society presents plays in Yiddish; that its library contained books printed in a mysterious script, and that the society ran its own summer camps for children — surely a suspicious activity.

On April 19, 1968, the 25th anniversary of the Warsaw ghetto uprising, *Glos Koszalinski*, a provincial newspaper, reported the expulsion from the Party of some Jewish tailors who had failed to condemn Israel with sufficient vigor and who had conveniently absented themselves from a meeting at which the 1968 student riots were condemned.

On April 28-29 the Wroclaw *Slowo Polskie* reported the discovery of yet another outrage. This time the target chosen for attack was the Jewish artisans' cooperatives, set up in postwar Silesia to provide employment for Yiddish-speaking

4. On April 21-22, 1968, *Slowo Polskie*, a newspaper published in the Silesian city of Wroclaw where relatively many Jews settled after 1945, revealed to its readers that, in the past, any Jew who visited the Israel embassy — even if only for a chat — received from the embassy a "gift" of 1,000 zlotys. The article was buttressed by a list of real persons who allegedly were recipients of such largesse. The implication of espionage was obvious.

5. *The Anti-Jewish Campaign in Present-Day Poland: Facts, Documents, Press Reports* (London, Institute of Jewish Affairs, 1968), p. 39.

tailors, shoemakers, mechanics and others, who, for obvious
psychological reasons, preferred to work with other Jews.
As *Slowo Polskie* interpreted it, this meant that true Poles
were the victims of employment discrimination in their own
country. The newspaper also accused the Jewish cooperatives
of importing raw materials from abroad. In fact, these raw
materials were donated by Jewish philanthropic agencies
abroad, and were thus gifts rather than imports. [6]

In keeping with Soviet historian Pokrovsky's famous
dictum that history is but politics projected into the past,
Polish publications began to minimize the extent of wartime
Jewish resistance to the Nazis. Thus, a reviewer of *The
Resistance Movement in the Bialystok Ghetto* by the late
Communist scholar Bernard Mark claimed that there actual-
ly never was any Jewish resistance movement in the area —
there were just a few Jews who were hidden in the forests by
Polish peasants. [7]

The most "rational" explanation of the success of the 1968
anti-Semitic campaign was written by Andrzej Werblan, a
leading Party theoretician, in a long monograph published in
the June 1968 issue of *Miesiecznik Literacki:*

> Why is it that among certain groups of the intelligentsia in our
> country . . . there are comparatively many people of Jewish
> origin? . . . It was their cosmopolitan [i.e., Jewish] background
> that gave rise to the unjustified accusation of anti-Semitism,
> hurled at those comrades who understood that no society will
> tolerate an inflated representation of a national minority in its
> elite, particularly in national defense, security, propaganda,
> and diplomatic service. . . . Experience has demonstrated that
> the majority of the personnel under discussion was ideologically
> alien, and subsequently chose the path of revisionism, while
> many have embraced Zionism. [8]

6. A similar charge that Jewish cooperatives were guilty of defrauding the
    Polish Treasury appeared in the specialized economic publication *Zycie
    Gospodarcze* on April 17-18, 1968.

7. *Gazeta Bialostocka,* May 4-5, 1968. Since then, Polish sources have con-
    sistently minimized the extent and importance of Jewish anti-Nazi
    resistance, while simultaneously emphasizing Jewish collaboration with
    the Nazis in Poland, e.g., *Judenrate,* and the complicity of Western
    Jewish organizations.

8. This part of Werblan's article was also reprinted in *Trybuna Ludu,*
    June 16, 1968.

And further:

> Among the revisionists, both academic personnel at Warsaw University and the students involved in hostile revisionist activity, a considerable role was played by a large group of people of Jewish origin. The existence of specifically nationalist and ethnic solidarity exerted a powerful influence on the course of events in Warsaw academic circles. . . . The favoritism demonstrated in the rapid advancement of persons of petit bourgeois Jewish origins, people who had no strong ties to Communism and often remained under Zionist influences, can only be ascribed to sheer thoughtlessness or to a clannishness based on racial ties.

According to Werblan, the evil's root was to be sought in the fact that, before the war, Jews constituted too high a percentage of Polish Communist Party membership, and that this detracted from the party's popularity with the Polish masses, who justly regarded it as "Jewish." Thus, in Werblan's opinion, the once excessively "Jewish" profile of the Polish Communist Party led it to oppose Poland's national independence:

> The distorted nature of the [pre-war Polish] Communist party's ethnic make-up would not have been a major problem were it not linked in a way with problems of ideological nature. Thus, the programmatic position of the Polish Communist Party (KPP) on the problem of Polish independence was for a long time burdened with the errors of Luxemburgism.[9]

The circle was thus closed. The Jews of Poland stood accused not only of being allied with Poland's enemies, but also of blackening the country's name abroad, subverting its might at home, exploiting it economically, engaging in espionage, and of ruling Poland. And, according to Werblan, they have even traditionally opposed the existence of Poland as an independent state.

At the July 1968 meeting of the Central Committee of the Polish Communist Party (officially called United Polish Workers' Party), some voices were raised in opposition to the anti-Semitic orgy. Thus, for example, Zenon Kliszko complained that "Jews are being equated with Zionists" (*Trybuna Ludu*, July 8, 1968), as did Boleslaw Ruminski, another Cen-

---

9. Rosa Luxemburg (1871-1919), a Polish-born Jewess and one of the founders of the German Communist Party, was, for doctrinal reasons, opposed to the idea of Polish independence.

tral Committee member, who declared that the struggle
against Zionism occasionally resulted in anti-Semitism
(Trybuna Ludu, July 10, 1968). Even Gomulka warned in a
Radio Warsaw speech on July 12 that the anti-Zionist campaign was creating "an unfriendly attitude toward Jews in
general." Gomulka's appeal for moderation went unheeded,
while the much stronger warning by Minister of Finance
Jerzy Albrecht that "all Jews, including good Communists,
are sometimes being lumped together as Zionists" *(Trybuna
Ludu,* July 10, 1968), may have contributed to his dismissal
from the post the very next day. In fact, between 1967 and
1968 there existed within the Polish ministry of interior a
special "Department of Zionist Affairs" headed by Colonel
Tadeusz Walichnowski of the secret police who, within two
years, produced seven "anti-Zionist" pamphlets under his
name. The department was said to have maintained a card
file of all persons of Jewish origin residing in Poland. According to some sources, the department was ordered closed only
after it began investigating the antecedents of Premier Jozef
Cyrankiewicz and then Defense Minister Marian Spychalski.

At first, the Soviet authorities demonstratively applauded
Poland's "anti-Zionist" purges. [10] Later, their enthusiasm
cooled when it gradually became apparent that Polish anti-
Semitism, originally unleashed to avert an anti-Soviet out-
break, might ultimately revert to its original target. Gomulka
who, in the meantime, had demonstrated his fidelity to the
Soviet cause by his all-out support of the Soviet invasion of
Czecholsovakia, represented the "moderates" during the anti-
Semitic purges.

Anti-Jewish articles continued to appear in Poland's
press. Thus, on December 28, 1968, the Warsaw daily *Zycie
Warszawy,* in a somewhat questionable attempt to shore up

10. Thus, for example, the Soviet army newspaper *Krasnaya Zvezda* wrote
on August 17, 1968, that "the Polish comrades have convincingly demonstrated that anti-Zionism is not anti-Semitism." More authoritative support allegedly came from Vladimir Semyonov, Soviet deputy minister
of foreign affairs who is rumored to write under the pseudonym "K.
Ivanov." He approvingly repeated the Polish assertion that support of
Zionism was tantamount to support of imperialism *(International
Affairs,* Moscow, June 1968).

Franco-Polish relations, gleefully pointed to the fact that
Poland and de Gaulle's France had common enemies — Baron
Guy de Rothschild and the German Jew Daniel Cohn-Bendit.
Truly pathological anti-Semitism may be found in Kazimierz
Sidor's book *Behind the Pyramids,* in which the author, a
recent Polish ambassador to Egypt, indiscriminately used
hundreds of anti-Semitic canards, ranging from the most
recently manufactured in Eastern Europe to those of the
ancient Greeks, who claimed that the Jews were descended
from lepers.

GERMAN DEMOCRATIC REPUBLIC

For obvious reasons, East Germany's Communist authorities long avoided anti-Semitism as a political weapon. Even
though East Germany was one of the two successor states to
Nazi Germany (with former Nazis occupying a number of
important positions), unlike West Germany it never paid any
restitution to victims of Nazi persecutions.[11] While, in the
wake of the Six Day War, denunciations of Israel's "aggression" were as virulent in East Germany as in the other Soviet
satellites, a really drastic reversal took place in the summer
of 1968, immediately before and after the Soviet bloc's armed
invasion of Czechoslovakia in which East German forces
participated. As in Poland, there were some purges of "Zionists," though necessarily on a smaller scale since East Germany had only slightly over 1,000 Jews in a total population
of 17,000,000. On August 25, 1968, within days after the invasion, *Neues Deutschland,* central organ of the East German Communist Party, charged that "Zionist forces have
taken over the leadership of Czechoslovakia's Communist
Party." A week later, on September 1, the same newspaper
carried an article entitled "Prague Is Ruled by the Zionists."

11. As Simon Wiesenthal, head of the Documentation Center of the Federation of Jewish Victims of Nazism in Vienna, pointed out at a press conference, September 6, 1968, former Nazis now active in East Germany
included Minister of Propaganda and press chief Kurt Blecha; Horst
Dressler-Anders, an employee of the propaganda ministry who had been
president of the Nazi state broadcasting system and editor of the *Kra-
kauer Tageblatt* in occupied Poland; Hans-Walter Aust, editor-in-chief
of *Deutsche Aussenpolitik,* a publication of East Germany's ministry of
foreign affairs; and Herbert Kroeger, staff member of the same journal,
the one-time head of the Gestapo in Cologne.

By a macabre coincidence, Hitler's *Voelkischer Beobachter* carried the headline "Prague Is Ruled by the Jews" several days after Nazi Germany's invasion of Czechoslovakia in 1939.

There has been little change in East Germany. On March 14, 1970, *Pravda* published an article by Fritz Noll, deputy editor of the Essen paper *Unsere Zeit*, in which the East German journalist pointed an accusing finger at those West Germans who "presently charge our country's democratic citizens with anti-Semitism because they condemn Israel's aggressive policies."

CZECHOSLOVAKIA

As already stated, by East European standards Czechoslovakia has traditionally been remarkably free of anti-Jewish prejudice. In the weeks following the Six Day War, Czechoslovakia's official reaction, then formulated by the Stalinist regime of Antonin Novotny, did not differ from that of its Soviet-bloc neighbors. Inevitably, the anti-Israel hysteria brought about a wave of anti-Semitism which affected the country's approximately 15,000 Jews. However, there was some vocal opposition to it, as there was also criticism of the government's unconditional support of the Arab cause. The most eloquent was the defection of the Slovak novelist Ladislav Mnacko, who demonstratively went to Israel in order to denounce the Czechoslovak government's position on both issues. The rapid liberalization in the spring of 1968, which resulted in Novotny's downfall and swept into power Alexander Dubcek's liberal Communist government, muted the anti-Israel campaign, and temporarily brought to a halt state-inspired anti-Semitism.

However, anti-Semitism was soon to re-emerge as one of the most important weapons of the enemies of Czechoslovakia's liberals, both within the country and in the other Soviet bloc nations — first and foremost, in the USSR. Some of the anti-Semitic propaganda was open; much of it was clandestine and took the form of anonymous letters and pamphlets. Thus, for example, Eduard Goldstucker, a Jew who was president of Czechoslovak Union of Writers and deputy rector of Prague's Charles University, made public in

the June 23, 1969, issue of *Rude Pravo*, the central organ of
the Czech Communist Party, an anonymous letter sent to
him, which said in part:

> You are not content to rule in Israel alone; as Zionists, you want
> to rule the whole world. Here you have something in common
> with Hitler. And we know for a fact that the ringleaders of the
> latest events here and in Poland are Zionists who are planning
> the final victory of international Zionism. . . . In any case, it
> will soon be all over with you; your days are numbered, you
> loathsome Jew. [12]

An anonymous pamphlet declared:

> The Federal [German] Republic is an agent of the USA, and Is-
> rael is an agent of the Federal Republic. . . . Our working class
> understands that financial power is controlled by international
> monopoly capital, and that Jewry is an international race. And
> against these two enemies the international proletariat is taking
> its stand with the slogan "Let us unite." The words of the Party's
> present leader [Dubcek] bear no relation to Socialism. They
> employ, it is said, the tactics of international capitalism "which
> in our country is represented by Jewry and its agents." This
> "Jewry" shrinks from no kind of crime. [13]

A few days after the invasion, on August 26, 1968, the still
defiant Czechoslovak radio commented:

> At last we have learned who is responsible for the nonexistent
> Czechoslovak counterrevolution. We have been told this by the
> official press of the occupiers, and they have done so in their
> usual refined and euphemistic way. They did not say outright
> "the Jews"; they said "international Zionism." Apparently, our
> East German friends have been experts on this subject ever since
> World War II. . . . Two million people allegedly are involved,
> and, after their liquidation, the soldiers apparently are to leave
> the country. . . . Why cannot these two million Zionists be found
> if the Soviet army command, or perhaps *Neues Deutschland*,
> wishes to find them? At any rate, today the Germans are the
> only real experts capable of distinguishing with absolute accura-
> cy between Aryans and inferior races.

The height of the insidiously anti-Semitic Soviet drive
against the liberal Communist Czechoslovak regime was
reached when, on September 4, 1968, two weeks after the in-

12. *Frankfurter Allgemeine Zeitung,* July 20, 1968, quoted in *Wiener Li-
    brary Bulletin* (London, Fall 1968).

13. *Ibid.*

vasion, *Izvestia*, the official newspaper of the Soviet government, printed a scurrilous attack on Jiri Hajek, Czechoslovakia's foreign minister who vainly attempted to mobilize world public opinion in support of his country's cause. Wrote *Izvestia:*

> A question suggests itself: who is that J. Hajek? Who was Czechoslovak Socialist Republic's minister of foreign affairs? . . . . People say that, during the German occupation of Czechoslovakia, J. Hajek, in order to save his life, wrote flattering articles for the Gestapo. And that it was the Gestapo that saved J. Hajek's life, but that Hajek had to "earn" it by doing quite a bit of work for the Nazis. It was perhaps for that reason that he had, eventually, changed his name from Karpeles to Hajek. During the last two weeks Hajek-Karpeles had been running all over the world, from city to city and from village to village. He has been to Belgrade and to Vienna, to New York and to London, to Zurich and to Geneva. . . . Some people intimate that he is getting ready to go overseas once again, to the United States. One of his "friends" there promised him a "big job" with an advertising agency.

The purpose of the article was all too transparent. The Soviet government's aim was to "expose" the liberal Czechoslovak minister as a shifty Jew, and a Nazi collaborator to boot. "Karpeles" is a fairly common Jewish name in Czechoslovakia. Jiri Hajek's answer appeared in the October 19, 1968, Prague magazine *Reporter*, one of the last issues of the publication. He stated that attacks on him had appeared in newspapers of certain (unnamed) Socialist countries:

> Some of these attacks had a distinctly racist character and were without foundation. It is not true that I am of Jewish origin. But I must add that I would not be ashamed of it if I were, because I think a man should be judged on the basis of what he does and how he behaves, and because I think that, in this country, racism was disowned long ago.

Ultimately, *Izvestia* acknowledged its "innocent" error. Yet it is difficult to believe that the "misunderstanding" was anything but intentional (it is hardly likely that the biography of a cabinet minister of a Soviet-bloc country was a secret in Moscow), but even if it were, the article would be no less revolting. The Soviet press continued to blame the "Zionists" for the events in Czechoslovakia, though it was nearly two years since its occupation by the armies of Warsaw Pact countries.

Thus, N. Gasarov, writing in the January 1969 issue of *Sovetskie Profsoyuzy*, the trade union journal, blamed the Czechoslovak liberal interlude (and also, while on the subject, the 1956 workers' uprising in Poland) on the "Zionists," and ominously added that "since diplomatic relations between the Soviet Union and Israel were broken off, Israeli intelligence and Zionist organizations have been using Jewish citizens of other capitalist countries for conducting subversive activities aimed against the USSR." On March 8, 1969, *Izvestia* quoted the left-wing Lebanese newspaper *Al Dunia*, which claimed that Israel was privy to all of Czechoslovakia's state secrets (including details of recent secret Czechoslovak-Soviet negotiations) "because many Jews residing in Czechoslovakia . . . occupy important political, scientific, and cultural positions, and favor the abolition of Socialism in Czechoslovakia and the restoration of a capitalist regime which would favor Israeli interests." Then, on January 28, 1970, Moscow's *Literaturnaya Gazeta* printed an article by one Radoslav Cermak, judging from his name a Czech, which asserted that responsibility for the Czechoslovak debacle did not really lie with Dubcek, who was merely a figurehead, but with Smrkovsky, Kriegel and Sik. Of the three, Kriegel is a Jew and Sik is always described as one. The statement was reinforced by being ascribed to Ludek Pachman, a Jew, who allegedly gave this information to the Israeli newspaper *Al Hamishmar* on December 27, 1968.

SOVIET RUSSIA

The year 1967 marked a watershed in the use of anti-Semitism as a policy tool within the USSR proper. The Soviet Union's unconditional support of the Arab cause was motivated by a number of considerations. There was, first of all, the desire to gain a foothold in the Mediterranean — an old dream of Russian statesmen, czarist and Soviet alike — which the Soviet rulers hoped to realize by backing the numerically and otherwise much stronger side in the conflict. There was also, no doubt, the hope of propping up the anti-American forces within the neutralist bloc still smarting under the impact of ignominious defeats in Ghana, Indonesia and the former Belgian Congo. There was also, no doubt, the need to demonstrate to the Afro-Asians that the Soviet Union, and not Communist China, could be counted on to bail out its allies, should the need arise. Then, of course, support of the Arabs would gain the Soviet Union the sympathies of Moslems everywhere, not least among Russia's own Turkic minorities along the now sensitive Chinese frontier. Last, but not least, an anti-Israel stance would of necessity result in some spillover of anti-Semitism, a posture that might alienate small segments of the Soviet liberal intelligentsia, but one that would prove popular with more numerous and more significant segments of the population, including the army and the party bureaucracy.

Chronologically, the wave of state-inspired domestic anti-Semitism in the USSR followed, rather than preceded, similar campaigns in the satellite states. This situation was not without precedent: the anti-Semitic witchhunts in Czechoslovakia (including Slansky's trial in 1952) antedated by approximately one year the announcement of the discovery of the Soviet "doctors' plot." One gets the impression that, in the wake of the Six Day War, Soviet propaganda planners decided, as it were, first to "experiment" with the various uses of anti-Semitism on the satellites, and then, depending on the results, either denounce it as an aberration alien to true Marxism-Leninism, or adapt it for domestic use. For the time being, Soviet propaganda spewed out anti-Semitic materials in Czechoslovakia, and offered at least encouragement and moral support of anti-Semitism in Poland. However, at first, at least until the end of 1967, precautions were taken not to allow the anti-Israeli rhetoric to degenerate into ordinary anti-Semitism.

It may be argued, of course, that, given the intensity of Soviet propaganda and the sharp awareness of ethnic identity in the USSR, this desire to steer a middle course was unrealistic; and events of the last three years certainly bear out this belief. One could not, in the USSR, wage an embittered propaganda war against the Jews of Israel without contributing to the already tensely anti-Semitic atmosphere in the country. Every Soviet citizen remembered that when the USSR was attacked by Nazi Germany in 1941, all persons of

German descent, including tens of thousands whose ancestors had settled in Russia centuries before, and even the dedicated Communists among them, were deported.

In the summer of 1967 the Soviet Union's unconditional support of the Arab cause resulted in a frenzied anti-Israeli campaign which made abundant use of traditional anti-Semitic stereotypes, particularly in cartoons that usually accompanied articles in Soviet newspapers and magazines. Then, early in 1968, came the stream of expressions of support for Poland's "anti-Zionist" drive and, some months later, the barrage of anti-Semitic propaganda unleashed against Czechoslovakia's liberals. But "anti-Zionism" and "anti-Judaism" began to grow increasingly fashionable within the USSR itself, and, in the absence of *any* attempt to combat them, could not but contribute to an exacerbation of anti-Semitic tensions within the country. Last but not least, an anti-Semitic tone was injected into the growing campaign against dissident Soviet intellectuals, among them a significant number of persons of Jewish origin, e.g., Pavel Litvinov, Larissa Daniel, Alexander Ginzburg.

A precursor of the resurgence of officially sponsored anti-Semitism was the reappearance in print of Trofim Kichko, a former Nazi collaborator, whose *Judaism Without Embellishment*, a crude anti-Semitic tract published in 1964 was, after vehement protests abroad, disowned by the ideological commission of the party's Central Committee. On October 4, 1967, an article by Kichko appeared in *Komsomolskoye Znamya*, a provincial newspaper published in the Ukraine; and on January 20, 1968, *Pravda Ukrainy*, the Republic's central newspaper, reported that Kichko was being rewarded with a scroll of honor for his "services to atheist propaganda," i.e., in effect his previously disowned tract. Soon thereafter, a new book by Kichko made its appearance. Its title, *Judaism and Zionism*, directly linked the practices and beliefs of Judaism to a hostile political ideology.[14] One of the book's central theses was the claim that Judaism — i.e., faith

---

14. Trofim K. Kichko, *Iudaizm i sionizm* (Kiev: "Znanie," 1968) was published in a very inexpensive edition of 60,000, at 14 kopeks per copy.

practiced by many of Russia's 3,000,000 Jews — bears much
of the responsibility for the "crimes" of Israeli "aggressors":

> There is a direct connection between the morality of Judaism
> and the actions of the Israeli Zionists. Weren't the actions of
> the Israeli extremists during their latest aggression against the
> Arab countries in keeping with the Torah?

But then, Kichko continued, this should not be surprising.
After all, "the Talmud does not even consider someone of
another faith a man, but merely a creature created in the
image of man." And, further, according to Kichko, Judaism
claims that "the entire world belongs to the Jews."

Kicho's book was followed by Yuri Ivanov's monograph
Beware, Zionism! [15] If anything, Ivanov's book was even more
poisonous than Kichko's. Raising the bogey of an international Jewish conspiracy, it said: "The Zionists are using the false
and reactionary concept of a 'world Jewish nation' in order to
establish control over citizens of diverse countries, as long as
they are of Jewish origin." It intimated that Soviet Jews
may not be immune to its blandishments by pointing out that
Zionism's — and, by extension, American imperialism —
slogans "have evoked a response among some circles of the
working Jewish intelligentsia" (author's emphasis). [16]

And, to top it all, it asserted that "Judaism is characterized by hatred of man, by preaching (in various forms and
ways) genocide, by cultivating love of power, and praising
criminal methods for achieving power." [17] All this prompted
a Soviet reviewer to point out approvingly that, "in contrast
to other varieties of modern nationalism, Zionism, as Yu.

---

15. Yuri Ivanov, *Ostorozhno, sionizm!* (Moscow: Gospolitizdat, 1969), 173
    pp.; published in an edition of 75,000, at 27 kopeks per copy.

16. The thesis had been advanced somewhat earlier in *Krasnaya Zvezda*,
    the newspaper of the Soviet armed forces, on August 17, 1968: "The
    Zionists stubbornly strive to make all Jews, regardless of citizenship
    and Party loyalties, partners in the Israeli aggression and in the dirty
    actions of the Jewish big bourgeoisie and of international imperialism,
    which are aimed at the camp of peace and Socialism. . . . Similar strata-
    gems were once resorted to by the Nazis in order to form their "fifth
    columns..." It also noted that Israeli intelligence was trying to recruit
    "persons of Jewish origin *residing in Socialist countries*" (author's em-
    phasis). Similar ideas were put forth in the January 24, 1969, issue of
    Sovetskaya Rossiya.

Ivanov convincingly demonstrates, is completely devoid of any democratic elements" (*Mezhdunarodnaya Zhizn'*, Moscow, April 1969). The equation was thus completed: the world's most inhuman religion spawned the world's most vicious nationalism, the only one without any redeeming features. At one time or another, this assertion has been advanced by scores of Soviet publications. [18]

In the last three years, sinister pictures of worldwide Jewish conspiracy have become a regular feature of Soviet periodicals. An article in *Komsomolskaya Pravda*, a Moscow youth newspaper, of October 4, 1967, offered a typical example of the genre:

> Zionism is an invisible, but huge and mighty, empire of financiers and industrialists, an empire not to be found on any map of the world, but one which nonetheless exists and operated everywhere in the capitalist camp. . . . The practical application of Zionism to Middle Eastern affairs includes genocide, racism, treachery, aggression and annexation. . . . As testified by a series of foreign sources, Zionist adherents in the United States alone number between twenty and twenty-five million. There are Jews and non-Jews among them [sic]. They belong to associations, organizations, and societies that play a dominant role in America's economy, politics, culture and science. Zionist lawyers comprise about 70 per cent of all American lawyers; the physicists, including those engaged in secret work of preparing weapons for mass destruction, comprise 69 per cent, and the industrialists, more than 43 percent. Adherents of Zionism among American Jews own 80 per cent of the local and international news agencies. In addition, about 60 percent of the large publishing houses serve the aims of the Zionists.

These strikingly "exact figures aroused the curiosity of some researchers who ultimately succeeded in tracking down the "series of foreign sources" referred to by the Soviet news-

17. Cited in *Jews in Eastern Europe* (London), January 1970, p. 61.

18. To cite two random examples from the central newspapers of the two union republics with the largest Jewish populations outside the Russian Federation: Zionism "promises the Jews that they will rule the entire world." (*Pravda Ukrainy*, Kiev, September 6, 1967); "He [Moshe Dayan] is a believer. He professes Judaism. In accordance with the tenets of his religion he considers himself 'God-chosen' "; and that is why, according to the Minsk *Sovetskaya Belorussiya* of March 9, 1969, he ordered fourteen Arabs buried alive, ostensibly in reprisal for the Baghdad "spy" hangings.

paper. It has now been established that the Soviet journalist's authority was a pamphlet published by *The Police Gazette*, a Cairo journal, in 1957, i.e., at a time when Egypt's propaganda apparatus was headed by Johannes van Leers, a Nazi fugitive and a former associate of Hitler's Propaganda Minister Joseph Goebbels.[19] Of late there were indiciations that Soviet propaganda was resorting with increasing frequency to Arab sources which, needless to say, were overtly anti-Semitic. At the same time, the USSR increased the import of Arab "cultural materials," such as feature films, with predictable results. Thus, on October 17, 1969, the London *Jewish Chronicle* reported that anti-Semitic demonstrations followed the showing of an Egyptian film portraying bloodthirsty Israeli villains, in Bessarabia, a Rumanian province annexed by the USSR in 1940.

In March 1970 the Soviet Union unleashed an unprecedented campaign of anti-Israel and "anti-Zionist" vilification, in which virulent attacks on Israel were completely merged with protestations that Jews in the USSR were a contented ethnic group, with no desire to leave for Israel. The latter element of the drive was a clear response to Western and Israeli protests against the disabilities suffered by Russia's Jews, who continued to be deprived even of those elementary rights granted to other ethnic groups in the USSR, such as schools, theaters and publications, all essential for the perpetuation of Jewish identity. For the first time, statements began to appear making official what had been known for a long time — that the Soviet authorities would do everything in their power to hasten the disappearance of Russia's Jews as a distinct ethnic group. Cultural genocide has now been acknowledged as the aim. A particularly odious feature of the campaign — still in full swing at the time of writing, after a brief intermission for the Lenin centennial observances in April 1970 — was the fact that the denunciations of

19. Yaakov Moriah, *Anti-Semitism — Tool of Soviet Policy* (Tel Aviv, 1968), pp. 7-8. It is curious that the Soviet sources mistranslated "physicians" as "physicists," and then proceeded to improve on the Egyptian original by adding the words "including those engaged in secret work of preparing weapons for mass destruction."

"Nazi-like" Israeli actions and protestations of absolute contentment of Russia's Jews with their position were all presented as having been voiced at "spontaneous" meetings organized by Soviet Jews and in letters written by them. Thus, among the authors of such declarations — now numbering in the hundreds — have been Jews from all walks of life, ranging from military specialists to scientists and poets, and from ordinary workers to Moscow's aging rabbi and Russia's greatest ballerina.

The best explanation of the rationale making anti-Semitism an attractive policy tool for the authorities in the Soviet bloc countries miraculously appeared in the Czechoslovak journal *Zitrek*,[20] named after the journal of pre-war democratic Czechoslovakia's President Eduard Benes. The article was published on March 19, 1969, well after Czechoslovakia's occupation by Soviet troops, and its tone of sad irony was typical of that country's journalism in those tragic days.

Written by Vilem Hejl a young novelist who was information officer of a now banned organization of former political prisoners during the Czechoslovak "liberal" period, it said in part:

> In a classical recipe for saving an unsuccessful or shaken regime, or for saving power, it is advisable to channel dissatisfaction, resistance, and hatred in a direction which is not a threat to that power, and which may even be useful to it. Non-Aryans need not necessarily be the target, although it is precisely they who are tested and well-tried objects.
>
> Jews can be more easily set apart and defined than, for instance, intellectuals, the opposition, or deviationists. Neither janitor nor mailman can be one hundred per cent certain that an attack on the intelligentsia is not somehow also aimed at him. The term "opposition" or "those extremist forces" are even more oblique and flexible. But every Aryan knows quite definitely that he is not a Zionist. This ensures that he will not feel endangered, and that he will not object if an apparatus of espionage and repression is created because, after all, it is only the Jews who are affected. Therefore, even if he is not sufficiently "high-principled" to cooperate, at least he won't obstruct it.

20. The journal was published by a group of liberal Czech intellectuals and was suppressed shortly after in published this article.

Hejl continued:

At first, the psychological mechanism [of blaming everything on the Jews — author] works reliably. Scapegoats are found, at the same time, there must be something positive for all the Aryans exempt from the effects of repressive measures. . . . All but the members of the minority under attack are automatically promoted to a caste of citizens of higher quality: this is Krone-wetter's Socialism for imbeciles. Simultaneously, a generous amnesty is declared. The blame for negligence is shifted to those affected by it. If water is not running in a new building, it is not the Aryan plumber who is to blame, but the Zionist surgeon living on the second floor. This cheap, but tested, fiction increases the number of those who share in the power, and a degree of social consolidation immediately results. . . . [But] after the first minority, the other minorities' turn inevitably must come. And everyone belongs to some minority — whether by origin, religion, profession, or by degree of commitment. And, the second time around, everything will go much more easily because the apparatus has had its workout in the first round. Coercion has come to be one of the well-tried and accepted methods of governing the state; and its success in solving the Jewish problem also intimidates those whose turn comes later.

Most of Hejl's observations do not appear to the Western reader as strikingly original. However, to the reader who was reared in Stalinist Czechoslovakia they must have been a revelation. Hejl's gloomy predictions unfortunately are being realized one by one, as a new era of repression gradually replaces the short-lived "thaw," not only in his homeland, but throughout the Soviet bloc.

September 1970

The Limits of Reform in Russia

Julius Jacobson

The many reforms in Russia since Stalin's death provide a seeming basis in fact for an all-too-popular image-transformation of Russia from a demonic force under Stalin, to an acceptable society under Khrushchev. A system which, current clichés advise us, is "dynamic," in "a state of ferment" and with "creative factors at work" organically evolving toward its historically determined liberal, democratic end. This view is not only projected by many who consider themselves radicals and socialists; it is far more popular than that. There is the case of George Kennan, a highly cultivated man of somewhat conservative tastes who, in an interview with Melvin Lasky (*Encounter*, March 1960), made the statement — astounding for a man of his background — that "in the main the goals and trends of Russian Communism lie along the same path as those of Western liberal-industrialism."

(Perhaps it is this recently unearthed liberal dynamic which encourages Kennan, in the same interview, to disparage "as most doubtful in point of adequacy to the needs of the time . . . the system of political parties and parliamentary institutions" known to the West and to advise us that ". . . for the endless varieties and gradations of normal [!] authoritarianism we in the West can afford to manifest a relaxed and even sympathetic toleration." Added to the cynicism of the "sympathetic toleration" for "normal authoritarianism" is the confusion arising from Kennan's promise that Russia, in the main, is moving onto the path of *liberal*-industrialism and the suggestion that the same country is settling down to a "normal" *authoritarianism.)*

Indeed, there have been many changes in Russia, and any balanced analysis of the meaning of the reforms, their implications and limits must mention, at least in summary fashion, what has prompted them and what areas of Russian life have been affected by them.

The labor discipline that was required for Communist Russia to industrialize in the 1930s—even when one discounts the excesses of Stalin—was an anachronism even before Stalin's death in 1953. The continued growth of the economy no longer depended on a relentless intensification of labor, forced labor camps or the Stalin-directed transfer of millions from the countryside to cities. Labor had to be more efficient to be more productive and for this it was necessary to provide political and economic incentives via relaxation of terror and rising living standards.

For the sake of science and technology it was indispensable that the hundreds of thousands of scientists, technicians, professionals engaged in manual labor in slave labor camps be released (along with millions of others removed from the normal work force and engaged in unproductive labor).

Terror and slave labor were not only without the same economic and political rationale of the thirties, they were also liabilities for Russia's new level of involvement in international politics after World War II.

Another inspiration for the post-Stalin reforms that must not be underestimated was the thinly disguised fear in the Kremlin that the peoples' hatred of Stalinism, unless mollified, might overwhelm a totalitarian system momentarily weakened by the loss of its main engineer.

Finally, and this must be underscored, the bureaucracy, for its own sake, *wanted* to relax. The bureaucrats wanted their class privileges and they wanted to live to enjoy them. This privilege of living was not certified so long as Stalin dominated the ruling Party. The Party Presidium had good reason to suspect that just before his death the "Great Mountain of Himalaya" was planning to bury some of his imminent pallbearers. Less certain was the identity of the victims...a disquieting state of affairs!

The bureaucrats not only wanted a greater assurance of normal longevity, they wanted — and needed — a set of procedures in the Party and laws in the country to live by which were explicit, ameliorative and predictable in operation to replace the Vyshinskyite "philosophy" of law that established the legal basis for the murderous and unpredictable whims of Stalin.

In a word, then, the bureaucracy sought to "normalize" its rule.

Almost immediately after Stalin's death, reforms were effected. The slave labor system was sharply curtailed in the amnesties of 1953 and 1955. The pernicious Doctrine of Analogy and Confession as Queen of Proof were eliminated in the letter of Russian law. The power of internal security agencies and secret services used by Stalin was reduced.

Wages were raised, the work week shortened and added free social services provided for the workers. A rise in consumer goods production made pay increases more meaningful.

There has been a vast extension of free educational facilities. And in the cultural thaw of 1955-1956 creative talents could produce with a modicum of artistic integrity for the first time in over 20 years. The cultural atmosphere has tightened since then but remains many degrees above the Stalin freeze. It was still possible for Ilya Ehrenburg recently to write of Pasternak not approvingly, but with some compassion. Also, limited debates are now permitted on such topics as the meaning of life and socialist humanism.

Then there is the great overall change: the reduction of terror coupled with Communist efforts to win the approval of the masses.

THE REALITIES OF RUSSIAN LIFE

Before reviewing the theory of a self-democratizing Russia, it is important to look first at the realities of Russian life for two reasons: first, to help correct the false image

created by the superficialities of Stalinoid journalism and
sightseers' tidbits; second, the level of social, political and
economic life in Russia today reveals something of the very
definite limits to Russian reforms.

The most common misimpression is that Russia is in the
process of political "democratization." But lessening of terror
and growth of democracy are separate propositions. To understand this is essential to comprehending the nature of
Russian society and the limits of the reforms. There was not
a single democratic institution under Stalin. There is not a
single democratic institution under Khrushchev: no right
to organize a critical press; no right to organize political
parties; no right to freedom of speech; no right to free
elections. The denial of these rights is codified in many
sections of Russian law. For example, in the statutes on
"State Crimes," Article 7, labelled "Anti-Soviet Agitation
and Propaganda" outlaws:

> Slanderous fabrication defaming the Soviet State and social
> system, or the dissemination, production or keeping of the litera-
> ture of such content for the same purpose.

Obviously, any organized movement of opposition to the
Party line via a political party, press, publication, speech,
etc., would be for the purpose of "slanderous fabrication
defaming the Soviet State and social system," punishable by
imprisonment for up to seven years or exile and banishment
for two to five years.

There were no trade unions under Stalin. There are no
trade unions under Khrushchev. By trade unions, we mean
the organization of working men in independent bodies which
advance the interests of their members through the right to
strike, to boycott, to pressure, to engage in political action. In
Russia, there are *institutions* called trade unions with no
internal democracy which exist as an integral part of the
State. While the leaders of these misnamed trade unions
handle workers' grievances occasionally and administer in
other respects to some of their needs, the main function of
these Party-State adjuncts is to discipline the labor force and
see to it that production goals are met. As Khrushchev put it:

> At present, the most fundamental, the most essential task of the

Soviet trade unions lies in mobilizing the efforts of the great working masses . . . for the timely fulfillment of the Seven Year Plan.

Simple freedom of physical movement is still sharply curtailed in Russia. All citizens are required to carry internal passports and permission must be granted by the police before one can change his locality. Without this passport, a worker cannot get a job and, in certain key industries such as coal and armaments, management is required to take away workers' passports in order that they be sealed to their jobs.

The campaign for "socialist legality" has eliminated some excesses of Stalinist terror; but *socialist* legality under Khrushchev remains a brutal hoax.

Despite improved living standards, the Russian people are worse off than almost any other people in a modern, industrial nation. Their pay is less, they eat less (during the first quarter of 1961 there was a 13% drop in meat processing) and they enjoy fewer comforts of life.

In the Seven Year Plan—which is to introduce Russia to the lower range of the higher stages of communism — the average wage of the Russian worker is to increase by a grand total of 26%: a rise from 78 to 99 rubles a month after five years. In dollars, from $86 to $109 per month by 1965. About $25 a week for the average worker! Even if the percentage increase is doubled, that would still leave the average weekly take home at about $30.

Much is made of the "free" social services provided for the Russian worker. There is something to this. Perhaps this adds the equivalent of another one-third to his paycheck (surely, a generous estimate). That still leaves him with a meager income by bourgeois standards, not to speak of the standards of a nation charging toward Communism. On the other hand, what needs to be emphasized no less is the worker pays through the nose for these "free" services via the infamous "turnover tax" — a tax on consumer goods added to the normal price, which socialists have traditionally fought. In Russia, the government revenue from this tax, borne mainly by the poorer classes, came to approximately $35 billion in 1960. Some consumer foods are taxed as high as 50%

of their normal selling price. Thus, a pair of men's shoes in Moscow costs about 32.50 rubles ($36.00) or considerably more than a week's pay. The same pair of shoes in New York costs about $10 and is of superior quality.

Other revealing prices: a dozen eggs — $2.33 (about $.55 in New York); a pound of sugar — $.45; a man's overcoat — $166.50 (one that retails for about $40 in New York); a four-cylinder car — $2,775 (nearly three years pay for the average worker).

But there have been widely touted tax reforms in Russia! By 1965, the personal income tax is to be completely eliminated! This will mean a saving of about three-quarters of one ruble per week for the average Russian worker in a factory or an office! Peasants with income from private plots are not even granted this insignificant relief.

How many times have we heard that if wages are low and taxes high, at least the Russian worker lives virtually rent-free! What is often omitted, however, is that the working class lives virtually space-free, as well.

In 1960, there were approximately seven square yards of living space for each Russian worker. This provided one averaged-sized room for every three people. The average family had little more than one room with a kitchen shared by other families and a communal toilet.

By the end of 1965 — if the Seven Year Plan quota is met — there will be eight square yards of living space for each person. Assuming that this is oversubscribed heavily, it is still doubtful that the average Russian family will have much more than one-half the living space currently enjoyed by the average urban family in bourgeois America. And the average family in an industrial Russian city will not have much more living space than its parents had in 1917!

One of the worst outrages of the Stalin era was the mass persecution of the Jews. Stalin practiced a policy that hinted at racial genocide. That he killed thousands of Jews for being Jews is now denied by few outside the hard core of Communist party members.

In the present period Jews are not murdered by the regime en masse. That is certainly an improvement. But the false image of Russia as a self-reforming system blurs the view of a society in which anti-Semitism has been raised to a thinly veiled government policy. Russia, today, is the most anti-Semitic of any industrial nation.

On every internal passport, a Russian citizen must mark his nationality. A Georgian puts down "Georgian"; a Great Russian puts down "Russian"; but a Georgian *Jew* or a Great Russian *Jew* must mark down as his nationality — "Jew."

This gross anti-Semitic act has its bitter irony: the Jew, forced to write "Jew" as his nationality, is deprived of all the cultural rights of a national people, as well as of a cultural and religious minority. There is no Yiddish theater, no Yiddish publishing house, no Yiddish national organization permitted.

(It appears that one Yiddish publication may be tolerated in the near future — this is hailed by some apologists as disproof of anti-Semitism.)

In the past several years, a rash of anti-Semitic stereotypes have appeared in the Russian press. We are told, for example, that rabbis "were active in spreading anti-Soviet slander and, with foaming mouths, called on the Jewish bourgeoisie to finance the intervention against the U.S.S.R."

In the Ukrainian language, Radio Kirovograd ranted that "Jewish ministers and circumcisers execute the rite of circumcision, which has a strikingly nationalistic character" and accused religious Jewish leaders in Kirovograd of praying "only to the Golden Calf: how to collect more money from believers for their own needs and to pray for the militant spirit of the Israeli militarists. Thus praying, they call for the killing of all those who deny the Pentateuch — the Jewish prayerbook."

Is it any wonder that against this background there have occurred desecrations of Jewish cemeteries and synagogues, that Jews have been beaten, even killed in this society reported on the path of "Western liberal-industrialism?" And is it surprising to learn that in a Moscow suburb a "Beat the Jew Committee" distributed a circular demanding that the "Jew be thrown out of commerce where he damages socialist property" and bemoans that "we rescued them from the Germans who treated them more wisely"?

I have acknowledged the cultural relaxation — the famous thaw — that has been effected in Russia. But after these reforms are acknowledged, what remains is a society most reactionary in its government restrictions on cultural freedom and most primitive in cultural and intellectual thought generated. Where else but in Russia does one find as a typical party-encouraged attitude a denunciation of "Freudianism, [as] a typical product of bourgeois ideological reaction in the epoch of imperialism, [which has been] employed by bourgeois ideologists as a means of benumbing the masses in the interests of imperialism and as an ideological weapon in the struggle against Marxism."

And in what other country can one find a parallel to Khrushchev's following instructions on literary matters to a Central Committee Plenary session:

> Among the writers in our country are individuals who say: How can there be Party guidance of literature? We tell such people: Do you mean to say, my dear fellow, that you do not recognize Party guidance? What is Party guidance? It is the will of millions of people, the will of millions of minds, the collective wisdom of millions. But one writer or another may sit at his country house, hatching a sniveling book, yet want it to be recognized as an expression of the sentiments of the people of our times, of all the people. Is that not a real cult of one's own personality, which, you see, does not want to suffer the guidance of the Party, expressing the will of millions? And such a man with his contrived book wants to rise above the Party, above the people. How many different kinds of people there are! This is, of course, a departure from the norm, a psychological phenomenon, so to speak, and such deviations evidently will take place with some individuals even under Communism.

The writer of a "sniveling book" in Khrushchev's inspirational message on literary criticism was Pasternak. Pasternak was permitted to live, even after he wrote *Doctor Zhivago*. That *is* a reform compared to what would have occurred during the Stalin era. Pasternak's punishment was meted out posthumously by Khrushchev with his vengeful sentencing of Mme. Olga Ivinskaya, Pasternak's Larisa, and her daughter,

Irina, to a prison labor camp for eight years and three years respectively. Such is the true measure of the limits of reform . . . "sniveling" authors impinging on beloved and reforming tyrants.

KHRUSHCHEV'S BRAND OF TERRORISM

Under Stalin, bureaucratic purges and extorted confessions were endemic to the system. That remains the case under Khrushchev. In the earlier instance, bureaucrats were purged of life itself; since Stalin's death — with a few deadly exceptions — the purges bureaucratically deprive bureaucrats of position, prestige and power — but not life.

Only someone totally blinded by Stalinophobia could dismiss the difference as unimportant. On the other hand, it usually takes a special kind of mentality to disregard or minimize the horror of a society where purges and confessions continue on a massive scale. And if the victims do not confess with the same degree of abjectness, this is not to say that the style and form of Russian confessions do not remain a distinct contribution to political psychopathology: Malenkov "could see with clarity [sic] my guilt and responsibility for the unsatisfactory state of affairs in agriculture." Molotov realized that his "formulations [are] theoretically erroneous and politically harmful"; Pervukhin grew "profoundly aware of my guilt before the Party"; while that old war horse, Bulganin, was forced to confess with some of the old flavor:

> What, then, is Molotov . . .? Molotov is a person who has cut himself off from the life of the Soviet people and is totally [!] ignorant of both industry and agriculture. Kaganovich is an intriguer who proved himself capable of every sort of vileness... in 1957 I joined them, supported them and . . . later shared with them all the anti-Party filth.

A society without a single democratic institution, without a free labor movement, with a populace ill-fed, ill-housed and ill-paid; with all the "normal" trappings of an abnormal society: anti-Semitism, cultural barbarism, large-scale purges, bizarre confessions and an antediluvian code of justice — all this remains in Russia after the reforms. Yet, it is this frightful society that has captured the imagination of many; looked upon by some as a socialist society, by others as kind of socialism, and by yet others as a society evolving toward liberalism or democracy or socialism.

What more distressing evidence can there be of the decline of radical culture and the loss of nerve and intelligence?

AN APOLOGIA FOR STALINISM

The new mood of toleration for the Kremlin has removed from unwarranted obscurity the names and works of such historians as Edward Carr and Isaac Deutscher. It is the latter, above all others, who was much maligned and misunderstood by those who misconstrued his distaste for the excesses of Stalinism as the emanations of a virulent anti-Sovietist. How wrong they were, many now realize. For it is Deutscher who has elaborated a grand historical apologia for Stalinism (and Stalinist terror) which now meshes with a growing Stalinoid mood.

According to Deutscher, Marxism was originally a body of thought that was rational, humane, democratic and alien to chauvinist prejudices. However, Marxism in its pure form failed; neither in Marx's time nor after has there been a single successful proletarian revolution. This failure was not without its compensations. For, Deutscher writes, "Marxism has spread to the East; and by the efforts of the intelligentsia and a young and small working class it has conquered primitive peasant nations . . . . At the middle of this century Marxism has become in a sense displaced from the West and *naturalized in Russia and China.* Where it has survived as a mass movement in the West, in France and Italy, it has done so in its *'Orientalized'* form: and it exists there as a broad reflex of the Russian *metamorphasis* of Marxism" (emphasis added).

What, more explicitly, is meant by Marxism's "Orientalized" form? Deutscher obliges: "In the East, Marxism has absorbed the traditions of Tsardom and Greek Orthodoxy." And, in a similar vein, "Stalinism represented the amalgamation of Western European Marxism with Russian barbarism."

Moreover, Deutscher finds accompanying Orientalized Marxism a parallel to the primitive magic of tribal cults in the complex totem and taboos of Stalinism. Thus, Stalinism is not only Orientalized Marxism, it also "appears as the mongrel offspring of Marxism and primitive magic."

It is not this writer's purpose to conduct an extended polemic over such matters; that is reserved for another occasion.* But I must note my view that what Deutscher has conveniently concocted with his mongrelized-barbarized-orientalized-mysticized-metamorphized *Marxism* is a poisonous brew that is fatal for socialism.

To believe that socialism can be itself *and* its negation is not a paradox, which is a *seeming* contradiction; it is pure absurdity. It is one thing to say that Marxism is being touched, even influenced, by totalitarian methods or concepts; it is another thing to say that there is such a beast as "Autocratic Socialism" (to use Deutscher's phrase) in which "autocratic" (or "barbaric" or "oriental") is used to *describe* or *define* Marxian socialism.

Marxists believe that there was a liberal dynamic to *capitalist* industrialization. But its existence was not proved by abstract references to industrialization as a force generating democracy. The democratizing dynamic was established only after the concrete workings and class relations of capitalism were carefully examined; only after it was established that in the nature of capitalism, despite all its misgivings about democracy and for all its violence against revolutionary democratic movements, capitalism itself was obliged, from within, so to speak, to permit individual freedom and democratic institutions to a degree unthinkable under the old order. It was shown that there was no permanently irreconcilable conflict between capitalism and parliamentary democracy; capitalist parties and socialist parties could coexist up to a point; the growth of a legally and politically *free* working class was necessary for capitalism and its organization in *free* trade unions presented no direct fundamental challenge to the social rule of the bourgeoisie.

Because industrial growth impelled the formation of a large and homogeneous working class and an intelligentsia,

---

*   A two-part critical study of Deutscher by Julius Jacobson is reprinted in
    this volume, pp. 86-162.

and provided leisure, education, culture, etc., it multiplied the physical agents and conditions for further democratization within the widely permissive limits of capitalism.

Now, if it can be shown that a free working class, trade unions, antagonistic political parties, parliamentary democracy, free press, free speech, cultural freedom, etc., can coexist within the limits of the Russian social system (even as these freedoms have a limited coexistence with most advanced capitalist nations today) the overwhelming probability is that the continued expansion of Russian industry will generate political freedom. But this has never been proven, for two related reasons: one, because it is impossible (in my opinion); two, it is far easier to be a prophet-apologist for Stalinism on the basis of broad, sweeping generalizations than to relate them to the realities of Russian class rule.

Nor is anything clarified by endlessly repeating the mystique of Russia as a Planned Economy with a Nationalized industry and therefore freed from the limitations placed on democracy by capitalism. It is a logical fallacy to suppose that because Russia is relieved of the liabilities of capitalism it is therefore possessed of a special sociological disposition favoring democratization.

Soviet apologists see the precondition for Russia's democratization as the growth of the productive forces. As the link between Stalinism and socialist freedom they must be free from excessive external interference.

Should the exigencies of the cold war oblige the Kremlin to over-invest in heavy industry and in the means of destruction, then, it is possible, they inform us, that the whole process of de-Stalinization would be impeded, perhaps forced into reverse gear. An excessive military budget would only penalize consumer industries; this, in turn might exacerbate the dissatisfaction of the Russian people; and a dissatisfied populace might oblige the Kremlin to resort to more repressive measures.

In this manner, the Russian social system is exonerated in advance of basic responsibility for the failure of domestic reforms to move forward. Instead, it would be the fault of those outside of Russia who resist the Kremlin's ambitions in West Berlin or protest the Russian "sphere of influence" in East Europe. This, of course, in the age-old argument of all apologists for imperialism who attribute retrogression in their favored land to its obligation to defend itself against alien subversion, or foreign imperialism. It is the counterpart of those who apologize for American imperialism in Cuba or Latin America as a purely defensive move against Communist aggression.

Given this self-contained system, the only way one could conclusively check the democratic potential of Russian industrialization abstracted from the real world of international conflict would be for the Kremlin to eliminate the capitalist third of the world and absorb the uncommitted third. Then, we could really see if Russia, freed from the restraining influence of the cold war would evolve toward democratic socialism.

This is a test we can readily forego.

Let us look at one implication of any theory which makes a virtual law of the industrial-freedom relationship.

Under the guidance of the Fuehrer and his Nazi party (a party ridden with totems, taboos and primitive magic), Germany recorded industrial advances impossible under the old, weak, vacillating, internally divided Weimar Republic. Under the pressure of internal needs and external threats, its technology and science led the world, its unemployed were put to work, and a limited sort of economic rationalization was introduced. It is true that this economic progress was achieved by barbaric methods equalled only by Stalin's superindustrialization during the same period. But historical necessity leaves little room for sentimental moralizing. Human rights and democracy come later.

The dynamism of the German economy was evidenced by Germany's ability to fight the entire world almost singlehandledly for four bloody years. That it was brought to its knees was no sign of weakness. (Had Germany been matched only with Russia during the war, Nazism's social superiority would have been proved.) But what would have happened if the Nazis had conquered Europe? We have no illusions about

the immediate political consequences. National boundaries
would have been destroyed, millions murdered and terror
would have beset an entire continent. Germany's industrial
expansion, however, would have been incalculable as it accumulated the wealth, the talent, the manpower and other
resources of subjugated Europe.

But with the methods of terror, it could go so far and no
further. Yet, the demands for continued expansion would be
there, generated by the economic ambitions of German
capitalists and the political ambitions of the Nazi party.
Since neither the German bourgeoisie nor the Nazi party
would have been prepared to pay the penalty of stagnation,
they would have been obliged to eliminate, gradually, the
grossest of their terroristic excesses and slowly, reluctantly,
to move toward democracy.

Germany would have had to release her aircraft designers,
unmuzzle her intellectuals and provide the working class
with the incentive of freedom as a political investment to
raise the productivity of labor. Thus, Nazism, with the weapons of barbarism, would have been the source of its own
democratic negation. (Unless international tensions would
have set back these democratic reforms.)

I know that some will answer this Nazi analog by saying
that the German bourgeoisie (and all capitalism) could not
possibly extend rights to the people that ran counter to the
"rights" of the bourgeoisie to exploit the worker and produce
goods for a profit on the market; and the Nazi party could not
afford to extend political or social democracy to the masses
since democracy ran counter to its ideology. The matter of
ideology I will come to shortly. It is the first part of the answer that is interesting here, not because it is wrong but, on
the contrary, so correct. Certainly, the limits to democracy
under capitalism are set by the "rights" of the capitalists to
exploit and to make a profit. But these are considerations of
class and *class relations* which do not enter into the calculations of the apologists for Russia. The point of this analogy is
that if one judges Nazism without any serious discussion of
class relations, it is possible to build a rationale for Nazism
similar to that of the Stalinist apologists.

THE MYTH OF STALINIST IDEOLOGY

Commonly added to the mystique of Industrialization and Planning is the myth of Stalinist ideology as a force impelling democratization.

Inherent in Communist ideology, so the argument goes, is commitment to freedom. Even during the worst years of Stalinist terror, when ideology was warped by "primitive magic," Communism was obliged to speak of national independence, racial equality and the future classless society where all men will be brothers. It also placed on required reading lists many Marxist classics. This "ideal inherent in Stalinism," Issac Deutscher wrote in his political biography of Stalin, "has remained the inspiration" in Russia, although the ideal was "given a grossly distorted expression" by Stalin.

If this "remained the inspiration" under Stalin, how much more inspiring it is today! For, as economic advances have brought Russia beyond the point where terror is required, the idea of freedom inherent in Communist ideology takes on new and more powerful meaning. The masses, who do not have to be convinced of the value of freedom, are made even more conscious of its absence. They press for freedom, and the bureaucracy, with less reason to resist such pressures, and themselves under the "inspiration" of Communist ideology moves, slowly, gradually — sometimes reluctantly — to bring reality into conformity with ideological commitment to freedom. There is also a more educated and confident intelligentsia in Russia, many of them young and uncompromised by personal responsibility for Stalin's terror. They find positions on all levels of government and industry. They, too, are "inspired" and encouraged by the relaxation and become a potent force for democratization.

There is something to be said for this popular thesis only as a "grossly distorted expression" of the truth.

Ideology *is* of tremendous moment in the Communist system. Its greater importance as compared to capitalism is rooted in the fact that Russia is ruled by a propertyless class whose authority is established by its political power. By contrast, the social power of capitalists resides in their private ownership of the means of production in a market

economy. As long as government protects the sanctity of free
enterprise, there is no absolutely compelling reason for
capitalists to concern themselves with ideology. Doctrine can
become a subject for pedants; politics for politicians.

In Russia, there is no such division between economics and
politics. The means of production are owned by the State.
And those who collectively control the State own the means
of production. Where social power is thus politically determined, the ruling class rules directly, and the ruling agency
— in Russia, the leadership of the Communist party — becomes in a most literal sense "the executive committee of the
ruling class." Clearly, politics for this "executive committee"
implies the highest levels of political sophistication and *class
consciousness*. This consciousness is invested in the complex
and well-tended ideology with which the ruling class struggles against opponents, justifies its rule, gives itself purpose,
fights for popular support outside and inside Russia.

This is not to say that the politics of the bureaucratic class
is determined by its ideology. On the contrary, it is more concerned with power than consistent principles. But a class
ideology does not require consistent principles. Indeed, a
basic function of Communist ideology is to provide a broad, Je-
suitical system to prove all contradictions to be nothing more
than strategic shifts, or new responses to new situations, all
of them consistent with the larger historical purpose of
Communism and therefore consistent with each other. Thus,
with its medieval casuistry called ideology, the contradiction
between Popular Front and the Nazi-Soviet Pact becomes a
logical sequence of strategic moves; totalitarianism becomes
freedom, subjugated nations becomes People's Democracies,
and, as we shall see, the future classless society in Russia
means the dictatorship of the Communist party, whose authority becomes even more absolute than in Stalin's day.

This totalitarian class, and its ideology, did not arise out
of the efforts of an indigenous, prerevoluntionary force in
Russia, contending for power with the armies and ideologies
of socialism and Czarism. It arose gradually, without any
clear perspective, out of the ranks and leadership of the
Communist movement — a movement already festering in

the early twenties—filling a vacuum created in that unhappy land by the inability of socialism to survive in isolation, and the impossibility of any other class to assume power. The Stalinist faction in the Bolshevik party — the Russian ruling class in embryo — to satisfy its own needs, to win support in and out of the Party, was obliged to speak in the name, and with the idiom, of socialism. It would do nothing else and nothing else would do. As it manipulated socialist language and concepts, it set the stage for transforming the Party, murdering its leaders and subverting everything that gives meaning to socialism.

(I should add here, just in passing, that when I speak of the Communists' ideological manipulation of language, I do *not* mean that they do so out of purely evil and undirected motives. Ideology fulfills an indispensable moral and psychological need for the bureaucracy. If the Russian leaders, even the most evil of them, were so many Iagos without a higher moral rationale, deceiving and manipulating for the pure joy of doing evil, we would not be discussing either a social system or an ideology, but a vast lunatic asylum.)

This writer, then, understands the historic roots of Communist ideology and why some (not all) of the socialist idiom has become a fixed ideological feature, and why it is obliged to bring to the public some (not all) books of some (not all) great socialist figures of the past.

But, after this is established — and exaggerated — what is there about these *aspects* of Communist ideology which gives them such force that the basic foundations of Communist class rule will gradually give way?

The answer might be given that "there are objective laws in Russia as in any society and these laws are more important than what this or that bureaucrat wants to do."

To which one might well reply: what laws? I know of economic laws under capitalism which exist independently of the whim of this or that capitalist. However, as has been pointed out, those who rule in Russia make their own laws. Their rule predicates *conscious* direction of society and they know, not by blind instinct but through consciousness, that their special privileges and prestige as a class rests on their control of the State and that this control is secure only as long as they can prevent contenders from arising. Khrushchev knows this; so does Suslov; it is known to that drab, anti-Semitic Minister of Culture, Mme. E. A. Furtseva; it is known to Brezhnev, to Mikoyan, to all Party secretaries from *Raions* up to the Central Committee; it is known to the Communist heads of the so-called trade unions; it is known to the super-annuated Komsomol chieftans. It is known, as well, to the editors of *Izvestia, Pravda* and *Party Life.* They all know that the limits to reform are set in this conscious class resistance to democratic institutions. They know that political parties, free press, free unions and similarly alien institutions can come to Russia only over their dead bodies — figuratively speaking, of course.

PENETRATION OF SOCIALISM

Yet, there is a liberalizing force generated by the language and texts of freedom. But it is not the dynamic that is going to see the self-redemption or self-immolation of a "historically progressive" totalitarian class.

The basic ideas of socialism did break through the curtain of Communist ideological falsification even during the era of Stalinist terror. They penetrate with even greater force in periods of relaxation. As terror becomes more latent, the ruling class is compelled to rely more on persuasion. It removes socialist books from the Index; it permits greater freedom of discussion of a wider range of subjects. It produces the "intellectual ferment" familiar to all. This may have made the masses hopeful at first. But the bureaucracy cannot possibly eliminate those glaring contradictions between the realities of its rule and the promises suggested by the reforms. The working class will not be permitted to enjoy either leisure or freedom; students and intellectuals will grow increasingly aware of the difference between Marx's promise of Communism as "the true resolution of the strife between existence and essence, between objectification and self-confirmation, between freedom and necessity, between the individual and the species" and the actuality of a one-Party system where the Party grows stronger and man remains the alienated object of class exploitation.

The dynamic of democratization, then, which inheres in Communism is to be found neither in its commitment to the socialist idiom, nor in its reforms. The dynamic resides only in the ability of these circumstances to educate, arouse and encourage the people to resolve the permanent contradiction between Communism and freedom in massive democratic struggles from below which aim not at reforming the ruling class but destroying it.

Any "ideal inherent" in Stalinism is but the "false consciousness" of a ruling class. A truer image of Communism can be found in the specific doctrines and general concepts inherent in a bastardized ideology that crosses some of the language and concepts of socialism with the strategic and fundamental social needs of a totalitarian class. It is not the ideal of racial equality or the brotherhood of man, but the theories of "socialism in one country," "social fascism," "Popular Frontism," which truly *inhere* in Communism. More than such reactionary notions, tribal rites, hero-worship and cultism continue under Khrushchev, as they will continue under his heir. The magic potion is less heady today, but it is there, and in recent years the cultist brew has taken on more of the stench of Stalin's day.

In addition to its inherent and unique antisocialist doctrines and "primitive magic" the true role, essence and measure of Communist ideology has been the corruption of the concepts and definitions which are at the very heart of socialism.

The Communist Manifesto states that the "first step in the workers' revolution is to make the proletariat the ruling class, to establish democracy." Stalinist ideology can neither ignore nor permit such formulations. Thus, according to the 1959 edition of the *History of the Communist Party of the Soviet Union*, Russia today is a "socialist democracy ... which secures to all citizens genuine freedom of speech, of the press, of assembly, meetings and demonstrations." Here, the *History* recognizes that democracy does mean freedom of press, speech, meetings, demonstrations. But the decisive *content* of democracy is denied and thereby redefined by the assertion that democracy *in practice* is exemplified by what *exists* in Russia. This gross redefinition of democracy is one edge of a multi-bladed ideological knife thrust into the heart of the whole humanist ethic of socialism: the disjunction between freedom and socialism, between "political democracy" and "economic democracy."

Such notions existed before Stalin, but it is Communism which made them a central feature of an ideology, and promoted it throughout the world. How effective this campaign has been can be seen in all the pseudosophisticated jabberwocky of those who assume that Russia has a "socialist economy" with a "political dictatorship," that it is a "workers' state" and, in the same breath, that its working class is disfranchised. This loss of concern in the left wing world with the relevance of freedom to socialism implies surrendering the values of both.

Stalinist ideology was always concerned with the future. To be sure, it was not the socialist future envisioned in broad outlines by socialist theoreticians. Stalinism had to weave the totalitarian reality into the egalitarian vision. In Stalin's day, this took the form of two grotesque theories: as the State moves toward the classless society, the class struggle becomes sharper; and, second, once in the classless phase, the State not only doesn't wither away but becomes more oppressive.

Ideological concern with the future is further heightened today under the impetus of a totalitarian regime trying to substitute persuasion for the naked use of a now latent terror. If only the peasants produce more, the workers meet quotas, everyone keeps his proper place and capitalism doesn't upset the schedule, then in 1970, or thereabouts — when American levels of production are reached — Russia will move into its higher Communist phase. (As though all that has to be done to reach Communist abundance is to match capitalist America's production figures!) Khrushchev feels the need to discuss the future not only for the sake of economic incentives, or to win favor, or because Communism is imminent. It also relates to the most important sociological change in Russia — the role of the Communist party.

Since this change provides the clearest evidence of the limits to Russian reform, it is worth a brief review; after which we will see that these changes have inspired reversals of Marxist thought similar to those contributed by Stalin.

THE COMMUNIST PARTY

The Communist party under Stalin — and under Khrushchev — was a vast coordinating agency embracing individuals on various levels of authority: factory managers, technicians, scientists, army men, teachers, intellectuals and the host of officials associated with non-Party government agencies.

However, within the Party structure there were not only government officials and the like, but the Party Specialists — the apparatus men who rose to prominence not by serving any special branch of government or economy but by serving the needs of the Party.

It was inevitable that *within* the Communist party conflicts would arise between the 3% which composed the Party machinery and other leading Party members prominent in government or military agencies. Army men, for example, who were Party members, had their own apparatus outside the Party. They developed narrower interests, thought more of combat training than of Party indoctrination. To a lesser degree, this was true of Party members who headed government ministries where they built private machines to which they had to cater, bringing them into conflict with professional Party functionaries. Certainly the ministers of various security agencies who had their own economic empires in slave labor camps and a powerful military apparatus under them, did not and could not have an identity of interests with the Party specialist.

It was a conflict between the Party machine, which must think in terms of power and be concerned with questions of ideology, foreign strategy, etc., and those whose loyalty to the Party competed with their own special interests as government officials.

This conflict between ministers and functionaries in Stalin's Party had its corollary in broader conflicts between the Party as a whole and non-Party technicians, managers and administrators. These conflicts which generated intrigues, purges and inefficiency were essential for the rule of the personal dictator. Stalin remained on the peak of each hierarchy and through his unique position, he could play one force against another and thereby see to it that no hierarchy or individual in either the Party or the government could ever challenge his supreme authority as the final arbiter of all disputes.

To maintain a kind of equilibrium of power, subordinate to his own, Stalin consciously set about to weaken (not destroy) the primacy of Communist party organizations in various government ministries. For example, it was expressly stated in the Party rules in 1939, and repeated in 1952, that the Party organizations in local industrial enterprises were not to dictate policies in the event of disputes with local managers.

When Stalin died, he left no heirs. Without his decisive voice and with no other to replace it immediately, heads of Party and State openly spoke of "panic and disarray," and within the Party the rivalry between *apparatchiki* and government ministers grew less restrained. This conflict has been resolved in the only way possible for the more viable functioning of a totalitarian system. The *apparatchiki* has become supreme in the Party, and the Party has become supreme in the country. And, once again, there is a personal dictator.

The Presidium of the Communist party after Stalin's death consisted of ten full members and four candidate-members. Of these, only one was a Party specialist who held no ministerial post: Nikita Khrushchev. All but one of the others have been purged: Beria was executed and his Ministry of the Interior eventually subdivided and rendered powerless as a potential threat to the supremacy of the Party; Malenkov tried to build his machine in the government apparatus as Premier and he was purged. Bulganin, who took over Malenkov's job, was purged, as were Pervukhin, the economic specialist, Kanganovich, Minister of Heavy Industry, Molotov, head of the Foreign Ministry, etc.

Of the original post-Stalin Presidium, only one minister, Mikoyan, remains. And between the Presidium as it stood in 1953 and today, there have been several turnovers with purges of governmental leaders a continual process until there has emerged, today, a Presidium of the Communist party on which only a minority have any leading ministerial posts.

Evidence that this struggle broke out openly in the Party immediately after Stalin's death was provided by the frame-up and execution of Beria. (He was accused of being in the pay of foreign imperialism during the civil war!)

Whatever motives others may have had in liquidating the head of the powerful Minister of Internal Affairs, the Party apparatus men feared this powerful Ministry as well as threats to the Party's primacy.

Pravda announced immediately after his arrest:

> The party organization must exercise regular and systematic surveillance over the work of all organizations and governmental offices as well as the activity of all leading officials. In line with this, it is necessary to maintain systematic and continuous supervision over the activity of the organs of the Ministry of Internal Affairs. This is not merely the right, but the direct duty of the party organization.

Khrushchev makes little pretense about his objection to leading Communists who have special allegiances outside of the Party sitting on the Presidium. In the case of Zhukov, for example, it was explained:

> Zhukov pursued a line separating our armed forces from the Communist Party, of weakening the party organization and essentially of weakening the political organs in the Soviet Army. His work was clearly marked by a tendency to regard the Soviet Armed forces as his own domain.
>
> The Party, which controls and directs the activity of all organizations and agencies, cannot leave the armed forces outside its field of vision. Leadership of them cannot be outside the control of the Party, of its Central Committee.

The idea that what we have in Russia is a managerial society or a managerial revolution was given the death blow in 1957 in a series of economic changes pushed through by Khrushchev. In these changes, the state economic commission was emasculated and the country broken down into a large number of economic regions. This was advertised as designed to increase the efficiency of industry by removing bureaucratic control from the center and giving local managers an incentive to increase production. That might have been one purpose, but of no less significance, the economic "reforms"

of 1957 were designed to give the Party a better chance to
supervise the work of the managers and technicians. By
giving greater authority to local economic bodies, it became
easier for local bodies of the centralized Communist party to
oversee directly and supervise production schedules and the
behavior of economic managers. As explained in an editorial
in Pravda:

> The reorganization of the management of the economy on the
> territorial principle will increase immeasurably the respon-
> sibility of the *Party* agencies in the republics, territories and
> regions for the development of production. . . the *Party* will
> guide efficiently and concretely industrial enterprises and con-
> struction projects.

The growing power of the Communist party is also evidenced by the revival of Comrades Courts and the formation
of People's Guards. Hailed by many as "reforms," they are
no such thing. The "Comrades Courts are elected public
agencies charged with actively contributing to the inculcation in citizens of a spirit of a Communist attitude toward
labor and socialist property, and the observance of the rules
of socialist behavior," according to the Model Statutes on
Comrades Courts. They are organized everywhere: in schools,
enterprises, apartment houses, collectives. The court is
selected at a general meeting of workers, students. These
courts hear minor infractions of discipline and can pass
light sentences on a worker found guilty of "poor quality
work, allowing defective output or idle time resulting from a
worker's unconscientious attitude toward his duties," "foul
language," "petty arrogance" or "leading a parasitic way
of life."

In March 1959, by joint Decree of the Communist Party
and the Council of Ministers, the People's Guard was organized. These are "voluntary detachments" — over 2,000,000
strong — recruited locally, ostensibly "to stop violations of
public order and restraining violators mainly through persuasion and warning." That one of the more popular methods
of persuasion includes beatings with clubs, feet and fists is
commonly reported even in the Russian press.

These kangaroo Comrades Courts and vigilante Guards
have a number of purposes. Obviously, they are intended as

counterbalances to the lessening of terror and to "persuade" the people that relaxation does not mean that they can depart from what the Kremlin calls the "everyday laws of Soviet life." They have the related purpose of prying into and regulating the greater leisure time of the people since Stalin's death. (Leisure is anathema to totalitarianism, and the Kremlin makes no secret about its anxieties that free time might seduce people into subversive thinking, leading a parasitic way of life, or departing in any way from acceptable Communist behavior.)

However, what basically motivates the formation of these two extremely important "public organizations" is the Party's campaign to inject itself into every phase of Russian life — political, economic, social, cultural, juridical and personal. Neither the Comrades Courts nor the People's Guards has its own national ministry; both are under the effective control of local units of the Communist party. Thus, the Party arrogates police and repressive powers formerly held by governmental agencies at the same time as it more closely supervises the people.

The Comrades Courts and People's Guards are also further evidence that modern totalitarianism is not simply an authoritarian rule imposed *above* society but that it penetrates and sinks its roots into every nook and cranny of society. It not only extends and deepens its areas of supervision but requires ·the participation of wider and deeper strata of the people. Ultimately, like any great evil, it seeks to involve its victims — in this case, the personnel of the Comrades Courts and People's Guards — in its own system of immorality and corruption.

THE RETURN TO ONE-MAN RULE

Parallel to the extension of Party power there has now emerged a personal dictator — Nikita Khrushchev.

The return to one-man rule — though obviously Khrushchev does not have, and will not have, the same power as Stalin — is not accidental. The idea and implications of collective leadership strike at the core of the totalitarian system.

Collective leadership implies the diffusion of power and diffusion of power among a committee of equals implies the organization of factions. If Khrushchev and Bulganin were equals, each would normally seek to bolster his power by currying favor among the lower echelons of the Party. And in the event of a dispute between equals, these factions would be contending for power. The factions, in turn, in order to strengthen their position, would seek support in non-Party institutions and might even turn to the masses for support. This would be catastrophic for the system.

These are the consequences of collective leadership. They are understood by the Kremlin leadership, which has the collective intelligence to understand that a supreme arbiter must be selected or win out in a power struggle confined to the highest circles of the Party.

Along with Khrushchev's rise as personal dictator, go the cultist trappings reminiscent of his predecessor.

At the Twenty-first Party Congress, we learned from A. N. Nesmayev, President of the Academy of Science, that "the theses of Comrade Khrushchev's report . . . point a clear road for biology." (And this accolade only a few months after Khrushchev dismissed the editor of Russia's leading botany publication for criticizing Lysenko!)

Minister of Defense, Marshal K. Malinovsky: ". . . thanks to the daily solicitude of the Communist Party, its Central Committee, and Nikita Khrushchev personally, our armed forces fully meet present day military requirements." Malinovsky learned well the lesson of Zhukov's fate.

And I cannot resist quoting the following sentence by P. N. Pospelov, Secretary of the Presidium:

We must say quite plainly, comrades, that in the great political, theorectical and organization work that has been carried out in all spheres by our Leninist Central Committee, beginning with the solution of the most complex and urgent international questions, the consistent struggle for the cause of peace, for the prevention of war, the solution of the most important question of the development of agriculture, the collective farm system, the reorganization of the management of industry and construction, and ending with the question of science, literature and arts, the question of enhancing links between school and life, the outstanding role belongs to the initiative, the rich political experience and tireless energy of Comrade Nikita Sergeyevich Khrushchev.

This, we are told, was followed by "stormy applause." These samples of the new cult of the individual are two years old! Since then, the "applause" has become "stormier," more "prolonged" and occurs at more frequent intervals.

What happens to Communist ideology in light of the growing power of the Party and the increasing concentration of power in the hands of one person? Political parties reflect class interest. How is it possible, then, for a ruling Party to become stronger as classes are dissolving with the State presumably, then, withering away? But these are not really such sticky questions for Party theoreticians. They resolve this dilemma with two ideological "thrusts." The first is simply a matter of linguistics. The Communist party becomes a "public organization" that will exist only for the purpose of enforcing the everyday rules of Communist life — and see to it, naturally, that competing "public agencies" do not arise to challenge the prerogatives of the supreme "public agency."

This is too disingenuous even for Communist theoreticians, so they go back to Stalin's text to let us know that, after all, under special circumstances, the State might be obliged to exist under Communism.

Thus, Suslov, a reputed theoretician and member of the Party Presidium speaks:

> Marxist-Leninist theory and historical experience have established that after the victory of the socialist revolution the state remains in existence not only under socialism but, in certain historic circumstances, under communism as well, if capitalism remains a threat to it.

In the same vein, Party historian M. V. Khuralmov also gives credit when credit is due:

> He (Stalin) . . . boldly posed the question of the insufficiency of the well-known formula of F. Engels about the withering away of the state, and gave a new formulation to the question of the possibility of preserving the state even under Communism, if the danger of attack from outside still exists.

The Russian Party's new Draft Program talks of the "withering away of the state" and simultaneously asserts the need for the Party to "strengthen discipline, control the activities of all the elements of the administrative apparatus, check the execution of the decisions and laws of the Soviet state and heighten the responsibility of every official for the strict and timely implementation of these laws."

Herein is the evidence from Communist ideology that the theoretical limit to reforms in Communist countries is set where freedom begins.

By way of summary and conclusions:

a) Reforms have considerably improved the overall conditions of life for the people. Russia, however, remains a totalitarian system in the most precise meaning of that term: a society where all power is in the hands of a single Party, where this Party must have a personal dictator at its head, where Party and dictator are removed from all popular control by the people (at the same time as they seek to establish their authority among the people through coercion, persuasion and corruption with the assistance of "public agencies"), and where the Party has developed its own ideology reflecting and reinforcing its rule.

b) This ruling Party is not a political party as is commonly understood. It is the heart, brain and nervous system of a totalitarian ruling *class*. To the extent that this Party has substituted itself for other repressive, non-Party bureaucracies, there has been a tightening of Communism's totalitarian fabric since Stalin's death, along with the relaxation of terror.

c) There is nothing to justify viewing industrialization as though it were possessed of some mystical qualities, teleologically pulling a totalitarian society to its democratic destiny. Far more important than the alleged imperative of democratization in Russia's planned economy is the totalitarian imperative inherent in the consciousness and ideology of a bureaucratic class whose economic rule is established by its political control of the State.

d) The Russian ruling class cannot move toward democracy. Neither can it revert to Stalinist terror — except as a means of suppressing overt revolutionary discontent. This dilemma is, indeed, an "internal contradiction."

But it is inconceivable that the people, encouraged by the

more relaxed atmosphere, will not take advantage of the reforms and make their demands upon the regime for more of the same and eventually for some of what the regime cannot possibly give — political freedom.

Opposition is inevitable and there are already many signs among Russian workers, peasants, youth and intellectuals that totalitarian reform has generated discontent, not apathetic consent. We can expect to see this discontent grow, not only among these groups, but even among elements of the bureaucracy itself which, under the pressure of events and their own inner moral resources, will rise above their own class and weld their strength to that of the masses below.

It is only this discontented populace, acting in revolutionary concert, which can finally resolve the "inner contradiction" of Communism.

September 1961

Isaac Deutscher: The Anatomy of an Apologist

Julius Jacobson

Issac Deutscher published his biography of Stalin 16 years ago. Since then he has produced a small book on Russian trade unions, several collections of essays and lectures, a three-volume biography of Trotsky and scores of newspaper and magazine articles analyzing contemporary developments in the Communist world. Not only is Deutscher a scholarly biographer and active political journalist, he also has had experience in the Polish Communist and Trotskyist movements. This combination of qualifications has helped him gain a position of special eminence in the expanding world of Kremlinology.

Deutscher's image of himself, skillfully conveyed in his writing, is that of the objective historian concerned with the larger movements of social forces, the broad sweep of events. He shows an edge of disdain for "political philosophers and moralists" who venture judgements (other than his own), who see only the horror of Stalinism at the expense of a larger historical perspective. (When asked recently whom he blames for the deterioration of Russo-Chinese relations, Deutscher answered: "I don't blame either of them — I am an outsider. I simply analyze a process without apportioning blame or praise.")

It is, perhaps, this affected detachment that has enabled Deutscher to elude any precise political identification. Many anti-Communist radicals take it for granted that he shares their antitotalitarian passions — and not without apparent cause. After all, did he not author a sympathetic biography of Trotsky? And didn't his earlier political study of Stalin expose the Vozhd's falsifications of history and the monstrosities known as the Moscow Trials? Because of all this, expressed in a brilliant literary style laden with Western culture, Deutscher was widely seen as a Marxist historian in the authentic socialist, anti-authoritarian tradition.

This view is belied by a more thorough reading of his work.

It is Deutscher's position that the special circumstances surrounding the Russian Revolution — cultural and economic primitiveness inherited from Czarism, exhaustion after seven years of war and civil war, defeat of the revolution in the West — necessitated the suppression of proletarian democracy in order to safeguard the basic social conquests of the revolution. This, for Deutscher, was the positive function of Stalinism, a function it fulfilled with excessive, historically superfluous brutality.

Moreover, Stalinism, according to Deutscher, did not arise solely because of the revolution's adverse context. There is also operative, in his opinion, a law of revolution which dictates that the heroic period following all great revolutions must succumb to moral and physical fatigue. It then becomes the responsibility of a small elite to establish its dictatorial rule over the masses in order to smash the old order and consolidate the revolution, thereby permitting the eventual realization of the revolution's long-term social objectives.

Stalinist terror, then, for all its excesses, preserved the basic conquests of October 1917, just as Cromwell's dictatorship over the nation consolidated the social rule of the British bourgeoisie. (The analogy is Deutscher's.) This historical rationalization for Stalinism is not confined to Russia. There is also the parallel apologia for the Stalinist conquest of Eastern Europe. Where Napoleon brought the revolution to much of Europe on the points of French bayonets, so did

Stalin bring the promise of socialism to other lands — "in the turrets of Russian tanks," as Deutscher puts it.

It becomes clear enough that the democracy Deutscher foresees has little to do with political freedom. What he proposes has the character of a benevolent dictatorship. This is not merely a critic's deduction. For, as if mulling over the consequences of his restrictive reading of democracy, Deutscher, later in this interview, notes of his promised democratic socialist Russia: "It may well be that what is coming won't take the form of a multiparty system."

This discussion will document the charge that Deutscher's well-deserved reputation as a talented writer stands in marked contrast to his unwarranted reputation as an insightful analyst of specific events and changes in the Communist world. Here his performance is replete with distortions, a biased selection of material, quotation marks around dialogue he never heard, unfulfilled predictions, statements which contradict the facts and sometimes each other.

TO THE DEFENSE—IN TIMES OF CRISIS

In the United States we have liberals who extol academic freedom at the same time as they would deny Communists their right to teach. This is the mark of the Cold War "critic" whose liberalism collapses when confronted by threats to his basic social allegiances. It is also the mark of Isaac Deutscher. Often indignant over social injustice in Russia, he rushes to the defense of the "autocratic socialist" system whenever its viability is threatened. This happened during the June 1953 uprising of the Berlin workers; during the Hungarian Revolution and in the Polish upheavals of 1956-1957.

The Berlin barricades had hardly been overrun by Russian tanks on Stalinallee when Deutscher rushed into print with an article in the English paper, *The News Chronicle* (July 13, 1953), repudiating the action of the Berlin workers:

> The Germans who on June 16-17 descended on the streets, assailed the People's Police and met Russian tanks with a hail of stones, may have had their genuine and long suppressed grievances which demanded an outlet. Nevertheless, their action had unfortunate consequences in Moscow. It compromised the men who stood for reform and conciliation. It gave fresh vigor to the die-hards of Stalinism and other irreconcilables . . . .

Thus, the German workers not only committed a disservice to themselves, they compromised the movement for
reform throughout the Communist world. They should have
been more patient and trusted Deutscher's assurances that
there were men in Moscow now who were prepared to right
justifiable grievances. Reform would come — from above and
all in good time.

Deutscher describes the socialism he sees in Russia and East
Europe as "autocratic" socialism (as contradictory a phrase
as "totalitarian freedom"). However, the terror, by "raising
Russia from the plough to the tractor," planted and nourished
the seeds of its own destruction, since terror becomes an
obstacle to the continuing economic growth of an industrialized nation. The institutions of terror are dismantled and
liberalization effectuated, though slowly and somewhat
unevenly. Thus, democracy will come to Russia primarily
from above, with the Party of socialist terror transformed into an instrument of socialist democratization. In an essay
written in 1957 for his *Russia In Transition*, Deutscher
wrote that in the immediate post-Stalin period political relaxation "could come only through reform from above" and
that "reform from above could be the work of Stalinists
only." By 1957, Deutscher still feared that "a spontaneous
mass movement" for freedom might only "become a factor of
social disruption and chaos." Mass pressure on the Kremlin
could acquire "a very stormy momentum" not in accord with
Deutscher's delicate historical timetable, and the whole
process of democratization reversed. History cannot be
rushed. (It puts one in mind of those who urge gradualism
and moderation in the American South. There, too, we are
told that history cannot be rushed by impatient Negroes who
want their Freedom Now.)

However, the "democracy" that Deutscher sees as the
glorious culmination of reforms from above in Russia is
somewhat lacking in democratic content. In a recent, remarkable interview appearing in *The Review* (Vol. V., No.
3, 1963) published by the Imre Nagy Institute, some details of
his vision of a democratic, socialist Russia are revealed:

To speak about tolerating Socialdemocracy in Russia is a completely unreal question. *In abstracto*, I would say that after nearly fifty years, the Russian Revolution should be able to tolerate any party. But after nearly fifty years, a Social Democratic party can hardly exist in Russia. It is just as if you wanted to resurrect in the England of today the parties that existed before the Wars of the Roses! Socialdemocracy makes sense only within the capitalist order, because the "ideological" difference between the Socialdemocrats and the Communists is or was whether capitalism can be overthrown only by revolution, or whether it can be transformed peacefully into socialism.

If what you [the interviewer] have in mind is freedom of debate, freedom of criticism, freedom of expression, freedom of association, well, I think this is what Communism must accept, will accept, and is driven to accept! . . . I believe that Russia is ripe, or nearly ripe even for a multiparty system. By this I do not mean anything like a reproduction of the multiparty systems of the bourgeois West, but a political regime, in which there would be room for various trends and various programmes all based on the foundations of the revolution . . . .

There is no room in Russia for bourgeois parties (since, obviously, they could not be "based on the foundations of the revolution" according to Deutscher in an interview from *The Review*, Vol. V, No. 3, 1963), no room for a Russian equivalent of the British Labor Party or other social democratic parties, no room for "anything like" the multiparty system of the bourgeois West, and if, as is clearly implied, there is room only for various *"trends"* based on his vague "foundations of the revolution," what remains of his envisioned freedom of debate and criticism that is politically meaningful? Indeed, one of the "foundations of the [socialist] revolution" is precisely the right of opposition parties to exist and legally challenge the leading position of the party in power.

Deutscher overlooked a number of facts. The Berlin revolt, spearheaded by the building trades workers, began as a protest against a decree on May 10, 1953, increasing their production norms by 10%. This *new* oppressive order was put into effect several months *after* Stalin's death, at a time when Deutscher assured readers of his *Russia: What Next?* (1953) that the new day of liberalization from above was already under way in the Communist world.

It is also important to note that on July 29, the intensified production quota was cut down and on July 31, two days after

Beria's fall (whose execution, according to Deutscher, was symptomatic of a new Stalinist resurgence brought on by the Berlin revolt), German reparations were sharply reduced. These concessions won by the German workers could hardly have been gained so readily had they passively awaited the benefits of Deutscher's promised liberalization from above.

Partly to justify his opposition to the Berlin workers, Deutscher has written articles on Germany which, despite his talents, are simply bizarre. In 1962 (*Observer*, January 28, 1962), he wrote that Malenkov and Beria "advocated a unilateral Russian withdrawal" even if the Americans would not pull out of West Germany! Moreover, Malenkov and Beria "took it for granted that this (Russian withdrawal from East Germany) would mean the end of Communist rule in East Germany. . . ."

Deutscher's fantasy includes "the partly hypothetical interpretation" that after Khrushchev was in power, and the rift with China already of several years duration, Khrushchev was "seeking to provoke Ulbricht into switching his allegiance" from Moscow to Peking which would permit Khrushchev to carry out "a withdrawal to the Oder and Neisse with relatively little loss of face." [1]

There is method to Deutscher's fantasy. He is not only minimizing the force of Russian imperialism, but is trying to bolster his thesis that it is self-defeating for those under the Russian yoke to defy the Kremlin. That is why he wrote, nine years after the Berlin events, that "the Berlin rising of June 16-17 saved Ulbricht." It is now 12 years since the uprising and Ulbricht is still there although the German workers have made no break for freedom since 1953, not even during the Hungarian Revolution. How long must they be penalized for

1. This view of Malenkov and Khrushchev prepared to sacrifice Communism in East Germany does not prevent the same Deutscher from writing the exact opposite elsewhere. Thus, in *The Great Contest* when discussing Eastern Europe (he explicitly includes East Germany as a part of Eastern Europe) he wrote: "To be sure, Stalin's successors cannot and will not preside over the liquidation of the Communist regimes in Eastern Europe" (p. 52). As we shall see, such blatant contradictions are an integral part of Deutscher's special style of apologetics for totalitarianism.

having flouted Deutscher's dictum that they can be delivered
from oppression only by their oppressors?

In October 1956 — the month of the Hungarian Revolution
— an article by Isaac Deutscher described Kremlin-satellite
relations as follows:

> The Soviet worker [!] has begun to "finance" in all earnestness
> the industrialization of the underdeveloped communist coun-
> tries; and he "finances" it out of the resources which might
> otherwise have been used to raise his own standard of living....
> Here indeed two aspects of de-Stalinization — Russian domestic
> reform and reform in Russia's relationship with the entire
> Soviet bloc — can be seen in actual conflict with each other
> [*Partisan Review*, Fall 1956].

These euphoric lines about Russian benevolence (and
sacrifices by Russian *workers*, no less) were written by
Deutscher just before the Hungarian Revolution. They were
in keeping with his glamorized view of Stalinist conquest of
Hungary and Poland expressed earlier in *Stalin: A Political
Biography:* "In Poland and Hungary the Communist-inspired
land reform fulfilled, perhaps imperfectly, a dream of many
generations of peasants and intellectuals" (p. 535). Now
compare the quotation from *Partisan Review* (and from
Stalin) with the following, written when the smoke of revolution was still smoldering in Budapest and the countryside.

> Yet the Poles and Hungarians struggled for political freedoms
> as well as for national emancipation, and they rose against the
> *Stalinist police state* through which *Russia* had dominated
> them. Last but not least, *they revolted against an economic
> policy that had sacrificed their consumer interests to industrial-
> ization and armaments and had plunged them into intolerable
> misery (emphasis added*).*

One could have bought, on the same day and from the
same newsstand, both the Fall 1956 issue of *Partisan Review*
and the November 15, 1956, issue of *The Reporter.* In the
former he would have read with relief, or amusement, Deutscher's statement that the Russian "workers" and a benevolent
Kremlin were sacrificing themselves for the sake of raising
the living standards in underdeveloped Communist nations.

---

*   All emphases in quotations in this chapter have been added unless otherwise noted.

Then the reader could have opened the pages of *The Reporter* and there have learned from the same Isaac Deutscher that the people of Poland and Hungary were in revolt because they were plunged into intolerable misery by a Russian-dominated police state.

Deutcher's evaluation of Russo-satellite relations in his later *Reporter* article was not in the spirit of self-correction. He seldom admits to errors of judgement or analysis. Nor should the reader confuse his sudden compassion for the Hungarian people with support of their revolution. In the same article in which he admitted to the misery which provoked the Hungarian people to armed insurrection, he *condemned the revolution* itself. There he wrote that the revolution began as an effort to "regenerate the Communist revolution" but subsequent Hungarian Stalinist provocation and armed Russian intervention permitted anti-Communists to win the initiative in Hungary, at which point "a *Thermidorean* situation arose." Of course, there was no Communist revolution in postwar Hungary for anyone to regenerate; only a dictatorship imposed by force of foreign Russian arms. But we will let this pass for the moment. More relevant at this point is Deutscher's summary judgement which appeared in his *Russia In Transition:*

> . . . it may be said that in October-November, the people of Hungary in a heroic frenzy tried unwittingly *to put the clock back*, while Moscow sought once again *to wind up with the bayonet*, or rather with the tank, *the broken clock of the Hungarian Communist revolution.* It is difficult to say who it was who acted the more tragic, and the more futile or hopeless role (p. 26).

The Hungarians, driven to heroic frenzy by justifiable grievances, were unwittingly turning back the clock of revolutionary progress as the insurrection moved into its counter-revolutionary "Thermidorean" phase; while the Russians sought to rewind the clock with bayonets. Not content with paradoxical clocks, Deutscher also repeated, in more civilized and temperate manner, some of the most malicious Communist canards against the Hungarian revolution.

> The ascendancy of anti-Communism found its spectacular climax with Cardinal Mindszenty's triumphal entry into Buda-

pest to the accompaniment of the bells of all the churches of the city broadcast for the whole world to hear. *The Cardinal became the spiritual head of the insurrection. A word of his now carried more weight than Nagy's appeals.* If in the classical revolutions the political initiative shifts rapidly from Right to Left, *here it shifted even more rapidly from Left to Right.* Parties suppressed years ago sprang back into being, among them the formidable Smallholders' Party (*The Reporter,* November 15, 1956).

More slander could not be compressed into so few lines.

Deutscher notwithstanding, one of the more illuminating aspects of the Hungarian Revolution was the rapidity with which the persecuted clerical Prince of this overwhelmingly Catholic nation was eclipsed by a revolution which he could neither fully accept nor reject nor even understand. (Incidentally, does Deutscher think that winding up the clock of progress means keeping priests in jail regardless of charge or guilt?) Upon his release from prison, Mindszenty baptized the Revolution with the cold water of doubt, equivocation, confusion and contradiction. He realized that there could be no return to the old order (and, perhaps, he did not want it) so he told the people that he was in favor of a "classless society" and supported "justified historical development." Yet, he could not speak in or accept the Marxist idiom so repugnant to him, so he spoke also of the need to return to "private ownership" but immediately qualified this with the stipulation that it would be private ownership "restricted by the interests of society and justice." Listen for a moment to how Deutscher's confused "spiritual head" addressed his revolutionary flock with the artificial voice of Christian charity and tolerance, so out of keeping with the temper of an embittered, imprisoned people locked in deadly combat with their jailers:

> Private revenge has to be avoided and eliminated. Those who have participated in the fallen regime carry their own responsibility for their activities, omissions, defaults, or wrong doings. I do not want to make a single denunciatory statement because this would retard the start of work and the course of production in the country. If things proceed decently according to promises made, this will not by my task *(La Revolte de la Hongrie d'Apres les Emissions des Radio Hongroise,* October-November 1956, Editions Pierre Horay, Paris, 1957, p. 179).

Do these lines sound like the militant call to arms of the ascending "spiritual head" of a "counterrevolution," or are they the irrelevant pieties of a man soon pushed offstage into the wings of history by a revolution which gave him no more than an enigmatic nod?

The slander spread by Stalinists that Mindszenty finally presided over the Revolution was motivated by such malice that Jean-Paul Sartre — hardly an enemy of Communism — was moved to write the following:

> As regards Cardinal Mindszenty, the Stalinist press has made him into its bugbear, but it is not enough to reproduce the words of an old man worn out by suffering and strongly motivated by his resentments, to discover behind him an army of fascists ready to act. Which are the forces he relied upon or was believed to rely upon? He had been isolated from the world for 8 years, then suddenly freed. Can we believe that he had a clear idea of the situation? The Communist press wanted to see a deep connection between his dreary voice which drawled over the radio waves and the slaughter that went on in the sewers. Those who believed this were moved by emotion. Only Stalinist paranoia prevents them from seeing the truth; that is, that this old, isolated priest and those headhunters are separated by an immense gap (*Temps Modernes*, November-December, 1956, January, 1957, Whole Nos. 129-131).

The Revolution did move in October-November — steadily leftward, in a socialist, and therefore anti-Stalinist and anti-capitalist direction. The opposition of the revolutionary Workers Councils — the backbone of the Revolution, something which escaped Deutscher — to anything resembling a capitalist restoration in Hungary is, or should be, known to all. On October 28, the Workers Committee of Gyor declared: "We do not wish to return to the old capitalist system. We want an independent and socialist Hungary." On the same day Radio Miskolc broadcast a revolutionary manifesto demanding "a new provisional government, one truly democratic, sovereign and independent, fighting for a free and socialist Hungary, excluding all ministers who served the Rakosi regime." Two days later, Radio Szombathely broadcast the demands of the National Committee for County Vas: ". . . we want a free, independent, and Socialist Hungary headed by the government of Imre Nagy."

These are a minute sampling of the demands made early in the Revolution. Had things shifted to the right by early November? The record is no less clear. On November 2, the Workers Councils of Borsod-Abauj-Zemplen County declared: "We will not return the land to landlords, nor the factories to the capitalists, nor the mines to the mining barons, nor the Army command to the Horthyist generals." When the Russians called upon the armed Hungarian forces in Dunapentele to surrender, the revolutionary military command answered: "Dunapentele is the foremost Socialist town in Hungary. The workers will defend their own from fascist excesses . . . but also from Soviet troops . . . . There are no counterrevolutionaries in the town . . . ." The Revolutionary University Students Committee proclaimed: "We want neither Stalinism nor capitalism. We want a truly democratic and truly Socialist Hungary, completely independent from any other country." In November, the Armed Revolutionary Youth called "For a neutral, independent, democratic and Socialist Hungary!" At approximately the same time, it became known that the Revolutionary Committee of Hungarian Intellectuals believed that "all of the factories and the mines are the property of the workers."

One of the most moving Hungarian appeals was transmitted by Radio Kossuth on November 7, the anniversary of the Russian Revolution. It was directed to the Russian soldiers:

> Soldiers!
> Your state was created at the cost of bloody fighting so that you could have freedom. Today is the thirty-ninth anniversary of that revolution. Why do you want to crush our liberty? You can see that it is not factory proprietors, not landowners, and not the bourgeoisie who have taken up arms against you, but the Hungarian people, who are fighting desperately for the same rights you fought for in 1917.

Ordinarily, Marxists, socialists and democrats consider the legalization of Stalinist-repressed parties as one of the major achievements of the Hungarian Revolution and evidence of its radical maturity. It is interesting that Deutscher mentions by name only the "formidable Smallholder's Party." He conveniently overlooks the names of socialist and radical organizations which also sprang back to life. He also distorts the picture by describing the Smallholders Party as "formidable," which was not exactly the case in October-November 1956. Moreover, he ignores the change in this Party (it had liberal and conservative wings before its suppression in 1918) which so sharply illustrates the progressive force of the revolution. In a speech to the reconstituted Smallholders Party on October 31, Bela Kovacs, one of its leading members and a minister in the Nagy government, noted:

> The Party has full rights to reassemble, but the question is whether on reconstitution the Party will proclaim the old ideas again. No one must dream of going back to the world of Counts, bankers and capitalists: that world is over once and for all.

This is hardly the voice of bourgeois reaction, encouraged by a Thermidorean counterrevolution.

Deutscher also subjected anti-Stalinist militants of the Polish 1956 October to his unique style of abuse. In an interview conducted by Aleksander Ziemny which appeared in the Polish weekly, *Swiat*, October 7, 1957 ("An Evening at Deutscher's"), he accused the liberalized (i.e., "revisionist") Polish press of opening its pages to "writers who try to justify the mistakes of pre-September regimes." To realize the enormity of this charge, one must understand that "pre-September regimes" refers to fascistic Polish regimes before September 1939! Of course, Deutscher does not — he cannot — name any Polish anti-Stalinist writers who were justifying anything that smacked of Pilsudskyism; just as he could give no documentation for his charge that a reactionary Church hierarch had become the spiritual head of the Hungarian Revolution. In the interview, he went on to speak contemptuously of the rebellious Polish youth who were attracted to Marxism because they viewed it as a "religion of social justice." Instead of viewing Marxism in this humanist light, and *acting* accordingly, Deutscher urges them to spend their time studying the "scholarly treasures" of Marxism. This quietism which he advocates is logically followed by his rebuke to those young Poles who don't realize, as he does, that "de-Stalinization is the work of people brought up in the Stalinist school — and with this fact one has to come to terms regardless of any subjective speculation." As for Polish rebels who preferred self-reliance to Deutscher's promised reform from above, he found many of them guilty of "cocky and loud-mouthed criticism."

Deutscher's real function as critical-rationalizer of totalitarianism did not escape Polish anti-Stalinists who followed his work. In a sharp rebuke to Deutscher for his advocacy of quietism,[2] as against militant, active opposition to Stalinism, one Polish writer, Andrezj Braun, wrote a polemic in *Nowa Kultura* (March 7, 1957), which accurately accused Deutscher of proposing "a position alien to action" which "would mean here [in Poland] agreement with all the evil around us."

DEUTSCHER AND MARGINAL SLAVE LABOR

There is a vast body of literature available on Russian concentration camps penned by former inmates, defectors from the Kremlin apparatus, and by scholars throughout the world. One student of Russian affairs, though, who has been reluctant to discuss the details of this singularly atrocious aspect of Stalinism is Isaac Deutscher.

Deutscher reserved his most detailed comments about the facts of the camps for a lesser work, *Russia: What Next?* It is worth quoting his discussion almost in its entirety.

> How much of Russia's industrial expansion has been due to planning, and how much has been achieved by, for instance, the use of forced labor?

> It is important to make a distinction between the fundamental elements of the Soviet economy and its marginal phenomena. A few years ago the number of the inmates of Soviet concentration camps was most implausibly estimated by Western commentators at from 12 to 20 millions. *If these figures were correct the whole Soviet experiment in planning would be only of negative significance to the rest of the world, for it would represent nothing but the recrudescence of slavery on a staggering scale.*

> However, much laborious research and some evidence from inside Russia have reduced these speculative figures to more plausible proportions. Dr. M.N. Jasny, for instance, an able but also a most extreme Menshevik critic of Stalinist economic policies, has reached the conclusion that at the height of the deportations the total number of inmates to those camps may have amounted to three or four millions. Morally, this makes little difference:

2. As expressed in an earlier article by Deutscher in *Nowa Kultura*.

the use of forced labor is equally repugnant and its condemnation equally valid whether four or twenty million people are involved. But a more precise idea of the dimensions of the problem helps to bring the economic picture of the Stalin era into more realistic focus. It disposes of the theory that the Soviet economy could not function without forced labor.

In an economy in which the total number of workers and employees is about 40 millions — it was over 30 millions before the Second World War — and in which further scores of millions work on collective farms, the labor of four million convicts is a marginal factor. The brunt of the industrialization has been borne by a working class which has been severely regimented, disciplined, and directed, but which is essentially a normal working class (pp. 71-72).

Having duly registered his repugnance at the fact of slave labor, Deutscher promptly extenuates it out of any significance. The fact that slavery might account for a mere 10% of the labor force is morally deplorable, at least repugnant, but of little historical significance because the economy could function without it. (The naivete of this dissociation between slave labor and planning is truly remarkable. If the number, function and location of slave labor was part of some plan, how is it possible to know whether the Soviet economy could have functioned without it?)

Was Russia a modern slave state as some have called it? No, says Deutscher; it only had 3,000,000 to 4,000,000 slaves. Give him a minimum of 12,000,000 and he is ready to recognize Russia as "nothing but a recrudescence of slavery on a staggering scale." But if the difference between 4,000,000 and 12,000,000 slaves is so decisive for his evaluation of Russian society, how then account for his Olympian dismissal of the "Western commentators" with their big numbers, without as much as a nodding analysis or refutation of what he claims to be the fundamental fallaciousness of their figures? Deut-

3. Deutscher did not footnote his source. It had to be uncovered. Naum Jasny's article appeared in the October 1951 issue of *The Journal of Political Economy*, published by the University of Chicago Press. Deutscher does not mention that in the August 1952 issue of the same journal there is a critical review of Jasny's essay by A. David Redding, which, in this writer's opinion, was as effective as Jasny's subsequent rejoinder was unconvincing.

scher prefers the 3,000,000 to 4,000,000 figure mentioned by "most extreme Menshevik," Naum Jasny.[3] While Mr. Jasny is a Menshevik, he is not a "most extreme" (or an average extreme) Menshevik. Deutscher tacks this on for a clear enough purpose: if even a "most extreme" anti-Communist downgrades the number of slave camp inmates then surely he is closer to the mark than those who see much larger figures. If Deutscher were more concerned with truth than scoring an apologist's point, he might have bothered to investigate Jasny's method of arriving at his figures. In this case, he would have been obliged, also in the interest of truth, to report some basic flaws in Jasnys' article.

One of the most glaring defects in Jasny's calculations is that they were based on an economic report of 1941—10 years before his article appeared and 12 years before Deutscher's. In the period immediately before, during and after the war, there were vast numbers, possibly millions, of East Europeans, Baltic peoples, national minorities in Russia, those from the Balkans, in addition to Russian soldiers who had to be reeducated after their contact with Western decadence, who were shipped off to slave labor camps. These numbers do not enter Jasny's estimate. If we were to add the post-1941 recruits to slave labor armies, the figure would swell enormously. While Jasny did not estimate the number of those who flooded the slave labor camps after 1940, he did acknowledge that they arrived en masse.

Deutscher also fails to mention Jasny's reservation that his estimated figure *"does not include children, full invalids, people too old to work, etc. I have no evidence by which to estimate them."* Since Jasny is interested in arriving at the truth, he footnotes this failure to include children, invalids and old people in his estimates by noting that one of David Dallin's[4] sources — a former chief of police of a large concentration camp — testified that only 50% to 60% of the inmates

4. In David Dallin's *The Real Soviet Russia* (Yale University Press, 1944) and his *Forced Labor In Soviet Russia*, co-authored with Boris Nicolaevsky (Yale University Press, 1948), the number of camp inmates is placed within the 7-12 million range on the basis of exhaustive research and painstaking analysis.

in his camp were engaged in productive labor. The rest were invalids, in hospitals, engaged in various services, etc. If this was typical of the Russian slave labor camps, then Jasny's figures would indeed have been a serious underestimation.

Deutscher's cursory discussion of slave labor camps is typical of his method. By omission and commission he misinforms his readers about the tangible realities of virtually every sensitive area of contemporary Russian life. In a 1959 lecture, printed in his collection, *The Great Contest,* Deutscher could say that today the Russian worker "cannot be punished for minor industrial offenses or branded as an enemy of the people when he tries to speak out for himself." This was said at a time when thousands of Comrade Courts had already been set up on factory levels and were zealously exercising their explicit authority to punish minor industrial offenders. At the same time many constituent union Republics had already adopted their "anti-Parasite" laws — soon extended to all of Russia — for the purpose of inflicting major punishment for minor sins. Sentences of up to five years of prison, exile or "corrective" labor were given to industrial offenders, to those who believed that they could "speak up" for themselves, and for other "antisocial" behavior (e.g., writing poetry).

When glamorizing Russia's economic growth, Deutscher (in *The Great Contest)* asserts that in 10 years, i.e., by 1969, Soviet standards of living "are *certain* to have risen above Western European standards." Or he writes of the "new deal for the working class" with its "promise" of a 30-35 hour work week sometime in the sixties. He discourses about the Kremlin's "continuous efforts to increase the output of consumer goods faster than had been planned and to mitigate the appalling housing conditions." Deutscher is always guaranteeing *the future* to the Russian people (on condition that they don't get too rambunctious and upset his calendar of reform). Why doesn't he support his optimism with some facts about living standards today? What is the average wage? What is the price of milk, butter and meat? What are housing conditions actually like and how much will they improve if housing plans are met? He seldom deigns to report and analyze such "details" of Russian life. And on the rare occasions he does discuss facts, he usually accepts Russian sources at face value.

When he writes of Russian legal reforms, he usually produces an abbreviated rosy progress report without any detailed study of the statutes, debates and actual practice of the law. Surely, the large number of death sentences meted out for "economic crimes" deserve a serious, thoughtful article.

What about the charges of Russian anti-Semitism? Deutscher is certainly familiar with the facts from his reading of the Russian press. How do systematic anti-Semitic acts, sponsored by the "reformers" in power, fit his theory of Russia's organic evolution to socialist democracy? Instead of an honest confrontation with reality, Isaac Deutscher informed a London audience, at a time when Russian anti-Semitism was already well documented, that the resurgence of Communist internationalism "must provide a source of hope to Jews of all political convictions" (quoted in Leopold Labedz's excellent article on Deutscher in *Survey*, April 14, 1962). This news will hardly console the families of several hundred Jews who have since been executed in Russia.

HISTORICAL NOVELIST WITH THE KEYHOLE VIEW

Deutscher's journalistic output reveals his talents as an historical novelist. He pretends access to closed councils of the Russian Communist Party, reports dialogue (quotation marks and all), discloses the inner psychic drive of Kremlin leaders in a manner that would put a Freud to shame. The unconscious yearnings of a Khrushchev or a Mikoyan — private thoughts which they could not even admit to themselves — are laid bare by Deutscher's scalpel-like pen. To give Deutscher his due, his literary skill makes his little stories and vignettes spring to life; they are a veritable tour-de-force.

Below are selections from his writings about the Twentieth Congress, an event that easily lends itself to fictionalized dramatization.

Here is how Deutscher discussed Mikoyan's speech at the Twentieth Congress in *The Reporter* (March 22, 1956):

when Mikoyan urged the Congress to wage a "merciless struggle " against "bureaucratic centralism" and for a full reinstatement of Lenin's "democratic centralism," he *consciously borrow-ed these terms, as well as many other ideas and formulas, from none other than Trotsky,* who coined them. And it was in an almost characteristically Trotskyist manner that Mikoyan hinted at Lenin's testament . . . ."

How does Deutscher — here the psychological dramatist — know that Mikoyan "consciously borrowed" from Trotsky? He doesn't. But it makes exciting reading and serves his political purpose to write such nonsense. And what, incidentally, are the other ideas "borrowed from Trotsky"? But never mind, here is more insight gained from Mikoyan's speech and its reception:

> When Mikoyan finished, the Congress gave him an ovation such as it accorded no other leader, except Khrushchev and perhaps Bulganin. But while Khrushchev and Bulganin received the homage due their offices and ranks, Mikoyan was applauded *for what he had said* and *for the manner* in which he had said it.

It is as though Deutscher were equipped with some ultrasonic applausograph device which not only measures the volume of clapping (from the Kremlin to Surrey!) but discloses the different motives behind each thunderous ovation. In the above quote, for example, Deutscher's applausograph tells him that Mikoyan and Khrushchev received the same stormy ovations. But it was the same in volume only. For the applausograph is so sensitive that it revealed that Mikoyan was cheered "for what he had said" and "for the manner" in which he said it, while the same volume of applause for Khrushchev shows up on the applausograph's screen as only respect for his high position. The marvels of (political) science! Of course, this reading fits in well with Deutscher's political predilections. If Mikoyan is the real de-Stalinizer who "consciously borrowed" ideas from Trotsky, and is applauded for his views, it becomes confirming evidence of irresistible reforms from above [5]

5. Malenkov also addressed the Twentieth Congress. His speech, we can be sure, was not given a stormy ovation since he was already in disgrace and his confession in preparation. But according to Deutscher, in the same article quoted above, "it was in *Malenkov's* heyday that the Stalin cult was in fact undermined." If this is the case, what is to stop one from reading Deutscher's applausograph as follows: the delegates to the Twentieth Congress applauded Khrushchev (the man who wanted to

What raises Deutscher's applause-analysis from the implausible to the absurd is his sentence which immediately precedes the above quotation.

> While many delegates certainly understood what Mikoyan was driving at and how far-reaching were the implications of what he said, the less informed missed the nuances and believed that Mikoyan merely toed the Khrushchev line, or that Khrushchev was in full agreement with Mikoyan.

If the import of Mikoyan's near-Trotskyist speech was missed by a number of delegates, that makes them near-idiots, and if Mikoyan's differences with Khrushchev could only be detected by "nuances" that makes Khrushcev a near-Trotskyist. And how does this mesh with the applausograph's recording? If the "less informed" — how many were there? — thought that Mikoyan and Khrushchev were in "full agreement" why should their applause for Mikoyan have a special significance as against their applause for Khrushchev?

There is more to the Mikoyan saga:

> Mikoyan's speech is a remarkable political and human document if only because he himself had been an *ardent Stalinist at least since 1922* . . . and Khrushchev and Kaganovich owed their careers entirely to Stalin; Mikoyan had risen in the party in Lenin's day, and his mind had been formed in Lenin's school.

These two sentences are to soften one for what follows:

> His speech was something of an *old Leninist's* recantation of the part he had played in helping Stalin to ascendency. It was not a recantation in the familiar Stalinist style, but a *seemingly genuine confession, if only implicit* of grim and grave errors, and of a desire to undo some of the still rampant evils of Stalinism.

The "ardent Stalinist" since at least 1922, becomes an "old Leninist" in just three miraculous sentences! This complex creature of Deutscher's imagination offers the world a confession which is "seemingly genuine" although it is "only implicit." How genuine was Mikoyan's "desire to undo some of the still rampant evils of Stalinism" was exhibited seven months later when this penitent ardent Stalinist-old-Lenin-

---

compromise the fight against Stalinism) as much as it applauded Mikoyan (practically a Trotskyist in his assault on Stalinism) and barely acknowledged the existence of Malenkov (in whose heyday the Stalin cult was undermined) because they wanted to call a halt to de-Stalinization!

ist-semi-Trotskyist played a special role in the slaughter of Hungarian revolutionaries.

The chief antagonists of the Twentieth Congress, our raconteur has told us, were Khrushchev and Mikoyan. The former feared too open and rash a break with Stalinism; the latter insisted upon it. Of this alleged controversy, Deutscher writes:

> That Mikoyan was permitted to state his views from the platform of the Congress is in itself an important precedent. Again, this is no evidence yet of any real reinstatement of Leninist "inner party democracy." In Lenin's day, when there was disagreement in the Central Committee over an important issue, it was customary for the majority to express its views in the official report of the Congress, while a spokesman of the minority came out with a frankly controversial "counter-report." Mikoyan, *it may be surmised, may have intended to come out with such a counter-report,* but the Central Committee refused to permit at this stage any open clash between two members of the "collective leadership." A compromise was reached, under which Mikoyan was allowed to state his views in a positive form, without making it explicit where and on what points he dissented from Khrushchev.

With this, Deutscher has taken us right into the closed sessions of the Russian Politburo. He speculates ("may be surmised, may have intended. . .") that Mikoyan considered coming before the Congress with a minority report. This speculation is only an immodest way of saying that he, Isaac Deutscher, has no evidence that this was actually the case. This doesn't inhibit him from discussing his speculation in the very next breath as though it were a fact and telling us precisely how this surmised report was actually disposed of by the Central Committee. It is typical of Deutscher's leap from the speculative to the assertive. It is not enough for him to tell us what the response to this surmised counterreport *might have been* on the Central Committee. With the storyteller's skill, he takes us into the closed chambers of the Central Committee to tell us precisely how it decided to handle this breach in its ranks, how it effectuated a compromise and exactly what Mikoyan was permitted to do.

Deutscher, who has taken us on a guided tour of Mikoyan's subconcious, is a novelist with a keen sense of balance. What is performed with Mikoyan's psyche cannot be left undone

with that of his (alleged) antagonist — Nikita Khrushchev.
Thus, the Dostoievskian touch is supplied for him, too, in
another chapter of his writings, also dealing with the Twentieth Congress. In *Russia In Transition*, he writes of Khrushchev:

> How is it, one must ask, that *a man of so sturdy a character, of a*
> *mind so inherently independent*, and of so eruptive and untame-
> able a temper could at all survive under Stalin, and survive at the
> very top of the Stalinist hierarchy? How did Khrushchev manage
> to control himself, to keep his thoughts to himself, and to hide
> his burning hatred from Stalin? How did he behave under the
> dictator's scrutinizing gaze when the dictator snarled at him:
> "Why do your eyes look so shifty today?"
>
> . . . *in this miner and miner's son risen to his present position*
> *one can still feel something of that tenacious, patient, yet alert*
> *and shrewd spirit which once characterized the old Russian*
> *worker when from the underground he bored under the Czar's*
> *throne.* To that spirit are now joined *new mental horizons*, a new
> capacity for organization, and an unwonted modernity. As one
> watches Khrushchev (*even, as I have watched him, with a cer-*
> *tain bias against him*) one comes to think that he is probably
> still the Russian (or the Russo-Ukrainian) worker, writ large —
> *the Russian worker who inwardly remained true to himself*
> even in the Stalinist straitjacket, who has over the years gather-
> ed strength and grown in stature and grown out of the strait-
> jacket. One might even say that *through Khrushchev the old*
> *repressed socialist tradition of the Russian working class takes*
> *a long-delayed and sly revenge on Stalinism.*
>
> Yet, Khrushchev also makes the impression of an actor who,
> while he plays his own part with superb self-assurance, is only
> half aware of his own place in the great, complex, and somber
> drama in which he has been involved. *His long, aggressive mono-*
> *logue is a cry from the heart, a cry about the tragedy of the Rus-*
> *sian revolution and of the Bolshevik Party; but it is only a frag-*
> *ment of the tragedy* (p. 34).

Khrushchev reminds Deutscher of the old Russian worker
who bored under the Czar's throne! He conveniently forgets
that Khrushchev never bored under any throne; that although
he was 23 years old at the time of the revolution he did not
participate in it and did not join the Communist party until
1918. And his record in the Party? Deutscher knows it all too
well. But he cannot tell it here for how would it fit into the
picture of a man inwardly "true to himself," with "so sturdy
a character" and of a "mind so inherently independent." He

does not tell us that from the very beginning Khrushchev lined up with the Stalinists in the Party. That for his *voluntary* services to the Stalinists in the early twenties, he was promoted by Kaganovich and later taken under Stalin's wing; that during the purges in the thirties, this Khrushchev was responsible for the deaths of thousands of real and imagined enemies of the Stalinist regime; that he was in charge of the purges in the Ukraine and soon became Party Secretary of the Ukraine and made a full member of Stalin's Politburo in 1939. And he does not see here the assassin of the Hungarian working class. [6]

Khrushchev's speech was a "cry from the heart, a cry about the tragedy of the Russian Revolution and of the Bolshevik Party." This, however, is only "a fragment of the tragedy." The other tragic fragment is soon unearthed:

> He himself [Khrushchev] did not expect to burst out with this cry. Only a few days before he made the secret speech, he did not know that he was going to make it; or any rate, he did not know what he was going to say (p. 35).

How does Deutscher know that Khrushchev did not know that he was going to burst forth this cry from the heart? The lyricist's intuitive insights? How does this insight jibe with the story about Mikoyan's alleged "counterreport" mentioned earlier? In that tale, the Central Committee refused to let Mikoyan make a report "counter" to Khrushchev's, which can only mean that the Central Committee knew about Khrushchev's report in advance and that certainly Mikoyan—Khrushchev's antagonist, remember — had a preview of it.

Moreover, a few pages after Deutscher reveals Khrushchev's tortured and indecisive frame of mind, he springs the following on us:

> Khrushchev builds his case against Stalin on three sets of facts: on Lenin's denunciation, in his testament, of Stalin's "rudeness and disloyalty"; on Stalin's role in the purges; and on the faults of Stalin's leadership in the war. Under each count of the indictment he treats the facts *selectively* so as to turn the evidence against Stalin rather than against the Stalinist faction (p. 42).

6. In the *New Statesman*, April 17, 1964, Deutscher draws a more accurate portrait of Khrushchev that reads like a point by point refutation of his earlier glorified sketch.

A legitimate and obvious point. But how does this "selectively" prepared speech correspond to the picture of Hamlet-Khrushchev torn by indecision, not knowing if he should make the speech, or what kind of speech it should be, until a few days or a few moments before his "impromptu" revelations?

Not content to lead us into closed Party meetings and take us on psychic tours of the Kremlin leaders, Deutscher probes and lays bare the mass psychology of the Russian people. To sell his readers on the Seven Year Plan, he assures them that "the new Plan undoubtedly gives the Soviet people the exhilarating sense of a tremendous social advance." We suspect that Deutscher was more exhilarated than the Russian people. But if he can be so all-knowing about the emotional responses of the entire Russian people in some instances, he can also admit to a revealing ignorance of mass psychology at other times — an ignorance which he insists is not unique to him. Thus, in an article which tries to discuss the ill-fated super-collectivization in China in an objective tone, he confesses his ignorance of how the Chinese peasants might react to this "blow that Mao has struck against private property and the traditional way of life of rural China." And what Deutscher claims not to know, no one can know, not even those in Peking: "It is difficult not only for outsiders and foreign travelers, but even for the rulers in Peking to judge what is going on in the hearts of a mass of half a billion people."

How can Deutscher know what is going on in the souls of 200,000,000 exhilirated Russians and be so dense about the collective inner mind of 500,000,000 Chinese victims of a brutal collectivization program?

DEUTSCHER AS ANALYST AND PROPHET

As this is written, Khrushchev has been removed and Mikoyan's position is not certain. Less familiar names have come into new prominence: Brezhnev, Kosygin, Podgorny, etc. We await one of Deutscher's *romans de séance* to disclose what these gentlemen really mean when they say things they don't really mean, or only half mean; whether they are sincere, genuine, corrupt; whether they "cry from the heart" and what makes their psyches tick.

While awaiting the benefits of his psychological wizardry, it can be reported that Deutscher did not wait more than 48 hours after Nikita Sergeyevich Khrushchev (a man "of so sturdy a character, of a mind so inherently independent, and of so eruptable and untamable a character") crumbled under a single blow from his colleagues, to predict one new (and certain) political course to be taken by his successors. In the October 18, 1964, issue of England's *Sunday Telegraph*, he assures us that "they will *certainly* soon go to Peking on a pilgrimage of penance and reconciliation, just as Stalin's successors went to Canossa — to Belgrade — in 1955. They will carry with them an offer to resume Soviet economic aid to China, the aid which Khrushchev had stopped abruptly and totally."

Three months have gone by and the certain pilgrimage to Peking has not come to pass. Instead, there is the clinking of ideological armor as Moscow and Peking have renewed their duel over conflicting national and international interests.

This prediction, almost immediately repudiated by events, leads us into a discussion of Deutscher's worth as a prognostician and prophet, and what his analysis and predictions reveal of his political bias.

In both areas — as analyst and prophet — Deutscher has exhibited a degree of vanity as unmerited as it is extreme. In *Russia in Transition*, he boasts in his preface:

> Readers will find here developed even further the views I have expressed in my *Stalin, A Political Biography* (1949) and more particularly in my *Russia: What Next?* (1953). This last book appeared shortly after Stalin's death and *forecast explicitly and emphatically the whole chain of events, with all its twists and turns*, which is now commonly described as de-Stalinization.
>
> . . . Readers are invited to check *in every case* the date of the original publication and to judge for themselves to what extent events have confirmed or refuted my analyses and anticipations.

One difficulty in picking up this gauntlet and checking his "analyses and anticipations" is that critical and climactic paragraphs in Deutscher's writings are peppered so often with such phrases as "it may be surmised," "seems to have been," "not quite groundless," "it may be assumed," "it is probable," "it will almost certainly follow," "it has so far proved," "were apparently," "it cannot be ruled out," etc. We are not abusing the idea of caution. But if similarly massive dosages of hedging phrases were employed by a less skillful writer, his reputation would soon be confined to a small circle of tolerant family friends. Actually, these qualifying phrases are often used by Deutscher for either an unwarranted suggestion of democratization in the Russian camp or to rationalize a particularly obnoxious move by the Kremlin.

There is another difficulty in checking Deutscher's analyses and anticipations. That is: which analysis and which anticipation about the same event? There are so many of them, inconsistent and contradictory, which undermine his self-claimed infallibility. They need to be sampled for what they show of his analytical talents and of his need to say different things at different times (sometimes at the same time) to shore up his defense of the totalitarian road to socialism.

Who stands for what, and what are the factional line-ups in the Communist world? This is one of Deutscher's favorite subjects. The trouble is that his answers depend on which of his articles one happens to pick up, which page one happens to read and what he is trying to prove at the time.

Analysis: Who is Malenkov?

Version A: The De-Stalinizer and Precise Executor of Trotsky's Will (all quotes in Version A are from *Russia: What Next?*).

> He [Malenkov] has come to the fore in the role of the rationalizer striving to put in order the Stalinist legacy and to disentangle its great assets from its heavy liabilities (p. 152).

> . . . Russia's urge to shake off the worst of Stalinism has become so strong that it compelled Stalin's arch-devotee [Malenkov] to become the liquidator of the Stalin era (p. 156).

> The masters of terror were themselves terrified, and the mass of the Soviet people must have been thrilled by the mere thought that henceforth they might be free to defend their rights against their persecutors. *Malenkov's government explicitly assured them of this* (p. 177).

> Malenkov's first preoccupation was to free Soviet foreign policy from its irrational Byzantinism and to make it more worldly and subtle (p. 186).

Version B: Opposed to Drastic de-Stalinization.

Several quotations in Version A originally appeared in an article in *The Reporter*, April 14, 1953. In using the article for his collection, *Russia: What Next?*, he omitted the following:

> Malenkov has come forward not as one of a triumvirate but as the autocrat's autocratic successor. [This version of Malenkov the "autocrat" was in turn contradicted by the same Deutscher who wrote in *Russia In Transition* (1957) that "it is nearly four years now since the U.S.S.R. has ceased to be ruled by an auto-crat."]

In *The Reporter* (August 8, 1957), in the course of an apologia for the Khrushchev regime, Deutscher disposes of the now disgraced Malenkov in the following fashion:

> [Malenkov] favored a pro-consumer line in economic policy and a relaxation of tension in foreign policy; *but he was opposed to drastic de-Stalinization* and probably also to decentralization of industrial management.

Analysis: Mao-Tse-Tung: Who and What Is He?

Version A: Anti-Stalinist and Socialist Democrat.

> . . . Mao's words are giving a new and powerful impulse to de-Stalinization. He has come to the rescue of the intellectual opposition in Russia . . . .
>
> . . . Now Mao tells the Russian workers that they have the right to strike, that if he downs tools not he but the bureaucrat must be blamed . . .
>
> Mao's address . . . represents a most radical repudiation of Stalinism.
>
> Mao attempts in effect to redefine the whole concept of proletarian dictatorship and to restore to it the meaning Marxists generally gave to it before the onset of the Stalin era.
>
> . . . the collectivization of farming is progressing by slow degrees and subtle transitions; and confiscation of property and the use of coercion are avoided *(New Statesman, June 29, 1957)*.

Version B: The Stalinist.

> The initiative to call this dramatic and bloody halt to de-Stalinization (the execution of Imre Nagy) has come from Peking — *Mao Tse Tung has been the chief promoter of the drive against revisionism. Hesitantly and at first reluctantly, Khrushchev has toed Mao's line (The Reporter, July 10, 1958).*
>
> . . . *there exist also undeniable affinities between Maoism in power and Stalinism,* affinities *rooted* in the contradiction be-

tween the socialist strivings of the revolution and the primitive
pre-industrial structure of society.[7] And so, despite all his de-
viations from Stalinism and a momentary determination to
transcend it, Mao has not been able to go beyond Stalinism; and
when he attempted to do so, he retraced his steps in a panic, and
came to the fore as the defender of Stalinist orthodoxy *(New Left
Review*, January-February, 1964).

Analysis: Molotov: Architect of Anti-Stalinist Foreign Policy or Symbol of Stalinist Diplomacy?

Version A (before he was purged by Khrushchev): Architect
of Anti-Stalinist Foreign Policy and Nice to Neutrals.

> In Stalin's day Moscow had only derision for the advocates of
> any "third force" and treated them as hypocritical agents of the
> Atlantic bloc. In the last few months both Moscow and Peking
> have heaped praise on Nehru; they *no longer treat India and the
> so-called Colombo grouping of nations as "puppets of western
> imperialism."* On the contrary, *the neutrals are now spoken of
> with sympathy and respect.* "He who is not with us is against
> us" seems no longer to be a guiding principle for *Molotov* or
> Chou-En-Lai; they have abandoned the slogan to certain poli-
> ticians and diplomats in the West.

Version B (after he was purged by Khrushchev): Symbol of
Stalinist Diplomacy and Nasty to Neutrals.

> Molotov, indeed, viewed suspiciously the nations that remained
> neutral in the cold war, and *he treated the governments of India,
> Burma, Indonesia, and Egypt as mere stooges of western imperi-
> alism.*

Version A (before he was purged): Force for World Peace.

> The cease-fire in Indo-China that was arranged last July in Ge-
> neva throws new light on Soviet foreign policy. This is the second

---

7. Apart from the obvious contradiction in these two versions, there is a
deeper, more fundamental methodological contradiction. Deutscher
believes that because of Russia's backwardness and isolation, political
repressions were inevitable there. Now, China today is more backward,
economically and culturally, than Russia of the late twenties and thirties, and was even more primitive seven years ago. How was it possible,
then, for Deutscher to find a free, democratic socialist welfare state
emerging in China in 1957 when, by his own reasoning, the "affinities
between Maoism in power and Stalinism" should have been even closer
than today? If there is a "contradiction," as he calls it, between democratic socialist strivings and "China's primitive pre-industrial structure
of society" in 1964, how could that contradiction have been overcome
seven years earlier?

armistice agreement concluded since Stalin's death in March, 1953, the first being the agreement on Korea. *Soviet Foreign Minister Molotov may be regarded as the prime mover of both.*

Version B (after he was purged): Isolationist Boor.

Molotov was almost a symbol of the isolationism of the Stalin era, with its obtuseness and lack of sensitiveness to the outside world; this was reflected even in his lack of fluency in any foreign language.

Version A (before): Polite and Flexible.

Freed from the paralyzing fear of Stalin, Molotov surprised the western ministers by a *tactical elasticity* and *politeness of manner* of which they had held him to be incapable.

Version B (after): Rude and Aggressive.

Molotov carried a rather short stick during most of the time when *he spoke so rudely, but he found soft speech uncongenial* even after the stick had become much bigger.

Deutscher's Version A can be found in *The Reporter* of September 23, 1954, the contradictory Version B, in the same magazine, June 28, 1956.

Analysis: *Nikita Khrushchev: The Logic of His Actions: Toward Stalinism or Away From It?*

Version A: Toward Stalinism.

But Khrushchev has probably achieved more than he intended. He meant to defeat his rivals and to deprive them of all influence, but not to stage a purge in the old Stalinist style. *Now, however, the logic of his actions drives him to do precisely this (The Reporter,* August 8, 1957).

Version B (9 months later): Away From Stalinism.

He [Khrushchev] has won [against the same Kremlin rivals as in Version A] at a price that makes it *extremely difficult for him to use power in a tyrannical and autocratic manner* [*The Reporter,* May 1, 1958].

Analysis: *Is the Path Back to Stalinism Still Open or Barred?*

Version A: The Path Back is Barred.

. . . the Soviet Union today is in every respect a much freer country than it was five years ago, and *it can hardly be robbed again of its newly won, though very limited, freedoms (The Reporter,* May 1, 1958).

The road back to Stalinist orthodoxy and discipline is barred,

because that orthodoxy and discipline belong to an epoch which
has come to a close *(Russia in Transition,* p. 55).

Version B: The Path Back is Open.

The trend against de-Stalinization, which began after the Hungarian rising in October, 1956, and continued with the drive
against "revisionism" and the revival of the anti-Titoist campaign, has now reached a decisive point. Even now the Soviet
bloc has not lapsed back into the full darkness of the Stalin era,
*but once again the phantom of the Stalinist terror and the threat
of the purge haunt heretics from China to East Germany (The
Reporter,* July 10, 1958).

Analysis: Has Stalinism Atomized the Russian Working Class?

Version A: Yes (they are hardly capable of formulating de-mands).

The workers have not yet been free enough to voice such demands (for equality) or to make their voices heard. *They may not
even been capable of formulating demands as people accustomed
to autonomous trade union and political activity would do.* . . . It
is more than thirty years since as a class they had ceased to have
any political life of their own. They could hardly recreate it over-
night, *even if those in power had put no obstacles in their way
(Russia in Transition,* pp. 11-12).

Version B: No (the traditions of the Revolution are alive).

With public ownership of the means of production firmly established, with the consolidation and expansion of planned economy,
and — last but not least — *with the traditions of a socialist revolution alive in the minds of its people,* the Soviet Union breaks
with Stalinism in order to resume its advance toward equality
and socialist democracy *(Partisan Review,* Fall 1956).

Analysis: What Does the Intelligentsia Want?

Version A: They Dreamed of Overcoming the Social Inequal-ities of Stalinism (when Stalin was alive).

The only relatively free debate which occurred in mid-century
Russia was concerned with the "transition from socialism to
communism." To outsiders this was bizarre scholastic quibbling
over esoteric dogma; and this in part it was. But to those engaged
in it the dispute offered an occasion for dreaming aloud, *dreaming about the day when the nightmares of the present would dis-
solve, when the State with its all too familiar terrors would
wither away, after all, when the social inequalities of the Stalin*

era would be overcome, and when the mastery of man over man
would become a memory of the past (Russia in Transition, p. 99,
based on articles written in 1951).

Version B: Now They Want To Preserve the Social Status Quo (under Khrushchev).

The men of the intelligentsia have been intensely interested in
political "liberalization," but socially they are conservative. It is
they who have benefitted from the inequalities of the Stalin era.
Apart from individuals and small groups, who may rise intellectually above their own privileged position and sectional viewpoint, they can hardly wish to put an end to those inequalities
and to upset the existing relationship between various groups
and classes of Soviet society. *They are inclined to preserve the
social status quo (Russia in Transition, p. 11).*

Analysis: The Role of the Russian Military — Bloody Conquerors or Militant Reformers?

Version A: Bloody Conquerors.

The day on which a Russian Bonaparte rises in the Kremlin may
see the end of all self-containment, for the Bonaparte would dis-
perse the party secretaries and ride in blood and glory to the
English Channel *(Russia: What Next? p. 207).*

Version B: Militant Reformers

It was no accident that in June, 1957, Marshal Zhukov threw his
weight behind Khrushchev. Perhaps more strongly than any
other group, the officers' corps had *resented the Stalinist purges,
and it was convinced of the urgency of economic and administrative reform*[8] *(The Reporter, November 19, 1959).*

Version C: Opponents of a Tough Line.

. . . Khrushchev himself adopted a tough line in foreign policy
and spoke in a voice that sounded almost like Molotov's. . . . *Zhu-*

---

8. There may be no logical contradiction between these two versions, since
    it is *theoretically* possible that a Russian general riding over Europe in
    blood and glory would also try to institute reforms at home. But it is
    only theoretically possible. Any such adventure, as Deutscher must
    understand, would bring on a full-scale atomic war. To think that in a
    total atomic war, a Russian Bonapartist regime either could or would
    want to ameliorate the harshness of Russian life is to lose contact with
    the realities of this world.

    The more obvious contradiction is in Version C where Marshal Zhukov,
    the chief "Bonapartist" contender who would ride in blood and glory (in
    Version A), turns out to be a bit of a pacifist who resented Khrushchev's
    adoption of Molotov's hard and militaristic foreign policy.

kov, who had backed Khrushchev *against Molotov*, *was in no mood to go on supporting him when he began to speak in Molotov's voice (The Reporter,* November 14, 1957).

Analysis: Dmitri T. Shepilov (Molotov's momentary successor): Was His Middle East Course a Notable Success or a Fiasco?

Version A: A Notable Success (when Shepilov is in power).

. . . Shepilov insisted on the need for Soviet diplomacy to encourage neutralism *and to treat India, Burma, Indonesia, and the Arab states with the consideration and respect due to independent nations.* He castigated Molotov's tactical rigidity and lack of initiative. He carried the day within the Central Committee. His was to some extent the initiative for Khrushchev's and Bulganin's visit to India; *he undertook to test his line in Egypt, which he did with notable success; and he had the satisfaction of being able to listen to Molotov's "selfcriticism" at the Twentieth Congress of the Soviet Communist Party (The Reporter,* June 28, 1956).

Version B: A Fiasco (after the purge of Shepilov).

This was his (Shepilov's) first trip abroad in his new capacity. He was in fact the initiator of the Soviet diplomatic offensive in the Middle East. Consequently, by dismissing him the Soviet leaders have acknowledged that this offensive has ended in fiasco *(The Reporter,* March 7, 1957).

What Malenkov's government is carrying out now is *precisely* the "limited revolution" envisaged by Trotsky (p. 215).

Having sampled some of Deutscher's "analyses" let us look at a few of his "anticipations."

Anticipation: In *Russia: What Next?,* the book that "forecast explicitly and emphatically the whole chain of events" following Stalin's death, he contemptuously dismisses those who predict dissension:

In the weeks before and after Stalin's death, the newspapers were full of speculation about the secret rivalries in the Kremlin, the many-sided plots in which now Beria was supposed to be trying to oust Malenkov and Molotov, now Malenkov and Beria were supposed to oust Molotov, while in still other versions Bulganin and Beria were preparing a coup against all the others. There were probably a few sparks behind this tremendous output of journalistic smoke (p. 12).

To ridicule someone else's prediction is a prediction in its own way. When Deutscher sneers at the journalists' prediction of dissension as little more than a "tremendous output of journalistic smoke" he is denying the essential validity of their speculation of a struggle in which, specifically, Beria, Malenkov, Bulganin and Molotov were trying to oust one another.

What is the proven reality? Beria, Malenkov, Molotov and Bulganin were all purged, the first executed, the others disgraced.

Anticipation: The End of Extracted Confessions.

> Officials who had the extraction of "confessions" on their conscience must have read with a shudder the communique about the release of the Kremlin physicians. The shudder must have been felt in every dark office of the political police throughout Russia. Every man, high and low, in the service must have wondered whether, if he ever again tried to extort confessions, he would not be made to pay for it with his head or at least his freedom *(Russia: What Next?*, p. 177).

Since writing these words in praise of the Malenkov government, Beria was framed up and shot, and confessions were extorted from Malenkov, Molotov, Kaganovich, Shepilov and Bulganin (the latter confessed twice; his first was not satisfactorily self-flagellating) and others. The world awaits Khrushchev's.

Whether the confessions were extracted by physical torture or not is hardly the point. Even under Stalin, not all confessions were obtained through torture. The important point here is that Khrushchev succeeded in extracting ridiculous public confessions from real or imagined rivals in the Kremlin.

Anticipation: No Group in the Central Committee Would Have Dared Defy the Army.

> For some time past Marshal Zhukov had been a virtual umpire vis-a-vis the opposed factions; and he now threw his decisive weight behind Khrushchev. Whatever various groups at the Central Committee may have felt about it, none dared to defy the Army *(The Reporter*, August 8, 1957).

What is the proven reality? This analysis could not withstand the test of the next few months when the officer corps was clearly put in its hierarchical place by Khrushchev, General Secretary of the Communist Party, who not only defied the army but ousted Zhukov from political leadership and chose his own military chieftain.

Anticipation: If There Is Not "Collective Leadership" the Army Is Certain To Take Over.

> Malenkov, Khrushchev and Molotov would have to shelve their own differences and actually exercise "collective leadership" in order to hold their ground jointly vis-à-vis the army. If they fail to do so, and if they try to preserve the party's corporate predominance vis-à-vis the army and at the same time give free rein to their competition for autocratic party leadership then *the outcome of this double contest cannot be seriously in doubt.* A deep cleavage in a leadership not based on a democratic rank and file *is a standing invitation to the army to step in* and "safeguard law and order."

This prediction was made 10 years ago in an article in *The Reporter* (February 2, 1954). Since then:

a) Malenkov, Khrushchev and Molotov failed to shelve their differences.

b) Competition for autocratic leadership of the Party continues.

c) The Communist Party has preserved its corporate predominance vis-a-vis the army.

Anticipation: The Old Bolsheviks Will Be Rehabilitated Soon.

> The inescapable conclusion is that the defendants in those trials, Zinoviev, Kamenev, Rykov, Bukharin and others (perhaps even the absent and impenitent Trotsky) were innocent of the crimes attributed to them. The Soviet leaders have so far still hesitated to say this in public clearly and frankly. But the logic of de-Stalinization will soon compel them to muster courage and to carry out this most difficult act of rehabilitation.

This anticipation is now six years old. We know that Deutscher has a broad historical view, but how soon is soon?

Deutscher's most persistent and fundamental prophecy was his repeated forecast of a democratic flowering of Russian political, intellectual and cultural life. However, the Russia of today is so far behind his calendar of change that even he was obliged to admit to error. "I say frankly, I was mistaken on one point—I expected ten years ago that there would be more *political* freedom in Russia than there is now." In the same (1963) interview he notes "the slow pace in intellectual, literary, cultural affairs, in the moral political atmosphere. I would have expected by now an open political debate to be possible in Russia. In this respect I was mistaken."

It was an unusual concession on Deutscher's part, but then he goes on to say: "I have misjudged the pace but not the direction that events have taken."

It is this writer's opinion that Deutscher has misjudged pace, direction, events and all. And these errors — reflected in his selective research, inconsistencies, half truths and apologetics — are encouraged by theories which we have touched only lightly here. It remains, then, to discuss Deutscher's writings on the social nature of the Russian state, his comparison of Stalin to Cromwell, his "law of revolution," industrialization as a force for democratization, the role of ideology and consciousness. What is involved is nothing less than a discussion of whether basic socialist concepts continue to have meaning in the modern world.

DEUTSCHER VERSUS TROTSKY

It is sometimes thought that Deutscher's views on Communism are akin to Leon Trotsky's. This misconception is due partly to Deutscher's sympathetic three-volume biography of Trotsky, but it is also promoted by the surface resemblance of Trotsky's definition of Russia as a "degenerated worker's state" to Deutscher's characterization of Russia as a form of "autocratic socialism." The similarity is more terminological than political. For whatever this writer believes to be the flaws, inconsistencies and dangerous implications of Trotsky's theory, it seldom served to compromise his opposition to the Kremlin. His politics were infused with a democratic, revolutionary consciousness absent in and alien to Deutscher. For Trotsky, the Kremlin was a totalitarian regime, "symmetrical to fascism." He shared none of Deutscher's illusions that a democratic socialist society could emerge from a totalitarian incubus. On the contrary, Trotsky believed that the socialist regeneration of the October Revolution was contingent on the ability of the Russian people to destroy the Stalinist political system. Where he viewed the liberation of the working class as the job of the working class alone, Deutscher assigns a major share of this mission to the autocratic masters themselves. It is the difference between one who would have hailed the Hungarian revolutionists and one who rationalized their "historically progressive" Stalinist assassins.

This difference was obliquely acknowledged by Deutscher himself in a remarkable passage in the last volume of his Trotsky biography *(The Prophet Outcast)*. Trotsky wrote that if the Marxist program proved impracticable it becomes "self-evident that a new minimum program would be required to defend the interests of the slaves of the totalitarian bureaucratic system." Deutscher comments:

> The passage was characteristic of the man: if bureaucratic slavery was all that the future had in store for mankind, then he would be on the side of the slaves, and not of the new exploiters, however "historically necessary" the new exploitation might be. Having lived all his life with the conviction that the advent of socialism was a scientifically established certainty and that history was on the side of those who struggled for the emancipation of the exploited and the oppressed, he now entreated his disciples to remain on the side of the exploited and the oppressed, even if history and all scientific certainties were against them. He, at any rate, would be with Spartacus, not with Pompey and the Caesars.

Here, Deutscher is not simply noting — and admiring — Trotsky's idealism. He is also summing up the difference between himself and a revolutionary who identifies with slaves even should this fly in the face of "history and all scientific certainties." For it is in deference to the alleged imperatives of history that Deutscher has fashioned his apologias for totalitarianism.

THE LACK OF A COHERENT FRAMEWORK

Deutscher's reputation as a creative or original thinker has grown far out of proportion to his intellectual contributions. He has advanced no coherent conception of the Russian system and, in place of debate, he perfunctorily dismisses views which are uncongenial to his teleological vision of Russia's drive for socialist self-fulfillment.

In *The Prophet Outcast* it did appear that Deutscher would break tradition and confront the arguments of those socialists who have long maintained that the Russian system is a new form of class exploitation — a bureaucratic collectivist totalitarian society antithetical to both socialism and capitalism. According to this theory, the nationalization of industry is an economic form whose progressive or retrograde character depends on who "owns" the state that controls the nationalized economy. In summary fashion, the view is developed as follows: While economics is primary under capitalism, there is no simple one-to-one relationship of economic and political power. Fundamentally, the social power of the capitalist class inheres in the private ownership of the means of production in a profit-motivated market economy, but these narrower economic concerns can bring the capitalist class (or sections of it) into sharp conflict with a national (capitalist) political administration. In a nationalized economy this limited autonomy of (sometimes antagonism between) economic forms and political institutions is largely dissipated. Politics and economics tend to fuse in a state that owns, controls and plans the economy. Given this relationship, to describe a collectivized economy as being "economically democratic" but "politically dictatorial" becomes an illogical and reactionary notion. For the only manner in which a collectivized system can manifest any economic democracy is in the democratically organized political controls of that economy. A socialist state, then, presupposes the conscious political rule of the broad mass of people which can be established only through political democracy — the exercise of free elections, competing political parties, right of recall, genuine trade unions, guaranteed civil rights, full cultural freedom, etc. Conversely, in a state where the bourgeoisie has been expropriated and the economy nationalized but where the people are subjected to the domination and whims of a totalitarian ruling party, we are confronted with a new form of political, therefore economic, class oppression.

In *The Prophet Outcast*, Deutscher presents a detailed review of the bureaucratic collectivist position, attributing its origins to the Italian leftist, Bruno Rizzi, and its further development to a group of former American Trotskyists, led by Max Shachtman [9] and James Burnham. After his sum-

mary, one had reason to expect that Deutscher would try to
expose what he believes to be the fallacies in their arguments.
Not only does he fail to give battle or at least provoke a skir-
mish, he doesn't even make contact with the enemy. Instead,
he tries to dispose of the theory in a couple of sentences. In
one sentence he writes:

> Implicitly or explicitly, they (Burnham and Shachtman) attack-
> ed national ownership of industry and national planning, saying
> that these served as the foundations for bureaucratic collectiv-
> ism and totalitarian slavery.

This is absolutely untrue. Deutscher simply transformed
the idea that the value socialists give to nationalization
should depend on the political nature of the ruling powers to
read that nationalization per se is evil. I know of no socialist
with the bureaucratic collectivist view who doubts that
nationalization and planning, as the economic corollaries of a
socialist society, are a necessary, but insufficient, condition
for socialism.

His other sentence meant to be damaging to the bureaucratic collectivist view is:

> Burnham, Shachtman, and those who followed them, found
> themselves rejecting the Marxist programme point after point.

Even if this were true, it is hardly a refutation of their
views. In any case, it was not true. The bureaucratic collectivist view of Russia which so heavily accents the indivisibility
of socialism and democracy is wholly in the Marxist-Leninist
tradition and was presented in that light. It was Marx who
wrote that the "first step in the revolution by the working
class is to raise the proletariat to the position of the ruling
class, to establish democracy." Engels explained that to accomplish the socialist revolution "the proletariat seizes political power" and then "turns the means of production into
state property." And it was Lenin who wrote, as if anticipa-
ting Deutscher, that "whoever wants to approach socialism

---

9. There is a note of special pique in Deutscher's references to Max Shacht-
    man. One reason may be that Shachtman is the individual most respon-
    sible, in this country, for developing the theory of bureaucratic collectiv-
    ism. Another explanation may be found in the fact that Shachtman is
    the author of a series of brilliant polemics directed against Deutscher
    and his theories. Needless to say, Deutscher never replied.

by any means other than that of political democracy will inevitably arrive at absurd and reactionary conclusions."

If Deutscher discusses neither seriously nor competently views which he finds distasteful, and if he doesn't present any developed, coherent picture of Russian society, that does not mean he avoids all characterization of the Russian social system. In fact, his characterizations of Russian society during the Stalin era are somewhat less than enlightening. In Stalin's defense of the nationalized forms of the Russian economy, Deutscher saw the progressive, Marxist aspect of Stalinism. In Stalin's terrorism, he recognized aspects of barbarism. To define Russian society under Stalin, Deutscher simply adds socialism to barbarism and there you have it — Stalinism was a form of socialist barbarism. In his words, Stalinism was "the mongrel offspring of Marxism and primitive magic."

Deutscher's more recent contributions to an understanding of Russian society after Stalin are hardly more illuminating. In an article explaining "The Failure of Khrushchevism" (published in *The Socialist Register,* 1965) we are informed that what was a "mongrel offspring" only yesterday and which, I believe, he still considers a form of "autocratic socialism" is today a society free of the maledictions of class conflict. In that article, comparing the extent of police persecution under the Czar to police persecution today, Deutscher finds that "evidently the antagonism between rulers and ruled is now different in kind, and less fundamental, for it is not a class antagonism." I doubt that the Russian poets and writers recently sent to Siberian camps would be considerably warmed by the thought that their persecution is less fundamental than the Czarist exile of Dostoyevsky to the same wintry region. But how less fundamental is this admitted antagonism between rulers and ruled? And if the antagonism is not a class conflict, what sort of antagonism is it? Is it possible that in the three decades of barbaric and autocratic rule, the barbarians and autocrats in the Kremlin have not been able to develop the necessary degree of social cohesion to justify their definition as a ruling class?

This disavowal of class conflict in Russia means, among

other things, to displace the responsibility for conformity in Russian life from the shoulders of the rulers to those of the ruled. The conclusion is made by Deutscher, himself, in the same article: "It is not so much police persecution that has prevented any progressive Soviet opposition from crystallizing and acting on a national scale." Instead it is the "apparent inability of those below (i.e., the masses) to exercise control" because they have not been able to overcome the stultifying effects that years of Stalin's rule "have left in their political thinking and social initiative."

How can Deutscher blame the Russian people for their oppressive circumstances? How can one so carelessly sweep under an historical rug the fact that, despite unquestioned relaxation, Russia is still governed by a single party with opposition parties excluded by law, that fundamental criticism if made publicly incurs the risk of jail or a madhouse, that free trade unions are prohibited and strikes outlawed, that cultural experimentalism is treated as subversive and criticism made abroad as treason; that tens of thousands of Russians have in recent years been sent to labor camps, jail or exile as "social parasities," etc. In fact, in "The Failure of Khrushchevism" Deutscher admits that in Russian universities a number of clandestine opposition student groups were organized, "membership of which has been punished as high treason." He also admits that "there has been no lack of industrial strikes, local street demonstrations, even food riots" in Russia, though he does not reveal that they were violently suppressed by the rulers of a country in which there "is not a class antagonism."

STALINISM AND BOLSHEVISM

The study of Lenin and Bolshevism has become a national industry. At least half a dozen well-published volumes on these subjects have been dumped on the market recently, ranging from Robert Payne's hard-covered comic book called *The Life and Death of Lenin* to Louis Fischer's ponderous misunderstanding of *The Life of Lenin*. Although the quality of these works varies, they usually share in their estimates of Leninism as a totalitarian doctrine, of the Bolshevik Revolution as a minority coup d'etat and of the emergence of Stalinism and its concomitant barbarities as the natural heir to Leninism and the Russian Revolution.[10]

While Isaac Deutscher shows nothing but contempt for many of these Sovietologists he has far more in common with them than he would like to think. For Deutscher, too, believes that in basic respects Stalinism was continuous with Leninism, though his judgements and political conclusions may differ. To the bourgeois critic of Bolshevism, the insistence that Stalinism flows from Leninism is used to expose the dangers of socialism; for the right-wing socialist critic, it reveals the pitfalls of revolutionary socialism. But for Isaac Deutscher, who accepts the socialist legitimacy of the Russian Revolution, his qualified acceptance of the Leninism-Stalinism sequence is used as a qualified historical justification of Stalinism.

The relationship between Leninism and Stalinism is not an academic question. At stake is the political and moral worth of socialism itself. For if anything remotely resembling Stalinist terror can be proved to be a necessary accompaniment of socialism then socialism itself becomes an unworthy and evil objective.

However, nothing in Deutscher's discussion of the Leninist-Stalinist relationship is sufficiently convincing to weaken one's socialist convictions.

In his *Russia: What Next?* Deutscher demonstrated the terrible confusion that follows from arguing that the basic

10. In this writer's view, the Bolshevik Revolution was by far the most inspiring and democratic social revolution in all history. Its scope had no precedent, its heroism and aspiration not matched until the Hungarian Revolution of October 1956. The Revolution's relevance for socialists today is — or should be — in the evidence it afforded that even in backward Russia, the majority of the politically conscious and oppressed could be *persuaded* (not coerced) — even if only briefly — to accept the leadership of a sophisticated revolutionary socialist party which hid neither its program nor its aims. Never before did the majority of the class in whose interests a revolution was organized prove to be its major, active supporters and soldiers.

This is not to deny that either Lenin or Leninism or the Soviet regime in its first years are deserving of critical review. The mistakes were many from the standpoint of revolutionary democratic socialism, but that is the subject for another article.

social conquests won by the Bolsheviks were continued and guarded by Stalinism:

> Stalinism developed out of Leninism, preserving some of the features of Leninism and discarding others. It continued in the Leninist tradition; but it also stood in a bitter and unavowed opposition to it.

To stand in bitter and unavowed opposition to a tradition and at the same time to continue that tradition is another of Deutscher's dialectical acrobatics. The proposition imposes the responsibility of clarification which he attempts later in the same book:

> In one fundamental respect Stalin did, of course, continue Lenin's work. He strove to preserve the State founded by Lenin and to increase its might. He also preserved and then expanded the nationalized and State-managed industry, in which the Bolsheviks saw the basic framework of their new society. These important threads of continuity between Leninism and Stalinism were never cut.

So there are threads (at least) of continuity. The first is that Stalin tried to preserve and strengthen the state. The question remains, however: what was the nature of that state? The term state is an abstraction, and the truism that all rulers try to strengthen their states hardly suggests a common bond or continuity between capitalist and socialist societies or between Leninism and Stalinism. The second thread that Deutscher spins (Stalin "also preserved . . .") is Stalin's loyalty to nationalized property. No one can question this. Both Lenin and Stalin believed in the basic importance of state-managed industries. But why is this a continuity with Leninism or the Leninist tradition which implies ideas, principles, programs and methods which defined Lenin and his followers?

Deutscher cannot tell us concretely how Stalin preserved the Leninist state if only because in passing he does accurately note some of the essential elements of this same Leninist state:

> But Leninism also committed itself in 1917 and afterward to respect, to guard, to promote, and to extend in every possible way the political freedom of the working classes, *who should have been the real masters in the new State. This* was the *meaning* of "proletarian democracy," which should have supplement-

ed, *or rather formed the basis of,* the dictatorship (emphasis added).

Deutscher was never more correct. Leninism meant the political freedom of the working class and the "meaning" and "the basis" of proletarian democracy (or proletarian dictatorship) is that the politically free working class should be "the real masters in the new state." In what respect then, did Stalin continue the Leninist state if he destroyed its very basis — proletarian democracy?

We should also point out that immediately after the passage informing the reader that Stalin preserved, in one fundamental respect, the Leninist state, Deutscher continues:

> But when Stalin took over the State its direction was in such a condition that it could be preserved only by being politically refashioned almost into its opposite.

The picture is now complete — and utterly incomprehensible. For in a dozen pages Deutscher has flung the following contradictory propositions and conclusion at his readers without the slightest display of self-doubt:

a) Stalinism continued in the Leninist tradition; Stalinism stood in bitter opposition to Leninism.

b) The Leninist state was inseparable from proletarian democracy; Stalin politically refashioned the Leninist state "almost into its opposite."

Conclusion:

c) Stalin, in a "fundamental respect" preserved and extended the Leninist state.

BOURGEOIS AND SOCIALIST REVOLUTIONS

Deutscher's apologia for communist totalitarianism is firmly woven into an elitist philosophy which rejects the socialist conception that the broad mass of people can emerge triumphant from a revolutionary struggle, retaining its élan and ability to manage its own affairs. Instead, he promulgates a virtual law of revolution according to which "each revolution begins with a phenomenal outburst of popular energy, impatience, anger and hope. Each ends in the weariness, exhaustion and disillusionment of the revolutionary people." While the people are exhausted,

> the Party of the Revolution knows no retreat. It has been driven

to its present pass largely through obeying the will of that same people by which it is now deserted. It will go on doing what it considers to be its duty, without paying much heed to the voice of the people. In the end it will muzzle and stifle that voice. Moreover,

> The rulers acquire the habits of arbitrary government and themselves come to be governed by their own habits. What had hopefully begun as a great warm-hearted popular venture gradually degenerates into a narrow and cold autocracy *(Stalin: A Political Biography*, pp. 173-175).

Thus a "narrow and cold autocracy" would have arisen in Russia under the best of postrevolutionary circumstances; backwardness, primitivism and isolation only served to accelerate the degenerative process and to foreshorten the Revolution's heroic period. It becomes utopian sentimentality not to realize that the "Calendar of Revolution" (one of Deutscher's favorite expressions) required the rule of a dictatorial elite to govern Russia in the long-term interests of the people and to prevent the revolution from shifting into reverse gear.

The weight of historic evidence is certainly on Deutscher's side. The great revolutions of the past were made in the name of popular causes and gathered enormous mass support. Yet, in each case, in England, in France as well as in Russia, a victorious elite emerged which violated the revolution's proclaimed democratic principles and institutions and eventually repressed the revolutionary peoples themselves.

If Deutscher is correct, that this is an inevitable historic pattern from which not even a socialist revolution can be excepted, then again socialism must be rejected as a hopelessly archaic, utopian and dangerous package. For the very heart of Marxist politics is its reliance on the ability of the working class to regulate its own affairs.

Related to this law of revolution is the grand parallel Deutscher finds between the Russian Revolution and the English and French bourgeois revolutions. The parallel is repeated in each of Deutscher's books and in many of his essays. In the French Revolution, above all, he finds "the passions, the spirit, and the language of the Russian Revolution. This is true to such an extent that it is absolutely necessary for the student of recent Russian history to view it every now and then through the French prism" *(Russia In Transition,* p. 143).

Deutscher sees the French and Russian revolutions as having established the power of socially progressive forces. Both revolutions revealed initial egalitarian, democratic impulses and mass enthusiasm. But given the force of the law of revolution, neither the Jacobins nor the Bolsheviks could possibly meet the expectations of the multitudes they inspired and led. The frustrated French plebians grew as disillusioned with the intangible results of their sacrifices as the Russian working class grew apathetic and even hostile toward a Bolshevik party that could provide it with none of the material benefits for which so much blood was shed. Consequently, the popular, democratic phase of the French Revolution, which reached its apex with the Jacobin triumph in 1793, inevitably succumbed, first to the Thermidor and then to Bonapartism. Similarly, the analogy goes, the Russian Revolution reached its inspirational heights in the first years of Bolshevik rule only to give way to one-party dictatorship and then to one-man tyrannical rule. The analogy continues: although Napoleon crowned himself Emperor, he neither wanted to nor could reverse the rising power of the French bourgeoisie established in the heroic period of 1789-1793; on the contrary, Napoleon defended the basic social objectives of the French Revolution at the necessary expense of its egalitarianism. Similarly, Stalin dissipated the egalitarianism of Russia's October Revolution, emerging as a personally fiendish dictator who nevertheless defended the socialist interests of the very working class he brutalized by preserving, consolidating and extending nationalized urban property within and without Russian borders.

Therefore, in Deutscher's view, "the Russian counterparts to the Jacobin, Thermidorean and Bonapartist phases of the [French] revolution have in a curious way overlapped and merged in Stalinism." Thus Stalin becomes a curious sort of socialist Napoleon, and his political personality is even more complex since he also emerges in Deutscher's writings as a barbaric kind of socialist Robespierre. (Or, depending on the specific national-historical focus of the analogies, Stalin is,

always in a qualified and curious way, reminiscent of Cromwell, Bismarck, a blend of "the Leninist and Ivan the Terrible," among other star billings including the Emperor
Constantine.)

Deutscher acknowledges that there are limits to the
analogy. In the first paragraph of his essay, "Two Revolutions," wholly concerned with an analogy of the French and
Communist revolutions, he counsels his reader that "in drawing any analogy it is . . . important to know where the analogy
ends." And he hopes not to "offend badly against this rule."
This promising beginning is followed by a series of compari-
sons between the two revolutions, some interesting, others
preposterous, but no indication of where the analogy finds its
limits. Yet, it is the incongruities far more than the similarities which sharpen the socialist image by way of contrast.
What these differences reveal is that the Russian (socialist)
Revolution represented a much sharper and more profound
break with the past than was the case with the French (bourgeois) Revolution. It is worth noting some of the important
differences:

a) The revolution of 1789-1793 brought the conflict between bourgeois and aristocrat to a head and out of that contest the supremacy of capitalism was hastened and assured
by the shattering of feudal restrictions to free competition,
to the development of manufacturing, to the right to exploit
both labor and partitioned lands; it relieved the bourgeoisie
of the burden of intolerable tithes and discriminatory taxa-
tion and permitted the realization of the bourgeoisie's dream
of a French nation state. However, vast as these changes
were, the French Revolution meant the triumph of one propertied class over another propertied class.

By contrast the Russian Revolution witnessed, for the
first time, the economic and political expropriation of prop-
erty-owning classes by a propertyless working class.

b) The French bourgeoisie had established its economic
and political beachheads within the old regime long before
the call for the Estates General. "Creeping capitalism" was an
irrepressible fact of life throughout the reign of Louis XVI.
Bolshevism, on the other hand, could not establish any

beachheads under Czarism (nor could socialism assert its authority within the framework of American capitalism in the future). For, under socialism, the individual worker remains propertyless but his class becomes the owner of the means of production through its political control of the state. It is patently impossible, then, for socialism to grow within capitalism since the working class cannot win political control of a nationalized industry in this or that sector of a capitalist economy.

If one accepts just these obvious differences between the two revolutions, the whole elegant structure of Deutscherism begins to sag, since one of its major underpinnings—his use of the analogy of bourgeois and socialist revolutions—turns out to be a numbing hallucination. There can be no curious sort of merging of Jacobinism-Thermidoreanism-Bonapartism, or their alleged "counterparts," in a socialist society. While Bonaparte deprived the bourgeoisie of many of its political rights, he nevertheless contributed enormously to the consolidation of capitalism in that he continued to battle the remnants of feudalism, created more congenial conditions for the expansion of capital and in his wars of conquest performed similar services in foreign lands bringing them into greater harmony with the needs of French capitalism.

But — as Deutscher's use of the analogy suggests — how could a socialist Bonaparte or a semi-socialist semi-Bonaparte deprive the working class of its political power and at the same time perform services for that class comparable to what Napoleon did for the French ruling class when the working class can be the ruling class only if it has political power? Deprive the workers of political power and they are once again an economically exploited class.

c) The French revolution — as with all bourgeois revolutions — was fought and won primarily by classes alien to the bourgeoisie. What there was of a French bourgeoisie was weak and vacillating though, for a brief period, sections of the Third Estate did develop a Messianic vision and fanaticism in the course of their struggle against the nobility. Left to their own resources, however, their triumph would have been much longer in coming. To break the back of the aristocracy, the bourgeoisie was obliged to form temporary and uneasy alliances with elements it feared and upon whom it would turn in fury. The necessary violence with which the aristocracy was defeated within France and the armies raised to resist foreign invasions in defense of the bourgeois revolution were primarily the achievements of the revolutionary Jacobin left whose mass base was largely found among those insurrectionary plebian elements who had far less to gain than the bourgeois class in whose historic interests they fought. Indeed, in the years immediately following the fall of Robespierre, with the victory of the revolution more or less secure, the Jacobin left and its plebian supporters were subjected to a white terror at the hands of conservative bourgeois and aristocrats in tacit alliance that far outdid the violence of Robespierre's Committee of Public Safety.

This contrasts sharply with a socialist revolution, which can be fought, won and sustained only by the working class and its natural allies — or not at all. The armies of socialism cannot possibly be recruited from the bourgeoisie, while the armies of the bourgeois revolution had to be plebian in composition.

d) The decisive function of politics in a socialist society and the above-noted necessity for the self-mobilization of the oppressed implies a fourth difference between socialist and bourgeois revolutions: the role of consciousness. To achieve power the working class must be moved by an awareness that is on a qualitatively higher plane than that required of a bourgeois class (which had the economic leverage of expanding capitalist enclaves within the old feudal order). And the organized leadership of a socialist working class must be moved by an ideology that is clear, consistent with its objectives, sensitive to the needs of the working class and whose aims are never hidden from the people. On the other hand, the social rule of the capitalist class is not dependent on a comparable sustained high level of class consciousness.

Deutscher would rather not dwell on the importance of consciousness as a socialist criterion since he is anxious to pass Russia off as a form of socialism at the same time as he recognizes the absence of popular direction of Russian society and has repeatedly asserted that the people are lacking in class consciousness and must relearn the habits of political thinking.

e) The success of a bourgeois revolution is not contingent on the support of the majority of people; a bourgeois government represents the interests of a minority class which may or may not have majority support. A socialist revolution, on the other hand, must have the support of the majority of urban and agrarian wage earners or feel assured of such support in the course of a struggle for power. Napoleon could force bourgeois change down the throat of European society with bayonets; socialist revolutions and socialist societies cannot impose socialist systems on a hostile majority, either at home or abroad, with tanks, bayonets and armies, as Deutscher tells us Stalin did in Russia and Eastern Europe.

Where Deutscher does point to dissimilarities between the French and Russian revolutions, they are seldom the basic ones and, more damaging, they are often used to demonstrate either implicitly or explicitly, the social superiority of Stalin as against Robespierre, and of Stalinism against the French Thermidor. An example from *The Prophet Outcast*:

> Another difference is even more important: Thermidor brought to a close the revolutionary transformation of French society and the upheaval in property. In the Soviet Union these did not come to a halt with Stalin's ascendancy. On the contrary, the most violent upheaval, collectivization of farming, was carried out under his rule. And it was surely not "law and order," even in a most anti-popular form, that prevailed either in 1923, or at any time during the Stalin era. What the early 1920s had in common with the Thermidorean period was the ebbing away of the popular revolutionary energies and the disillusionment and apathy of the masses. It was against such a background that Robespierre had sought to keep the rump of the Jacobin Party in power and failed; and that Stalin struggled to preserve the dictatorship of the Bolshevik rump (i.e., of his own faction) and succeeded.

First of all, the Thermidor did not bring to a close the revolutionary transformation of French society. It only brought to a close the Jacobin chapter in that transformation. In fact, the victory of the Thermidoreans over the Robespierrists assured the continuation of the basic social-economic changes in France. While the Robespierrists were com-

mitted to bourgeois property rights they also advocated
democratic political and economic policies — such as universal suffrage and price ceilings — which galled the more conservative bourgeois elements, many of whom fell under the
guillotine of Robespierre's "reign of terror." In bringing
Robespierre to account after Thermidor, the bourgeoisie
rejoiced not because the revolutionary transformation of
French society and the "upheaval in property" ground to a
halt, but because the bourgeois upheaval in property would
be less constrained by restrictions imposed by the plebian-
based left wing of the revolution. In this decisive sense the
Thermidoreans, despite their lessened vigilance vis-à-vis the
aristocracy, were the continuants and consolidators of that
revolution and those upheavals destined to establish the
supremacy of bourgeois property relations.

By placing a period to the French upheavals in property
after Robespierre's fall and by implicitly (and falsely) equating
the essence of the Russian Revolution with such upheavals as
"collectivization of farming," Stalin and Stalinism emerge
as superior creatures (even if, admittedly, somewhat odious)
in Deutscher's analogous heap. Stalin "succeeded" where
Robespierre failed, and Stalin carried out revolutionary upheavals where the Thermidoreans supposedly brought them
to a halt.

Shortly after this revealing comparison, Deutscher gives
forth in the same intellectual spirit with both a similarity
and a difference between Stalin and Robespierre.

> The historically far more justified charge that Trotsky could
> have levelled against Stalin (i.e., that Stalinism represented the
> Russian Thermidor) was that he instituted a reign of terror like
> Robespierre's, and that he had monstrously outdone Robes-
> pierre.

That Stalin monstrously outdid Robespierre in the use of
terror will be challenged by no responsible person. That
Stalin's reign of terror was anything "like Robespierre's"
is to monstrously abuse Robespierre and history.

There has been a tendency, perhaps, for socialists to
overdress Robespierre in revolutionary democratic robes, to
glamorize the man and the faction he led. Robespierre's
terror was not only directed against the aristocracy and the

Gironde. It moved against his opposition on the left, Hébert and the Enragées, using false accusations, drumhead trials and the guillotine in a violent and futile effort to consolidate Robespierre's power. Despite the similarities, to place Robespierre's terror in a "like" category with Stalin's terror is somewhat like comparing a gourmand to a cannibal because both are meat-eaters.

The fact is that the brunt of the French terror was felt by the aristocracy, by those who speculated in the welfare of the people, by bourgeois elements who grew to fear the sans-culottes more than the nobility and by those who gave aid and comfort to foreign armies fighting on French soil. Now, if Stalin's terror was "like" Robespierre's, only more thorough, then it would seem that Stalin's terror was primarily and more effectively, directed against comparable elements in Russia — against Czarist restorationists, agents of foreign imperialism, swindlers, etc. But this was not the case, of course. Stalin's terror was directed against workers, peasants, intellectuals, socialists, as well as against the top and secondary leadership and tens of thousands of rank and file members of the Communist Party. How was this like Robespierre's terror?

APOLOGIA FOR FORCED INDUSTRIALIZATION

Deutscher does believe in democracy and he does look forward to socialist democracy in Russia. At least he has so assured us in his writings. But when it comes down to the here and now, who one should support, which system is progressive, democracy becomes a secondary consideration. And in any conflict between democracy and what be believes to be the needs of industrialization in a nationalized and collectivized economy the former is denied any decisive merit. This is borne out, above all, in Deutscher's treatment of "primitive socialist accumulation" in which his value judgements are evident.

The Russian economy, weak to begin with in 1914, was shattered by more than seven years of war and revolution. The defeat of the revolution in the West was an even heavier blow to the industrial needs of the Soviet regime. Confronted with famine, apathy and mounting hostility, the Leninist

Party led the country into the New Economic Policy (NEP) period which was highlighted by a general relaxation of economic controls. Forced grain collections were eliminated and the market in the agrarian section of the economy was reintroduced to encourage the farmer to produce. This served to stabilize Russian society; anti-government violence subsided in the countryside, more food was produced by the profit-motivated farmer and famine was thereby averted among urban consumers.

The blessings of NEP, however, were of short duration and never unmixed. It was initiated by an already bureaucratized party that counterweighted economic relaxation with still tighter Party political controls. With the declining caliber of the party and Stalin's ascendancy, it served the latter's purposes to give the NEP, originally designed as a temporary stopgap, a more permanent place in Party ideology. A new class of more prosperous farmers (kulaks) was advised by the Stalin regime to "enrich yourselves." This, of course, they tried to do, one technique being to withhold produce from the once again hard-pressed urban consumer in the late twenties. The farmers sought not only to keep the price of their produce at a profitable level but were incensed over the prospect of their profits being wiped out by the rising price of urban manufactured goods produced by an inefficient and neglected Russian industry. By 1929, Stalin was confronted by a hungry proletariat, a weak industry, an insurrectionary peasantry and a rising class of capitalist-oriented kulaks. Stalin set about to strengthen the Communist party and his position in it with a radical and sudden departure from the policies of 1923-1929. This was to be the period of forced collectivization and forced industrialization. These objectives could be achieved by Stalin in only one way: through the most massive, systematized and historically unrivalled application of mass terror. Forced collectivization required a veritable civil war in which millions of peasants were killed by gunfire, famine and the rigors of labor camps. Industrialization was advanced in similar fashion. The political auxilliary of these new economic policies was the consolidation of totalitarianism, one-man dictatorship and mass purges.

The human misery wrought by Stalinist industrialization and collectivization is detailed by Isaac Deutscher. But for all his lamentation over Stalin's barbarities, Deutscher's final political judgement is essentially indifferent to totalitarianism's deprivation of life, liberty and the pursuit of happiness. In his balance sheet of history, forced collectivization and industrialization are in the historical black, so to speak, since Stalin preserved and extended the "socialist" nature of the economy. It was Russia's "Second Revolution" which, we are told, could only be carried out brutally and required the extirpation of democracy.

The logic of Deutscherism is inescapable. Given his views of socialism, which eliminate democracy as an integral part of socialism, and given his conviction that only the inevitably ("predetermined") evolved system of Stalinism could bring this good about, there is no ground for repudiating Stalin's methods other than an irrelevant squeamishness. Perhaps it was not necessary to slander the old Bolsheviks with the charge of being agents of foreign imperialism and on Hitler's payroll, but whatever reasons might be advanced, from Deutscher's point of view and analysis, if logic prevails, the old Bolsheviks had to be removed one way or another, since it can easily be established that their very existence was a serious menace to the consolidation of Stalinism politically and therefore an impediment to its historic "socialist" mission of raising Russia from the wooden plow to the tractor.

More generally, Deutscher has created a theoretical justification for terror whose practical significance today lies in its contribution to totalitarian tendencies which seek, on similar grounds, to justify the use of terror and the liquidation of democracy and democrats in Cuba, China, North Vietnam and elsewhere on the ground that such terror is historically conditioned and necessary for the sake of social progress.

A basic merit of industrialization in Deutscher's view is that it provides the economic catalyst for Russia's evolution from authoritarian socialism. This optimistic vision is presented in Marxistical terms, although what emerges is a crude form of economic determinism that shares nothing with Marxism.

In the Marxist view, political institutions, philosophical ideas, legal concepts, national customs and habits are shaped and influenced by the material conditions of life. These material factors include: a) all the limitations and propensities inherent in natural conditions — climate, waterways, topography, etc. — and b) the level and form of economic activity. Since the conditions of nature are relatively constant, it is to the variable factor, economic conditions, that the historian must turn to understand the complexities of social evolution. The changes in the level of productivity, the means whereby the product is exchanged, the economic relations into which men are obliged to enter with other men, become the underlying sources of social transformation.

Marxism did not limit itself to promulgating a philosophical view of the world. It sought to examine concretely the economic relations men entered into with one another; to establish the causes and consequences of economic conflict; to learn what is needed to permit man to overcome the limitations of nature. In the class struggle, Marxists found the "locomotive of history"; in the capitalist mode of production they found inner contradictions which would lead to the expropriation of the capitalist expropriators; and *in the growth of the productive forces Marxism saw the prerequisite of man's emancipation from exploitative class society.*

It is in this latter condition for freedom — the growth of the productive forces — that the modern authoritarian socialist finds it possible to mask economic determinism with a protective Marxist cloak. Did not Marx find that capitalism, as against feudalism, was a progressive form of society because it meant a vast growth of the productive forces? And if capitalism was an historic advance because it meant the triumph of the machine process over feudal agrarianism, is not Stalinism a progressive form of society because in Russia it transformed an agrarian economy into a highly industrialized one and created a large industrial working class? In the words of the dean of authoritarian socialism:

> In spite of its "blood and dirt," the English industrial revolution — Marx did not dispute this — marked a tremendous progress in the history of mankind. It opened a new and not unhopeful

epoch of civilization. *Stalin's industrial revolution can claim the same merit (Stalin: A Political Biography,* pp. 342-343).

There is so much wrong with this analogy between Stalinist industrialization in modern times and the growth of the factory system more than a century ago, that we must limit ourselves here to itemizing a few critical observations:

a) The victory of capitalism was achieved at the expense of a retrograde feudal society. The victory of Stalinism had as its precondition the defeat of a socialistic Russia.

b) For all of its hesitations and misgivings about democracy, for all of its violence against the working class, even in its earliest days, the victory of the European bourgeoisie over the nobility witnessed an extension of individual rights and political freedom which was unthinkable under feudalism. And what the bourgeoisie would not willingly concede to the nation in the way of democracy could often be won by democratic forces within the framework of the bourgeois social order. What is disastrous for Deutscher's analogy of capitalist and Stalinist industrialization is that the latter was effected under the auspices of a totalitarian force which can remain in power only as long as it can prevent the emergence of democratic institutions.

c) One progressive contribution of capitalism was the creation of a large, socially homogeneous industrial proletariat which is, in the Marxist view, the indispensable agent for liberating society. This class, unique to capitalist society, was "freed" from any ownership of the means of production but it was, of necessity, also freed from the political servitude of feudalism. This political freedom is atypical of Stalinism's working class and would be inimical to its totalitarian collectivized economy. The Russian working class is *not* the same as the industrial proletariat described by Marx.

d) To increase the wealth of nations there was no alternative to a capitalist reorganization of society. The economic basis of socialism had to be developed and a working class of weight and experience had to appear. It has yet to be proved that despite the degree of Russia's economic backwardness, and given the economically advanced character of the capitalist world, the only way to modernize Russia was through its Stalinization.

Moreover, Stalinization in Russia cannot be considered in isolation. It meant the corruption of the world Communist movement, reducing foreign parties to little more than adjuncts of the Kremlin. It meant sacrificing socialist principles and national revolutionary ambitions throughout the world for the sake of securing the degenerated Russian Communist party in power. Before dismissing the possibility of Russia industrializing in a democratic manner, one must consider the very real possibility that a genuinely communist, i.e., revolutionary socialist, movement in Germany might have taken power in 1932 which would have changed the political map of Europe and provided the technological assistance for which the Bolshevik leaders of 1917 thirsted.

e) The most telling difference between Marx's treatment of England's industrial revolution and Deutscher's view of Stalinist industrialization is the following: Marx never used his view of capitalist industrialization to underplay the attendant horrors of British exploitation on the ground that England's economic growth was largely contingent on the sun never setting on its empire; in Deutscher's hands, by contrast, the alleged progressiveness of an industrializing nationalized economy is used to cloud reality and to cast Stalinist imperialism in a progressive mold.

But, it is said, forced industrialization is a thing of the past, and even if it was a nasty business, look at how it has transformed Russia and improved the living standards of the Russian people today. However, even where these highly touted economic advances are concerned, we are less impressed than Isaac Deutscher and the whole coterie of Stalinoid aficionados of the statistic whose spirits soar with every new orbiting Sputnik or rise in the production of steel or pigs. The growth is certainly real, but the important thing for socialists, apart from the question of who controls the expanding economy, is to know who are its beneficiaries. One thing is certain — those benefitting least are the workers and peasants. *The truth of the matter is that by American standards the vast majority of Russian wage-earners would qualify for assistance under the Washington Administration's antipoverty program and be eligible for supplementary relief from local welfare agencies.*

In February of this year the USSR Central Statistical Administration, reporting on the final year's achievement of the Seven Year Plan (1959-65), stated that the "average monthly earnings of workers and employees in the national economy increased from 90 rubles in 1964 to 95 rubles in 1965 or by 5.8%." The higher figure means an average weekly wage of approximately $25.00 on the basis of the dollar-ruble exchange rate. What about the many fringe benefits that Russian workers are said to receive? The following figures given in the report reveal how modest they really are: "If the payments and benefits received from public funds are added in, the average earnings increased correspondingly from 121 rubles [in 1964] to 128 rubles per month [in 1965]." Even if these figures are not exaggerated the combined wage and public fund benefits would come to about $33.00 per week, or slightly over $1700 a year.

What does the Five Year Plan (1966-1970) recently adopted at the Party's 23rd Congress hold in store for the workers in Deutscher's socialist Russia? Premier Kosygin's report to the Congress on the Five Year Plan Directives lets us know: "The average monthly wages of production and office workers will go up during the five years by an average of not less than 20% and *by the end of the new five-year plan* will amount to about 115 rubles; if payments and benefits from the public consumption funds are included, the total will reach approximately 155 rubles per employed person." In other words, after another five years of reaping socialism, the average workingman can look forward to a total income from pay and benefits of around $40 per week. And these are figures for urban industrial and white-collar workers. If we averaged in agricultural earnings, the figures would be still lower.

While this will be the average income (if the goal is fulfilled), whole categories of workers will receive considerably less. According to the section of the Five Year Plan concerned with "Raising The Material Well-Being and Cultural Level of the People" we are informed of the Party's ambition "to raise the minimum wage in the (national) economy to 60 rubles a month." Sixteen dollars a week — by 1970! As this is to be the minimum wage if the Plan is successfully completed, it is reasonable enough to assume — and there are statistics to bear it out — that today there are categories of unskilled workers who receive no more than $13 to $14 a week. How much culture and well-being can be raised on this pittance?

While there has been some levelling of income in Russia, it is nonetheless the case that in Deutscher's socialist economy there are top academicians and administrators who receive up to $10,000 a year (apart from such little extras as dachas and chauffered limousines). Between high and low earnings, then, there is a differential of 14:1 compared to a spread of 5:1 in equivalent categories in Western bourgeois countries.

In Russia there is an income tax. It is not high by American standards, but high enough given the low wages. It begins with incomes of only 60 rubles a month and discriminates against the poor since it is not a highly graduated direct tax system. Instead, a family of four earning 50 rubles above the 60 ruble exemption pays 10% of those 50 rubles while a top administrator who earns 800 rubles above the 60 only pays 13%. A continuing major source of revenue is the turnover tax which continues to add about 30% to retail prices. This, too, discriminates against the poor who must pay the same 30% on the price of goods as the affluent professional or bureaucrat.

The situation for Russian worker-consumers is even more morbid than the above figures suggest since the prices they must pay for basic necessities of life are outlandish. The prices of butter and meats were raised 25 to 30% in 1962. The increases have not been rescinded. A pound of salted butter costs $1.75 in Moscow, and the average buyer must work well over three hours to earn enough for the purchase. In New York the comparable figures are 75¢ a pound and 19 minutes worktime for the average factory worker. The price of beef is approximately the same in Moscow and New York, but the Moscow worker must work five times as long as his New York counterpart to make the purchase. The story is the same for such items as sugar, bread, potatoes, eggs and milk, where the Muscovite must work from 400% to 1900% longer than the New Yorker to purchase these necessities. It is the same in clothing where, for example, an average Russian worker must be prepared to spend five weeks pay for a suit of moderate quality that would require 23 hours worktime for a New York worker. Other Moscow figures: four weeks work for a radio set, two months for a TV set, while even the lowest priced car is for bureaucrats only since it would require three to four years of worktime.

The statistics on food costs are based on state-fixed prices. However, since there is a continuing shortage of these basic goods, the consumer is often obliged to buy on the open market where farmers sell their goods for considerably higher prices. (It is true that on the positive side of the economic picture are the considerably lower rents in Russia compared to the United States. On the other hand, the Russian family gets considerably less for its money. Russian dwellings are notoriously inadequate in quality and terribly overcrowded with a total floor space per person of 100 square feet (10' x 10') including kitchen and bathroom.)

Compare these economic facts of Russian life with Deutscher's "certain[ty]" of surpassing Western European standards (by 1969) and consider the moral enormity of a view that considers Russia to be reaping the benefits of socialism (as far back as 1959).

APOLOGIA FOR IMPERIALISM

Deutscher's obscuring of the full scope and criminality of Stalinist industrialization is matched by his presentation of Russia's postwar conquest of Eastern Europe as if it were merely a distorted and unsophisticated application of the Marxist concept of the socialist revolution in permanence. In his introduction to *The Age of Permanent Revolution: A Trotsky Anthology*, published less than two years ago, he found that just as Stalin was the manager of the ideas in domestic affairs developed by the man he murdered, so was he the executor of Trotsky's will to world socialist revolution:

> . . . his (Stalin's) single-country socialism was indeed, as Trotsky maintained, a pragmatist's Utopia. The Soviet Union abandoned it to all intents and purposes towards the end of the Second World War, when its troops, in pursuit of Hitler's armies, marched into a dozen foreign lands, and carried revolution on their bayonets and in the turrets of their tanks.

This socialism by foreign tanks and bayonets is one of

Deutscher's pet themes that deserves a more detailed view. In discussing the battle of the Vistula, which witnessed the decisive defeat of the Red armies at the gates of Warsaw in 1920, Deutscher wrote (in *The Prophet Armed)* that the battle "did not change the course of history, as its contemporaries believed — it only delayed it by a quarter of a century." In other words, Stalin succeeded in Poland where Trotsky and Lenin failed a quarter of a century earlier! Of course, as Deutscher knows and acknowledges, the earlier Russian invasion of Poland took place under entirely different circumstances and with altogether different motives than Stalin's military conquests.

In 1920, the Red Army invaded Poland as a continuation of a war which had begun as a defensive operation. Large sections of the Ukraine had already been occupied by Polish troops who amused themselves by inflicting all sorts of atrocities upon the Ukrainian people. The enmity of the Ukrainian peasant to Pilsudski's troops facilitated the Bolshevik military victory in the Ukraine, and when the Red Army reached Polish borders it pursued the retreating Polish armies into Poland proper. This military venture, however, was undertaken against the advice of Trotsky, who did not believe that Russian bayonets were a proper substitute for an absent socialist consciousness of the Polish people. Lenin and the majority of the Bolsheviks did order the continuation of the war into Polish territory but even for them a victorious Red Army was not intended as an occupying force to stuff freedom down Polish throats with Russian bayonets. They were convinced that the Polish people would respond favorably to the Red Army; and perhaps an even greater consideration for the Bolshevik majority was its conviction that a Red Army on the Polish-German border would provide a moral and political impetus to the developing revolutionary consciousness of the German working class. In any case, the 1920 Polish adventure came to be looked on by Lenin and his party as a mistake for precisely those reasons advanced by Trotsky at the time of his minority opposition to the war — socialism cannot be advanced in foreign countries on the points of bayonets.

By contrast, the Russian occupation of Poland in 1945 did

not follow the expulsion of Polish troops from Russian soil. (The fate of the Polish armies had been sealed five years earlier in the aftermath of the Nazi-Soviet Pact of 1939.) And Stalin's conquest of Poland had nothing to do with an anticipated rise of Polish socialist consciousness and nothing to do with providing the catalyst for a revolutionary upheaval from below of the West European working class.

Deutscher is actually aware of how removed his concept of socialism by foreign bayonets is from revolutionary socialist principles. He has written, for example, that "it had been a canon of Marxist politics that revolution cannot and must not be carried on the point of bayonets into foreign countries," and that this canon "also followed from the fundamental attitude of Marxism which looked to the working classes of all nations as to the sovereign agents of socialism and certainly did not expect socialism to be imposed upon peoples from outside."

Deutscher, with his foreign "socialist" bayonets, is privileged to violate what he recognizes to be fundamental Marxist attitudes. But he has no right to do so and simultaneously pose as a Marxist.

What term other than imperialism can more accurately describe the foreign politics of a country which, by the use or threat of armed force, imposes its will and, at times, its social system on weaker nations? This imperialism may not be generated by the economic drives peculiar to monopoly capitalism, but imperialism, generally defined, is not unique to capitalism. Caesar's marauding imperial legions were not driven by a need to offset a falling rate of profit. Russia is a modern case in point of a noncapitalist imperialism. It was not impelled to export capital in postwar Europe. It merely exported its social system at bayonet point.

Deutscher frequently waxes wroth over the manner and consequences of Russian "expansionism." But he is incapable of presenting a clear, consistent repudiation of this imperialism given his view that the Kremlin was exporting revolutionary progress along with some unsavory practices. Even his criticisms of Communist methods often prove to be disarming preludes to contradictory political conclusions rationalizing some of the cruder aspects of Stalinist imperialism. In his *Stalin,* where we find the most explicit and detailed apologetics, he wrote: "Between the two wars [World War I and II] nearly all those peoples [of Eastern Europe] had been stranded in an impasse; their life had been bogged down in savage poverty and darkness; their politics had been dominated by archaic cliques who had not minded the material and cultural retrogression of their subjects as long as their own privileges had been safe. That whole portion of Europe had emerged from the Second World War and from the hideous 'school' of nazism even more destitute, savage and helpless."

This grim, sweeping canvas of Eastern Europe is drawn in somewhat exaggerated strokes, particularly if one includes Czechoslovakia. But there is method in Deutscher's levelling postwar Eastern Europe to one pathetic, helpless, savage mass. He is actually preparing us for East Europe's postwar liberation — by Stalin — who apparently was not a savage! by the Russian Communist Party — which we all know was neither a clique nor archaic! by Russia — which had so firmly established itself as a culturally enlightened nation!

In his words, following his chilling image of pre-Stalinist East European barbarism: "It may well be that for its peoples the only chance of breaking out of their impasse lay in a *coup de force* such as that to which Stalin goaded them." Apart from the suggestion that Stalinist conquest of East Europe, with its executions, purges, deportations and overall savagery, provided the "only chance" for freedom, there is the insidious suggestion that Communist regimes were not actually installed by the Kremlin but by Czechs, Poles, Hungarians, etc., merely spurred on by Stalin.

Moved by his own rhetoric, perhaps, Deutscher next reveals more of his hand. "In Poland and Hungary the Communist-inspired land reform fulfilled, perhaps imperfectly, a dream of many generations of peasants and intellectuals. All over eastern Europe the Communists, having nationalized the main industries, vigorously promoted plans for industrialization and full employment such as were beyond the material resources and wit of native 'private enterprise.'..."

The new Peoples' Democracies "did much to calm nationalist vendettas and to promote co-operation between their peoples. In a word, they opened before eastern Europe broad vistas of common reform and advancement. It was as if Russia had imparted to her neighbors some of her own ways and methods of communal work and social organization. Considering the vastness and the radical character of the upheaval, it is remarkable that Stalin and his men brought it off not without terror, indeed, not without indulging in a long series of *coups*, but without provoking within the Russian orbit a real civil war such as that waged in Greece."

Thus Deutscher's vision. Ours is somewhat less euphoric. In Russia's postwar aggrandizement we see armies of occupation; the threat and the use of force; trumped-up elections; mounting hatred by peasants, workers, intellectuals; political suppression; bureaucratic inefficiency in industry; low living standards; national indignities. We also see the mass graves of Hungarian revolutionaries — workers, peasants, intellectuals, children — who chose the path of armed resistance since they could nowhere find on totalitarianism's political map the "broad vistas of common reform and advancement" conjured up by Deutscher.

To soften the imperial edge of Russia's foreign policy Deutscher has offered some extraordinary explanations for Russian expansionism, including the theory that Stalin imposed Communist satellite regimes on Eastern Europe virtually against his will. In discussing the Teheran, Yalta and Potsdam agreements, Deutscher, in his *Russia: What Next?* wrote:

> It may, of course, be argued that Stalin's behavior during the war was nothing but make-believe, and that all his solemn vows of non-interference in the internal affairs of neighboring countries were dust thrown into the eyes of his Allies. On the other hand, Stalin's deeds at the time lent weight to his vows. . . . The point is that both Churchill and Roosevelt had solid evidence that Stalin's policy was, in fact, geared to self-containment. They saw Stalin acting, not merely speaking, as any nationalist statesman would have done in his place — they saw him divested, as it were, of his communist character. He was approaching the problems of the Russian zone of influence in a manner calculated to satisfy nationalist Russian demands and aspirations and to

wreck the chances of communist revolution in those territories.

If we believe Deutscher, Stalin was committed to a policy of Russian self-containment and shrank from the prospect of imposing Communist regimes in Eastern and Central Europe. What kind of governments did Stalin want in Eastern and Central Europe? Bourgeois governments! At least so Deutscher tells us: "He (Stalin) expected, of course, that victorious Russia would enjoy a position of diplomatic and economic preponderance in neighboring countries, ruled by 'friendly governments,' to quote the insiped cliche then fashionable. *But he also expected that those governments would remain essentially bourgeois.*"

If Stalin preferred friendly bourgeois governments why did he impose Communist regimes on Eastern Europe? Deutscher is quick to answer:

> . . . at least three factors combined to undo Stalin's policy of self-containment: genuine revolutionary ferment abroad; the revolutionary urge in Stalin's own armies; and the jockeying for position among allies rapidly turning into potential enemies *(Russia: What Next?,* p. 106).

The first of Deutscher's three factors is patently false since the regimes the Kremlin imposed on Central and Eastern Europe could in no sense have been a response — either positive or negative — to internal Communist ferment. In Czechoslovakia, Poland, Rumania, etc., Communist parties existed in varying degrees of strength, but in no case, except Yugoslavia, were these parties in a position to take power relying solely upon their own resources. It is Deutscher himself who wrote (as we have quoted above) that Eastern Europe had emerged from the war and from the hideous school of Nazism "even more destitute, savage and helpless" than before the war. By what dialectical contortion is it possible to find, at the same time and the same place, both a state of barbarism (and helplessness) and a state of "genuine revolutionary ferment"? The contradiction is too apparent to dwell upon. The only consistent element is that Deutscher uses each part of his contradiction for the same purpose of rationalizing Russian imperialism.

The second reason offered for Stalin's abandoning his alleged non-imperialist policy of self-containment — that it was a response to a global revolutionary urge welling up in the ideological breasts of Russian army personnel — is even less serious than the first. It is incredible to think that if Stalin really wanted to maintain capitalism in Eastern Europe after the war, he would succumb, on such a decisive matter, to the allegedly internationalist Communist aspirations of army officers. If these idealistic Communist generals could passively abide Stalin's murderous purge of the armed forces in the 1930s and then swallow the Nazi-Soviet Pact, is it conceivable that they would be put in a mutinous frame of mind by Stalin's supposed policy of self-containment?

The third reason given — that Russia abandoned its pre-war policy of self-containment because former war-time allies were becoming potential enemies — has merit. But this is in no way reduces the fact and culpability of Communist imperialism. (One can also point to Washington's need for political or strategic defense to explain American intervention in Guatemala, Cuba and Vietnam. That would hardly vindicate Washington or absolve it of the charge of imperialism.)

Life and politics are complicated enough in the modern world without needlessly adding to them such exotic political motivations as Deutscher claims to find behind Russian expansionism. What the Kremlin successfully sought was to plunder the economies of East Germany, Central and Eastern Europe. It robbed these countries of enormous wealth (called reparations in the case of East Germany), forcibly imported thousands of workers and technicians to help rebuild Russia's war-torn industry, and dictated terms of economic trade most favorable to Russia. Thievery was not Russia's only objective. The Cold War was under way before the smoke of World War II had lifted in Europe and Asia. Only two great and inimical powers emerged from the war, the United States and Russia, and the Kremlin instinctively sought to secure its position, politically and militarily, in Europe. In addition, to achieve its immediate economic, political and military objectives, Russia was obliged to frustrate, whenever possible, the independent revolutionary potential that inhered in the anti-Nazi resistance movements throughout Europe.

Stalin understood that these ambitions and needs could not be met in deals with bourgeois governments, but through the direct annexation of foreign territories or the imposition of Russian-dominated Communist regimes wherever this could be done with some show of plausibility (such as trotting out old Czarist claims to parts of Poland) and a minimum risk of war with the United States. To believe that Stalin, out of conservatism or a dogmatic allegiance to his theory of socialism in one country, was reluctant to fulfill these imperialist ambitions is to be guilty of misreading history or of underplaying the venality of Stalinism or, as in the case of Deutscher, to be guilty of both.

A recent example of Deutscher's apologia for Russian imperialism was his performance at the nationally televised Teach-in held in Washington, D.C., in May 1965. There Deutscher rejected the reciprocal responsibility of Washington and Moscow for the Cold War, arguing, instead, that it was the exclusive, initial responsibility of Western imperialism. Evidence offered of Russia's pacific intentions included his claim that Russian armed forces had been reduced to "less than three million men by the end of 1947." This is an example of a man shaving a statistic to fit a theory, since by the end of 1947 Russia's armed forces were closer to 4,000,000 than 3,000,000 men. But even accepting Deutscher's pared figure, approximately 6% of the adult Russian male population was in the armed forces. The actual figure is closer to 8% and both figures are considerably higher if computed on the basis of able-bodied men under the age of 60, and further increased if we add the well-equipped armies of secret police and other paramilitary organizations.

Considering that this commitment to the forces of destruction was made by a country horribly drained of economic and human resources we have a better measure of Russia's postwar militarism. And we get a clearer image of Deutscher's design when we remember that he conveniently omitted from his picture of Russia's military posture such factual details as the strength of Stalinist armies maintained in subjugated, occupied countries: 22 divisions in East Germany, two divisions in Poland, two in Hungary, two in Rumania, troops in Austria, Finland, Port Arthur and the Baltics (gobbled up in 1940) and other thousands of supply troops in these areas and in Russia to keep the imperial fighting legions in combat readiness.

In the same Washington speech and in the same spirit of apologetics, Deutscher went on to claim that the Kremlin never did "threaten to overrun Europe" and, what is more, "I don't think that the attack on Stalin's government on the basis of its alleged threat to peace of the world was ever justified." One difficulty with the first statement is that Stalin did, in effect, overrun one-third of the continent outside of Russian borders — East Germany, Poland, Rumania, Bulgaria, Hungary, the Baltics; and that Stalin had designs on West Germany is part of the historic record. That Russia did not directly threaten the rest of Western Europe does not mean that such fears had no basis in reality. As for his denial that Stalin's government "was ever" a threat to the peace of the world, it is at such variance with history from the time of the Nazi-Soviet Pact (was this not a threat to world peace?) until Stalin's death, that it is perhaps best to let the remark speak for itself.

THE RESTORATIONIST BUGBEAR

An age-old device of apologists for reaction is to defend what exists, wicked as it is acknowledged to be, lest sudden upheaval bring on something worse. Deutscher is an old hand at the game. Whenever Communist imperialism has been threatened by revolution he admits that life was bad for the people but it would have been worse if the insurgents won. We would have had, among other things — bourgeois restoration! Accordingly, in *The Prophet Unarmed*, written shortly after the Hungarian Revolution, Deutscher wrote: "Eastern Europe (Hungary, Poland, and Eastern Germany), however, found itself almost on the brink of bourgeois restoration at the end of the Stalin era; only Soviet armed power (or its threat) stopped it there" (p. 462). This is Deutscher — parentheses and all.

Earlier in this essay, in a summary of the actual program, objectives, leadership and conduct of the Hungarian revolution, we refuted Deutscher's slander against the Hungarian people. Here let us look at Deutscher's more general bugbear

of "bourgeois restoration," a hoax so untenable that he can
do no more than mention it in footnotes and in passing although the thought is of the greatest theoretical and political
significance.

Consider some relevant facts about Hungary. There, as in
other Eastern European countries, the bourgeoisie was never
strong. Much of Hungary was controlled by foreign capital.
In part to protect what it could of its industry from this
predatory grip of foreign financiers, the pre-war Hungarian
governments nationalized a good deal of the native industry,
thereby further undercutting the power of Hungarian capitalists.

During the war, Hungary was a German ally. As a result,
about one-third of Hungarian industry fell into the hands of
German capitalists and the Nazi state. Excluding land and
buildings, around one-fourth of Hungarian wealth was German controlled. With Germany's defeat, the power of Hungarian capitalism was further weakened since much of her
industry, left ownerless, had to be taken over by the state.
Other industries, owned by Hungarians who collaborated
with the Nazis, were also taken over by the state.

That Hungary was a German ally became the legal basis
for Russia to occupy that country. As conquerors, the Russians proceeded to destroy what was left of the Hungarian
bourgeoisie, dismantling, looting and taking over outright
ownership of considerable sections of Hungarian industry.
When the Russians installed their puppet Communist government, the two forces combined to uproot and decisively destroy the residues of capitalism.

How can capitalism be restored in Hungary in light of
the above? Capitalism requires capitalists. Who are they?
Even if they could be brought back from the beyond how
could they divide a nationalized Hungarian industry, much of
it built during the past 20 years?

Capitalism in Hungary is dead. It is merely Deutscher's
Frankenstein, created to frighten the unthinking and to
shore up his opposition to the Hungarian Revolution.

In *The Prophet Outcast*, Deutscher even tracks down
bourgeois elements still operating in Russia itself! It is a

discovery pertinent to our discussion of his apologia for Russian imperialism as can be seen in the first sentence of the following quotation:

> The Stalinist state [Russia], by promoting or assisting for its own reasons revolution in eastern Europe and Asia, created formidable counter checks to its own bourgeois tendencies. The post-war industrialization, the immense expansion of the Soviet working class, the growth of mass education, and the reviving self-assurance of the workers tended to subdue the bourgeois elements in the state; and after Stalin's death the bureaucracy was compelled to make concession after concession to the egalitarianism of the masses. To be sure, the tension between the bourgeois and the socialist elements of the state continues; and, being inherent in the structure of any post capitalist society, it was bound to persist for a very long time to come (p. 308).

After nearly 50 years of revolution, civil war, nationalization, collectivization, industrialization, terror, purges, slave labor camps, deportations and war, to discover bourgeois elements in Russia strong enough to produce tension in their conflict with the "socialist elements of the state" is no less astounding than if Deutscher had announced that he had unearthed descendants of the Lost Tribes of Israel boring from within the Kremlin walls. (We assume that Deutscher has more in mind than peasants who prefer to work their own private plots to working on the collective or state farms, and that he will not bring up the Liberman plan as an example of bourgeois forces or plots in Russia.)

Yet 17 years ago, Deutscher wrote on the same subject in an altogether different vein:

> Finally, the whole structure of Russian society has undergone a change so profound and so many sided that *it cannot really be reversed.* It is possible to imagine a violent reaction of the Russian people itself against the state of seige in which it has been living so long. It is even possible to imagine something like a political restoration. But it is *certain* that even such a restoration would touch merely the surface of Russian society and that it would demonstrate its impotence *vis-à-vis* the work done by the revolution even more thoroughly than the Stuart and the Bourbon restorations had done. For of Stalinist Russia it is even truer than of any other revolutionary nation that "twenty years have done the work of twenty generations" *(Stalin: A Political Biography,* p. 569).

If Deutscher knew before 1949 that capitalism was reduced to impotence how can he find significant struggles with
bourgeois elements after nearly another 20 years of that
revolution (which presumably does the work of another 20
generations)? It all depends on what Deutscher wants to
prove at a particular moment. In the earlier quotation from
Stalin he is trying to demonstrate Stalin and Stalinism's
superiority to Hitler and Nazism, for which he finds evidence
in the permanence with which Stalinism has destroyed capitalism, whereas Nazism proved to be a savage historic interlude that neither fundamentally nor permanently altered the
German bourgeois order. In the more recent quotation,
Deutscher reincarnates tension-producing bourgeois forces
to show, among other things, the basically progressive
feature of Russian expansion in Eastern Europe, since this
expansion, he says, served to "countercheck" the alleged
bourgeois elements in Russia itself.

DEUTSCHER: THE BERNSTEIN OF TOTALITARIANISM

The conception of a society's democratic evolution through
its massive industrial growth is not the original "socialist"
contribution of Isaac Deutscher or the lesser apologists for
totalitarianism. It is reminiscent, above all, of the Revisionist school which first made itself felt as a force in the socialist
movement before the turn of the century. Under the tutelage
of Eduard Bernstein, this school advanced the concept that
capitalism would bow peacefully before the requirements of
its industrial development, furthered in its natural evolution
by reforming pressure from the mass of people, and finally
emerging as a full-fledged democratic socialist society.

Where Marx saw industrial growth and concentration of
capital sharpening the antagonism between capital and labor,
Bernstein saw the opposite tendency in the growth of vast
cartels and the credit system. In Bernstein's estimate, the
expansion of the modern corporation entailed the emergence
of a new middle class of property-controlling shareholders
which would continue to grow at the expense of the social
power of the industrial magnate. This new middle class would
be able to adjust itself to the needs of an expanding economy
and, through the continued growth of trusts and the liberal

use of credit, overcome the anarchy of production and eliminate economic crisis.

Economic growth and diffusion of wealth via the growth of the trusts would encourage the adaptive new middle class to discard the laissez-faire doctrine that that government is best which governs least. Government would learn to perform the role of mediator and benevolent regulator of society, and the middle class could permit, might even encourage, the extension of progressive social welfare legislation and political democracy. In the meantime, the working class through its political parties, trade unions and cooperative societies would assert itself as a democratizing influence on society as a whole.

Revisionism gained considerable strength in the German socialist movement after Engels' death since its predictions of growing prosperity, democratic reform and peace corresponded to the experience of the past thirty years: after 1871, Germany's industrial indices pointed upward; the ten-year periodic crises predicted by Marx did not occur; the Social Democratic party gained many adherents and victories at the polls; cooperative societies sprouted all over the nation; democratic and social reforms were effectuated; and there had been no major European conflict since the Franco-Prussian War.

Indeed, the case that Bernstein made for evolutionary socialism was a thousand times stronger than that presented by modern authoritarian "socialists."

Bernstein's basic revision of Marxian socialism, similar to Deutscher's, was in his substitution of automatic laws attendant to industrial expansion for the mobilization of the mass of people as the catalyst of social revolution. The working class would not have to emancipate itself; socialism was free to come from above (although Deutscher pays occasional lip service to the necessity of a developing socialist consciousness of the Russian people as a precondition for full democratization of communist society).

This schema had its predictable political effect. Since the laws of capitalist development insured its socialist negation, these laws were not to be interfered with by extremist anticapitalist activities and there was no longer the need for a socialist party to wage a revolutionary struggle for political power. The socialist movement, perforce, need only be a responsible movement of reform. And, since Germany was the advanced capitalist vanguard of Europe, Revisionism, despite the pacifism of its leading personality, prepared the German socialist movement for its chauvinist course a decade later (just as Deutscherite revisionism, despite its predilection for the Marxist idiom, prepares sections of the left-wing world for totalitarian rationalization).

In place of the adaptation of a corporate middle class to social progress, the Revisionists adapted themselves to bourgeois parliamentary democracy.

Where the Bernsteinites followed their theories through politically to the advantage of capitalism, their modern methodological cousins come to the aid of Stalinism. If Russian totalitarianism is the precursor of socialism, then despite its moral shortcomings, Stalinism must be defended against all comers, be they the forces of Western capitalism or the rebellions of its oppressed.

Most striking — and damning — in the parallel between Bernstein and Deutscher is the consistent application of their respective theories to the point of crass apologetics for the imperialist ambitions of Kaiserism and Communism.

In his book, *Evolutionary Socialism*, Bernstein described Germany as a nation "which has indeed carried out, and is carrying out, its honourable share in the civilising work of the world." This civilizing function of German colonialism was spelled out:

> If we take into account the fact that Germany now imports yearly a considerable amount of colonial produce, we must also say to ourselves that the time may come when it will be desirable to draw at least a part of these products from our own colonies. However speedy socialists may imagine the course of development in Germany towards themselves to be, yet we cannot be blind to the fact that *it will need a considerable time before a whole series of other countries are converted to socialism* (emphasis added). But if it is not reprehensible to enjoy the produce of tropical plantations, it cannot be so to cultivate such plantations ourselves. Not the whether but the how is here the decisive point. It is neither necessary that the occupation of tropical

lands by Europeans should injure the natives in their enjoyment of life, nor has it hitherto usually been the case. *Moreover, only a conditional right of the savages to the land occupied by them can be recognized. The higher civilisation ultimately can claim a higher right. Not the conquest, but the cultivation, of the land gives the historical legal title to its use.*

Bernstein's brief for German imperialism is clear and direct. Deutscher's rationalizations for Stalinist imperialism, wary and subtle. But the basic similarities are there.

In the earlier period, socialists were cautioned against excessive denunciations of Germany's overseas adventures because her fate was related to the rest of the world: so long as "it will need a considerable amount of time before a whole series of other countries are converted to socialism" it was neither realistic nor desirable to demand that Germany abandon her imperialist policies. Similarly, today, the distance of Western countries from socialism is used to excuse Russian imperialism: so long as Western powers pursue a colonial policy, socialists have no right to demand of Russia that she voluntarily relinquish her East European sphere of influence and thereby weaken her status as a world power.

For Bernstein, the "right of savages" to their land is "conditional" upon the "higher right" of a "higher civilization." Whoever has followed the authoritarian apologia for Stalinist imperialism knows that it is largely based upon almost identical reasoning: instead of the lower order of savagery, there is the lower order of capitalism whose national entities cannot be given priority over the higher right of a superior "socialist economy" brought by Russia to all of Eastern Europe and the Baltic lands at the point of Russian bayonets; the Polish bourgeoisie may have had a formal legal title to Poland but it is Russia which Deutscher implies had the historical legal title.

At least the gentle Bernstein was concerned with the method of German expansionism ("not the whether but the how" of colonialism is the "decisive point") and his inexcusable defense of German imperialism *was* a defense of a culturally superior country's exploitation of lower, sometimes savage, societies. The modern authoritarian revisionist, on the other hand, does not find the methods of Stalinist expansionism the "decisive point," and no one can refer to pre-war Poland and Czechoslovakia as primitive societies; on the contrary, Poland had as great a cultural heritage as its Russian "liberators" and Czechoslovakia a more advanced technology.

The analogy between Bernstein and Deutscher, between Revisionist and modern "authoritarian socialism," does not hold at every point. There are differences as well as similarities and the differences are illustrative, in their own way, of the intellectual and moral debilitation of the socialist movement today. One dissimilarity is a matter of deception. The earlier Revisionists presented their views as a criticism of Marxism; the authoritarian Revisionists feel compelled to pass off their apologias as the last word in Marxist thought.

The paramount difference can be found in a conflicting evaluation of democracy. To the extent that the socialist movement accepted the Revisionists' reliance on the economic dynamism of modern capitalism, circa 1900, its revolutionary militancy was subverted and its capitulation to reaction potential. But the early Revisionists did not look upon political democracy as a luxury, expendable for a few decades or so. On the contrary, the primary practical concern of the Revisionists was social reform and political democracy at home; these, in fact, were the fetishes of Revisionism which induced Bernstein to shock the socialist movement with his famous cryptic declaration that for him the movement and the present means everything and the socialist future nothing. The modern authoritarian socialists, on the other hand, have adapted the Revisionist concept of a progressive, self-evolving economic system, but they have muted the Revisionists' immediate concern with democracy. This emasculated Revisionism is then drawn to a consistent and pernicious conclusion and placed to the intellectual advantage of a politically uncivilized totalitarian regime. Bernstein's dictum is, in effect, transposed by the authoritarian revisionists to read: the present is nothing and everything must be subordinated to Russia's predestined socialist end.

Deutscher endows Communist ideology with the power to propel autocratic socialism onto democratic paths. Presumably, the distorted socialist trappings adorning Communist ideology and the circulation of selected, sometimes censored, socialist classics serve to effect a democratic transformation as industry continues to expand and undercut the economic rationale for totalitarian practices. However, the socialist texts and slogans are only a light travelling case in the Party's intellectual baggage. While the Kremlin is obliged to incorporate much of the Marxist idiom in its propaganda, its major ideological thrust is, and must be, designed to tear the heart out of socialism in order to justify, morally and politically, the continuation of one-party rule with its concomitant suppression of democracy, denial of civil liberties, etc.

Nevertheless, there is some truth to Deutscher's claim. For reasons which we need not elaborate here, the Kremlin is obliged to bring millions into contact with socialist ideas. This is one of the internal dilemmas — or contradictions — of Communism, since reading Marx and Lenin undoubtedly serves to heighten awareness of the contradiction between Communist reality and socialist theory. This nourishes democratic, oppositional moods from below which is an altogether different proposition from Deutscher's vision of an ideologically fed, self-reforming ruling Party. There is reason to believe that those who are influenced by the socialist aspects of Communist ideology will be driven into more active forms of opposition to the Kremlin hierarchs.

REFORM AND REALITY

Yet there is reform in Russia, and here the authoritarian "socialist" believes he has his trump as he plays the relaxation of terror and improved living standards to prove that his theories and predictions are in harmony with reality.

Reform *is* a fact in post-Stalin Russia and a welcome one. But to welcome reforms is not necessarily to welcome the society within which they are achieved. The Kremlin's political relaxation does not imply relaxation of socialist opposition to the continuing totalitarian system in Russia.

The reforms are welcome for their own sake and for the additional specific reason that they are in part a response to pressure from below. In this we find confirmation of a fundamental humanist assumption that man is moved by an elemental instinct to gain and enjoy freedom and a further repudiation of the melancholy view that totalitarianism reduces man to an isolated atom, incapable of expression, pliant, terrified, demoralized, inept, adaptable. This theory received its most heavy-handed elaboration in the writings of Hannah Arendt. But it is also explicit and implicit in Deutscher's elitism that the Russian people lost the ability to think and act as a result of Stalinist terror and therefore had to rely on dispensations from a self-reforming ruling circle.

We also welcome the reforms because we have learned from history that they do not always pacify a dissatisfied population but rather encourage people to demand more and act in their own behalf. In Russia we have reason to hope that this process will assume revolutionary proportions as the spiralling demands for reform rise above the theoretically permissive limits of a totalitarian society, drawn at the point where institutionalized democratic forms begin.

Also encouraging are those changes which are not strictly reforms in the sense of a direct and immediate alleviation of the hardships of life for the majority of people under totalitarianism. We have in mind, above all, the so-called economic reforms inspired by Yevsey Liberman, designed to streamline the nationalized economy through providing greater local autonomy for economic managers, money incentives and bonuses to managers and workers based on plant profit instead of production and permitting prices to shift in response to changes in the market. (The Liberman Plan has nothing to do with a reintroduction of capitalism as some writers think.)

Raising totalitarianism's economic efficiency does not inspire any hosannahs in this corner, even if some economic benefits eventually filter down to the producers. But the struggle of economic administrators to overcome Party resistance to the Liberman proposals reflects a growing cleavage in Russian society between the men of the Party apparatus and the technicians and economic managers who are more concerned with efficiency and their own authority than with ideology and Party controls, although the division is not always clear and political and economic authority overlaps.

Since one-party control is the natural state of affairs in a totalitarian society, any move by any other segment of that society, be it the economic managers, the scientists, the military, the governmental administrators, to encroach upon the supremacy of the Party in a particular sphere places enormous stress on the monolithic character of the system. In this sense, the new authority which the economic managers have gained with the Liberman proposals tends to loosen important strands in the totalitarian fabric. And this we welcome most heartily; not because we think that economic managers are liberal or progressive, but because it tends to encourage resistance from below to the overall repressive policies of both the Party leaders and economic managers on top. Also, as competition of various bureaucracies with each other and with the ruling Party intensifies, each may feel obliged to seek wider support in lower social and political echelons thereby further weakening the system as lines are drawn more firmly and larger numbers become more directly involved in the struggles.

For all the changes and reforms in Russia, the system remains totalitarian. The Party is still firmly in control and not a single democratic institution is even on the horizon. Only the Communist party is permitted a legal existence. The law, despite additional reforms in the past year, remains, in the sum of its theory and practice, the most reactionary of any advanced Western nation. The "trade unions" despite a greater degree of automony have not lost their essential Stalinist function of supervising and disciplining the working class in the interests of Party control and greater productivity. Strikes are forbidden and the few recent spontaneous strikes we know of have been brutally suppressed. The manifestations of anti-Semitism have abated somewhat but are far from eliminated. Culturally, Party policy after Khrushchev still belongs to the dark ages despite concessions forced out of the regime by a restive and emboldened younger gereration.

Russia remains a society where the people have less freedom and less to eat than in any industrialized capitalist nation. If it should be accepted in the left-wing world that such

a nation can be defined as socialist in the spirit of Deutscherism, then socialism will have been crowned with the thorns
of reaction and its humanist and democratic soul crucified
on the cross of nationalization and ideology.

November 1965

Russian Law Enters the
"Final Stages of Communism"

Julius Jacobson

The following discussion of Russian law was written toward
the end of 1963. Rather than update the material, I have
added footnotes wherever I thought necessary. Nothing more
extensive than this was done for two reasons: first, to update
the essay would destroy whatever value it has in a developmental sense, that is, it would destroy the picture of
Russian law in theory and practice as it actually was at a
given time in history; second, there really is not that much
to change. For all the talk about Russia in ferment, there has
probably been less change in procedural and substantive
law in Russia than in the United States in the past eight years.

Of course, there have been some changes. In some areas the
law has become more harsh; in others, more relaxed (at least
on paper). On the whole, however, the tendency in recent
years has been to greater severity. Perhaps the most important examples of added stringency since 1963 can be found in
the following legislation: a) The Principles of Corrective-
Labor Legislation, drawn up in late 1969 and approved earlier
this year by the Supreme Soviet of the USSR, which reduces
the categories of convicts elegible for parole after serving
half their sentences and sharply increases the number of
prisoners who will now have to serve at least two-thirds of

their sentence before they can apply for parole. b) The USSR Law on Additions to and Changes in the Principles of Criminal Legislation of the USSR and the Union Republics, which amplify and, in some respects, intensify the severity of the fundamental Principles of Criminal Legislation passed in 1958 which are discussed in the essay. As with the new Principles of Corrective-Labor legislation, it sharply limits a convict's opportunity for parole. c) In the same period, we are confronted with the Statute on Preventive Detention in Custody which empowers the authorities of Union Republics, under certain circumstances, to hold a person suspected of having committed a crime in preventive-detention cells for 30 days. d) The Decree of the Presidium of the USSR Supreme Soviet "On Increased Liability for Hooliganism," issued in 1966, represents an escalation of the permanent war against "antisocial" elements. The Decree divides hooliganism into three subcategories: "petty hooliganism," plain "hooliganism" and "malicious hooliganism." The petty hooligan can be imprisoned for 15 days by decision of a judge or police official. He has no right to appeal and cannot correspond, receive messages or parcels or purchase food and is not provided with bedding. The malicious hooligan can be sentenced for up to seven years in prison.

The antihooligan decree is not really a new phenomenon. The campaign began years ago and the new decree merely confirms the analysis provided below.

Khrushchev's "revelations" at the Twentieth Congress of the Russian Communist party sparked a relatively intense discussion in Party, government and legal circles on the problem of "socialist legality." Though the exchange had been initiated shortly after Stalin's death, it assumed the unprecedented form of a limited national debate only after Khrushchev's 1956 speech.

The large-scale — but not total — dissolution of the concentration camps in the period from 1953-1957 is evidence enough to dismiss any foolish notion that this debate was merely the permissive window dressing of a totalitarian regime making wholly insincere gestures to the Russian people. Russia's rulers genuinely wanted to rid themselves of the excesses of an unrelieved and self-victimizing system of terror under Stalin. New rules and regulations — i.e., laws — were called for to establish both wider boundaries and more definite guides of conduct within which heads of Party and state could maneuver without the constant paralyzing fear that, for no ostensible reason, they would be dispatched to a concentration camp or to their ancestors. (This relaxation, necessarily codified in new national legislation, could not possibly be restricted to the bureaucratic class alone. Its benefits inevitably filtered down to the masses, though not without pressure from below and reluctance above.)

That the post-Stalin relaxation required new laws does not mean that to measure political changes in Russia from 1953 to 1963 one need only compare Stalin's laws to Khrushchev's. Laws and dogmas can be circumvented or flouted with comparative ease in a one-party system. For example, Stalin's Constitution of 1936, with its promises ranging from an independent judiciary to political rights of national minorities, hardly corresponded to the reality of a regime that was its own judiciary and which threatened entire national minorities with genocide. Nevertheless, even under Stalin, there was some consistency between law and its practice as he sought, paradoxically, to rationalize arbitrary terror via more explicit legislation inspired and embellished by Vyshinsky's savage "philosophy" of law. Under Stalin, confession was the "Queen of Proof"; the accused was obliged to prove his innocence; a man "probably" guilty was doomed; there was the pernicious "Doctrine of Analogy"; the rights of a defendant and his counsel were reduced to less than nothing by specific provisions of the law; to whisk away people in the dead of night, to arrest without charges, to sentence without trial and to execute without cause were actually all provided for by murderously vague and permissive statutes. Thus, there was a kind of law of lawlessness, a degree of codification of total terror; and its study offered special insights into a system given to the mass murder of its own people.

If the law provided clues to understanding Russia under Stalin, it is even more instructive in assessing Russia under

Khrushchev. The reason, it should be obvious, is that the post-Stalin relaxation requires laws which, on the whole, are less stringent, more precise and in greater conformity with the realities of life. Above all, it is Russia's new criminal legislation, the most significant of all reforms and changes in Russian political life, which sheds most light on what is meant by "the struggle for socialist legality."

I

It is now more than ten years since Stalin's death and much of the debate on "socialist legality" has been resolved. This does not mean that the debate is over or that no new changes will be made — for better or worse — but in 1963 it is possible to examine a new body of national criminal legislation as well as some new laws of Russia's constituent union-Republics. This is so, largely because of a series of statutes pertaining to criminal law passed by the Supreme Soviet in December 1958.

A Major Reform

In one of the statutes, the Principles of Criminal Legislation,[1] there is tersely stated in Article 3 what is perhaps the most significant reform in current legal dogma:

> Only persons who are guilty of a crime — that is, who have deliberately or through negligence committed a socially dangerous act *specified by criminal law* — may be held criminally liable and subject to punishment.
>
> Criminal punishment may be applied only upon sentence of the court.

The concepts embodied in this Article had several purposes explicitly stated in the preliminary debate over the forthcoming legal reforms.

In the first place, it was designed to replace the notorious Doctrine of Analogy. According to this doctrine, if an individual committed a "socially dangerous act" not specified in law, the authorities could inflict the penalty specified for the crime which, in their opinion, most closely resembled the

---

1. All national statutes quoted can be found in English translations in the *Current Digest of the Soviet Press*, Vol. XI, Nos. 4 and 5, published by the Joint Committee on Slavic Studies, New York, unless otherwise footnoted. Emphases have been added.

alleged offense committed. Now, with Article 3 of the new Principles, a man is to be convicted of an offense only if it is *"specified* by criminal law."

Second, the stipulation that one can be punished only for a specified crime was intended to undercut the odious practice during Stalin's reign of holding relatives of a criminal legally responsible as accessories to the crime.

Third, by specifying that a criminal can be punished "only upon the sentence of the court" this Article legally repudiates past techniques whereby concentration camps had been filled, not so much by the actions of Russian courts, as by administrative decrees — particularly those of the dreaded Ministry of Internal Affairs. Previously, a Russian citizen could be abducted by the secret police and promptly shipped to Karaganda. Now, so Article 3 formally states, it is necessary to prove that a specific legal provision has been violated — and this is to be determined only by courts of proper jurisdiction— as contrasted to arbitrary actions of administrative state organs.

However, this new legal concept has its loopholes, not only in other criminal legislation, but in the fact that the Republics of the USSR have passed administrative decrees permitting nonjudicial bodies of local citizens to sentence those found guilty of a "parasitic mode of life" to banishment and forced labor, subject to confirmation by public administrative bodies. We will return to these "antiparasite" codes.

Presumption of Neither Guilt Nor Innocence

One advanced, democratic legal concept is the presumption of a defendant's innocence. In Stalin's time just the reverse was the case: the defendant was presumed guilty unless he could prove himself innocent. According to this conception the prosecuting authorities were men of such high civic consciousness that they would not think of pressing charges against an accused if in their preliminary investigation the prosecutor and agents of investigative bodies were not convinced of the incontrovertible guilt of the accused.

The question of presumption of guilt or innocence was one of the most heatedly debated legal concepts. The debate continues because of the ambiguity of Article 14 of the Prin-

ciples of Criminal Procedure which dodges the problem as
follows:

> The court, prosecutor, investigator, and person conducting an
> investigation do not have the right to place the burden of proof
> on the accused.

This, of course, is an evasion since there is no explicit
statement of presumed innocence. Even as an evasion, this
Article represents progress over what existed in the past.
But it cannot be correctly evaluated — even if abstracted
from the limiting context of the Russian political reality —
without understanding that it was a concession to appease
more liberal elements who had been pressing hard for codify-
ing as an unambiguous maxim of Russian law that a man is
innocent until proven guilty.

For example, the Lithuanian deputy B.S. Sharkov *who introduced the Statute under discussion* to the Supreme Soviet
rebuked those who insisted that the presumption-of-innocence concept be legislated:

> Efforts to include into our theory and practice obsolete dog-
> mas of bourgeois law, for instance, the presumption of inno-
> cence, deeply contradict the essence of Soviet socialist law. The
> presumption of innocence was proposed to be included in the
> Principles of Criminal Procedure by using a formula like the
> following: 'The defendant shall be considered innocent until his
> guilt is established by the final court of judgement.' Perhaps
> lawyers can understand the meaning of such a complicated
> formula, but great masses of people could hardly understand it
> (quoted in W.W. Kulski, *The Soviet Regime, 3rd ed., p. 453).*

Deputy Sharkov, reporter to the Supreme Soviet, who
thought that "perhaps lawyers" (but not the "great masses")
could understand the presumption-of-innocence principle,
continued his attack on the defeated advocates of this "ob-
solete dogma" with this concrete example:

> Take a case like this: a murderer, a bandit, is caught at the
> scene of the crime with the goods on him. The investigator and
> the procurator make a careful investigation in full conformity
> with the law and establish the guilt of the bandit, *though even
> without that his guilt was evident to everyone.* On the basis of the
> law and the indisputable evidence collected, the investigator
> and the procurator not only have the right but are obliged in
> duty to hold the murderer to criminal liability and place him
> under guard. At the same time, law, the investigator and the

procurator would be obliged to consider that bandit innocent....
The absurdity of such a state of affairs from the viewpoint of
common sense is beyond dispute.

Everyone can understand this, lawyer and great masses
alike.

The same sentiment was voiced by Nikita Khrushchev,
speaking at the Fourteenth Congress of the Young Communist League in April 1962:

> Some people reason that even if a man has stolen something
> but has not been caught he cannot be called to account, although
> many people know him to be a thief. But this kind of morality
> is characteristic of Bourgeois society, where people say "a man
> isn't a thief until he has been caught." Our principles should
> be different. . . . We should not wait until he is caught redhanded
> to indict and try him (Merle Fainsod, *How Russia is Ruled*
> (rev. ed., 1963), p. 452).

If the letter of the law does not assume the innocence of
the accused[2] and it is all but denied in life — what of the
accused's defense counsel? If there is one function that a
defense counsel should have, by definition, it is to assist his
client's plea of innocence or if a guilty plea is entered to light-
en his client's sentence. This elementary notion is not accepted as self-evident in Russia and, though still debated,
remains alien to the spirit and practice of law.

This was adequately demonstrated in the remarks of another reporter to the Supreme Soviet session of December 25,
1958 — D. Rasulov, Chairman of the Commission of Draft
Legislation of the Soviet Nationalities. Mr. Rasulov summed
up his concept of the role of defense counsel:

> Soviet defense counsel must serve the great humane cause of
> defense of socialist society, law, truth and justice. That is the
> way to define his course of conduct in the defense of the accused—
> that is where the task of the defense counsel lies, and not in the
> defense of illegal chicanery on the part of the accused, which
> would inevitably grow into defense of a criminal and thus of

2. In recent years legal theory has moved in the direction of presumption of
    innocence. Article 77 of the Russian Republic Criminal Procedures Code
    now makes more explicit that a defendant's confession must have other
    supportive evidence before proof of guilt is established. But it remains,
    nonetheless, a formal legal concession. The Russian press is replete with
    incidents indicating that an accused is at an enormous disadvantage
    once charged with a crime.

the crime (quoted in Leon Lipson, "Socialist Legality: The Mountain has Labored," *Problems of Communism*, March-April, 1959).

If one strips this passage of prettified phrases ("the great humane cause of socialist society, law, truth and justice") similarly used in the era of "violations of socialist legality," Chairman Rasulov reveals the still-widespread attitude that confuses the role of counsel for the accused with counsel for the prosecution.

Some Principles of Criminal Procedure

Several of the ugliest aspects of criminal procedure in Stalin's day have been carried over in less grievous and more covert form.

The writ of habeas corpus remains alien to Russian law. The Principles of Criminal Procedure permit either a prosecutor, the police or an agent of an investigative agency to place under arrest a Russian citizen suspected of a crime that carries a prison sentence. If the arrest is by order of an investigative agency, that arrest must be reported within 24 hours to the *prosecutor*, but not necessarily to the court — i.e., to the very agency that will act as the arrested person's adversary in the event of a trial. The prosecutor is then given two days before he is obliged either to release the suspect or "sanction the imprisonment." Actually the statutes would permit pretrial arrest *for a total of nine months without notifying the courts!*

A person held for nine months before either being released or having his case brought before the courts would, in all likelihood, be accused of a "state crime," say "anti-Soviet propaganda and agitation" — a most serious criminal offense. During this preliminary investigation the accused is not entitled to defense counsel. He can be held virtually incommunicado. His longest conversations are with those preparing or investigating the case against him.

Before May 1963, he had to contend mainly with two adversaries — the prosecutor and an agent of an investigatory body. In an April 1963 decree by the Presidium of the Supreme Soviet, the accused could be obliged to contend with a third adversary in preliminary investigations. In that month it was ruled that, "for the purpose of intensifying the fight against crime and further strengthening and expanding democratic principles of Soviet Court procedure," the accused would now be obliged to submit to investigation by newly created "agencies for Safeguarding Public Order."

The investigator — i.e., a representative of special administrative bodies — determines the line of investigation. Should the prosecutor feel that no case can be made against the accused, the investigator has the right to appeal this decision to a higher prosecuting authority. The investigator can also appeal the classification of the alleged crime and the scope of the indictment.

Damaging to the rights of a defendant are the relations of the courts to the Procurator General's office (Attorney General would be the United States equivalent), and of both institutions to the Communist party. According to Article 10 of the Principles of Criminal Procedure, called "Independence of Judges and Their Subordination to the Law," we read:

> In administering justice in criminal cases, judges and people's assessors are independent and are subordinate only to the law. Judges and peoples' assessors decide criminal cases on the basis of the law in accordance with socialist legal consciousness and in conditions *precluding outside influence on judges.*

If this concept corresponded to other legal provisions and to the facts of political life we would be discussing a society undergoing a fundamental democratic transformation. But a moment's reflection is all it should take to recognize the hypocrisy of Article 10. Can anyone picture any Russian court "precluding the outside influence" of the Communist party since to preclude such outside influence has no meaning unless the courts are privileged to make specific decisions which run counter to or overrule the will of the Party? It will be the heroic magistrate, indeed, who declares a Khrushchevian edict unconstitutional or frees an accused criminal in the face of explicit Party pressures. The truth is that the judiciary is not a whit less free of Party control today than during Stalin's reign. (Under Stalin, too, the Constitution gave assurance in Article 112 that "judges are independent and only subject to the law.") Also (Article 10 notwithstanding), the courts are supervised by the procuracy, i.e., by state prosecutors. This is made explicit in the Constitution and in Article 14 of the more recent (1958) statute on the Principles of Legislation On the Judicial System, which gives to the "U.S.S.R. Prosecutor General and the prosecutors subordinate to him" the right to "exercise supervision over the legality of and grounds for sentences, judgements and decisions and orders handed down by court agencies and over the carrying out of the sentence."

A related obstacle to a defendants' rights resides in the organization of lawyers collegiums which include all defense lawyers. For example, in a statute passed by the Russian Republic in July 1962, "The Russian Republic Ministry of Justice exercises general supervision of the lawyers collegium in the Russian Republic and control over their work." (The Ministry sees to it, among other things, that lawyers display "moral purity and irreproachable conduct.")

Thus a state organ — the Ministry of Justice — supervises the activities of the lawyer defending a man accused by the state, and he is tried by judges who are subject to the general supervision of the office of the prosecutor presenting the state case against him.

The inquisitorial character of criminal procedure is further illustrated in Article 21 of the procedural statute which establishes the "Rights of the Accused." Here, the accused is told that he has the right to appeal, to know the charge and to offer an explanation, to submit evidence and to petition — all of which is impeccably just. But the same Article also permits him "to familiarize himself with all the materials of the case *upon completion of the preliminary investigation.*" The significance of our italicized passage needs no comment. What must be added is a note of pertinent history: the discrepancy between this Article, as passed by the supreme Soviet, and what had been proposed in the draft. The earlier draft version of Article 21 included the right of the accused to receive "a presentation of evidence" during the pretrial examination. This was obviously considered too radical a departure from Stalinist techniques and consequently deleted in the final, adopted version. Article 22, concerned with the "Participation of the Defense Counsel in Criminal Procedure," limits his right to defense counsel until *after* the pretrial arrest and examination is completed. [3]

Furthermore, when an alleged crime is investigated by the prosecutor's office, the defense counsel is permitted to enter the case only from the time that the accused is informed of the completion of the preliminary investigation. This is a serious enough denial of an accused's rights. More pernicious is that when a case has been investigated by the militia the defense counsel is often not allowed to participate in the case until it is heard in court. According to a December 1962 article in a Russian law journal, "the militia agencies now investigate approximately half of all crimes, including those for which the law provides quite severe penalties."

Both the accused and his counsel are additionally handicapped by the fact that Article 16 of the criminal procedure statute permits the introduction as evidence into open court of all material collected during the pretrial investigation when the suspect, deprived of right to counsel, was at an enormous disadvantage.

Is it any wonder, then, that a court hearing is usually little more than a public, ritualistic affirmation of a pretrial verdict?

The new procedural code offers little protection to the individual, his home and personal correspondence, against administrative incursion. On the contrary, Article 35 permits an inquiry agency or an investigator "with the sanction of a prosecutor" to search a person and his premises, seize mail at postal and telegraph offices. There is no need to go to the courts first. In some "urgent cases" investigative agencies need not even get the prosecutor's permission to carry on search and seizure of mail.

---

3. There has been a modest improvement in the rights of the accused. In August 1970 the USSR Supreme Soviet Presidium revised Article 22 so that defense counsel must participate in the case from the moment a charge is made when the accused is a minor or cannot defend himself because of mental or physical handicaps; the defense counsel can participate in a trial from the time a charge is presented, on a ruling by the prosecutor. Only in cases involving possible capital punishment is the defense counsel obliged to enter the case when the preliminary investigation is completed.

Double Jeopardy Remains a Law of the Land

Article 46 of the procedural code contains the following reform in its first paragraph: "In hearing a case by way of appeal, a court may reduce the penalty set by the court of original jurisdiction or apply a law governing a less serious crime. . . ."

Had the new statutes governing the appeal system continued in this spirit, we could point to them as highly significant reforms in Russian criminal law. Under Stalin, a higher court could impose a *more* severe penalty on the basis of a defendant's appeal. According to the paragraph quoted above, an appeal from a defendant can earn him either a reduced sentence or a confirmation of the original but not one which is more severe. However, the new code also provides that on a defendant's appeal, a higher court can remand a case to lower court for a retrial in which the defendant could be charged with a more serious offense and sentenced more severely.

Much else that appears on the subject can only lead to the conclusion that reforms in the appeal system are modest compared to what has been retained from the past. Double jeopardy remains a codified principle. It is not only the defendant who has the right to appeal but the prosecution and/or the "injured party" which have similar privileges. This is codified as follows:

> A sentence may be rescinded because of the necessity of applying a law governing a more serious crime or because of leniency of penalty only if the prosecutor has lodged a protest on this ground or the injured party has submitted a complaint (Article 46).

Not only may a sentence be increased on the protest of the prosecution or that of the injured party, but it is established in Article 47 that even an acquittal may be rescinded "on the protest of the prosecutor," thereby forcing a defendant to risk the jeopardy of a court the second time, for the same charge.

Technically, a decision is considered final if the allocated time for an appeal has expired or if the appeal court refuses to rescind the verdict. However, this "final judgement" is not really final for there is still Judicial Supervision whereby a verdict that has entered into legal force can be submitted once again to review upon the protest of *the prosecutor, the court chairman or their deputies. A convicted person is not similarly privileged.* Under this supervisory system two previous acquittals — the first by the court of original jurisdiction, the second by a court of appeals — can be reversed if the court finds that a judge misused his authority, that there was false evidence or there is new evidence, or "new circumstances are found" (Article 48 and 49).

The court of judicial review may not only reverse two previous acquittals, it can also set new sentences — either lighter or harsher — if it finds "a discrepancy between the penalty set by the court and the gravity of the crime or the personality of the convicted person."

During an appeal or judicial review the prosecutor is obliged to participate in the proceedings but the defendant is not permitted to testify on his own behalf except on the special sufferance of the court.

There is a relatively modest improvement from Stalin's time: the state's protest of an acquittal on the basis of new evidence under this system of judicial review must be made within "one year from the day of their discovery." But there is no limit on the lapse of time from the acquittal to the point that the alleged new evidence is unearthed.

One final point here: the Supreme Court of the USSR and those of the union-Republics not only pass on the legality of the action of lower courts, they also pass sentences.

Law on Criminal Liability for State Crimes

Although the 1958 provisions of the Statute on State Crimes is less harsh than what existed in Stalin's time, they nonetheless reveal the continuing totalitarian character of Russian society.

Article I is concerned with "Especially Dangerous State Crimes." Here, high treason is defined as "an act deliberately committed by a citizen of the USSR to the detriment of the state independence, territorial inviolability, or military might of the USSR: defection to the side of the enemy, espionage, handing over a state or military secret to a foreign state, *fleeing abroad or refusal to return to the USSR from abroad, helping a foreign state to carry on hostile activity against the USSR*, or conspiracy for the purpose of seizing power. . . ." [4]

The above crimes are punishable by death!

Article 7, labeled "Anti-Soviet Agitation and Propaganda," outlaws the dissemination "of slanderous fabrication defaming the Soviet State and social system, or the dissemination, production, or keeping the literature of such content for the same purpose." This crime of "agitation and propaganda" is punishable by imprisonment up to seven years and exile or banishment for a period of two to five years.

This is the legal codification of political dictatorship. It need hardly be argued that the Kremlin could find *any* anti-Soviet propaganda, agitation or criticism of the social system to be a "slanderous fabrication" or "defamation" and contrary to law. (How would those beguiled by Russia's new "liberal dynamism" react to the American citadel of world capitalism outlawing all agitation and propaganda that was "slanderous fabrication" aimed at the capitalist "social system"?)

The penalties imposed by this article are stringent enough but given the broadness of its formulations and those in Article I, it is possible, depending on the given inclination and need of the regime in power, that with only the slightest stretching of the point, anyone charged with violation of Article 7 could be prosecuted under Article I, which carries the death penalty. For example, spreading "slanderous fabrications" or "defaming" the Russian social system could be said to be "helping a foreign state to carry on hostile activity against the USSR" — an offense punishable by death.

In Articles 6 and 8 are similar provisions, unique to the Stalinst mode of thought and operation. The earlier one is devoted to "wrecking," which is described as "an act of commission or omission" designed to undermine industry or a state agency. Conviction on this count carries a penalty of eight to fifteen years in prison. In a similar vein, Article 8 illegalizes "war propaganda." For this offense — "regardless of the

---

4. In January 1960, the Supreme Soviet amended this article so that a person who has ties with a foreign power but has not actually committed a criminal act in her behalf will not be held criminally responsible if he voluntarily informs a responsible agency of this association.

forms in which it is contained" — there is a penalty of three to eight years.

Article 9 outlaws any organizational activity or the establishment of an organization having the aim of committing any one of the gamut of crimes listed in Articles 1-8, "wrecking," "anti-Soviet agitation and propaganda," defection, espionage, etc. — with penalties provided by the previous articles.

Capital and Other Forms of Punishment

Theoretically, Russian law is designed to rehabilitate the criminal. A maximum of persuasion and a minimum of coercion are to be used. So Khrushchev says, and all Russian legal experts nod approvingly. Perhaps Russian courts are heavily infiltrated by evangelists. Otherwise how could judges hope to regenerate those they condemn to death unless it be in a hereafter? And "death by shooting," often without the right to appeal, is increasingly common in Russian courts.

We have already noted that the statute on state crimes permits the death sentence for social and political crimes. Other 1958 statutes allow the death sentence, except for minors and pregnant women, to be applied in cases of premeditated murder and some cases of banditry. These statutes were inhumane enough but since then a series of grim decrees have extended the applicability of capital punishment — decrees so barbarous that if all else was just in Russian Law it would remain the most atrocious of any modern legal system. The first of these new decrees, passed by the Presidium of the Supreme Soviet in May 1961, permitted "capital punishment by shooting" for "pilfering of state or public property in especially large amounts." In July of that year another death-dealing decree determined that "speculation in voluta valuables or banknotes conducted as a business" is punishable by death, as are speculating in foreign currency and "giving or receiving a bribe under aggravating circumstances." In addition to economic crimes, the same method of persuasion was extended to other offenses. The May 1961 decree allows the death penalty for dangerous convicts who "terrorize prisoners who have taken the path of reform, or who commit attacks on the administration or organize criminal groupings for this purpose or actively participate in such groupings." (If this were the law in the United States, thousands of prisoners who participated in recent violent outbreaks against prison administrations could be executed.)

On Feburary 12, 1962 the Soviet Presidium ruled that rape committed by a group or by an "especially dangerous recidivist" is henceforth punishable by death. A few days later, the Presidium ruled that merely the *attempt* to take the life of a People's Volunteer could be punished by death.

According to the 1958 Principles of Criminal Legislation, where the death penalty is not applied, the maximum penalty for an habitual offender or for committing a serious crime is 15 years "deprivation of freedom." Exile and banishment, two other forms of punishment, are not to exceed five years.

While prison sentences were lessened, this reform was partially offset by an added harshness of the parole system: it was made *more* difficult for some prisoners to receive time off for "good behavior." The remarks of Deputy D. S. Polyansky, Chairman of the Legislative Proposals Committee, speaking before the rubber-stamping session of the Supreme Soviet, reveal the purpose and severity of the new parole system more clearly than the bland legalistic idiom of the new code:

> In rejecting excessively long terms of deprivation of freedom, the committee proceeds from the view that the system of commutation should be fundamentally improved or abandoned altogether, so that no one except the court could change the term of punishment set by court sentence. "No indulgences for dangerous criminals" is the people's demand. And our duty is to meet it.
>
> Proceeding from this, parole can be applied only to those convicted persons who have served at least half their sentence and have shown by exemplary conduct and honest attitude toward work that they have reformed. Persons convicted of grave crimes may be paroled after serving at least two-thirds of the sentence. As for especially dangerous recidivists, this measure should not apply.

Since 1958, parole has become even more inaccessible to those categorized as "dangerous recidivists."[5] Also, the punishment of a crime, apart from the extension of the death sentence, has grown more severe in the last five years.

According to Roman Rudenko, Procurator General of the USSR, this is in the best tradition of socialist humanism. In his words, "There cannot be the slightest leniency toward criminals; they must be punished mercilessly — that is the demand of socialist humanism." While some courts are criticized for being too severe, it is only for the overzealousness with which courts interpret Rudenko's bizarre "humanism." A more common complaint against the courts was voiced at the July 1963 plenary session of the Supreme Soviet, against "some courts [which] have recently relaxed their work to combat lawbreaking by minors," and there was more sweeping criticism of some courts for softness and not showing the necessary "strict and unflinching observance of the requirements of the 12 February 1962 Decree [widening the applicability of the death penalty]. . . ."

Concept of Social Danger

By any democratic concept of law, the order of punishment is relative to the degree of the willful, conscious intent of a crime. In fact, even where intent exists but insanity can be demonstrated, there is mitigation of punishment.

In Russia's new criminal legislation some articles acknowledge the importance of establishing intent, and they make allowances for insanity. However, the General Principles of Criminal Legislation dealing with definitions of crime tend to blur distinctions between acts of omission and commission, between negligence and intent. This can be seen in Article 7 of the Principles, which defines a crime as follows:

> A crime is recognized to be a socially dangerous act (of commission or omission) specified by criminal law which violates the Soviet social or state system, the socialist system of economy, socialist property or the person or political, labor, property or other rights of citizens, or any other socially dangerous act specified by criminal law which violates the socialist legal system.

This definition, in principle, of crimes as "socially dangerous acts" is so vague that it simply does not lend itself to any precise implementation in specific criminal statutes which

---

5. As already noted, the recent Corrective-Labor Legislation still further restricts the opportunity for parole.

can adequately distinguish between crimes of omission and commission. It falls, then, to the none-too-tender mercies of the courts and parajudicial organizations to substitute their will for the imprecision of the law, always fitting their interpretations of crime to the ruling Party's fluid political concerns of what constitutes a more or less grave social danger. Since "social dangers" are infinite in number, and therefore impossible to detail, the Party's frequent admonition to the courts to consider the personality of the offender, to seek to reform rather than punish (this appeal is usually confined to obviously minor offenses) has a hollow ring.

A related issue is found in Article 15 of the Criminal Principles where it is stated that "punishment for *preparing* to commit a crime or for *attempting* to commit a crime is prescribed by law stipulating responsibility for the given crime." By a more humane concept of law, a man might be punished if found guilty of preparing or conspiring or attempting to commit murder. But the order of punishment could not be the same as if an overt act of murder took place. However in Russia, as the law makes clear, men can be — and often are — shot if found guilty of plotting or attempting a murder that never materialized. This is suggestive of a quintessential totalitarian concept which equates preparations of acts with overt performance. Where preparation to rob or kill can be tantamount to the act of robbery or murder, then thought and speech can be made the equivalent of overt acts and failure to support the regime through omission or negligence can be viewed as an overt act against the regime.

The severity with which negligence is handled is typified by Article 13 of the Law on State Crimes which permits the courts to sentence a man to eight years in prison for losing a state secret due to not following regulations for handling such documents, i.e., negligence. According to Article 24 of the law establishing liability for military crimes, a recurring case of a "negligent attitude toward duty" can earn the careless soul 10 years imprisonment if there are grave consequences; in wartime such negligence is punishable by death.

One recent example of punishment prescribed for criminal negligence is the decree on "Criminal Liability for Criminal

Negligence in the Use or Maintenance of Farm Machinery,"
which makes one guilty of an "uneconomical and negligent
attitude toward tractors" and the like liable to one year in
prison or corrective labor for the first offense and up to three
years for further offenses. This is the stuff of which "socialist legality" is made.

"Necessary Defense" and "Extreme Necessity"

A legal manifestation of a totalitarian state, ruled less by
laws than by the ubiquitous Party, is its treatment of the
State as though it were a person — and a person with privileged status. To malign an individual is a crime; to abuse the
State is a more serious crime. To assault an individual is an
offense but to assault the State politically is intolerable. We
have already seen this in the special statute covering state
crimes but it has also been expressed in the Principles of
Criminal Law in two sections: in Article 13 dealing with
"Necessary Defense" and Article 14 captioned "Extreme
Necessity." The first of those two articles reads:

> An act which has the attributes of an act stipulated in criminal
> law but which was committed in the course of necessary defense,
> that is, *while defending the interests of the Soviet state*, public
> interests or the person or rights of the defender of another
> person from a socially dangerous violator, is not a crime if the
> limits of necessary defense were not exceeded. A clear discrep-
> ancy between the defense and the nature and danger of the
> violation is considered to be exceeding the limits of necessary
> defense.

If one can push through this underbrush of jargon he will
be rewarded with the following principle: if a man bloodies
someone's nose, not just in defense of his own person but
"while defending the interests of the Soviet State," he has
not necessarily committed a crime. All that has to be established to make this otherwise criminal act legal is to show
that there has been "no discrepancy between the defense and
the nature of the violation." But what is the gravity of smash-
ing someone's nose compared to the heroic defense of the
interests of the Soviet State from the verbal assaults of a
"socially dangerous person"?

Article 14 — on "Extreme Necessity" — is substantially
the same as the above except that here it is not even obliga-

tory to prove "necessary defense" to legitimize an otherwise criminal act. To pursue the example of our friend with the bloodied nose: should he arrive at this painful condition because our vigilant and prescient Communist here simply *foresaw* the villain's *intended* antisocial acts, and took manly measures to avert this danger to the Soviet State, he would hardly be charged with assault. All that he would have to prove is that there was no time to warn the proper authorities and in "extreme necessity" therefore, he personally imposed Communist justice.[6]

Other Highlights of Russian Law

No Jury System. Whatever defects there may be in the jury system it is inestimably more advanced, tolerant and considerate of the rights of the defendant than is the inquisitorial nature of Russian justice.

One of the reforms sought by the more liberal of Russian legalists was the introduction of the jury system. That has been denied. In place of a jury, verdicts in criminal cases are rendered by a judge and two "peoples' assessors." These assessors are local judges "elected" at a general meeting of a specified district for a two-year term (formerly it was for a longer period) with the exact procedure of election established by each union-Republic. They rotate their services, each one serving approximately two weeks out of the year. No special knowledge of law is required.

In Russian court procedure the three judges (i.e., the judge and two peoples' assessors) act as judge and jury; they are permitted to participate in proceedings as an adversary of the defendant, berating or cross-examining him and then passing sentence. A majority is all that is needed.

Military Courts. Any liberal, humane philosophy of law must deny the right of a military court to try a civilian. Any proponent of this liberal philosophy would have a tough, up-

---

6. "Necessary defense" and "extreme necessity" are other areas which have been marked by retrogressive change in the past eight years. The press is filled with exhortations to ordinary citizens and members of control agencies to pummel or otherwise abuse suspected hooligans. The law permitting these attacks on those engaged in, or seemingly about to engage in "hooligan" behavior has been reinforced in various decrees, particularly those of 1966 "On Increased Liability for Hooliganism."

hill struggle in Russia. There, where Khrushchev is preparing the more advanced stage of Communism and complete democracy, the Decree on Military Courts (Article 9) gives such courts the right to try civilians on espionage charges. Article 11 extends the jurisdiction of military courts to all civilians involved in civil or criminal cases in areas where there are no general courts.

According to Article 12, a man accused of any number of crimes, only one of which is an offense that falls in the military jurisdiction, is tried on all counts by the military tribunal. According to the same article, all members of a civilian gang engaged in a variety of criminal acts must face the wrath of a military tribunal if only one of its members committed a crime within the jurisdiction of a military court.

II
"Socialist Legality" as a Living Process

Thus far, we have restricted our discussion of "socialist legality" to legal provisions. It is impossible, however, to gauge the legal temper of any society by reviewing codes whose dispassionate, technical idiom tends to obfuscate the meaning of the law itself. To the average person confronted with the jargon of legalese, the meretricious and the meritorious might seem to merge and overlap into one confusing jumble. And the Russians are past masters in exercising a judicious use of judicial language in their legal documents; as they are, more broadly, experts in the art of linguistic camouflage. Vyshinsky's Doctrines of Analogy and Confession as the Queen of Proof were the legal counterparts of Vyshinsky the inquisitor, torturer and legal assassin presiding over the mass murder trials of the 1930s. However, the Doctrines were *doctrines*, which is a lofty term; "analogy" is an educative word, and to describe a theory of evidence as the "Queen of Proof" seems harmless enough. The world had to await the purge trials to understand these concepts fully.

Similarly, our discussion thus far might give one the erroneous impression that all that is at stake here are technical legal quibbles. To find out the real meaning of the law, to get a less guarded picture of the state of law in Russia, one is obliged to observe the law as a living process.

One might think, from all the loose talk about "democratization" and "socialist legality," that capital punishment is seldom, if ever, applied. The truth is that in the last few years alone hundreds of Russians have been shot to death. How many it is difficult to say, but we know that approximately 175 people — about 60% being Jews — have been executed for *economic crimes* since the May 4, 1961 Decree. A random sampling of death sentences for economic crimes:

February, 1963: Two leaders of a ring accused of swindling the public for their own profit in the baking of meat and vegetable filled pies are sentenced to "death by shooting" by the Sverdlovsk Province Court. (They were accused of using less than the required shortening in the pies — 4 instead of 6 ozs. — and using the difference for their own gain.)

March, 1963: *Pravda* reports four men sentenced to death for speculation in the selling of old rags and old paper.

August, 1963: The director of a machine building plant sentenced to death as a bribetaker. "He only took large bills."

August, 1963: "Rabbi B. Gavrilov moved to Pyatigorsk from Samarkand" for the purposes of speculation, a Caucasian paper writes. He and two confederates engaged in all sorts of shady deals including melting down "dust and filings for plate and dental bridges" for speculative purposes. The Rabbi and his two friends were sentenced "to the supreme penalty — death by shooting."

A single issue of the daily paper of the Kazakh Republic Communist Party, reports 10 separate but *concurrent* instances of trials and trials-in-preparation of people accused of economic crimes. In one case, "the criminals have been arrested, and the investigation of the case continues." (But if the investigation "continues" how does the Party paper know that the suspects are "criminals"?) In another case, "the culprits have been arrested and will come to trial in the near future." (But if the trial is to be in the future then how does the Party paper know that the accused are "culprits"?)

An example of non-economic crimes bringing the death sentence is the recent case of five boys, mostly in their late teens, sentenced to death for rape. Another, in June of 1962, involved two young Armenians who unsuccessfully tried to seize a plane in flight to flee to the West. The plane crashed, the pilot was injured, "the traitors to the homeland" caught, condemned to death, and the Court ruled that the *"sentence is final and not subject to appeal."*

Ex post facto "justice" is theoretically eliminated in the letter of Russia's new laws. But not in life. Take, for example, the 1961 case of two men, found guilty of speculating and sentenced to 15 years deprivation of freedom. The USSR Procurator General found this sentence too lenient. He appealed to the Russian Republic Supreme Court. The Supreme Court — surprise! — upheld the Procurator General and the "light" penalty was changed to more suitable punishment to fit the crime — death by shooting from which "there can be no appeal."

Added to the horror of this story and more to the immediate point is that the legal basis for changing the sentence was the new decrees on economic crimes passed by the Presidium *after* the alleged crimes were committed.

In the press, the vulgarity, the hysteria, the brutality and the disregard of civilized concepts of justice can be found in letters to the editor, feature articles, editorials and accounts of criminal trials.

For example, while the formal texts concerning the right of a defendant to counsel are bad enough, studying them might not induce more than a yawn. They hardly prepare one for the more declamatory language of articles and letters appearing in the press denouncing defense lawyers as the bane of "socialism." Take a letter in *Pravda* signed by Karasov, a "Hero of Socialist Labor."

> It is not time in cases of gangsterism, murder and hooliganism to dispense with the service of paid lawyers who often try to prove that black is white and who "earn" their fees by expending the ardor of their eloquence in shielding patently vicious criminals? We must without fail, and more frequently than we do now, *organize show trials* and attract the attention of the wide public to them.
>
> . . . any contemptible person who raises his hand against a Soviet citizen must be destroyed.*

---

*   Unless otherwise noted, all emphasis has been added by the editor.

Whoever thinks this is just the cultural lag of an isolated, indignant worker, enraged at the sedate pleas of some legalists who would like to see defense lawyers admitted to the human race, is naive or ill-informed. Mr. Karasov represents the lynch mentality of Russian justice as it *is*, not merely as it is fuzzied up in legal texts.

Our typical "Hero of Socialist Labor" has his distinguished counterparts. Take the no-less-typical letter from a professor who sports the Honored Badge of Science. "No mercy for hooligans, the wreckers of human society" is his anguished plea. "They must be destroyed like rats and bedbugs. Unfortunately, however, there are some people who appeal for humaneness, resembling those Tolstoyans who didn't dare 'take the life' of a flea or cockroach."

In the letter from the "Hero of Socialist Labor" there is the appeal for more "public show trials." That such trials continue to exist in the land of "socialist legality" may come as a shock to many. It shouldn't. Public show trials — that is, trials where *the defendant is found guilty in advance, no defense counsel in any intelligible sense of the term is permitted, and the accused's fate is held up as a warning to all* — are common and integral elements of Russian justice.

Scores of public show trials have been held recently in Russia. One Moscow spectacular was performed in a public stadium before an audience of 2,000 jurors! This was the "trial" of five young "moral degenerates." Under the circumstances, one should hardly be surprised that the wages of their degeneracy was that they "be banished from Moscow and made to atone for their sins . . . through labor in harsh conditions." The period of atonement, it was later decided, would take five years.

These court spectacles are also traveling road shows. A March 1959 Party-State decree "requires institutions of internal affairs, agencies of the prosecutors office, justice agencies and the courts to intensify the struggle against anti-social phenomena and to conduct public trials of malicious violators of public order directly at enterprises, construction projects and state and collective farms."

Where court authorities are brought directly into factories

and collectives all semblance of legal rights for the defendant vanishes. An acquittal would make the show as irrelevant as a gladiators' arena without victims.

A particularly chilling "show trial" was announced in the October 20, 1963 issue of *Izvestia* under the head, "There Will Be No Mercy for Thieves!" It concerned an alleged ring of criminals led by two Jews, Shakerman and Roifman. Following is a summary of the *Izvestia* story:

Shakerman was recently widowed, but immediately after the period of mourning he started to shop around for a new wife. He set his lustful sights on the wife of a friend and relative and accomplished his objective. He had a new wife. To try to appease his forsaken friend and relative he gave him a sizeable sum of money. (These Jews, you know, think that money can buy anything.) The relative was not appeased. He informed the authorities that Shakerman was involved in some shady manipulations. (But Shakerman's Jewish friend and relative did not mention receiving money for his former wife. There is no limit to the perfidy and deceitfulness of these money-loving Jews.) The relative's information led to an investigation which proved, according to *Izvestia*, that Shakerman, a former doctor, together with a colleague and fellow-Jew, Roifman, were heading a vast complex of embezzlers, thieves, speculators, bribe-givers, etc. — all the things that merit death in the land of "socialist legality." Among other alleged activities *Izvestia* claims that the gang operated an illegal knitgoods enterprise installed in a psycho-neurological clinic with a production therapy workshop. The anti-Semitic undertones and overtones of this case are neither more nor less glaring than in so many other recent similar incidents. This charge of anti-Semitism is more substantiated than disproven by *Izvestia's* disclaimer that "we mention the Jewish surnames of people who were in this gang because we do not deign to pay attention to the malicious slander that the Western press stirs up from time to time."

But Russian anti-Semitism, the prevalence of which has been so brutally revealed by the economic trials, is not the subject of this essay. More to the point at the moment is that for these alleged crimes the newspaper *Izvestia* is demanding the death sentence. Not only does it demand such cruel punishment for people who have not even had the benefit of trial but it demands that the forthcoming "trial" of the criminals be *"a public show trial* that is widely publicized." To make it a real national spectacle *Izvestia* proposes that none other than the Procurator General of the USSR, Roman Rudenko, prosecute the case. Only worldwide protest could inhibit the Russian authorities from carrying out *Izvestia's* pretrial death verdict.

Another terrifying demonstration of Stalinist justice was yet to be revealed. On the heels of *Izvestia's* exposé and judgment of the Shakerman-Roifman "gang," an article in the October 30 issue of the Russian Republic newspaper, *Sovetskaya Rossiya,* published a demand by the Soviet Supreme *Court* for "public" trials of economic criminals to be given "wide publicity" in the press. Reflect for a moment. This is not a demand by the Party, or a prosecutor or the press or an individual. Here the demand for show trials is made by a court of justice — the Soviet Supreme Court at that.

Criminal cases of any importance are, as a rule, decided in advance. A man is accused of a serious crime and there follows a flood of letters and petitions to the press, denouncing the "criminal" and demanding his head. The trial may not have even begun. That is a detail, for where there is trial by press, court proceedings are a formality.

III

Some of the most important features of Russian justice are to be found in the presumably noncriminal decrees known as antiparasite laws and in extralegal institutions—Comrade Courts, People's Guards, Neighborhood Committees, euphemistically categorized as measures of public influence and heralded as milestones in democratization.

The Antiparasite Laws

One of the earliest of the antiparasite laws was introduced to the Azerbaijan Supreme Soviet in the summer of 1957 and passed the following year. The law "On Instensifying the Struggle against Antisocial Parasitical Elements" avowed that "there should be no parasitic idlers in Soviet society" and promised that those able-bodied citizens found guilty of an antisocial parasitic way of life may be sentenced to "exile by public sentence for a term of two to five years, with obligatory engagement in work at the place of exile."

All that was necessary for the law's execution was that a "street committee" in the cities, or a village soviet in rural areas, convene a meeting of residents in designated areas to pass judgment on a suspected "antisocial parasite." If a majority of the residents attended the meeting it was legal, and a majority of those present could, in open vote, pass "a public sentence of exile." Once the sentence was confirmed by a district of the city soviet, it took immediate effect with no recourse of appeal.

This vigilante law, passed in nine of the smaller union-Republics between 1957-1960, was so reminiscent of the arbitrary justice during the era of the "cult of personality" that it apparently met with resistance from more liberal elements within the legal profession, postponing its extension to the larger Republics. But resistance wilted before the clearly expressed determination of the Party to extend the anti-parasite laws. In May 1961 the Presidium of the Russian Republic Supreme Soviet passed its decree "On Intensifying the Struggle Against Persons Who Avoid Socially Useful Work and Lead an Antisocial Parasitic Way of Life."

The decree begins with the ceremonious but always startling news that "under the leadership of the Communist party, our country has entered the period of the full-scale building of communism." Of course the Soviet people are "working with enthusiasm . . . and respecting the rules of socialist society." However, in the countryside and in the cities "there are still individuals who are stubbornly opposed to work." These antisocial elements either refuse to work at all except in "forbidden business, private enterprise, speculation and begging" and the like, or else they do have jobs but only "for appearance's sake" as they engage in such skullduggery as "home brewing" and "undermining labor discipline." This parasitism is usually "accompanied by drunkenness, moral degradation and violation of the rules of socialist society."

To intensify the struggle against "antisocial parasitic elements," the Republic Supreme Soviet resolved that able-bodied adults who avoid socially useful work altogether, derive unearned income from speculation, etc., or generally "commit other antisocial acts" that permit them to live parasitically, are subject upon the order of a People's Court to deportation for a period of two to five years with "mandatory enlistment in work" at the place of exile. The court's decision "is not subject to appeal."

The other category of parasites — those who do have jobs but do not labor at them honestly — are subject to the "same measure of influence" except that they can be prescribed by either the court *or* a "public sentence" handed down by people working in the accused's shop, organization or collective. A "public sentence" is subject to the approval of the district (city) soviet executive committee "whose decision is final."

Orders for deportation by the courts or public sentence are carried out by militia agencies.

This 1963 decree differed in several respects from the earlier antiparasite laws passed by smaller Republics which have since been amended to conform with the Russian Republic's law. It is now necessary for agencies of the militia or the prosecutor's office to investigate a person charged with parasitism. If the charges are upheld, then a period of time is permitted the "parasite" to turn to the path of righteous labor to avoid being brought to trial before a court or a collective.

These changes represent a softening of the earlier parasite laws which denied all procedural rights to the accused. Nevertheless, as these are considered *administrative* decrees, the accused is still denied many of the limited procedural gains promised in the 1958 Statutes on Criminal Procedure. The new decree does not mention the right to a defense counsel and specifically denies the right of appeal. While the earlier decrees were even more stringent, they were the law only in smaller Republics with a small percentage of the national population. The present antiparasite laws are nationwide, and perhaps the most serious retrogressive step in Russian legality in the post-Stalin period.

This throwback to Stalin's technique recreates the quasi-legal basis for mass deportations to labor camps. This is not a theoretical possibility because thousands upon thousands of Russians have been recently sent into exile with "mandatory enlistment at work" for two to five years on the strength of the antiparasite laws, with the average sentence closer to the maximum five year period.

How many thousands have been deported is impossible to estimate. But the evidence is that the number is huge. An article by law professor Harold J. Berman (well respected in Russian legal circles and hardly an overmilitant critic of Russia's reformed legal system) in the *Harvard Law Review* (May 1963) suggests that there were at least 10,000 people accused under the antiparasite decree *in Moscow alone*, 2,000 of whom were sent into exile. This information was supplied to Berman by no less an authority than the Minister of Justice. Considering the nature of Berman's source it is reasonable to assume that both the number of accused and percentage banished were even higher. Also, this information was supplied to Berman in May of 1962, only one year after the decree took effect. Is there any reason to believe, given the intensified press campaign against "parasites," that the annual rate of accusations and deportations declined in the following year? And is there any reason to doubt that the provinces have been as vigilant as Moscow, especially if one recalls that the smaller Republics passed even harsher antiparasite laws several years before the larger Republics?[7]

The Comrade Courts

Comrade Courts are not a wholly new phenomenon. They functioned off and on, mainly to discipline labor, until 1940. But the present Comrade Courts, reintroduced in many smaller Republics in 1957 and in the Russian Republic four years later, are far broader in scope than their antecedents, as can be seen in the Model Statutes on Comrade Courts

---

7. In 1970, legislation was passed by a number of Union Republics which, on balance, provides for harsher administrative and criminal punishment of vagrants, beggars and against those leading "a parasitic way of life" and whose who "avoid socially useful labor."

passed by the Supreme Soviet in October, 1959 (translated in *Current Digest of the Soviet Press*, November 25, 1959).

According to the Model's first article, "Comrade Courts are elected public agencies charged with actively contributing to the inculcation in citizens of a spirit of a Communist attitude toward labor and socialist property and the observance of the rules of socialist behavior. . . ."

Where these courts are to be set up is established in Article 2: "Comrade Courts shall be set up at enterprises, institutions, organizations and higher and specialized secondary schools by decision of a general meeting of the workers and employers or of the students." In addition, "Rural comrade courts and comrade courts at collective farms, producers' cooperatives, housing bureaus, apartment house managements and street committees shall be set up." The next article determines that "those who receive a majority vote of more than half of those present at the meeting" are elected to the court. Those elected, "by open vote," choose the chairman, vice-chairman and secretary of the court. The courts report to the electors at least once a year.

Articles 5 and 6 specify the kind of cases to be heard. They include charges against a worker for "poor quality work, allowing defective output, or idle time resulting from a worker's unconscientious attitude toward his duties." Other chargeable offenses are violations of "labor discipline" including absence from work without a good excuse, lateness to work or leaving work before the end of the working day. Other cases heard include "the shirking of socially useful labor and leading a parasitic life," using abusive language, petty hooliganism (when a first offense), "foul language" and "petty arrogance."

Cases are to be heard at places of work or residence.

The "corrective measures" in the Model range from forcing apologies, issuing warnings and public censure, to more severe forms of punishment such as 100-ruble fines, ordering compensation up to 500 rubles [8] for alleged damage, "suggest-

8. This is in old currency. The corresponding figures in the new, devalued currency are 10 and 50 rubles. The latter fine is more than two weeks pay for the average Russian worker.

ing" to the plant manager that a worker be dismissed or demoted for three months and suggesting to the People's Court that the guilty party be evicted from his apartment. Finally, should the Comrade Court feel that a more serious penalty is called for involving an offense beyond its jurisdiction, it will have the right to turn over all relevant documents to the higher court.

Article 16 stipulates that "The decision of a comrade court shall be final and not subject to appeal" although trade unions or local soviets can ask for a rehearing. However, as Comrade Courts are under the direction of the local trade union committee or soviet (Article 19) it will be a rare instance when someone found guilty of "petty arrogance" or "poor quality work" finds his champion there.

In the Russian Republic, by a decree of the Presidium of the Republic Supreme Soviet in October 1963, the number and role of Comrade Courts were extended. It is no longer necessary for a collective to have at least 50 persons before a Comrade Court can be established, and an additional number of minor infractions of correct behavior were itemized — including "high handed acts" — that could lead the violator to a confrontation with a Comrade Court. This expansion of the jurisdiction of Comrade Courts in the Russian Republic will undoubtedly become the model for the smaller Republics.

One ostensible reason for extending the role of Comrade Courts is to relieve the regular People's Court of its heavy load and to soften the punitive nature of Russian justice. However, there are many boastful admissions in the Russian press that workers would rather confront a regular People's Court than risk the wrath of a Comrade Court. This is understandable, since an accused brought before a Comrade Court has few legal rights, is invariably found guilty or painfully humiliated and is tried by individuals with whom he is in close physical proximity and therefore in a position to harass him on or off his job. Far better then, many Russian workers feel, to take your chances before a more anonymous People's Court than be humbled by kangaroo courts whose job it is to probe and publicly review the most private corners of one's life, be it work quotas, family relations, style of dress, etc.

The personnel of the Courts is usually described in glowing terms; they are conscientious, stern but understanding comrades, eternally vigilant in their patriarchal supervision of their fellow workers or neighbors. In the words of one *Izvestia* correspondent: "a person who has broken the *everyday laws* of soviet life or *those of the production line* must answer before a stern but just comrade court." In a totalitarian society there are many "everyday laws" that can be broken, be it on the production line or in "soviet life" in general. Consequently the Comrade Courts have a busy time of it.

The Comrade Court is not only concerned with labor discipline and quality control techniques. It watches the worker at work, it acts as a court of human relations, it supervises the personal habits of all. As the *Izvestia* correspondents wrote, "It fights for Communist morals in everyday life and on the production line."

The Comrade Court system has its recognized excesses, too — incidents bordering on lunacy. For example, take the trial of a student before a Comrade Court consisting of his fellow students.

The accused is a student named Talis B. He has been charged with such offenses as stealing a ball, a girl's ribbon, a chess set and a sandwich. Found guilty, student Talis B. was expelled from the school by the court with the approval of the school director.

What we have not mentioned, however, is that Talis B. was eight years old, his court consisted of other second grade children and chairman of the court was all of ten years old! (This "case" was ridiculed in *Izvestia*. It was an excess. The question remains, though, how it is possible for such "excesses" to be manifested in the land that is approaching the final stages of Communism?)

By October 1963 there were nearly 200,000 Comrade Courts to discipline labor and defend everyday laws of Soviet life. [9]

9. According to an article in *Izvestia*, August 1, 1970 (trans. in CDSP, Vol. XX, No. 32), there are still approximately 200,000 Comrade Courts in the USSR.

The Druzhiny — The People's Volunteers

In March 1959, the Communist Party and the Council of Ministers issued a decree, "On the Participation by the Working People in Safeguarding Public Order," which ordered the formation of "voluntary detachments" of People's Volunteers *(Druzhiny)*. These detachments, which have their own local apparatus independent of the militia, have the duty to "stop violations of public order and restrain violators mainly through persuasion and warnings," and more broadly, to counter "those individuals in our Soviet society who do not observe the norms of public behavior."

An article in *Izvestia* of June 2, 1963, reports 130,000 People's Volunteer detachments with 5,500,000 Druzhinniki patrolling major Russian enterprises, farms, cities and towns. These figures reveal not only the importance attached to People's Volunteers but *one vigilante for every 40 Russians* is no less suggestive of a huge and increasing number of Russians defying Party "norms of public behavior."

A politically offensive remark, a drink too many, a carelessly tossed cigarette, a gaudy dress, a skirt too short or trousers too long or some similar evidence of "petty hooliganism" is offense enough for a People's Volunteer to bring the "hooligan" to headquarters for a little bit of persuasion. From there the offender can either be released or hauled before a Comrade Court or a regular People's Court.

The Druzhiny have attracted some of the worst elements in Russian life — the servile, the venal, the sadistic (mainly young Communist hooligans). That one method of persuasion includes beating with clubs, fists and feet, sometimes with fatal consequences, is widely known. Complaints of such excesses have even found their way into the Russian press. For example, a writer from Leningrad reported, more than a year after the Druzhiny was organized, that "young communist street patrols were literally hunting down young men wearing brightly colored shirts and young women wearing slacks. They ripped or slashed the shirts. The same fate befell the slacks." Moreover, "the method of knocking in someone's teeth is not . . . the best educational method" and "to chop off a girl's hair . . . is sheer violence."

That such actions are neither isolated instances nor to be reported in the past tense is evidenced by the continuing accounts of similar atrocities. Two *Izvestia* correspondents discussing the Druzhiny last year conceded that "not only in Leningrad but also in Moscow, Kiev and Minsk, people's volunteers at times act out of conviction that in the struggle against violators all means are fair." While "this does not mean that people's volunteers must fight hooligans with kid gloves" it does mean that "shaving someone's head for 'immaturity' is not the way."

The regime has apparently been unsuccessful in containing resistance to the Druzhiny. In 1961, the Armenian Communist Party reprimanded the Chairman and Vice-Chairman of that Republic's Supreme Court for "underestimat[ing] the social and political significance of cases of murder and violence against people's volunteers." More telling than the reported physical violence is the candid admission that the threat is not confined to a few allegedly criminal elements but is a problem of "social and political significance," i.e., the violence is a manifestation of wider and deeper popular resentment. By 1962, popular hostility and acts of violence had become so serious that on February 12 of that year the USSR Supreme Soviet passed a decree which makes anyone "insulting a member of the People's Volunteers in the course of fulfilling his duty" liable to six months in jail or one year of corrective labor. If insults are "accompanied by violence or the threat of use of violence" then penalties are raised to up to five years in jail. An *attempt* on the life of a druzhinnik "in the presence of aggravating circumstances" can result in the death sentence. Clearly enough, these harsh and cruel penalties are the Kremlin's response to the growth of mass hostility to the guardians of the proprieties of private manners and social behavior.

This decree could hardly be expected to persuade the Russian people of the benevolence of the paramilitia. And it even failed as a deterrent to violent forms of resistance. More than a year later, in July 1963, *Pravda* reported that a plenary session of the USSR Supreme Soviet was obliged to discuss "serious shortcomings that attest to certain court officials' underestimation of the social danger of attempts on the life, health and dignity of militia workers and people's volunteers by criminal and other anti-social elements." (Again, the source of the trouble comes not only from "criminal" types but other, broadly defined, "anti-social elements.") The plenum, *Pravda* notes, "called the attention of the courts . . . to the need for strict and unflinching observance of the requirements of the February 12, 1962 decree of the Presidium of the USSR Supreme Soviet" permitting capital punishment.

IV

Why the Organizations of "Public Control"?

Before discussing the role of Comrade Courts and People's Volunteers we should make clear what they emphatically are not.

They are not evidence of a society bursting the bonds of its totalitarian past and groping, hesitatingly and in a dialectically self-contradictory manner, as some apologists would have it, toward political freedom.

They are not symptomatic of a dictator "encouraging the people themselves, the rank and file, to participate in the running of the country" as Edward Crankshaw would have readers of his *Khrushchev's Russia* believe.

They are certainly not proof that "persuasion and education [are] becoming the principal method of regulating the life of Soviet society," as Khrushchev announced at the twenty-second Congress of the Communist Party. Our conviction is bolstered by Khrushchev himself, who, in the very next breath, emphasized that education and persuasion "do not imply relaxed supervision of strict observance of Soviet law, labor discipline and moral behavior." (Equally certain was that delegates to the Congress were "persuaded" enough to approve all his remarks and the new Party program unanimously, and "educated" enough to greet Nikita Sergeyevich with loud, tumultuous, thunderous applause.)

Now, had Russian law, in statutes and in life, grown less stringent in the past five years and had the sovereignty of the Communist party declined as the role of Comrade Courts and People's Volunteers was enhanced, then one might speak with some verisimilitude of the transfer of power to broader, more representative popular institutions. However, the law remains bitter and its practice cruel. Democracy is outlawed. Legal rights are more for the state than the accused. Thousands are being sent into exile under the arbitrary Parasite Laws. There are increasingly harsh penalties for crime. The rate of executions in Russia (of cases we know of) is about five times what it is in the United States. Men sentenced to death are sometimes denied the right to appeal. Men sentenced to long jail terms have been shot to death on the appeal of the prosecutor. Is it conceivable that those responsible for the modern world's most uncivilized legal system and customs are "encouraging the people to rule themselves" via Comrade Courts and People's Guards?

If the "organizations of public influence" were to become, in Khrushchev's words, "the principal method of regulating the life of Soviet society," power would be gradually transferred from the Communist party, the only political party permitted by law, to broader, self-regulating mass organizations, whose policies are self-determined and not subordinate to any political party. Would that this were so!

But the Communist party is surrendering none of its authority and is to grow stronger under communism, according to latest Party dogma. In fact, it is the Party drive to absorb many of the functions of, or direct control over, state and administrative institutions which is largely responsible for the existence of Comrade Courts, People's Volunteers and Party-State Control agencies. Khrushchev was only speaking the truth when he said that "our Party will continue to follow the course of handing over an ever larger number of *government* functions to mass organizations." But the *government* in Russia governs less than the Party, and the Party apparatus has always looked upon governmental institutions, which have their own bureaucracies and their own ambitions, as possible sources of friction. The best way to prevent friction is to eliminate its source, accounting for the Party drive to undercut state ministries, decentralize governmental agencies and to absorb or more easily supervise their operations. How the agencies of public influence fit into this scheme of things is simple enough. The Comrade Courts with their expanding area of competence have taken over many of the functions of the regular courts, and the People's Volunteers have become a virtual army of para-police paralleling the activities of the regular militia, thereby tending to displace the functions of several powerful Republic and USSR governmental bureaucracies. While the new public agencies weaken the authority of existing ministries, they are organizations *without any national apparatus* and with few full-time functionaries; they have mainly volunteer workers. This clearly delimits the possibilities of special bureaucracies arising within the new coercive institutions. Furthermore, given the local nature of their operations, they are more easily subjected to the "guidance" of local units of the Communist party.

To the extent that new public agencies have tightened the Party grip on Russia, they represent a retreat from "liberalization" since, in the context of "de-Stalinization," conflicts engendered by competing centers of power afford a far greater chance for liberal change than the consolidation of all authority in the hands of the Party. (Tighter Party control of the whole judicial process can also be seen in the following figures based on Russian sources and supplied by Harold Berman: in the 1949 elections to the judiciary, 47% of the candidates were Party members; in 1957, 93.9% of the People's Judges elected were Communist party members.)

There are additional reasons for Party sponsorship of public agencies, itemized in summary fashion below.

In the past half-decade Russia has become a vertical society. Everything is soaring: rockets, spacemen, industrial indices, parasitism and death sentences. At least, almost everything, one exception being the standard of living which remains horizontal, perhaps on a lower plane than any European nation, with no prospect of anything more than a slight perpendicular tilt.

Whatever pride the Russian people take in their scientists and engineers, there inevitably grows the realization that nuclear achievements are made at the expense of wage rates, that astronomical industrial growth statistics are indigestible as food for body or soul, and that vehicles in space do not provide space in which to live. Emboldened by the relaxation of terror, the resentment of the Russian people over their conditions of life and embitterment over poverty in the midst of huge expenditures for armaments and capital goods industries, have taken overt forms that were not so freely risked under Stalin. "Violations of labor discipline" in factories have become infinite in their variety while the peasant shows an increasingly flagrant disregard for the collective's production goals as he tends his own small private plot.

Indiscipline is not confined to worker and peasant. The intellectual, far from becoming docilely grateful to the Party for relieving the country of many of Stalin's excesses, is now more venturesome, even truculent and defiant. Among the youth, there is the impossible-to-hide conflict of generations: the contempt youngsters show for the Party bureaucrat in their efforts to escape the asphyxiating puritanism and philistinism of "Communist morality."

The repression of these "antisocial manifestations" provides an added and more obvious function of parasite laws and the ubiquitous agencies of popular control. In this view, these laws and agencies are not steps to loosen the social fabric of totalitarianism or to promote popular self-rule, as some Kremlinologists would have it, but are designed to stifle dissent and to brake the liberal impetus provided by the earlier weakening of the special instruments and techniques of Stalin's terror.

One specific target of the expanding network of public agencies and the parasite laws worthy of special notice is stealing. The most recent spectacular case concerns a Moscow "gang" (most of whom are clearly identified as Jews [10]) accused of embezzling operations involving 52 factories, artels and collective farms and stealing a total of three million rubles from the state. In another recent case, several leaders of the Kirghizan Republic were condemned to death for stealing more than 30 million rubles. (This "gang of thieves" involved 50 high Republic government and Party officials.) In Sverd-

10. The probability is that for anti-Semitic reasons the amounts allegedly stolen by Jewish defendants in the wave of economic crimes are highly exaggerated.

lovsk, 100 pounds of gold were cached by a "large band of gold thieves." A clerk in a Stavropol kolkhoz reputedly stole 500,000 rubles. A group of enterprising economic officials in Moscow are accused of having stolen "900 looms from the state and sold them." The head of the Moscow Oblast Economic Council Section for Distribution of Equipment performed his duties on the basis of the most generous giver, and in four years he sold on the side 50 motor cranes, 12 tower cranes, 11 electric welding machines and several mechanical trench-diggers and loaders.

Komsomolskaya Pravda reports in an article called "Thieves' Town" that an entire community was built next to the site of a Siberian metallurgical plant out of stolen material: "foundation blocks and panels of reinforced concrete, slag blocks and rails, drainpipes and preconstructed buildings," etc., were all stolen to construct the settlement. This is apparently not an isolated case since the paper concedes that despite efforts to curtail such activities with the assistance of the people's volunteers, "thieves' towns spring up in the old way." The same paper admits that stealing and embezzlement are common to entire all-Union or Republic organizations, from functionaries atop down to regional and local subordinates. In some factories, managers and their entire staffs have been replaced as many as five times — they all turned out to be thieves.

A special cause for Party grief and vigilance is the peasant who will expropriate whatever he can — due less to an innate acquisitive instinct than an average annual income of around $500 a year. Not only spades, shovels, rakes and milk-pails disappear; crops, too, vanish. At a Communist party plenum in 1961 Khrushchev reported that in the Ukraine "half of the cultivated maize was pilfered and plundered as it stood." If there has been any change since then, it has been an increase in agricultural thefts. Party activists and People's Volunteers have been organized in special squads to patrol the fields spending "difficult, sleepless [nights], no easier than a soldier's duties. . . . making the rounds, night watches." Grain is stolen in the fields, and bread stolen in the towns. *Sovetskaya Rossiya* (November 17, 1963) gives an account of

27 bread thieves who stole 11,330 leaves of bread in seven
months. [11]

Thus it is to curtail the incalculable financial drain on the
state and the even greater social threat to a ruling totalitarian
party from such a massive breakdown of "social discipline"
that we find another major motivation for the public control
agencies and parasite laws. [12]

The working day in Russia has been reduced. People have
more free time. A democratic society would welcome this
added opportunity for people to relax, think, read, write,
experiment in the arts and letters, resist some ideas and advance others. Not in Russia. There, and this is the trademark
of a totalitarian society, free time is considered fraught with
danger. Leisure begets not culture, but vice — unless it is controlled and policed by the Party-State. One theoretician,
writing in the Party's philosophical journal, formulates the
dangers of free time this way:

> The community must be increasingly concerned with organizing
> the leisure of the working people and the youth. Where this
> matter is allowed to drift, all sorts of unpleasantries may arise.
> We must not forget about the tenacity of the survivals of capital-
> ism, about the penetration of corrupting ideology among some
> channels in our midst.

To control "unpleasantries" born of free time, it is not
enough to harp on the theme in the press. The Party does not
rule through exhortations. Here, it is as agencies of time and
thought control that we find another reason for Comrade
Courts and People's Volunteers. Their organization on house
and neighborhood levels facilitates this assignment, as the
shock troops of philistinism, to root out old and newly arisen

11. Simple arithmetic shows that each "thief" stole an average of two loaves
     of bread a day. Whether this was done for profit or personal consump-
     tion is hard to say. For these crimes one salesgirl and a foreman received
     six-year prison sentences; the others were sentenced up to five years.

12. There is no evidence that the problem of theft has been eased since the
     above was written. On the contrary, there is every reason to believe that
     it has been aggravated. Along with the rise of thefts there has also been
     a rise in the number of decrees and directives for "intensifying the
     struggle against thefts of state and public property, violations of state
     and labor discipline, bribe-taking and other violations of the law."

symptoms of "corrupting ideologies" among the working people and youth.

Another function of these agencies concerns the Party's need to project a more popular image and build a broader base for itself. With the reduction of rule by terror, the Party is obliged to show greater concern for public opinion. It must appear stern, but benevolent, and this is reflected in its ideology and even in Party nomenclature for organs of repression. Kangaroo courts are Comrade Courts; posses and vigilantes are People's Volunteers. They are not to coerce, but to persuade and re-educate. They are "prophylactic" forms of "popular justice" to protect the many from the few remaining "loafers," "parasites," "hooligans," "drunkards," "degenerates," "swindlers," "speculators," "embezzlers," "petty thieves," "ideologically corrupted," etc. More to the point, however, is that the agencies of "social control" involve millions of people enjoying some degree or other of special status as Druzhinniki, pseudo court officials or other species of Party watchmen, who are thereby indebted to the Party. Their numerical weight becomes a significant mass social base for the ruling Party.

A more general explanation for quasilegal public control agencies and parasite laws is their usefulness to the Communist party as "checks and balances" against the Party's own reduction of terror. In the post-Stalin legal reforms, a number of extreme manifestations of arbitrary justice were formally removed from legal statutes. But arbitrariness cannot be dispensed with by a Party which does not rely on any democratic consensus for its power. Since the Party neither wants to return to all the methods employed by Stalin nor can it divest itself of arbitrary rule, it has found one way of circumventing legal restrictions: reliance on parasite laws and public control agencies which are not formal judicial bodies.

V

Socialist Legality and the Limits of Legal Reform

As law reflects social divisions and conflict it follows that where the law grows more severe, conflicts remain or become more intense. How is it possible, then, for Russia to be entering the final stages of Communism, which presupposes a final resolution of class struggles (not to mention a higher living standard than any bourgeois country), when its system of law, in the past five years, has extended the right of the Party-State to execute people and deprive them of liberty? Khrushchev's claim of imminent Communism, as the law grows more punitive, smacks of Stalin's theoretic contribution that as Russia attains the higher reaches of socialism, the class struggle grows ever sharper.

Nevertheless, recent retrogressive steps should not blind one to the considerable overall differences in legal concepts and practices between Russia today and Russia under Stalin. Mass deportations, mass frame-up trials, mass murder on a Stalin-scale are no longer typical of Russian justice. However, eliminating the excesses of Stalin's irrational terror is hardly proof of "socialist legality" or democratization. For what could socialist legality mean other than that the law is imbued with the rational, democratic and humane values of socialism? To be socialist, legality must mean that political freedom becomes a cardinal principle of law. Socialist jurisprudence would absorb, extend and consistently apply the best features of "bourgeois" substantive and procedural law. And as an advance over more primitive justice, socialist criminal law — in the statutes and as a living process — would be directed toward the rehabilitation of criminals; capital punishment would be frowned upon as a hideous relic of ancient times; and, generally, the punitive "eye for an eye" code would be a historic curio of the Scriptural Canons.

Socialist legality, then, implies all that is still denied in the letter or practice of Russian law.

Russia is not governed by an ill-defined social caste that will melt before the demands of some mystical historical process drawing it out of Stalinist primitivism, beyond the limited reforms of Khrushchevism and into the realm of socialist freedom. The Kremlin rulers are neither men of whim nor helpless creatures to be shunted aside by teleological winds blowing from the pages of apologists for totalitarianism. They are men of purpose, with their own sense of history, with an ideology. They hold a distinct, unique relation, as a hardened social class, to the means of production —

they own and control the nationalized economy through their control of the State via the rule of the Communist party. Their source of power, self-interest and self-consciousness impose relatively clear limits to legal (and other) reforms with the Party-State.

That is why, whatever legal reforms may yet occur in Russian law within the framework of a one-party dictatorship, political democracy will always be outlawed, and it is unrealistic to anticipate fundamental procedural reforms which protect the rights of the individual against the authority of the Party-State.

January 1965

The Breakdown of
Stalinist "Socialism"

Walter Kendall

Communist orthodoxy alleges that the Communist party is the sole authentic voice of the working class, that as such it is the irreplaceable agent of the proceeding world socialist revolution, that within the Soviet bloc, wherever the party rules, the working class in enthroned in power, while production goes ahead on uninterrupted, rationally planned lines in stark contradiction to the anarchy and chaos of capitalist society.

The contention of this essay is that all these claims belong more to the realm of myth than actuality. Further, these claims are being increasingly exposed by events and the monolithic character of world Communism is being destroyed; in short, in Marxist terms, the "breakdown" of Stalinist socialism is the order of the day. The Czech events, coming as they have done in the most advanced and cultured of the nations of the Soviet bloc, are in no sense an accidental aberration. Rather they indicate the future of the other members and in particular of Russia, where the problems which led to Czech decentralization are already exercising a marked and considerable influence on the progress of the economy and of society as a whole.

Lenin, writing in August and September 1917, quoted approvingly Marx's own opinion that the task of the socialist revolution was "not merely to hand the bureaucratic and military machine over from one set of hands to another — but to shatter it; and it is this which is the preliminary condition of any real people's revolution."[1]

In reality, the Soviet State which as sprung from the Russian Revolution is more bureaucratic than Czarist rule. The bureaucratic and military middle class exercises more power over the working class than in any other European state, with the doubtful exception of Franco's Spain.

THE MYTH OF PLANNING

The roots of this transformation lie in the isolated, primitive and backward conditions which existed in Russia at the time of the Revolution. These were the decisive objective conditions for the transformation. Yet within the limits predetermined by objective necessity men do not fail to make their mark on history. There can be no doubt that the process of centralization and bureaucratization in Russia, Eastern Europe and China has been markedly hastened and accentuated by certain false conceptions about the nature of "planned" economy itself.

In one of the closing chapters of *Anti-Dühring*, Frederick Engels draws attention to "the fact that the social organization of production within the factory has developed to the point at which it has become incompatible with the anarchy of production in society. . . ." "Anarchy in social production," he concluded, must be "replaced by conscious organization on a planned basis."[2]

The conclusion drawn by Soviet authorities was that the analogy between factory and society was not illustrative but exact. The whole gigantic, delicately balanced economy could and must be planned as if it were a single industrial plant.

1. Nikolai Lenin, *State and Revolution* (London), p. 49. The full letter, dated 12 April 1871, in a different translation will be found in Karl Marx, 'Letters to Dr. Kugelmann,' (Moscow, 1934), p. 123.

2. Frederick Engels, *Anti-Dühring* (London, 1934), pp. 304, 311.

"Our plans are not forecasts, nor guesses," warned Stalin majestically. "They are instructions."[3] The Soviet plan demonstrated the superiority of the "socialist" system to the anarchy of capitalist production.

In reality the "plan" of which Stalin and his parties spoke was a myth. The attempt to plan everything proved impossible. Capitalist anarchy was ended. A form of Stalinist "socialist" anarchy took its place. The party built a prison and pronounced it "socialism." The overplanning of the economy created a new ruling caste and *of necessity* excluded the working class from power.

Engels aptly described the socialist transition as "the leap from the realm of necessity to the realm of freedom." Oskar Lange, an economist of world renown, in 1960 Chairman of the Economic Council of Poland, offers the definition, "Under capitalism . . . production is done for private profit; under socialism . . . for the satisfaction of human wants."[4]

In reality, under the Soviet system the satisfaction of human wants is at the bottom of the scale of priorities; subsistence wages have been the rule for a past generation, while for most citizens the leap has been from freedom to necessity and not the other way around.

"We actually had a period in the socialist countries, maybe with the exception of China . . . when the output of the least important commodity was planned," writes Oskar Lange. "There was the famous joke of Poland — really it was not a joke, but it was true — that the production of pickled cucumbers is in the national plan. Another case which was not a joke either but was a fact — was that the State Planning Commission made a plan of the number of hares which will be shot during the year by hunters. At the same time you could not get, for instance, buttons, or hairpins for ladies, simply because they were *forgotten* in the national economic plan."[5] In Poland at this very moment toilet paper still ar-

3. Report of Central Committee to 15th Congress CPSU.

4. Oskar Lange, *The Political Economy of Socialism* (The Hague, 1960), p. 7.

5. *Ibid.*, p. 21.

rives in the shops on one day a month; he who fails to survive the queues on that momentous occasion goes raw and uncomfortable until the next great day of opportunity comes round again in four weeks time. "In Hungary," writes the Communist economist Janos Kornai, "the final draft of the annual plan was in some sectors not available until past the middle of the year of operation." [6]

The outcome of this situation has been that in many cases the plan has existed only *on paper*, as an abstract scheme which did not exist in concrete form. In many cases plans were made which were impossible of achievement because the objectives were overambitious. In all, the feasibility of planning all economic life from a single center was proved to be an illusion. The refusal to recognize this fact led to a necessary attribution of nonfulfillment of the plan to subjective "sabotage" and not economic impossibility. Penal sanction, witch hunts, death sentences, terror, followed as an inexorable consequence.

If the plan is too rigid the center cannot react to unforeseen developments at the base until it is too late. Corrections arrive behind time, underestimate or exaggerate the need. The plan begins to go "wild." "The central decision responds to a situation too late — unless there is decentralization, central planning becomes fictitious: what actually is obtained is an elemental development. For instance, in Poland in a certain period the amount of elemental processes became so great that you could ask whether there still exists a planned economy. On the one hand there was a plan, but on the other the economy produced results in a very elemental way." [7]

The myth of of a mammoth plan that goes like clockwork has been so well propagated by Stalinist apologists in the Western labor movement that these statements, despite their irrefutable source, merit some further documentation.

Stalin told an astonished party conference in June 1930, that industry was under orders to increase output by 50% in

6. J. Kornai, *Over Centralisation in Economic Administration* (London, 1959).

7. Oskar Lange, *Role of Planning in Socialist Economy* (The Hague, 1958), p. 25.

that single year. In 1928 Russia produced 3,5000,000 tons of pig iron. Stalin now ordered at all costs the economy must produce 17,000,000 tons in 1932. The target had still to be reached in 1941.[8] Stalin's totally "idealistic" and un-Marxist belief that "there are no fortresses which Bolsheviks cannot conquer" led to similar exaggerated targets not only in many other sections of Soviet economy but to precisely comparable costly absurdities in the satellites. "We mechanically copied the methods of building socialism accepted in the Soviet Union,"[9] Oskar Lange declares.

In Hungary, writes Kornai, "in order to secure early increases of the volume of output on as large a scale as possible, machinery production was expanded disproportionately faster than that . . . of materials, power, semi-finished products and components." New installations were being brought into operation at breakneck speed, but provision was not being made for providing necessary support for these advances. "In a number of fields, relative rates of growth have been the reverse of what would have been required for balance. The growth of machine manufacturing has outstripped that of iron and steel production, manufacturing industry has grown faster than the industries supplying power, coal, electricity, etc."[10]

The situation which Kornai describes is not unknown to political economy. The description is precisely that of a trade crisis under capitalism, typified by a dis-balance of factors of production, caused by the anarchic, unplanned character of the productive process. The distinction of Stalinist bureaucratism is that it has successfully planned the very chaos which capitalism itself produces only unintentionally and "by accident."

The analogy with the trade cycle is in no sense forced. The Hungarian plan requirements were assigned by monthly,

8. Isaac Deutscher, *Stalin*, (London, 1950), pp. 321-322.

9. Oskar Lange, *Some Problems Relating to the Polish Road to Socialism* (Warsaw, 1957), p. 9.

10. J. Kornai, *Over-Centralisation in Economic Administration* (London, 1959), p. 181.

quarterly and annual check/target figures. Economic, political and penal sanctions were applied to seek their fulfillment. As a result the periodic (but relatively long spaced) capitalist trade cycle disappears. In its place a new cycle "the peak always found to occur at the end of the month, quarter or year and the troughs at the beginning" takes it's place.[11]

Statistics from the Chief Planning Division of the Ministry of Light Industry in Hungary bear this out. The output of cloth and shoes during the single month of May 1956 varied as follows:[12]

Article	*Unit*	*1st 10 days*	*2nd 10 days*	*3rd 10 days*
Finished cotton cloth	1,000 sq.m	4,343	5,825	7,674
Men's shoes	1,000 pairs	40.9	37.2	50.4
Women's shoes	1,000 pairs	75.6	98.2	128.5
Children's shoes	1,000 pairs	103.6	115.2	133.5

Even when 100% plan fulfillment is achieved the result may well be illusory. "It is possible to 'juggle' to the tune of a few percent by manipulating stocks of semi-finished products and work in progress." "In the leather trade — the way out is to dump large amounts of raw hides into the tanks for soaking. In an hour they can throw as much as two wagonfuls into the tanks and these hides immediately appear in total production as work in progress. Net value added is practically nil, but the material instantly assumes a value equal to 75% of that of finished leather," for the purposes of reckoning total production. The plan is saved!

The use of production indicators is prone to lead to absurdities. A plan expressed in tons encourages the production of wastefully heavy commodities; factories making cement blocks manufacture large ones and the target is the more easily attained. Industrial machinery carries an excessive content of steel, becomes inordinately expensive and makes exceedingly costly demands on power supply if it is to function effectively. Change the plan target to rubles, no cheap

11. *Ibid.*, p. 139.

12. *Ibid.*, p. 145.

blocks will be produced: all will be unnecessarily dear. Plan roofing iron by square meters and it will become dangerously thin. Plan cloth by length, then width will be sacrificed to yardage. The "optique" of the plan, the easiest way to achieve targets, takes precedence over objective needs. The problem is acknowledged by Soviet authorities. A *Krokodil* cartoon once caricatured a factory which fulfilled its entire month's nail output program by the manufacture of one gigantic nail, which hung from an overhead crane extending the whole length of the workshop. [13]

Idle plant, unutilized labor, wastage of materials follow, directly created by the plan. In Hungary the plan consistently failed to make adequate provision for stocks. In several light industries in 1956 these amounted to barely 15 to 30 days' supplies. The stocks of cotton in the main capitalist importing countries during 1952, 1953, 1954 averaged respectively 140, 104, 108 days' supply. In Hungary the figure was 31, 36 and 40 days' supply. Since these stocks were very unevenly allocated between requirements the result was that the plant was constantly out of action for lack of material; costly waste through use of inappropriate materials resulted and inferior goods were produced. The short stock position was "planned"; it was in no sense accidental. One factory with stocks of six to 12 months under capitalism found them reduced to five to 15 days under Stalinist planning. [14]

Centralization breeds bureaucracy and contempt for the consumer. The "orders for the entire supply of woolen cloth for the whole country are placed by a single official of the Ministry of Domestic Commerce." "Even if the person had an excellent grasp of his business, is it right," asks Kornai, "that a single human being should decide in a matter such as this?" [15]

OVERPLANNING AND ITS CONSEQUENCES

The consequences of overplanning are in no sense acciden-

13. A. Nove, *The Soviet Economy* (London, 1961), pp. 157-158.

14. J. Kornai, *Over-Centralisation in Economic Administration* (London, 1959), pp. 54-55.

15. *Ibid.*, p. 188.

tal. A rigid party dictatorship creates the plan and gives it the force of law. The arbitrarily decided plan quotients necessitate the destruction of a free trade union movement whose activities might otherwise disrupt the achievement of plan targets. The total character of the plan makes impossible the exercise of consumer choice. The impossibility of fulfilling the plan targets in the form outlined leads to holdups, to endless corrective campaigns, to administrative sanctions, to penal sentences and, if the crisis grows bad enough, to purges on the scale seen in Russia in the thirties and in post-war Eastern Europe in the forties and fifties. The connection is not fortuitous. The sequence is a logical outcome of cause and effect.

The Ujpest leather factory in Hungary received between September 1 and December 31, 1955, no less than 102 specific instructions relating to production, excluding other more general requisitions.[16] To hold the line, a system of fines, reminiscent of the early industrial revolution and extending even to managerial staff was introduced. Thus among other instances the Hungarian official *Light Industry Gazette* recorded punishment of "top management staff for failing to make use of a steam engine," "for negligent warehouse management," "for not having visited the Ministry in person [!] about a payment of wages in excess of the planned amount." The repression develops as a *consequence* of the system and not as an excrescence upon it. The more impossible and absurd the plan, the more inevitable the consequence that the bureaucratic machine will grow disproportionately, the apparatus of administration, legal and penal sanction, mushroom in size; in other words the more the dictatorship of a bureaucratic caste over the nation and most important, over a disenfranchised working class, will grow powerful, vicious and all-embracing in its scope and consequences.

Courage, independence, initiative, intelligence, innovating capacity, are all at a discount. Creative activity retires within a protective shell. "The main thing really, is not so much to

16. *Ibid.*, p. 68

see that all is well in our factory, but to make sure that my superiors are satisfied. I must fulfill the indices which are most insisted upon: I must not make too many difficulties by arguing about plans." Abruptness, dictatorial methods, a tendency "to order people about in the course of their work" becomes the rule; it spreads like a contagious disease. Production suffers. Human beings suffer most of all. Socialism is to be introduced to free mankind. Stalinism in the name of freedom begins to turn society into one vast prison.

A bureaucratic group entirely divorced from the people possessed of a new supreme power begins to rule. Rationality loses its effect. To challenge an irrational command is to risk position, liberty and even life itself. As in Hungary under Rakosi, in Russia under Stalin, in Czechoslovakia under Gottwald, the brakes are off. Any insanity is possible, the limit of the oppression of the people is decided only by the possibility of revolt; the economic waste is limited only by the certain eventual "seizure" of the whole machine. Thus Czechoslovakia, in defiance of plan growth targets, experienced in 1963 a net decline in production. In unexcelled Stalinist gobbledeygook the party described this downturn as a "negative rate of growth." The Czech economy, once among the most advanced in Europe, now finds itself in a state of general qualitative decline, unable to compete effectively in markets held easily before the Communist coup. After 20 years of Stalinist "socialism" the wave of Czech tourists to the "West" in the 1960s was shocked beyond measure to discover that "socialist" Czechoslovakia had been overtaken and surpassed by neighboring capitalist nations formerly viewed as social and cultural inferiors.

THE STATE AS AN AGENT OF CAPITAL ACCUMULATION

The portrait of a smooth-as-clockwork execution of the state plan, of a steadily rising production graph, of a system divorced from cycles of production, unencumbered with economic waste and inefficiency, freely administered according to the will of the working masses — this portrait, so artistically created by Soviet propaganda, proves on examination to be almost a total reversal of the truth.

Hierarchical command replaces democratic decision.

Bureaucratic allocation replaces consumer choice. The waste of advertising is replaced by the maintenance of a superfluous bureaucratic administration and the vastly expensive secret police force which total command makes inevitable.[17] The capitalist trade cycle ends — the monthly, quarterly, annual plan cycle takes its place. The output graph, far from rising steadily upwards, suffers irregualr crises of its own; the limits to insensate waste provided by market force and democratic control have been equally eliminated. The whole of Soviet architecture comes to reflect the wasteful Victorian exuberance of Stalin's bad taste.

"The great intensity of the industrialization process" (in Eastern Europe), wrote Oskar Lange, "required methods reminiscent of war economy."[18] "Such methods are not peculiar to socialism — they are also introduced in capitalist countries too, in war time; they are rather certain techniques of war economy."[19]

Lange's statement is very revealing. The characteristics of war-time society are the very antithesis of those of socialism. What then has become of the "socialism" of the Soviet state? Nominally socialist, the Soviet state apparatus has in fact performed a role best described as that of a classic agent of rapid capital accumulation. "Capital," wrote Marx, "comes into the world soiled with mire from tip to toe and oozing blood at every pore." The growth of Stalinist society, the events which have accompanied the "planning" already described, provide illustrations as moving as those which Marx himself provided in the pages of Volume I of *Capital*. "The secret of the self-expansion of capital finds its explanation is this," wrote Marx, "that capital has at its disposal a definite

---

17. According to the London *Observer* of July 28, 1968, in post-1948 Czechoslovakia "there were probably 100,000 people imprisoned for long sentences . . . perhaps 2,000 died in prison from fever and other diseases. About 30,000 people served 15 years." According to one Czech estimate published in the *Guardian*, the secret police network numbered 200,000 men.

18. Oskar Lange, *Ibid.*, p. 17.

19. Oskar Lange, *Problems of Political Economy of Socialism* (Calcutta, 1962), p. 18.

quantity of other people's unpaid labor." As if to offer mute evidence of this fact, statistics show that "the purchasing power of money wages (in the USSR) in 1937, 1940 and (particularly) 1947 was below 1928." Capital for the expansion of Soviet industry has been obtained by forcing working-class living standards to subsistence level or below.

The word utopian comes readily to the lips of certain Communist ideologists. Yet, beyond doubt, the greatest utopians of the twentieth century are the Communists themselves. Sir Thomas More confined his "Utopia" to the field of literature. The Communists claim theirs exists in real life, in the Soviet Union, and this despite the fact that almost every aspect of reality confronts and denies its utopian portrayal.

COMMUNISM AND REVOLUTION

The Communists have sedulously propagated the myth that without their party there could be no proletarian social revolution. Yet, in reality, the only proletarian revolution seen in Europe since the war took place in Hungary and was directed against the Communists' own monopoly of power. Similar events took place in Eastern Germany and were only narrowly avoided in Poland.

The party's claim to hegemony over the colonial revolution has similarly collapsed. In Algeria, a non-Communist movement has concluded a successful revolutionary war against French imperialism. In Algeria, for a number of years, workers' control of productive processes in land and industry existed in forms more advanced than those in Russia after four decades of Communist rule. It becomes increasingly obvious that in defiance of Stalinist orthodoxy the former colonial states intend to avoid the bourgeois state altogether. The State, as in Nasser's Egypt or Nkrumah's former Ghana, begins to replace the idle or non-existent capitalist entrepreneur, and to do so quite without working-class democracy or support. Stalinist state methods begin to emerge — yet the Stalinist party is nowhere present.

Nor is this all. The central Leninist thesis commands that the revolution be led by the proletarian party at the head of the peasantry. In real life, in Poland, in Hungary, in Czechoslovakia, in Rumania, in Bulgaria, a statized transformation has taken place in which both workers and peasants have been passive observers, while the whole operation has been conducted by a party, a state, a police and a military bureaucracy.

"Salami socialism," to use Rakosi's cynical but expressive phrase, the technique of slicing off the bourgeoisie in layers by means of the forces of the bourgeois state, infiltrated from within, is in fact not a socialist technique at all. The precedent is clear and beyond question. It is that of Mussolini following the March on Rome in 1922 and Hitler following his installation as Reich Chancellor in 1933.

These facts in themselves are immensely damaging to the Communist world view. They do not exhaust the list. The greatest revolutionary transformation in world history, the Chinese overturn, was not only made in opposition to the "advice" of the Communist party of the Soviet Union, it was also a transformation effected by a military civil war based on the peasantry in which the working class played no part at all. The Chinese experience does not stand alone. Castro's revolution, itself opposed by the Cuban Communist Party, possessed an agrarian-military character which cannot be fitted within the framework of Marxist-Leninist thought.

Nor have the Russian-Chinese, and one might add, Yugoslav doctrinal divisions proved to be the end. In the years since 1945 the Russian-imposed regimes in Eastern Europe have been able to create new ruling bureaucratized strata of their own, with specific state and sectarian interests to defend as against those of the USSR. To the extent, as in Albania, Czechoslovakia and Rumania, that these bureaucratic groups have been able increasingly to maintain themselves *independently* of the Communist party of the Soviet Union, so separate and specific doctrinal and state interest disputes and divisions emerged. The level of development, historical and cultural traditions, economic problems of the Soviet bloc territories differ. To deny that in the future these differences will increasingly assume doctrinal form would be to deny the validity of the materialist conception of history.

"Just as our opinion of an individual is not based on what he thinks of himself, so we cannot judge of . . . a period of transformation by its own consciousness," wrote Marx in his *Contribution to the Critique of Political Economy.* "On the contrary, this consciousness must be rather explained from the conditions of material life, from the existing conflict between the social forces of production and the relations of production."[20]

Revolutions made without the Party (Algeria), revolutions made in opposition to the Party (Cuba), revolutions made with a peasant and not a proletarian party (China), revolutions made without either workers or peasants (Eastern Europe), revolutions made against the Party (Hungary), near-revolutions made against the Party from within the Party (Czechoslovakia) — these illustrate the contradictions which Communist dogma can no longer resolve or explain away.

The Nasser dictatorship in Egypt, strangely enough, gives a real clue to the so far unrevealed character of Communist regimes. War is a great forcing house of economic and political development. In a backward society the army is frequently the group most highly organized and educated in modern technique, a condition forced upon it by external circumstances. As such, it is both impressed by foreign superiority and dismayed by the backwardness of its own social base. Significant sections of the officer corps incline to national revival. As in Egypt, the hierarchic character of the officer corps, now extended, comes to form a spinal column for the state. The revolution is controlled, hierarchic, the masses are excluded, yet the social structure changes in a statized direction. Externally, a superficial similarity with the structural aims of socialism may be perceived. Internally, in social content, this is almost entirely lacking.

Exchange the army for the Communist party hierarchy and one finds the closest parallel with Eastern Europe.

The past characteristics of the Stalinist regimes have been those of backward and primitive societies accumulating capital at a rapid rate by means of statized economy. "All this

---

20. Karl Marx, Preface to *A Contribution to the Critique of Political Economy* (London, 1904), p. 12.

led to a system which today we call bureaucratic centralism," writes Oskar Lange in a description of postwar development of the Polish economy. "After a time this system becomes, to some extent an independent factor, growing beyond necessity by its own inertia and interested in deepening and spreading centralized methods of administration in the national economy. In time a social stratum was created with marked interests and opinions. It began to function as an independent factor in the national economy, in social relations and political life. Bureaucratic centralist methods in our country were methods of building socialism with the help of war economy, technical means which in certain situations during wars are also used by capitalist states. . . ."[21]

If we excise the reference to "building socialism" (which plays the same role for the Communist hierarchy as the "hereafter" for the Catholic church) the quotation from Lange gives an excellent account of the development of postwar Eastern European economy and of the ruling group. Stalinist ideology stands revealed as no more than a revised version of the Protestant ethic updated to fit a collectivist age. The Party and its bureaucratic apparatus substitutes itself for the working class and the "dictatorship of the proletariat" in the same way as Nasser's army substitutes itself for the "people" and the "nation."

Yet if this is socialism, then every army represents the dictatorship of the common soldier over the officer caste. If this is socialism, then our prisons are hitherto unrecognized prototypes of a planned society. The early socialists declared that property is socialist *because* it is owned by a workers' state, that is the organized working class in power. "The Stalinists declared that the state is socialist simply *because* it owns the property."[22] If that were so, the Catholic Church would be a socialist institution, the Peru of the Inca's and Pharaoh's Egypt both socialist states.

21. Oskar Lange, *Some Problems Relating to the Polish Road to Socialism* (Warsaw, 1957), p. 13.

22. Max Shachtman, *The Bureaucratic Revolution* (New York, 1962), p. 237.

Nor can it be argued that, like toffee and chocolate, socialism comes in varied brands dressed in different wrappings.
To argue that under one brand of socialism the workers may
rule and under another they may be enslaved is to deprive
the word "socialism" of all its meaning. One might as well
argue "that there are two brands of freedom, one in which
you are free and the other in which you are in jail." [23]

THE BUREAUCRATIC STAGE OF SOCIALISM

The true perception of Soviet reality has unfortunately
proved difficult for all sections of the socialist movement.
The world continues to treat the Soviet regime of 1970 as if,
despite aberrant failings, it remained essentially the same as
that of October 1917, an error as gross as equating the France
of Louis Phillipe with that of the Revolution of 1789.

The difficulty has been enhanced by the belief that in his
views on sociological development Marx outlined only three
stages, ancient, feudal and capitalist, whereas he had explicitly considered a fourth, "Asiatic," as anterior to all the
others. [24] This has led, in turn, to the fallacious belief that
property relations alone were the key to class rule as in the
case of slave, feudal and capitalist societies and to the total
neglect of the historical evidence for a further "functional"
mode of exploitation. As a result, otherwise intelligent and
honest persons, having proved to themselves that Russian
society was not capitalist, felt justified in asserting that it
must be both proletarian and socialist, a quite unjustified
and un-Marxist assumption.

In reality, history offers numerous examples, among them
those of Pharaoh's Egypt, Ancient China, India and pre-
conquest South American civilizations, within which social
domination was based less on property than on bureaucratic
functions, and this in a fashion which offers a striking and
illuminating parallel with modern Soviet society.

The essential thesis is simple to understand. In certain
climates and locations land is of little productive value with-

23. *Ibid.*, p. 278.

24. See Karl Marx, *Preface to the Critique of Political Economy* (London,
    1904), p. 13.

out water. The provision of water requires large-scale irrigation. A high level of technique, the capacity to deploy large
forces of labor in irrigation projects, the creation of a highly
centralized bureaucratic apparatus, become the preconditions
for the supply of water to the would-be rural producer. Real
power lies with the water "supply" rather than the land
"ownership." Water "supply" is a bureaucratic function. The
bureaucracy emerges as the ruling group. A vast, static
hierarchic, immensely powerful state machine, as in ancient
Egypt and the Chinese mandarinate now emerges. Exploitation exists but on a bureaucratic rather than on a property
base. The regime may last in this form for thousands of
years. [25]

One may well argue that in the twentieth century, the
complexity of society makes necessary a bureaucratic apparatus in the form of scientists, technologists, administrators, economists, propagandists, police, government and political functionaries who interpose themselves inevitably between the worker and his product in a similar fashion to that
of the ruling bureaucracy in former "Asiatic" society. The
intellectuals' monopoly of education in Marxist terms constitutes a form of property right by which they dominate
society. If this be so, then Stalinist society emerges as the
crude prototype of a new regressive social order. The Stalinist
parties manifest themselves as the nuclei of the new ruling
caste; the power monopoly of the Communist party of the
Soviet Union stands revealed as quite analogous to that of
the priestly caste in ancient Egypt. The phenomenon of
Stalinism thus becomes explicable as a manifestation of a
new force in its own right (which it plainly is) and not a degeneration from something quite different (which by now it
quite plainly is not.)

Such a hypothesis would give an excellent explanation of
the failure of all opposition Communist groups. Uniformly
under the illusion that they are defending "true Communism," they are in fact no more than idealistic enthusiasts
who have made the stereotype error of mistaking the move-

---

25. See for example, Karl A. Wittfogel, *Oriental Despotism* (Yale, 1957).

ment's ideological *form* for its true but concealed *reality*. In such circumstances the possibility of "true Communism" (whether of Trotskyist, Guevarist, Dubcek or any other variety) over the "degenerate" version, simply does not exist.

The treatment of the Communist ruling group by the state apparatus also becomes explicable. The members of the ruling group, like those of a feudal aristocracy, may be exiled, imprisoned or executed by the faction in command. They always retain more in common with one another than with the mass below. Imre Nagy, to whose courage and devotion one must pay full tribute, was no more prepared to raise the masses against the party than would have been any feudal lord to stir a peasant jacquerie against his king. Dubcek's rebellion, important though it was, sought always to remain within the court of the Czar. Rehabilitation, restoration with full privileges to the ruling group, is the prospect always open to those who survive the ultimate sanction. Once restored, they become as much a part of the power structure as any feudal lord restored to his confiscated estates after a forced exile in a foreign land.

The roots of such a development can certainly be traced to Leninism. Yet to argue that they are an inevitable consequence would be as unsound as to suggest that a man must die of *every* germ which transitionally takes hold of his body. What is plainly more important is that with two Popes, one in Peking and another in Moscow, with rebellious bishoprics appearing in most corners of the globe, the ideological uniformity of Stalinism has irrevocably broken down. The state interests of different ruling groups must in the nature of things continue to accelerate this process of fission. The ideological schema of Stalinism ever more plainly fail to fit the facts. Stalinism progressively abandons the whole field of scientific explanation to enter that of mysticism and "ideology." The characteristics and behavior of Stalinist parties and states prove capable of explanation without the necessity of crediting them with even a shred of socialist purpose. The domination which Stalinism has wielded over large sections of the labor movement is about to end.

In these circumstances, how prophetic sound the words of

Rosa Luxemburg, written in her critique of the Russian Revolution, completed in the closing months of 1918. "Socialism," declared Rosa Luxemburg, "by its very nature cannot be built by decree. . . . Without general elections, without unrestricted freedom of press and assembly . . . public life gradually falls asleep, a few dozen party leaders of inexhaustible energy and boundless experience direct and rule . . . a dictatorship to be sure; not the dictatorship of the proletariat, however, but only the dictatorship of a handful of politicians, that is the dictatorship in the bourgeois sense. . . ."

The socialist revolution, a socialist society, involves of necessity the self-administration of production and of society by the citizens and the producers on their own behalf and not by any self-appointed clique claiming to rule in their place. Viewed in retrospect the "Soviet Experience" appears significant not as a model for others to follow (as previously has widely been thought) but rather as indicative to a series of colossal errors they ought at all costs to avoid. It is the failure to appreciate and act upon this lesson that, more than any other factor, has led to the isolation and sterility of socialism in large areas of the modern world, not least in the United States where the Russian model could least of all be in any sense relevant. Socialists must live with the fact that there exist no textbook recipes for either revolution or socialist construction. The Soviet-Communist party experience is irretrievably exploded. Recognition of this fact is the precondition for any progress of the socialist movement not only in the United States but in all countries of the capitalist world.

March 1970

Behind the Polish Upheavals

Zbigniew Byrski

No one — not Gomulka nor Brezhnev, nor Western sovietologists — foresaw the strikes and riots of December 1970 in Poland. In the West, it was widely thought that the Communist system had succeeded in thwarting all possibilities of resistance. In Communist countries those who revolted and those who suppressed the revolt had assumed on the basis of previous experience that security forces, experts in preventing or crushing resistance, could control the mechanisms of rebellion.

Powerlessness, resulting from a conviction that nothing could be changed, was thought to be the guarantor of political stability. This pessimism was reinforced by the fact that people living under Communism, though undernourished, don't go hungry; though underclothed and living in poorly heated apartments, don't dress in rags and freeze. The masses receive little but are not deprived of everything. They are not pushed beyond the limits of endurance. Every Pole who is not in prison still has a lot to lose: he is not in the position of the character in Solzhenitsyn's novel who told his persecutor: "I am free since you deprived me of everything."

Thus, the perspective of revolt seemed hopeless. It should be clear now that such a judgement is much too simple. The possibility of popular action is real and must be considered, not only to understand the latest occurences in Poland but also the future of Eastern Europe and the USSR.

Totalitarian rule in Communist countries is unsettled. Since Stalin's death it has been subjected to those ebbs and flows of liberalism popularly called the "thaw." In Poland, since 1959, the thaw has been chilled by pressure from the bureaucracy, pressure which culminated in the anti-Semitic purges of the Party and the Administration in 1967-1968. The purges ended in 1969 with a large-scale exodus of Poles of Jewish origin, but "dividends" in the form of a terrorized population continued to some degree. Yet, although the screws were tightened and more liberal voices suppressed, there was no return to the mass arrests of Stalin's time. Terror halted at the prison door. A Pole could be destroyed economically and socially, but as long as he had not protested publicly he remained free.

When a totalitarian regime penetrates and controls all areas of life and renders opposition impossible, even underground, a sense of misery and resentment is repressed since its expression is dangerous for personal safety. This forced self-restraint results in an increasing desire for revenge. Such frustration can produce an explosion and that is exactly what happened in Poland in December 1970.

The earnings of dockworkers in Gdansk, Szczecin, Slupsk and Gdynia were not lower than average. On the contrary, they were higher. These workers did not go hungry. They had free medical care and were clothed, which by Communist standards means a great deal. They had free education for their children, and although their standard of living was not to be compared with the workers in the United States, England or France, it was not so low as to cause despair. In other words, the increase in the prices of food, fuel and clothing before Christmas meant lowering their already low standard of living but not to such an extent that they would be inclined to risk strikes and demonstrations which usually ended in a massacre or in bloodless but severe police repression. It was the government's deception and lies that exhausted people's patience; clumsy political lies which attempted to present the price increases as a necessity, the result of well-considered economic policies serving the interests of working people.

In Poland, as well as in other countries of the Communist bloc, the repertory of falsehoods is extensive and touches almost all fields of life. In the past, particularly during the most vicious period of Stalinism, Poles had tolerated all kinds of propaganda falsehoods which presented each new assault as a victory for the working masses. Why did they start losing their patience now?

During Stalin's terror, opposition to officially proclaimed "truth" resulted not only in economic repression (loss of a job) but also in imprisonment. Now, the threat of prison has disappeared and it will not return because, even under Communism, people cannot work under threat of exile, imprisonment or execution. All that remains is the threat of economic reprisals and that has turned out to be insufficient to maintain order and discipline.

As will all government decrees which worsen the living conditions of the people, the one of December 1970 was accompanied by a wide "explanation campaign," i.e., government-proclaimed lies conveyed by radio, the press, television and by Party orators at open or closed meetings. It was carried on by professionals for whom lying is as rewarding a profession as medicine is for doctors. But trouble arose among Party activists, not all of whom are paid functionaries, some of whom refused to participate. They understood that false propaganda could only worsen a tense situation. These activists were not essentially motivated by considerations of honesty but were simply afraid of the reaction of the masses; and when people in Poland start fearing the masses more than the Party, crisis is imminent.

Based on the experience of the last 15 years, there were two popular theories in the West about Communist countries. The first was that since the Communist bloc was attempting to approximate the industrial level of developed capitalist countries, at least in some fields of industry, Stalinist terror as a system of rule was no longer possible. The second said that the government, given its total control, would be able to maintain the stability of the system without resorting to mass terror so long as it provided the people with minimal subsistence.

The first view still has merit but the second has been exploded by the December events in Poland. The Polish government did provide minimum subsistence for its people, but that did not satify certain sections of the working class, and despite the fact that their material situation was not tragic and that there were undeniable risks involved, the workers revolted against the government. What followed was intervention by the army and the militia and a further escalation of events which ended with government concessions, one of which was the revocation of the economic incentive plan.

A concession of even greater importance was the cancellation of food price increases, something which Edward Gierek, Gomulka's successor, originally had no intention of granting but which he and the new leadership were forced to do a month later when the women in textile factories in Lodz went on strike in February 1971. This act was, in fact, a retreat forced on the government exclusively by pressure from the masses, the first time the people's struggle against Communist bureaucracy has been so effective since the period of the big thaw in 1956. (The demise of Gomulka and his crew cannot be exclusively considered a response to mass pressure since there were other factors involved — in-fighting within the Party elite and a split in the leadership.) These developments contributed to a growth of self-confidence among workers in Communist countries who, in recent years, seemed completely dependent on the good or bad will of their rulers.

BUREAUCRACY VS. THE PEOPLE

The recent events generally signify a growing crises of East European social systems. At the root of the crisis is a conflict which may be defined as the difficulty of maintaining unlimited bureaucratic rule in a society which emphasizes greater productivity while, at the same time, the people demand more freedom and an improved standard of living. The difficulty of satisfying these contradictory demands constitutes the very essence of the problem, a problem that has been chronic since the end of Stalinist rule when it became

obvious that the Communist countries were too developed
economically to be ruled by Stalinist methods. The conflict
does not always take the form of sharp crisis. The fact that
periods of political stability are relatively long and moments
of sharp crises sudden but short, blurs the otherwise obvious
truth that the conflict between the aspirations of the bureaucracy and the interests of the people cannot be resolved. It
can only be muted by dulling the sharp edges of some particular antagonism between the bureaucracy and the people. The
main hindrance to the cultural development of these nations
is the structure of the system itself: the monopoly of political-
economic power where goods markets and money markets are
controlled by the same center.

The interdependence of the two foundations of totalitarian
power — the economic system and its political-cultural super-
structure — is obvious. That interdependence does not mean
that it is impossible to make concessions in one field without
making them in the other. On the contrary, the bureaucracy,
without compromising the governing principles of totalitarianism, has more freedom to maneuver in economic matters
than in political ones so that, although it cannot afford to
permit a widening of democracy, it can easily satisfy some of
the people's economic demands.

During the past 18 years, it has managed to retreat many
times and to make concessions to the working masses. In
various countries, including the USSR, Communist governments, without compromising their preference for capital
investment, have actually reduced the sums invested in this
field in favor of greater production of consumer goods. They
have temporarily halted or reduced export quotas when the
situation in consumer goods industries reached a critical
level. The simultaneous attempts, from time to time, to decentralize and to increase the independence of individual enterprises mitigates the absurdities of central planning. Those
tendencies, whose spokesmen have been the so-called liberal
economists (of the Liberman type in the USSR), predominate
periodically, but as soon as the most urgent needs are satisfied
they are abandoned in favor of the old methods. "Liberalization of the economy," unlike political liberalization, has al-

ways been introduced at exclusive meetings of economists under the watchful eye of the *apparatchiki* who take care that the reforms remained within limits dictated by the bureaucratic power monopoly. In other words, there were *controlled reforms with no danger of escalation,* unlike the attempts at political liberalization. The latter are substantially more dangerous since they contain the threat of a chain reaction. Even limited concessions in this field not only embolden but facilitate further demands.

The difference between risking liberalization in the economy (within limits) and the attempt to weaken the Party's supremacy is obvious. To the displeasure of the bureaucracy, the events in Poland revealed, however, two facts of life: first, that economic demands are impossible without accents of political rebellion and second, that economic maneuvering is inadequate to meet those demands.

"The press is lying" is the slogan that was used by Polish students during their March 1968 demonstrations when they tried, with some success, to set fire to the building of the Polish daily, *Zycie Warszawy* (Warsaw Life) — a typical political incident. Two and a half years later, demands for political freedom were voiced by Baltic Coast workers as early as the second day of their strike. The political aspect of the strike should not be surprising. Each strike in Poland, directed against the only employer, the government, is by nature not simply economic. For a strike to have some chance of success, it cannot limit itself to factory or dock establishments, because the strikers would soon be isolated since there are no genuine trade unions, the normally active instruments of economic struggle. Trade unions in Communist countries are simply extensions of the government administration. To win a strike, workers must go out into the streets or, if they are strong enough, force the authorities to come to the factory. Either is a political act. And that is what the dockworkers did in December 1970. Once they went into the streets, the confrontation with the militia and later with the army was only a question of hours. If the dockworkers of Gdansk and Szezecin did not put the torch to the press buildings it was only because they were busy burning the Party and Security buildings. This was the heightened level of political struggle and proof that the decisive intention to win an economic strike logically develops into a political and revolutionary struggle. For 120 years Marxists have regarded the fusion of the economic and the political as the basis of any class struggle achieving a higher level. After all, Polish workers learned something in Party schools; at least they learned that the class enemy — Communist bureaucracy — has two faces: economic and political.

The Jaszcuk-Gomulka plan of economic incentives, which new Party leader Gierek was forced to rescind, was one of many unsuccessful attempts to lead Poland out of its economic impasse. It was neither worse nor better than previous plans. It suffered, however, from a critical fault: failure to tell the workers anything specific that could convince them of its probable success. Previous experience had led them to believe, and rightly so, that such "incentive plans" would only increase their work load without producing any benefits for them.

There is no reason to believe that the new Gierek crew has any effective plan for improving the economic situation. The so-called "new era" promised by the new leadership has been preceded by many "new eras" in the past which brought nothing but brief relaxation. Relaxation has taken place already, not because of any economic program but as a result of the increased supply of domestic consumer goods subtracted from export quotas and of reduced aid to some distant allies. This does not augur any economic breakthrough since the root of economic ills lies much deeper — in the unchanged economic structure of the country.

It is hard to tell what kind of people Gierek and his associates are, not that the intellectual qualifications of the new leadership would be of any importance. In a system functioning badly but possessing the potential dynamic for growth and change, the leader's personality could become the lever for releasing those possibilities. Unfortunately, what is characteristic of Communism is not so much its actual economic failure and other accompanying misfortunes, but the fact that it impedes the regenerating mechanism. For the past 15 years, the Communist parties have considered and still consider all attempts to reform their system dangerous. We must agree that they are absolutely correct.

SOCIAL BASES OF NEW LEADERSHIP

Gierek's opportunities do not lie in the economic or political fields. In economics, his maneuvering possibilities are very limited. As for politics, attempts at liberalization would be tantamount to playing with fire. Nevertheless, the new leadership has a wide and unique opportunity to maneuver in the Communist camp. It has a chance to balance the social forces by using these four existing factors: the small-scale individual peasantry; the unshaken position of the Catholic Church; the country's ethnic unity and the power of the peasant background of the Party elite.

Of course, these factors exist in all Communist bloc countries. Poland, however, is the only country where the Party leadership can benefit from the presence of all four elements; where even the position of the Church, hitherto weakening the power of the Party, can now be used to strengthen it. The core of the problem is that a favorable situation has developed for the Polish Communist Party which enables it to muster a combination of forces consisting of the Party bureaucracy, individual peasants and the Church against hostile urban industrial workers and the intelligentsia.

In addition, the ethnic uniformity that was achieved as a result of the expulsion of Polish Jews, including a large group of intellectuals, is favorable for the Party. The combination of factors is a result of the degeneration of Communism as an ideology, the conservatism and provincialism of the Church, the backward social attitudes of the peasantry and the reactionary posture of the Party bureaucracy primarily interested in maintaining its hegemony. For a better understanding of the situation, let us look at the changes in the composition of those forces which were hostile to the Party and those which supported it when it came to power.

When the Communist party took power in Poland in 1945, it had no support among the people. Its only support came from the Soviet Union and a hastily manufactured Security Police. A relatively moderate attitude toward the Party was taken by the numerically small radical intelligentsia which realized that the only alternative to Communism in Poland was the extreme right. These radical intellectuals accepted Communism as the lesser evil, believing that after the war Communism would develop more humanitarian features. The conservative peasantry was actively hostile to the new power, distrusting land reform and suspecting, not without justification, that the next step would be collectivization. Hostile also were the middle class, an overwhelming majority of intellectuals and the workers, among whom the Party had very little influence.

Not only did the Party lack a social base, it did not even have a substitute for it which, under Communism, is traditionally a bureaucracy. The Party machinery was embryonic and the fledgling state administration looked on the Party as an intruder. But the most important hostile element and the most difficult to neutralize was the Catholic Church.

Without going into the shift of social forces that has occurred since then, it can be said that the social composition of the anti-Party forces is now completely different. The socio-radical group which was a small minority among the intellectuals is now a majority. It is the intellectuals' devotion to social radicalism that makes them decisively hostile to the Party and its totalitarian government. As for the Polish bourgeoisie, it no longer exists. It vanished and with it the main reservoir of anti-Communist forces vanished as well. Small businessmen and artisans, deprived of the necessary supply of raw materials which could only be obtained from government sources, vegetated and no longer constitute any significant social force. They operate a semilegal black market tolerated by the administration. This *lumpen* bourgeoisie is a pathological social product of Communism, swindling the government and the people.

The workers do not constitute a homogeneous group. They are divided and their material situation is determined by the type of production in which they are engaged and the size of the establishment. For example, there is a difference between the material situation of a coal miner (not because of special attention by Edward Gierek, the former Party Secretary for

Silesia, but because coal was and is the main source of foreign currency for Poland) and that of a cooperative worker. There is a difference between workers in large industrial combines and those in light industry. Despite these differences, the working class as a whole has a decisively negative attitude toward the present system. Its reluctance to engage in active struggle is the result of its feeling of powerlessness and also the lack of an alternative to the system. Along with the intellectuals, workers constitute the most dangerous reservoir of anti-Communism. Since the position of the working class, especially those workers in heavy industry, is of key importance to the Party, it is an object of special concern to the government and the security apparatus. For the Party to achieve its ends, it must isolate the workers politically from the intellectuals. Previous experience (especially Czechoslovakia's) demonstrates that an alliance of these two forces could be explosive.

About 35% of Poland's population works in agriculture, 84% on individual farms. The period of collectivization begun in 1948-1949 ended in 1956 with a collapse of the collectives and a return to private farming. Poland is the only country in the Communist bloc (Yugoslavia is not part of the bloc) in which the overwhelming majority of peasants have their own farms. This exception to the monopolistic economic pattern is unusual since it allows a certain part of the population a large margin of economic freedom. That freedom, however, is limited, since the peasants, although they manage and work on their own farms, do not reap the benefits of a free market. They are obliged to deliver a substantial part of their wheat and dairy products to the state at government set prices. Mutually agreed-upon livestock prices are closer to free market prices since a large share of meat products is assigned for export and the government seeks to increase production, thereby offering relatively decent prices. A Polish peasant lives under far better conditions than a Soviet *kolkhoznik*. But, as is true for other social groups, his situation is not determined solely by economic factors.

Polish peasants are deeply attached to Catholicism, probably more so than any other group in Poland. It must be made clear that what is generally called "religion" in Eastern Europe has little relationship to a world outlook or confession of faith, except for a small group of Catholic intellectuals. Polish peasants are Catholics in a behavioral sense. They are deeply attached to the ceremonial and religious traditions which constitute a practice once rooted in holy belief; but dogma itself is almost unknown to the believers. This is true, by the way, not only for religion but for other areas, as well. People appear to be more attached to political and social rituals than to the principles that underly their philosophical or ideological basis.[1]

Because the Communist party did not understand that the power of Catholicism in Poland does not reside in the vitality of its dogmas but in the attraction of the rituals, it developed an unsuccessful (and therefore abandoned) strategy for fighting religion in Poland. Besides, the Church won its long struggle against the Party because it constitutes the only legal crack in the political monopoly of the Party. This was not of as much importance for the peasants as it was for the Polish intelligentsia, which looked on the Church as its ally in the fight for human rights.

After a quarter of a century of efforts designed to undermine the role of the Church in Poland, the Communist party has now reached the conclusion that since it cannot win over the Church it must cooperate with it and make the Church an ally. The "dogmatic" Gomulka was less suited to this role than the "flexible" Gierek. Gomulka and especially the Party ideologist, Kliszko, were somewhat burdened with old Marxist "prejudices" and had not accepted all the consequences of the most important Communist "doctrine": everything contributing to safeguarding the totalitarian power of the Party is right and good. If cooperation with the Church serves this aim, then this kind of alliance is worth far-reach-

1. If Pope Paul changed the dogma of the Trinity, it would cause a rebellion among Vatican theologians but millions of Catholics would not be affected. If, however, the ecumenical synod came to the conclusion that Jesus Christ was born, not on December 25, but in July, Catholics who would have to celebrate Christmas in the heat of summer would probably ignore the decision or leave the Church.

ing concessions. This discovery was made only recently on the central level. On the local level, Gierek's subordinates long ago decorated Party offices with renditions of St. Barbara, patron saint of the Polish miners. That on the same wall was a picture of the First Secretary did not disturb anyone, least of all the tradition-minded Silesians. Most probably they thought that First Secretaries come and go but St. Barbara remains. The alliance with the Church seems more urgently needed today than at any other time.

Just as Poland is atypical in the Communist bloc, the Polish Church is atypical in the Catholic realm. While the Church does not claim to occupy the mighty position it held in pre-war years, it remains convinced that it is synonymous with the character and aspirations of the Polish people. The Polish Church has not moved in the direction of the liberalized policies of Pope John XXIII, but rather in the opposite direction: the episcopate in Poland was and is against pluralism in politics, morality and philosophy.

It is possible then that given present conditions, the Polish Catholic Church may meet the Party more than halfway. The Church was successful in its long fight but not without suffering some serious losses. Material losses resulting from separation of Church and State, limitation of its activities in the field of public education, and the constant chicanery of Party and administrative organs were of secondary importance. Persecution has never harmed the Church. On the contrary, it has always emerged stronger. Rather, it is overprotection by the government that might cause harm, just as overprotection of the Orthodox Church under Czarism reduced it to atrophy, making it easy prey for the Bolsheviks.

The Church can exist without mass media, without access to public education, so long as priests are uttering God's words from their pulpits. But the Church cannot exist without a priesthood, just as an army cannot exist without noncommissioned officers and soldiers. In Poland, the number of candidates for the priesthood dropped to an alarming degree during the last decade, not because of difficulties created by the Party but rather because of social changes in the countryside. Up to the postwar period, the farm regions provided most of the candidates for Church seminaries because the road to the priesthood, an honorable occupation, was more accessible to poor peasant families than the difficult and more expensive road to other professions — medicine and the law. Since the war, the situation has changed. Industrial development, free education and urban growth has caused an extensive flow of youth from the countryside to urban centers. Because of these factors, plus the Party's desire to change the social structure of the intelligentsia, the priesthood ceased to attract even the sons of the poorer peasant families. The more able strived to become engineers, economists or doctors. The less talented went into government and Party jobs. Losing this prime reservoir of candidates for the priesthood was the most painful, if unintentional blow, inflicted on the Church. It has placed the Church in a position so difficult that now, more than ever, it may seek to cooperate with the Party.

The second factor contributing to Church cooperation is the further transformation of Poland's ethnic structure. This transformation has strengthened the Church. As a result of postwar territorial changes, Poland has become virtually an ethnically homogeneous country. There remained a group of Jewish Poles who, because of their social position, had a rather substantial influence on Polish political and cultural life. The obvious desire of the Party bureaucracy to remove Jews from these fields concurred with the traditional position of the Polish Church. Although the Church did not approve the brutal anti-Jewish Party propaganda in 1967-1969, and although it was against the policies which caused a number of Poles of non-Polish origin to leave the country, the results of these policies reinforced traditional Polish Catholic attitudes: the identification or equation of Polishness with Catholicism. That such a notion should exist in the second half of the twentieth century may be surprising but although every equation between Poles and Catholicism was, is and will remain a myth, it is a fact that Cardinal Wyszynski expressed just that view in 1957, when the government introduced religious instruction in the public schools for a short time on a voluntary basis.

AN ALLIANCE BETWEEN PARTY AND CHURCH?

Can differences in ideology and world view present an obstacle to the formation of the alliance between Party and Church? For the Party — certainly not; for it, the only obstacle is the necessity for preserving the Party monopoly threatened by the Church. It is much the same problem that exists in international relations between the capitalist 'and Soviet Communist camps. Soviet imperialism has global ambitions but, since it has been unable to accomplish that goal in 54 years, it must negotiate, coexist and even cooperate. Such necessities cause adversaries to limit their political ambitions. These same factors at work in international relations are present to an even greater extent within one country since the opponents are not separated by borders and oceans but live under the same roof. Since, after 25 years of open or behind-the-scenes warfare between the Church and the Party in Poland, neither could force the other side to capitulate, they must reach some compromise.

Both have been weakened by the fight. The Party has dangerous opponents undermining the Communist establishment: the workers and the intellectuals. Through the generations, the Church has supported existing social orders so long as their ideology did not challenge the basis of faith and infringe on the Church's rule over souls. Since the Communist world is now devoid of any ideology, the conditions for rapprochement, even symbiosis, are the best. That is why "Radio Vatican" could say in a broadcast for Polish listeners on February 12, 1971: "There is no obstacle to a dialogue between believers and non-believers. Our joint forces can also build socialism . . . fight against alchoholism and show our common concern to strengthen Poland's position in the international forum" *(Zycie Warszawy,* February 18, 1971).

A "dialogue between believers and non-believers" is, of course, a dialogue between Church and Party. In the present situation, the side which has to make concessions is the Party which finds itself in a critical situation and is forced to take remedial steps. The Catholic Church, with a 15-century rich tradition of struggles and pacts with worldly powers, will not be a weak party at the negotiating table.

The growth of nationalistic tendencies is a well-known phenomenon in Communism. It appeared and developed along with the Stalinization of the Soviet Union and the strengthening of the bureaucracy. Recognizable in the thirties, these nationalistic tendencies do not result, as many sovietologists in the West believe, from the general evolution of Communism in which international principles were compromised in favor of patriotism. The nationalism of the Communist parties in power is simply one of the means of maintaining a totalitarian system, a further sympton of freeing itself of ideology as impeding ballast. There is no reason why Communist parties should not take advantage of nationalism since it always finds such an easy response in the masses. However, considering the fact that the main value of this nationalism is preservation of the bureaucracy which needs the Soviet Union as its most important protector, it is never used to reflect unfavorably on the Russians. Therefore, despite the great possibilities of a rapprochement between Party and Church, nationalism in Poland, controlled and directed by the Party is not so much help as hindrance.

The Polish Church is traditionally nationalistic and all attempts to induce it to treat Russia differently than it treats other nations have to end in failure. Given Polish circumstances, the most natural outlet for national xenophobia, which always goes hand in hand with nationalism, may be the Russians.

The Party bureaucracy is the factor which guarantees self-perpetuation of the present social system. This heir of the former Polish middle class did not come into being as the result of a revolution or revolutionary change. The fact that it came into being as the result of a single act in a favorable international constellation weakened its position from the start.

By contrast, before the Soviet bureaucracy had degenerated and was reduced to the function of proprietor and guard of the new system, it had a short but heroic period as a revolutionary Party, enjoying great prestige among the Russian peasantry and working class.

The genealogy of the Polish *apparatchiks* did not even

allow them this modest possibility, because in Poland there was never a revolution. The Polish Party bureaucracy came into being by an order decreed from above; it could never lose authority since it never had it. From the very beginning, in rags or later in riches, it was looked on with contempt and, at best, disdain by all sections of the population. This situation has not changed, even though compared with days gone by the bureaucracy is mightier and more prosperous. Since it has power, it cannot be slighted; it can only be despised.

The Party bureaucracy consisted of a group so badly educated that it used to be referred to as the "semi-intelligentsia." The privileges enjoyed by an *apparatchik* generally remain inversely related to his intellectual qualifications. The same can be said about security functionaries but the police are traditionally rewarded for loyalty in any system, while the bureaucracy is a new creation without tradition and barely tolerated.

Although occupying an important position in the local and central power system, the Party apparatus is numerically small and, unlike the old large middle class, constitutes only a minute part of the population. In addition, it has no broad family ties to other sections of the population — neither with workers nor with intellectuals — and is therefore isolated in certain situations and disappointing and ineffective as we saw in Czechoslovakia. There is no doubt that even the least intelligent *apparatchik* in Eastern Europe is aware of the fact that the highest disposition center of his country is beyond its geographical borders.

Notwithstanding its isolation, the Polish Party apparatus has some opening to society via the peasantry from which the overwhelming number of Party activists stem. The peasantry, although smaller than it used to be, is of particular importance since it constitutes the only normally functioning economic sector and it produces provisions which Poland never has in such sufficient quantities to provide for both the domestic and export markets. In spite of its significant economic role, the peasantry's political role is limited because farmers are dispersed while workers, living and working in urban centers, can more easily act as an organized anti-government power. Aside from that, as already mentioned, the peasants have no compelling reason, nor do they desire, to oppose the authorities. At present, they too are rather a stabilizing factor.

Peasants are conscious of the fact that part of their labor is being pillaged by the bureaucrats. They need only compare the price the government pays them with the market prices. (Of course, this price differential was considerably larger under Stalinism than it is now.) In this situation, one might assume that since the farmer and the worker are both equally robbed by the bureaucracy, there is a common basis for anti-government opposition. The trouble is that the peasants know they cannot win since they cannot organize farmers' strikes. Such action would only result in deep animosities between the city and the countryside; the farmers would be presented as those attempting to starve the workers.

On the other hand, Polish farmers have an opportunity to bargain and obtain higher prices from the government for some of their produce which does not affect the cities. This might mean less income for the State but it is possible because farmers are important to the Communist bureaucracy, not only as food producers but also as a social power which could strengthen its position as a quasiclass. The young (in historical terms), unpopular Party apparatus needs the support of just such a social group which is considered perennial and indestructible. In every country, no matter its social system, such a social group always consists of people living on the land.

Should the bureaucracy-peasant alliance win the support of, better still, the participation of the Church, an even more perennial institution rooted in tradition, the Communist bureaucracy would strengthen its position in quite an unexpected manner. I do not say that these possibilities (which some students of Communism may consider fantastic) will be easily translated into reality. But I believe that they exist only for Poland. It should be sufficient to compare Poland to the Soviet Union where peasants live on collective farms which they would like to escape at the first possible moment, where the Orthodox Church has ceased to exist as an organization which could resist Communism, where the Party has increasing difficulties with the revived nationalistic tendencies of the various peoples constituting the Soviet Union, to come to the conclusion that the possibilities present in Poland do not exist in other Communist countries. What remains true for all the Communist parties is their drive for international stability to safeguard the status quo at any price. So far as that is concerned, Poland is no exception. Poland simply has more favorable conditions for achieving this aim.

May 1971

An Open Letter to the Party

Jacek Kuron and Karol Modzelewski

On November 27, 1964, Jacek Kuron and Karol Modzelweski, both lecturers at Warsaw University, were expelled from the Polish United Workers' Party. The basis for their expulsion was a document they had written analyzing the Polish economic and political system, attacking the regime and calling for workers' democracy. They were tried *in camera* in July 1965. Kuron was sentenced to three years in prison and Modzelewski to three and a half.

Appearing in the pages that follow are major portions of Kuron and Modzelewski's "An Open Letter to the Party," which was written after their original document was confiscated at the time of their arrest.

It is an exciting, extraordinary document, the work of intelligent, principled revolutionaries whose discussion of the new bureaucratic class is the most thoughtful we have seen from socialists in East Europe. And while they are uncompromising in their opposition to the "Eastern central political bureaucracy," they are no less firm in their opposition to Western capitalism. What gives the Open Letter added importance is that it was written by two young men brought up and educated in a closed society.

Their commitment to socialism and democracy is given depth by the high level of their understanding and political

242

sophistication; but Kuron and Modzelewski are obviously more than politically committed socialist revolutionaries. They are men of great personal courage who knew that their Open Letter, with its direct appeal to the Polish working class to resist the Gomulka dictatorship, meant "putting their bodies on the line."

"An Open Letter to the Party" was published in Polish under the title *List Otwarty Do Partii*, copyright Institut Litteraire, S.A.R.I.

THE RULE OF THE BUREAUCRACY

According to official doctrine, we live in a socialist country. This thesis is based on the identification of state ownership of the means of production with social ownership. The act of nationalization transferred industry, transport and banking into social property, and production relations based on social property are allegedly socialist.

This reasoning is Marxist in appearance. In reality, an element fundamentally alien to Marxist theory has been introduced: the formal, legal meaning of ownership. State ownership can conceal various class meanings, depending on the class character of the state. The public sector in the economies of contemporary capitalist countries has nothing in common with social ownership. This is true not only because there exist, beside it, private capitalist corporations, but because the worker in a capitalist state factory is totally deprived of ownership, since he has no real influence in the state and hence no control over his own labor and its product. History has seen examples of class and antagonistic societies in which state ownership of the means of production has prevailed (the so-called Asiatic method of production).

State ownership of the means of production is only a *form* of ownership. It is exercised by those social groups to which the state belongs. In a nationalized economic system only those who participate in, or can influence decisions of an economic nature (such as use of the means of production, the distribution of, and profiting from the product) can affect the decisions of the state. Political power is connected with power over the process of production and the distribution of the product.

To whom does power belong in our state? To one monopolistic Party — the Polish United Workers' Party (PUWP). All essential decisions are made first in the Party, and only later in the offices of the official state power; no important decision can be made and carried out without the approval of the Party authorities. This is called the leading role of the Party, and since the monopolistic Party considers itself the representative of the interests of the working class, its power is supposed to be a guarantee of working class power.

But if we are not to evaluate the system according to what its leaders think and say about themselves, then we must see what opportunities there are for the working class to influence the decisions of the state apparatus.

Outside the Party — none. For the ruling Party is monopolistic. It is impossible for the working class to organize in other parties and, through them, to formulate, propagate and struggle for the realization of other programs, other variants of dividing the national product, political concepts other than those of the PUWP. The prohibition by the ruling Party against organizing the working class is guarded by the entire state apparatus of power and force: the administration, political police, attorney general's office, the courts and also the political organizations led by the Party, which unmask and nip in the bud all attempts to undermine the leading role of the PUWP.

But more than a million Party members are ordinary citizens; among them, several hundred thousand are workers. What are their chances of influencing the decisions of Party and state authorities? The Party is not only monopolistic, but is also organized along monolithic lines. All factions, groups with different platforms, organized political currents, are forbidden within the Party. Every rank-and-file member is entitled to his opinion, but he has no right to organize others who think as he does to follow his program, and he has no right to organize a propaganda and electoral struggle for the realization of that program. Elections to Party offices, to conferences and congresses become fictitious under such conditions, since they do not take place on the basis of different programs and platforms (i.e., an assessment of political alternatives). Exercising political initiative in society demands organization, but in any attempt to exert influence on the decisions of the "top," the mass of rank-and-file Party members is deprived of organization, atomized, and therefore powerless. The only source of political initiative can be — in the nature of things — organized bodies, i.e., the Party apparatus. Like every apparatus, it is organized hierarchically; information flows upward, while decisions and orders are handed down from above. As in every hierarchical apparatus, the fountainhead of orders is the elite, the group of people who occupy conspicuous positions in the hierarchy and who collectively make basic decisions.

In our system, the Party elite is, at one and the same time, also the power elite; all decisions relating to state power are made by it and, in any case, at the top of the Party and state hierarchies there exists, as a rule, a fusion of responsible posts. By exercising state power, the Party elite has at its disposal all the nationalized means of production; it decides on the extent of accumulation and consumption, on the direction of investment, on the share of various social groups in consumption and in the national income; in other words, it decides on the distribution and utilization of the entire social product. The decisions of the elite are independent, free of any control on the part of the working class and of the remaining classes and social strata. The workers have no way of influencing them, nor have Party members in general. Elections to the Sejm and National Councils become fictitious, with only one list of candidates drawn up by the "top" and a lack of any real differences in the programs of the PUWP and the satellite parties (United Peasant Party and Democratic Party). This Party-state power elite, free of any social control and able independently to make all key economic decisions of nationwide importance (as well as all political decisions), we shall call the *central political bureaucracy*.

Membership in the central political bureaucracy is determined by real participation in reaching basic political and economic decisions that are made centrally and are effective on the national scale. It is probably impossible to draw the exact limits of this elite. Fixing its exact limits would require sociological research in an area which is completely taboo. For us, however, the most important thing is not the numerical strength and internal organization of the bureaucracy, but its role in society and in the social process of production.

If the Party rank-and-file is disorganized in terms of influencing the decisions of the bureaucracy it is organized to execute the bureaucracy's orders according to the principles of Party discipline. Whoever opposes it is removed, and outside the Party he has no right to organize and therefore to act. In this way the Party, which at the top of its hierarchy is simply the organized bureaucracy, becomes at the "bottom" a tool for disrupting attempts at resistance by the working class, while at the same time organizing the working class and other social groups in a spirit of obedience to the bureaucracy. The same function is fulfilled by the remaining social organizations directed by the Party, including the trade unions. The traditional organization of workers' economic self-defense, subjected to the leadership of the only organized political force, i.e., the Party, has become an obedient organ of the bureaucracy, that is of state power, both political and economic.

THE GENERAL SOCIAL CRISIS OF THE SYSTEM

No social system has collapsed solely because it exploited and oppressed the masses. On the other hand, no class can maintain its rule for any length of time if it is based only on coercion, victimizing the rest of society.

In the nature of things, the working class is the chief opponent of the bureaucracy. The worker stands on the lowest level of the social hierarchy with everyone from the foreman to the prime minister above him and no one below him. Because the exploitation of the worker constitutes the material basis maintaining the system, the entire apparatus of power and coercion is directed primarily against the working class. This is the way it was and the way it is now. But in the periods 1949-1955 and 1956-1959, the workers' lot improved, though for different reasons in each of these two periods. However, according to official statistical data which we have already cited, in the 1960-1963 period the average real income per capita among families of industrial workers only rose by 2.6% (0.6% yearly on the average). Taking into account that hidden increase in living costs due to changes in lines of goods and, in recent years, the price rise of articles of prime necessity, the standard of living of the working class has actually declined during the last four years. This state of affairs was particularly painful for the majority of families where no one advanced and the number of wage earners did not increase.

The plan for the 1967-1970 period provides for the creation of 1.5 million jobs at the enormous cost of 830-840 billion zloty, set aside for investment. Yet, according to the calculations of the demographers (Holzer's article in *Trybuna Ludu* published before the Fifteenth Plenum of the Central Committee of the PUWP), the increase in the working-age population during that period will amount to 2,000,000. This means that if the plan is fulfilled, there will be no jobs for about 500,000 people. At the Fourth Party Congress, no increases in real wages were promised; from published data (28% increase in individual consumption alongside an 18% increase in employment), one may conclude that, if the plan is executed ideally, the average real wage will increase by about 10%, by about 2% yearly, during the Five Year Plan period. However, Professor Kalecki has shown that necessary raises alone consume nearly 2% of the wage fund every year.

Apart from this, there is a growing differential between the earning levels of workers, on the one hand, and managers, engineers and technicians, on the other. According to official data, in the 1960-1963 period, the average real income per capita in families of white-collar workers employed in industry rose by 11.6%, while the increase for workers' families was only 2.6%. In the Central Committee report to the Fourth Party Congress, it was mentioned that the investment fund has been so calculated as to make possible "at least a stabilization of real wages," that is, on the brink of the inflationary barrier. This means that workers' real wages in the coming five years must be lowered somewhat if the plan is to be realized. But in all the 20 years of the Polish Peoples' Republic, investments always cost more than planned and were never completed within the allotted time. Nothing indicates that the coming Five Year Plan period will be an exception. The sum of 840 billion zloty will probably turn out to be insufficient for carrying out a businesslike program of investment and the collapse of this program will mean a drastic rise in unemployment. It will be necessary to find additional means for the realization of the investment program. Since these means can only be found by subtracting them from the consumption fund, the assumption that real wages can be stabilized will not prove correct. A substantial fall in real wages will result and the inflationary barrier will be broken.

The possibilities of supplementing the investment fund by lowering real wages are limited, however, for economic and political reasons. Therefore, it is likely that the investment program for the 1966-1970 period will not be fulfilled after all and no way will be found of creating the 1.5 million new jobs. The number of people for whom there will be no jobs will then exceed half a million.

The mass proportions of unemployment will probably compel the economic bosses to employ some of these people despite the shortage of jobs. In that case, the nominal wage fund will rise while production will not increase. This will cause a disruption in the balance of the market. Prices will soar and real wages will fall further while hundreds of thousands of people of working age will still find no work.

As can be seen, in a growing crisis the system not only deprives the working class of the prospect of an improved material situation, it is not even able to assure the maintenance of earnings at the present level or the retention of jobs.

By treating social consumption as a necessary evil, the bureaucracy tries to keep the earnings of numerous categories of hired workers at subsistence levels. This includes not only industrial, construction and transport workers, but also the large majority of white-collar employees in telecommunications, the communal economy, trade, the health services, education and the lower echelons of civil service. This mass of low-paid white-collar employees differs in no way from the working class in terms of their material situation and future prospects. Everything we have said about the workers' material conditions of existence when the system is in economic crisis applies to the large majority of all employees outside of agriculture.

Industrialization has brought a substantial improvement in the social and cultural conditions of the working class. Education has become universal and the young have been given an opportunity to advance since university education has become accessible to all. Many of these achievements — state housing at low rents, free medical care, social benefits, etc. — constitute an indispensable part of the historically determined subsistence level, given the low level of the working wage. In crisis conditions, the bureaucracy first limits all expenditures which might be called "investments in the human being" and this hits the poorest categories of the population hardest, the working class, the low-paid white-collar employees and the poorer peasantry.

Despite the very bad housing situation, Poland is one of the last on the European list in constructing housing. It has also adopted a cooperative system which is supposed to supply 60% of the apartments in the next five-year plan. That is why the costs of building apartment houses were transferred from the state budget to individual incomes which means that apartments will not be obtained by those who need them most, but by those who can pay for them. For a worker, whose wages are hardly sufficient to survive, it is practically impossible to get an apartment.

Cuts in cultural expenses together with higher prices in this area cause a decline in cultural activities. Theater audiences are smaller and periodical and book editions, including textbooks, drastically decreased. This particularly hurts workers' families which exist on a minimum subsistence level and for whom the higher prices of books, theater and movie tickets, etc., amount to giving up many elementary cultural goods.

Cuts in expenses for higher education, in particular for scholarships, student cafeterias and dormitories, make it difficult for youngsters from workers', peasants' and lower-middle-class families to attend universities. Their percentage in higher education decreases: a money standard limits their rights to education and social advancement.

In a growing crisis, working conditions inevitably deteriorate. The growing danger of unemployment makes managers and supervisors more willful and greatly facilitates official pressure on the workers. Formerly, exploitation was covered up by compulsory, sloganized and sometimes authentic enthusiasm. The powers-that-be liked to put on overalls and prided themselves on their working-class origins. They decorated shop workers and found it unfitting to pay the manager ten times as much as the worker. Today, the authorities wear elegant suits and the manager who knows best how to squeeze the surplus product out of the workers is a positive hero of socialist construction, while his villa and car are visible symbols of his social prestige and civic virtue. Today, exploitation is evident and visible to all, and its tool is not propaganda or forced enthusiasm but the whip of economic penalty, of administrative coercion and — in cases of organized attempts at resistance — of police violence. Today, the trade unions, jointly with the government and together with the managements, execute resolutions and decisions on firing workers (Operation "R").

Thus the crisis worsens the material, cultural and social situation of the working class, intensifies the degree of its captivity in its place of work and completely deprives it of prospects for the realization of its minimal interest within the framework of prevailing production and social relations. *It forces the working class to come out against the system in defense of the present level of its material and spiritual existence.*

The bureaucracy will not willingly give up to the working class even one zloty and, in conditions of economic crisis and lack of reserves, it has nothing to give up under pressure. In this situation, any large-scale strike action cannot but transform itself into a political conflict with the bureaucracy. For the working class, it is the only way to change its situation. *Today, at a time when the system is going through a general crisis, the interest of the working class lies in revolution:* the overthrow of the bureaucracy and the present relations of production, gaining control over one's own labor and its product, control over the production goals — the introduction of an economic, social and political system based on workers' democracy. The interests of the vast majority of white-collar employees coincide with those of the working class.

For the countryside, the crisis means mass reductions in the number of worker-peasants, the reappearance of rural overpopulation and the loss of sources of income outside agriculture which support poor peasants and a large number of small farms. For the majority of peasants, it means not only a lack of prospects for improvement but an absolute worsening of their material situation and a danger of their farms failing. Only the small minority of rich peasants can benefit from this through an increased supply of cheap labor and cheap land which will open possibilities for capitalization. But even this richest group feels the fiscal pressure of the state as a limitation on its possibilities of accumulation and capitalist development. Therefore, despite the fact that the present agricultural policy is relatively the most suitable from its point of view, its attitude toward the system is hostile and it will not lend active support to the ruling bureaucracy.

If society in general is deprived of perspectives, it is the *youth* who experience this most painfully. Unemployment is a disaster for the working class as a whole but young people just reaching working age are the first to be jobless. Transition to cooperative building deprives the majority of city dwellers of the chance to improve its housing situation, but young people about to marry and start a family find it most difficult to find a place of their own. The danger of rural overpopulation threatens the well-being of the majority of peasants, but would be worst for members of the younger generation who would not find jobs in industry, while at the fathers' or elder brothers' farms they would, at best, have the status of agricultural laborers. Inadequate investments for higher education retard the development of the whole of society, but inflict the greatest damage on the children of workers, peasants and small-town dwellers.

Since the youth are finding it particularly difficult to

secure a place in the life of the community and are among the most seriously hurt by the economic, social, ideological and moral crisis, it constitutes a potentially revolutionary element in every stratum.

It would appear that today the *technocracy* is the chief pillar of bureaucratic power in society since it is bound to the ruling class by its privileges and special role in the productive process. Reality would undoubtedly conform to appearance if this technocracy could achieve its natural aspirations within the framework of the existing system. Before 1956 it was a stratum of badly paid supervisors whose salaries were much smaller than those of the small pre-war groups of administrators at the service of capital. But along with the postwar impetus to industry, a managerial cadre emerged and the directors' chairs were filled by people who owed their advancement, and everything else, to the system.

Today, the technocracy has become a stable stratum conscious of its own interests. It enjoys the privileges of high consumption and is in conflict with the working class in its daily supervisory function and in its hankering for a form of "managerial socialism." On the other hand, we have seen that the class goal of production under the present system is alien to the interests of the technocracy, which acts against the goals set up by the bureaucracy whenever it has an opportunity to exercise any initiative. That is why the managerial stratum is deprived, not only of all influence on general economic decision-making, but also of the right to decide on matters of fundamental significance for its own plants and its own work. In the existing system, the technocrats can be nothing more than executors and supervisors who cannot realize their own aspirations. They yearn for decentralization of management based on the Yugoslav model, thereby seeking a change in the production relations. The slogan, "power to the experts," popular with this group, expresses both the managers' opinion of what the social range of democracy should be in their kind of socialism as well as their hostility toward the existing system and the central political bureaucracy at its head.

The interests of the technocracy, exceeding the limitations

of the existing system, drive it into opposition to the ruling bureaucracy.

We have seen also that the entire working class, the majority of low-paid salaried employees, almost the entire peasantry (with the exception of the richest group), the youth — in other words, the overwhelming majority of the population — have no prospect of improving their lot within the framework of the existing system. On the contrary, the growing crisis worsens their material, social and cultural living conditions. Under these circumstances, the bureaucracy is deprived of social support and must rely on blatant economic, administrative and political coercion which clearly reveals the class nature of its dictatorship. The control of the political police over society is tightened, not because it is again to become a Moloch that will devour the Party itself but because, in all strata, hostility to the ruling bureaucracy is sharpening and any autonomous organization of social forces in this situation signifies mortal danger of the system. The legislation of total Stalinist dictatorship — the so-called "Small Criminal Code" — has been dusted off.

By its very nature, the bureaucracy destroys social initiative since its rule is based on a monopoly of social organization and the atomization of independent social forces. This tendency is reinforced during times of crisis when any authentic social initiative becomes a more dangerous threat to the bureaucracy. Initiatives connected with the development of social thinking and with the enrichment of cultural and ideological life — discussion clubs, cultural societies, etc. — are subjected to strict control and treated by the authorities as a potential danger. The same applies to all signs of independent ideological-political activity and to discussions in the livelier youth and Party organizations, something that the members of the Party and SYU at the university know from their own experience.

Since it no longer has the possibility of imposing its hegemony on the rest of society, the bureaucracy has no ideology of its own; nothing has replaced the official Stalinist doctrine which was shattered in 1956-1957. The bureaucracy justifies its political and economic moves in the name of the

"national interest." The national interest, if it is not the
interest of the various classes and strata in society, can only
be the interest of the class in whose hands state power
resides. No matter how hard the bureaucracy tries to obscure
its class interest by presenting it as the general national
interest, nationalism preached from a position of power in a
period of social crisis has little chance of gaining social support.

Having no official, coherent ideological system, while at
the same time controlling the sum total of collective life and
all forms of ideological life in the country by means of organizational, administrative and police methods, the bureaucracy
seeks to eliminate all signs of ideological independence in a
time of general crisis. For ideology is the consciousness of
people acting socially in conditions of crisis. When the interests of the overwhelming majority of society can no longer
be satisfied within the framework of the system and when
they turn against it, then authentic ideology and social
activity reflecting the interests of given strata must, ultimately, turn against the bureaucracy.

This situation has especially sharp repercussions on the
creative intelligentsia, for its social function is the scientific
formulation of social thought and the artistic expression of
ideas. The ideological crisis in society signifies a crisis in
creativity for this stratum and all attempts to overcome it
and achieve ideological independence for its creative members
are administratively repressed. Engaged scholars, writers
and artists are discriminated against by publishing houses
and cultural policy makers. They are denied access to mass
media, i.e., the chance to practice their profession; socio-
literary periodicals which exhibit even a minimum degree of
independence are replaced by publications which are then
boycotted by the most eminent creative people; the intensification of censorship narrows down still further the already
small margin of professional freedom among the creative
intelligentsia. In this way, the ideological crisis becomes
the source of a crisis in cultural creativity.

The ideological crisis also brings in its wake a crisis of
moral values and norms, especially for youth in the process

of forming their views and ideals. What results is cynicism, crude careerism, hooliganism; mass thefts, too, are not just an economic phenomenon.

As the economic crisis cannot be overcome within the framework of present production relations, so, too, the general social crisis cannot be overcome within the limits imposed by prevailing social relations. A solution is possible only through the overthrow of prevailing production and social relations. *Revolution is a necessity for development.*

No social class sides with the bureaucracy in crisis. At best, the rich peasants and petty bourgeoisie might remain neutral. But only the working class, because of its conditions of life and work, *is compelled* to overthrow the bureaucracy. The essential origins of the economic and social crisis lie, as we have seen, in the production relations that prevail in the sector of heavy industry; that is, in the relations into which the working class and the central political bureaucracy enter mutually in the productive process. Revolution is thus, first of all, the conflict between these two fundamental classes in an industrialized society. That is why the working class must be the chief and leading force of revolution. The revolution that will overthrow the bureaucratic system will be a proletarian revolution.

It is often said that a tremendous power apparatus, having at its disposal modern means of material coercion, is sufficient for the ruling class to perpetuate its power even without any social backing. Despite appearances of modernity in the argument, this is an error as old as class society and the state itself. In October 1956 we saw that a powerful coercive machine in Hungary proved helpless and collapsed within a few days. The working class produces and transports weapons, serves in the armed forces, produces the entire material potential of the state. The walls of prisons, barracks and arsenals are durable, not because they have been built of solid materials, but because they are guarded by the authority of the powers-that-be, by fear and accommodation to the prevailing social order. These psychological walls allow the ruling power to secure its position atop the walls of brick. But a deepening social crisis undermines the psychological walls that are the real defense of the ruling power and as a revolutionary situation matures, the walls of brick, too, will crumble. In view of the impossibility of overcoming the crisis within the framework of the bureaucratic system, *revolution is inevitable.*

THE INTERNATIONAL PROBLEMS OF THE REVOLUTION

We are told: "We live in the center of European conflicts. The world is divided into camps, and both sides have atomic weapons. All revolutionary movements in this situation are crimes against the nation and against humanity. The Polish *raison d'etat,* following from the international situation and our geographical situation, demands our silence and obedience. Otherwise, we are menaced with atomic annihilation or, at best, with intervention by the tanks of a friendly power, as happened in Hungary. Under such conditions, to analyze social structures, to discuss surplus value, to work out political programs — these are occupations which are either irrational or simply harmful. In order to build socialism one must first of all *exist.*"

Since this is a political argument, who says it and why is not a matter of indifference. It is said first of all by the very representatives of the ruling state power although they do not always dot all the "i's." It is also said by people who reluctantly admit to connections with the government, but willingly suggest that, at the bottom of their souls, they are opposition-minded. They nevertheless proclaim obedience to the ruling state power, as they defend it. As propagandists of the system they speak; as alleged members of the opposition they are silent; their resistance does not go beyond the intimate area of their spiritual experience. In point of fact, therefore, they belong in the camp of the ruling state power and they plead the cause of the ruling bureaucracy.

This argumentation is, to put it delicately, somewhat equivocal: the leaders and propagandists of a system which has at its disposal all means of coercion and destruction call on the masses for obedience in the name of maintaining peace. As a typical argument "from a position of strength," this blackmail can be rational and convincing. Let us therefore calmly consider this reasoning without deluding ourselves that it is a form of gentle persuasion.

a) This thinking is based on the assumption that revolution is the result of a criminal conspiracy against internal or world peace. It is the traditional argument of all antirevolutionary ideologies and well known in the history of the workers' movement. It is typical police thinking. In reality, revolutions are the result of economic and social crises.

From the social point of view, revolution is always an act of force which pits the strength of a social movement against that of the ruling power. But revolution is the act of an enormous majority of society directed against the rule of a minority that is in political crisis and whose apparatus of coercion has been weakened. That is why revolution does not necessarily have to be carried out by force of arms. The possibility of avoiding civil war depends on such factors as the level of consciousness and organization of the revolutionary movement which limit the degree of chaos and the possibilities of armed counteraction. The real crime against the internal peace of the country is committed by the ruling bureaucracy, which first tries to disorganize the masses, deprive them of political consciousness, and then uses armed force to try to break their revolutionary movement. We remember Poznan and Budapest.

b) The argument of Soviet tanks. It is said that an eventual revolution in Poland would inevitably lead to Soviet armed intervention, the result of which, from the military point of view, is not open to doubt. Those who advance this view assume that everything takes place in "one country in isolation" which, by way of exception, is torn by class struggles while in neighboring countries there are no classes but only regular armies with a given number of planes and tanks. For them, the revolution neither crosses national boundaries nor has an effect beyond them.

This typical "political realism" completely contradicts historical experience. Revolutionary crises have always been of an international nature. 1956 was no exception, but the bureaucracy then had at its disposal economic and social reserves which enabled it to handle the crisis by a reform maneuver. This made it possible to put a brake on the development of the revolution in Poland, to prevent a revolutionary situation from arising in Czechoslovakia, the GDR and the

USSR and thereby permitted the Hungarian revolution to be isolated and crushed. The present phase of the crisis is marked by a lack of the necessary reserves for such a maneuver. This is true not only in Poland but also in Czechoslovakia, the GDR and Hungary and even of the USSR itself. It is difficult to foresee in which of these countries the revolution will begin; it is certain, however, that it will not end where it begins. The crisis in these countries cannot be mitigated, even temporarily, by reforms and concessions, because there is nothing more to concede or to reform within the framework of the system. Under these conditions, the revolutionary movement must spread to the whole camp, while the possibilities of armed intervention on the part of the Soviet bureaucracy (if it is still in power) will not be measured by the number of its tanks and planes but by the degree of tension of class conflicts within the USSR.

The antibureaucratic revolution undoubtedly undermines the political stabilization of neocapitalism though it obviously more directly menaces the central political bureaucracy. In any case, it is improbable that Western imperialism, which would gladly take the place of the overthrown bureaucracy, would resort to intervention for that purpose. The working class in the developed Western countries has won a relatively wide margin of democratic freedoms for itself and for society. Therefore, war requires proper preparation of public opinion. Understanding this, an armed crusade against the countries of the antibureaucratic revolution is most implausible since it would run counter to public opinion, lead to mass resistance and an active antiwar struggle by the working class which, over there, is a well-organized and powerful political force. Moreover, neocapitalism is threatened by the colonial revolution. A final deterrent to imperialist intervention against an antibureaucratic revolution is that it would threaten to escalate into a suicidal, worldwide nuclear conflict.

c) The atom bomb is a modern addition to the traditional arsenal of antirevolutionary arguments. Today, when the stocks of nuclear weapons are more than enough to destroy the world, the governing elites of the two great blocs which

share power in the world decry revolution as a crime against
internal peace and all humanity. Those who possess the arsenals filled with the means of nuclear annihilation, the
leading circles of imperialism and the international (central
political) bureaucracy demand obedience from the masses in
the name of avoiding a worldwide nuclear war.

A worldwide nuclear conflict would be absurd from the
point of view of the goals of both great blocs; it would lead to
the destruction, if not of the whole of mankind, at least of
the major powers and of the parts of the world that are most
thickly populated and economically and culturally advanced.
It would be suicide. The two great blocs don't want mutual
destruction in any case, but are engaged in an economic,
political and diplomatic competition based on a division into
spheres of influence. In their struggle against the revolutionary movement, atomic weapons are a means of blackmail.
It is a well-known fact, however, that since the end of World
War II, revolutionary wars are continually being waged in
various parts of the world, while at the same time, and
independent of them, the two great blocs, having atomic
weapons at their disposal, carry on their politics of tension
and rapprochement. This was pointed out recently by the
leaders of the Chinese bureaucracy when their conflict with
the Soviet bureaucracy and their attempt to strengthen their
independence and international position drove them to an
alliance with the forces of the colonial revolution.

The bureaucracy speaks a great deal about the need to
maintain peace on the basis of the status quo. But every time
its rule was threatened it did not hesitate to use armed might.
It used tanks against the demonstrating Berlin workers in
June 1953; it did the same against the Poznan workers in 1956
and against the workers of Novocherkassk in 1962; it launched a regular war against the working class in Hungary.

The leaders of the imperialist countries compete with the
bureaucracy in peace phraseology. But the history of the
last 20 years is filled with armed interventions and wars
against the colonial revolution: from the crushing of the liberalization struggle of the Greek partisans, through Korea,

Vietnam, Algeria, Cuba and right up to the Congo and the latest acts of aggression against the Democratic Republic of Vietnam.

d) It is understandable that the ideological spokesmen of the ruling classes do not like to reflect on the social causes of the war danger, while they refuse to admit the role of "surplus value considerations." In reality, this matter has never been as urgent as it is today, when the alienation of labor assumes material forms which threaten the existence of mankind, when the surplus product created by the workers of the West, by the nations exploited by imperialism and by the workers of the USSR is turned against them in the classical form of police, prisons, marines, tanks, to which is now added the means of atomic annihilation.

The sources of the war danger are the growing social conflicts which give birth to and deepen the crisis in the world rule of the system of antipopular dictatorship. This is true in the first place of imperialism which, being unable to maintain its rule over the backward countries, wages wars of intervention and continually embarks on new political adventures of "brinksmanship." But this is also true of the international bureaucracy; we remember the Berlin crisis of 1961, the provocative installation of Soviet rocket launching sites in Cuba and the threat to the Cuban revolution and world peace which followed; we remember the operations undertaken by Soviet tanks in Berlin and the war of intervention launched against the Hungarian revolution.

Every assault on revolutionary movements strengthens antipopular distatorships and increases the risk of war. The danger of war can be done away with finally only by eliminating its social sources — imperialism and bureaucratic dictatorship. The possibilities for limiting this danger today and of its complete elimination in the future are afforded mankind by an organized international revolutionary movement conscious of its goals.

e) Bureaucracy and the revolutionary movement in the world. The young Soviet republic was able to defend itself successfully against the intervention of the imperialist countries thanks to the struggle of the working class in the

West and the wave of revolutionary movements which shook the world toward the end of World War I and after the victory of the Russian revolution. The maintenance and general development of Soviet Russia as *a workers' state* depended on the results of the revolutionary struggles in other countries, especially in the industrialized countries of the West. Lenin, Trotsky and the other Bolshevik leaders realized that only another revolutionary power could be a genuine ally of the proletarian dictatorship. That is why the ideology and foreign policy of Soviet Russia in that early period had an internationalist charactèr. As the Soviet state became bureaucratized and the ruling elite was transformed into a ruling class, an international revolutionary movement could not serve as a natural ally of the Soviet bureaucratic class. The movement had to be — and was — subordinated to the directives of the Soviet bureaucracy to provide a convenient bargaining counter and tool for the realization of the state interests of the USSR's ruling bureaucracy. We know the results.

On the other hand, every independent and victorious revolution is a menace to the bureaucracy. For revolution is a sovereign act by the masses whose example and contagious ideas strike at the ideological hegemony of the bureaucracy over its own subjects. Moreover, victorious revolutions do not subordinate themselves to the dictates of the Soviet bureaucracy; hence they threaten the rule of the international monolith, which is also dangerous for the internal monolith. The first country where an independent, victorious revolution took place after World War II was Yugoslavia; the second, China. We know the results.

That is why the Soviet bureaucracy follows the principle: "socialism" will reach as far as its army. In the name of this principle, it first tried to subordinate to its own police and its own bureaucrats the Spanish revolution, which it then betrayed; it forbade the French and Italian Communists to carry on a struggle for power in the 1945-1946 revolutionary situation; it betrayed the Greek revolution; it tried to pressure the Chinese Communists to abandon the struggle against Chiang Kai-shek's army.

Snatching countries from capitalist domination had been, and is, a factor that favors the revolutionary struggle against imperialism. But the bureaucratization of those countries is a factor which puts a brake on the development of the colonial revolution and on the struggle of the working class of the highly developed capitalist countries. Through its foreign policy based on the sharing of spheres of influence with imperialism and on maintaining the status quo, through its ideology which sanctions this policy and finally through its influence on the official Communist parties, the international bureaucracy opposes the anticapitalist revolution. The colonial revolution, however, escapes its control; it is successfully organized and directed by groups which stand outside the official Communist parties. Witness Cuba; witness Algeria.

The control exerted by the international bureaucracy over the world Communist movement is going through a crisis that has been deepened profoundly by the first anti-bureaucratic revolutions in Poland and Hungary. A victorious antibureaucratic revolution will put an end to the dictatorship's control and prove to be the natural ally of the world revolutionary movement.

PROGRAM

Thus far we have considered the revolution as the gravedigger of the old order. It also creates a new society. Is the working class, which must be the main and leading force of the revolution, capable of developing a real, viable program?

The class interest of the workers demands the abolition of the bureaucratic ownership of the means of production and of exploitation. This does not mean that the worker is to receive, in the form of a working wage, the full equivalent of the product of his labor. The level of development of the productive forces in a modern society necessitates a division of labor in which there are unproductive sectors, supported by the material product created by the worker. Therefore, under conditions of a workers' democracy, it will also be necessary to set aside from the total product a part earmarked for accumulation, for the maintenance and development of health services, education, science, culture, social benefits and those expenditures for administration and for the apparatus of political power which the working class will recognize as indispens-able. The essence of exploitation is not that the working wage represents only a part of the value of the newly created prod-uct but that the surplus product is taken away from the work-er by force and that the process of capital accumulation is alien to his interests, while the unproductive sectors serve to maintain and strengthen the rule of a bureaucracy (or bour-geoisie) over production and over society, and thus in the first place, over the labor and social life of the working class.

To abolish exploitation means, therefore, to create a system in which the organized working class will be master of its own labor and the resulting product; in which it will set the goals of social production, decide on the sharing and use of the national income, hence define the size and purpose of investments, the size and disbursement of expenditures for social benefits, health services, education, science and cul-ture, the amount for the power apparatus and its current tasks. In brief, a system in which the working class will exer-cise economic, social and political power in the state.

How should the working class and its state be organized in order that it might rule over its own labor and its product?

a) If there is no workers' democracy in the factory, there can be none in the state on any long-term basis. For it is only in the factory that the worker is a worker, that he fulfills his fundamental social function. If he were to remain a slave in his place of work, then any freedom outside the place of work would soon become "Sunday freedom," fictitious free-dom.

The working class cannot rule over its own labor and its product without controlling the conditions and goals of its toil in the factory. To that end, it must organize itself in the plants into workers' councils in order to run the factories. The manager must be made into a functionary subordinate to the council, controlled, hired or dismissed by the council.

However, these days, all key decisions relating to the management of an enterprise are made centrally. Under these conditions, the workers' council would, in practice, be deprived of power. The manager is closely bound up with the offices which make the decisions — the central apparatus of

economic management. In this situation, the workers' council
would inevitably be reduced to an adjunct to the management, as is the case with the present-day Conferences of
Workers' Self-Government.

To manage enterprises through its workers' councils, the
working class must make the enterprises independent, creating the preliminary conditions for workers' democracy and, at
the same time, adapting management relationships to the
new class goal of production (as we have already shown, the
system of centralized management is an organizational tool
of production for the sake of production, whereas production
for the sake of consumption requires a decentralized system).
Thus, while taking the first step toward realizing its program,
the working class achieves that which is most far-reaching
and progressive in the program of technocracy: the indepen-
dency of enterprises. But the working class and the technocracy each imbue this concept with a fundamentally different
social content. To the technocracy, independence of an enterprise means that management has full powers in the factory.
For the working class, it means self-government for the working force. That is why the working class must go beyond plant
management by the councils. Workers' self-rule, limited to
the level of the enterprise, would inevitably become fictitious
and a cover for the power of management in the factory and
for the rule of a new technocratic bureaucracy; exploitation
would be maintained and the former state of chaos would return in a new form.

Basic decisions relating to the sharing and use of the national income naturally have a general social character; that
is, they are made on an economy-wide scale and, therefore,
they can only be made centrally. If these central decisions
were to remain outside the influence of the working class,
it would not rule over the product that it has created and over
its own labor.

b) That is why in addition to factory councils, the working
class will have to organize itself into a nationwide system of
councils of workers' delegates, headed by a central council of
delegates. Through the system of councils, the working class
will determine the national economic plant and maintain

permanent control over its execution. As a result, the councils at all levels will become organs of economic, political, legislative and executive power. They will be truly elective offices, since the electors, organized according to the natural principle of production, will be able at any time to recall their representatives and appoint new ones in their place. In this way, the representatives of working forces in the factories will become the backbone of proletarian state power.

c) If, however, the workers' representatives in the central council of delegates were to have only one draft plan for the division of the national income laid before them by the government or by the leadership of a single, ruling political party, their role would be limited to a mechanical act of voting. As we noted earlier, a monopolistic ruling party cannot be a workers' party; it inevitably becomes the party of the dictatorship over the working class, an organization of a bureaucracy designed to keep the workers and the whole of society disorganized and in line.

For the council system to become the expression of the organized will, organized opinion and organized activity of the masses, *the working class must organize itself along multiparty lines*. In practice, a workers' multiparty system means the right of every political group which has its base in the working class to publish its own paper, to propagate its own program through mass media, to organize cadres of activists and agitators, i.e., to form a party. A workers' multiparty system requires freedom of speech, press and association, *the abolition of preventive censorship*, full freedom of scholarly research, of literary and artistic creativity. Without the freedom to elaborate, publish, express various ideological trends, without full freedom for the creative intelligentsia, there is no workers' democracy.

In the workers' multiparty system, various parties will propose plans for the division of the national income to the central council of delegates, creating conditions for discerning alternatives and for freedom of choice for the central representatives of the working class and for factory workers electing and recalling their delegates.

We speak of a workers' multiparty system, although it

would neither serve any purpose nor even be possible to limit membership in the parties only to workers. The working-class character of the multiparty system would follow from the nature of the state power, organized as a system of councils. This means that parties seeking to influence the center of political power would be obliged to win influence among the workers.

By the same token, we are against the parliamentary system. The experience of both 20-year periods shows that it carried no guarantee against dictatorship and, even in its most perfect form, is not a form of people's power. In the parliamentary system, parties compete for votes. Once the votes have been cast, election programs can be tossed into the wastebasket. The deputies in parliament feel close only to the leadership of the party which nominated them. The electorate, artifically arranged in purely formal districts is atomized and the right to recall a deputy is fictitious. The citizen's participation in political life is reduced to reading statements by political leaders, listening to them on radio or watching them on television, while once every four or five years, he goes to the ballot box to decide which party's representatives are to rule him. Everything happens with his mandate, but without his participation. In addition, parliament is a purely legislative body, which permits executive power to emerge as the only real authority, dominated by men of economic power. Thus, in the parliamentary system, the working class and the whole of society, on the strength of their own vote, are deprived of influence on the center of power.

As against this formal, periodic voting, we propose the regular participation of the working class, through its councils, parties and trade unions, in economic and political decision-making at all levels. In capitalist society, above parliament stands the bourgeoisie, disposing of the surplus product; in the bureaucratic system, above the fiction of parliament, the central political bureaucracy rules indivisibly. In a system of workers' democracy, if it takes a parliamentary form, the working class will stand above it, organized into councils and having at its disposal the material basis of society's existence — the product of its labor.

d) The working class cannot decide directly, but only through its political representation at the central level, how to divide the product it has created. But as its interests are not entirely uniform, contradictions between the decisions of workers' representatives and the aspirations of particular sections of the working class are unavoidable. The very fact of separating the function of management from the function of production carries with it the possibility of alienation of the elected power, at the level of both the enterprise and the state. If the workers were deprived of the possibility of self-defense in the face of the decisions of the representative system, apart from their right to vote (i.e., apart from that very system), then it would turn against those whom it is supposed to represent. If the working class was deprived of the possibilities of self-defense in its own state, workers' democracy would be fraudulent. This defense should be assured by *trade unions completely independent of the state with the right to organize economic and political strikes.* The various parties, competing for influence in the trade unions, would struggle for the preservation of their working-class character.

e) To prevent the institutions of workers' democracy from being reduced to a facade, behind which the old disorder would make a comeback, their democratic forms must be the living expression of the activity of the working masses. Administrators, experts and politicians have the necessary time and knowledge to bother with public affairs while the worker is obliged to stand next to his machine. To take an active part in public life, the worker, too, must be provided with the necessary time and knowledge. This requires a certain number of hours to be set aside weekly from the required paid working time to insure *the universal education of the workers.* During those hours, workers grouped into production complexes will discuss draft economic plans submitted by different parties for the country, factory or region which are too difficult for popular presentation only if an attempt is made to conceal their class content. The representatives of political parties participating in these hours of workers' education will bring both their programs and the working class closer to each other.

f) In a workers' democracy it will be impossible to preserve the political police or the regular army in any form. The antidemocratic character of the political police is obvious to everyone; on the other hand, the ruling classes have had more success in spreading myths about the regular army.

The regular army tears hundreds of thousands of young people away from their environment. They are isolated in barracks, brainwashed by brutal methods and taught, instead, a mechanical performance of every order issued by their professional commanders locked in a rigid hierarchy. This organization of armed force is separated from society in order that it may more easily be directed against society. The regular army, like the political police, is by its very nature a tool of antidemocratic dictatorship. As long as it is maintained, a clique of generals may always prove stronger than all the parties and councils.

It is said that the regular army is necessary to defend the state. This is true in the case of an antidemocratic dictatorship where, other than by terror, it is impossible to force the large mass of people to defend a state that does not belong to them. On the other hand, if the masses were allowed to carry arms outside the military organization, it would create a mortal danger for the system. Consequently, a regular army is the only possible form of defense force for such a system.

We have already seen, during the revolutionary wars in Vietnam, Algeria and Cuba, that the armed workers and peasants — if they know what they are fighting for and if they identify their interests with those of the revolution — are not worse soldiers than those in the regular army. This is especially true for small countries threatened by the counterrevolutionary intervention of a foreign power. It has no chance with a regular army; it can defend itself successfully by a people's war. Regular armies are necessary for aggressors who undertake colonial wars and wars of intervention; they are necessary for the antidemocratic dictatorships in order to keep the masses obedient. This is evident especially in Latin American countries where the army has exclusively the internal function of the police. It can also be observed elsewhere — in Poland, for example, as we saw during the events in Poznan. Whether or not the army and the workers actually clash, the regular army always remains an instrument of tyranny over the working class and society, just as a club always remains a means of beating, whether or not its owner actually puts it to that use. In a system of workers' democracy, the regular army does not insure defense against the counterrevolution; on the contrary, it may become the source and the tool of the counterrevolutionary camp. It must therefore be abolished.

To make democracy indestructible, the working class should be armed. This applies, first of all, to the workers in larger industries who should be organized into a workers' militia under the aegis of the workers' councils. The military experts who will train the workers' militia will be employed by the workers' councils and remain subordinated to them. In this way, the basic military repressive force in the state will be directly tied to the working class which will always be ready to defend its own state and its own revolution.

For technical reasons, it is impossible to avoid maintenance of permanent military units within specialized divisions such as the navy, air force, rocketry, etc. The soldiers for those divisions should be recruited among the workers of heavy industry, and during their military service they should remain in touch with their factory teams and retain all their workers' rights.

g) Agricultural production plays an essential part in the economy, and the peasantry too important a role in society for the workers' program to bypass the affairs of the countryside. The future of agriculture lies, without doubt, with large, specialized industrialized and nationalized enterprises. The technical base for such an organization of agricultural production can only be created by the industrialization of agriculture. This requires enormous investments whose realization is a problem for the distant future. Under present technical-economic conditions, all attempts at collectivization mean depriving the peasant of the land he owns; this can be achieved only against his will through the methods of police dictatorship. The result would be a fall in production and a police dictatorship victimizing the working class itself.

Such collectivization can be reconciled only with a bureaucratic system; it spells death for workers' democracy.

The free, unlimited interplay of market forces, under
conditions of individual ownership of land, and given the
present structure of agriculture, leads to capitalist-type
farming. It deprives owners of small and scattered holdings
of the possibility of concentrating their means of investment,
necessary for their development, and consequently shifts the
major part of the means of investment in the countryside to
the richest farms. It means the rationalization of the rural
economy through a deep crisis, bankrupting the poorest holdings; and it means unemployment and high prices for necessities for the industrial working class. This is acceptable to
the technocracy which is naturally sympathetic to capitalist
farming but unacceptable to a workers' democracy.

For the working class, the goal of production is the development of improved consumption for the broad mass of people
who today live at subsistence level. As we have already seen,
the bureaucracy pushes the consumption of the majority of
villages even below that level, deprives the peasant economy
of its surpluses and agriculture of any prospects of development because it seeks to minimize the real expenditure on
labor and regards social consumption as a necessary evil.

The interests of the working class lie in overthrowing
these relationships between the peasant economy and the
state; it demands a rapid development of agricultural production — the basis for increased consumption — through the
development of the mass of small and medium individual
holdings. This makes the working class the spokesman for the
majority of peasants and creates the basis for a real alliance
between them. To realize their common interests it is necessary, first of all, to overcome the "price scissors" which deprives small and medium peasant holdings of the material
base for development, and to tax progressively the richest
farms. Second, that part of the product of the peasants' labor
intercepted by the state in the form of taxes or in any other
way must be — after subtracting sums corresponding to the
peasants' contribution to administrative expenditures — returned to the countryside in the form of social and cultural

investments and as state economic and technical aid to assist small and dwarf holdings.

To achieve this, the peasantry needs to organize itself on an economic basis and elect its own political representatives. It must set up its own production organizations and find new perspectives for the almost 60% of the peasantry which vegetates on small holdings and has labor surpluses; it is inadmissable to allow investments in industry to be blown up out of all proportion. This requires the proper use of labor surpluses in intensive additional production, such as livestock breeding, vegetable and fruit cultivation and such industries as meat packing and fruit canning. This is very difficult, and in the case of processing plants, impossible to achieve with the scattered forces of small holdings. The precondition for success is the creation of associations of small and medium holdings, having at their disposal a labor surplus. These associations, based on the land they possess, on cooperation and on state aid in the form of low-interest credits, participation in small investments, transport guarantees, etc., will then set up small processing plants and, also in common, organize their supplies and marketing. This is the cheapest way to increase the production of deficit-bearing agricultural produce and to invigorate the underdeveloped food industry. It is also the only way of intensifying the work of dwarf and small holdings and simultaneously employing, on the spot, the existing labor surplus.

Peasant holdings must be provided with conditions favoring specialization of production, without which there can be no rational husbandry. At the same time, in their contacts with state purchasing enterprises, peasant producers must be organized to defend themselves against artificial lowering of prices. For the isolated peasant producer who enters into a "voluntary" accord with the state is helpless when faced with the state's monopoly of the market. Accordingly, apart from creating production organizations, the rural population must form its own universal *supply and marketing organization* for the peasant holdings. The richest farms, which are relatively few in number but play an important role given their size and economic strength, will then have no chance to transform themselves into capitalist enterprises; they will be short of cheap labor and cheap land that would otherwise be provided by the failure of weak holdings. The richest farms, however, will have the chance to increase their production on the basis of their own means of investment provided they are able to solve the manual labor shortage through the use of machines.

Inasmuch as industry plays the decisive role in the economy, the direction of industrial production will determine the general direction of the national economy. And the working class, which will have control of its own product, will thereby create a general framework for the functions of the other sectors, including agriculture. But within these most general limits, determined by the level, structure and development of industrial production, the peasants must also control the product of their labor. The plans for development, for investments, for economic aid, should not be imposed by the state on the peasant population. Otherwise, a specific apparatus of control would come into being and would, finally, also obtain control over the working class. *That is why political self-government by the peasants* is a must for the good of workers' democracy. It is made possible because the interests of the workers and peasants converge.

Economic organizations of peasant producers are not enough to give peasants control over that part of their product taken over by the state and to be restored to the countryside in the form of direct state investments and state aid to peasant holdings. This can be assured only by the *political representation of peasant producers on a national scale*, elected on the basis of economic organizations and peasant political parties.

h) We do not consider the antibureaucratic revolution to be a purely Polish affair. The economic and social contradictions we have analyzed appear in mature form in all the industrialized bureaucratic countries: in Czechoslovakia, East Germany, Hungary and the USSR. Nor do we view the revolution as the exclusive affair of the working class in bureaucratic dictatorships. The bureaucratic system, passed off as socialism by official propaganda in both East and West, compromises socialism in the eyes of the masses of developed capitalist countries. The international bureaucracy and its leading force — the Soviet bureaucracy — fear all authentic revolutionary movements in any part of the world. Seeking internal and international stabilization of its own system, based on the division of the world into spheres of influence with capitalism, the bureaucracy suppresses revolutionary movements at home and uses its influence over foreign official Communist parties to impede the development of revolutionary movements in Latin America, Asia and Africa. The antibureaucratic revolution is, therefore, the concern of the international workers' movement and of the movement for colonial revolution.

Like every revolution, the antibureaucratic revolution threatens the established world order and, in turn, is threatened by the forces guarding that order. The international bureaucracy will try to crush the first country or countries of the victorious revolution in proportion to the internal forces it will still have at the moment of crisis. Western imperialism will try to take advantage of our revolution to supplant the dictatorship of the bureaucracy with the dictatorship of the capitalist monopolies, which is in no way better.

Our ally against the intervention of Soviet tanks is the Russian, Ukrainian, Hungarian and Czech working class. Our ally against the pressures and threats of imperialism is the working class of the industrialized West and the developing colonial revolution in the backward countries. Against an eventual accord between the international bureaucracy and the international imperialist bourgeoisie, which maintain systems of antipopular dictatorship in their spheres of influence, we utter the traditional working-class slogan: "proletarians of all countries, unite!"

The working class must carry out all these changes in the area of political, social and economic relations in order to realize its own class interest, which is the command over its own labor and its product. Is this program realistic?

With the initial step toward its realization — making the enterprise independent — the working class would create the conditions for adapting production to needs, eliminating all waste of the economic surplus and the proper use of the intensive factors of economic growth. The same would be carried out by the technocracy, the difference being that the production goal of the working class is consumption by many, not the luxury consumption of privileged strata. That is why workers' control of production would assure the most radical resolution of the contradiction between an expanded productive potential and the low level of social consumption which impedes economic growth today.

The workers separate class interest coincides with the economic interests of the mass of low-paid white-collar employees and of the small and medium holders in the countryside. In their combined numbers, they are the overwhelming majority of the rural and urban population. Since the slavery of the working class is the essential source of the slavery of other classes and strata, by emancipating itself the working class also liberates the whole of society.

To liberate itself, it must abolish the political police; by doing this it frees the whole of society from fear and dictatorship.

It must abolish the regular army and liberate the soldier in the barracks from nightmarish oppression.

It must introduce a multiparty system, providing political freedom to the whole of society.

It must abolish preventive censorship, introduce full freedoms of the press, of scholarly and cultural creativity, of formulating and propagating various trends of social thinking. It will thereby liberate the writer, artist, scholar and journalist; it will create, on the widest possible scale, conditions for the free fulfillment by the intelligentsia of its proper social function.

It must subject the administrative apparatus to the permanent control and supervision of democratic organizations, changing existing relationships within the apparatus. Today's common civil servant will become a man free of humiliating dependence on a bureaucratic hierarchy.

It must assure the peasant control over his product, as well as economic, social and political self-government. It will thereby change the peasant from the eternal. helpless object of all power into an active citizen sharing in making decisions which shape his life and work.

Because the worker occupies the lowest position in the productive process, the working class more than any other social group needs democracy: every incursion on democracy is first a blow against the worker. That is why workers' democracy will have the widest social base and will create the fullest conditions for the free development of the whole of society.

Because the workers' class interest most closely corresponds to the requirements for economic development and to the interests of society, the working-class program is a realistic one.

Will that program be realized? That depends on the degree of ideological and organizational preparation of the working class in a revolutionary crisis and therefore also depends on the present activities of those who identify with workers' democracy.

COUNTER-ARGUMENTS

In the last section of our text we mentioned those contemporary sociopolitical tendencies against which the working class must conduct a political struggle: the technocracy ("managerial socialism"), the farmer's group ("the good husbandmen's socialism"); and the petty bourgeoisie ("Christian democracy").

In connection with our program and in particular with the above-mentioned section, some basic criticisms have been advanced and we shall try to reply here. First, on relations with the technocracy.

"Managerial socialism" does not change the worker's position in the process of production. It maintains exploitation and is nothing but another form of dictatorship over the workers, over the majority of peasants and over the intelligentsia. We are not against it just for tactical reasons but because we have consciously chosen the other side of the barricades. We have been accused of aiming at proletarian revolution, whereas the technocratic program would also solve the crisis but could be realized by a combination of pressure from below and reforms from above — without revolution and its attendant dangers.

We believe, first of all, that those who subscribe to this view have also chosen their side of the barricades so that we argue from opposing positions. Also, it is they who are the utopians although they use so-called realistic arguments. The technocratic system in Yugoslavia did not replace a fully formed bureaucratic system, but rose directly from the fluid postrevolutionary period in a specific international situation under specific economic conditions. It would seem that there existed in Poland in 1956-1957 all the reasons and conditions necessary for the introduction of technocratic reforms: this would theoretically have solved the crisis and brought permanent stabilization. However, the bureaucracy did not allow this to happen. First of all, it was by then a fully formed ruling class and defended by all means available to it the existing conditions of production upon which its rule is based. We have seen, though, that technocratic reform would mean a change in production relations. If yesterday's Marxists consider this argument anachronistic, we can point out another, equally important. Technocratic reform would give rise to a conflict of social forces, a political struggle at the highest level, an acute political crisis and broader, if transient, political freedom. It would also give autonomy to the enterprise and then the workers' teams would not have to combat the anonymous power of the State, but their own management. During the tensions that existed in 1956, this could most likely have brought further progress in the revolution and the collapse of bureaucratic rule. That the bureaucracy did not opt for technocratic reforms eight years ago when the system still possessed economic reserves, and the new leadership undoubted authority, makes it most unlikely that the bureaucracy can effectuate such reforms today when it lacks both economic reserves and support in society. These are facts which not only a Marxist but an ordinary realist must take into account.

"Managerial socialism" can triumph, not in place of the revolution, but because of it, or after it. It may become a sort of Thermidor for workers' democracy. We do not see why we should work for such a solution. On the contrary, in our section on program, we tried to find ways to struggle against it.

We are also accused of not knowing what we are doing in pressing toward revolution. This, they say, can only lead to the victory of antisocialist forces (like the multiparty system, abolition of political police, etc.) because either the working class is in its mass reactionary or the bourgeois forces are so powerful.

Those who follow this reasoning have also chosen their side of the barricades. They want to defend the existing system which they consider socialist against the working class (which is supposedly antisocialist). In this line of reasoning the bureaucracy has been identified with socialism and the defense of its rule over the masses is represented as the defense of socialism.

We believe that the reality is just the opposite — something we have tried to demonstrate in these pages. The ruling bureaucracy is anti-working class, an enemy. It represents the most powerful reactionary force since it has both state power and power over production. The elements of the traditional Right have no economic base in any decisive sector: industry, transport, construction, etc. The petty bourgeoisie, so-called "private initiative" elements in the cities and the so-called "kulaks" in the countryside represent only a narrow margin of the national economy and the social structure. Of considerable importance, however, are rightist groups and currents, with the church hierarchy in the lead, which are attached to the old reactionary symbols.

The bureaucratic system provokes natural antagonism and hate among the masses; it identifies itself with socialism but ruthlessly suppresses all opposition from the Left, thus creating conditions favorable for spreading rightist ideologies among the masses. People look for ideological symbols to express their protest against the existing dictatorship, and in the absence of opposition from the Left expressing their real interests, they find the old symbols of the traditional Right. In this manner the bureaucratic dictatorship aids the tra-

ditional Right and even enters into agreements based on
collaboration with them as with PAX and agreements with
the Church hierarchy.

The only effective way of fighting the traditional Right is
not the defense of the bureaucratic dictatorship but an in-
sistent struggle against it, unmasking it from the Left. A
working-class program does not use nebulous symbols, but
social realities. In its criticism and its radicalism, this program differentiates itself from all nationalist and clerical
slogans. It turns against the very essence of the bureaucratic
dictatorship and corresponds to the interests of the masses.
Therefore, it has all chances of winning the support of the
masses. The struggle against the governing Right and the
Right in retirement is indivisible. To those who believe that
workers' democracy, by introducing a multiparty system and
abolishing the political police, will give the rightist forces
access to power, we reply: we are not talking of a supraclass
state but of working-class democracy. The representatives of
the workers' councils are the foundation of economic and
political authority. Therefore the working class will have the
decisive voice in the conflicts between the political parties.
There will also exist an organization which represents actual
power — the workers' militia — but unlike its present role,
this military force will not be anti-working class but directly
linked to the working class.

We believe that all this will give the workers a decisive
voice in the state and will safeguard it against rightist danger. We shall not argue with the thesis that the working class
in our country represents a reactionary force since it is a
meaningless anti-working-class bias.

Indeed, the fact that our program is based on working-
class leadership has also provoked criticism in academic
circles. It was said that we advocate workers' power without
any participation of other social classes, that our program is
anti-intelligentsia, that it is not "modern."

We are convinced that these critics do not really believe
in the model of the "general national state" which does not,
and most likely will never, exist anywhere outside the program of the PUWP.

Perhaps their criticism means that we failed to mention the forms of political representation within the framework of the workers' state, of society as a whole. These forms, however, are difficult to anticipate. We did not intend to write a future constitution, but a political program. In the nature of things we could only include what is decisive of the character of workers' democracy.

Since the industrial sector plays the decisive role in the economy, the power over industrial production and over labor is tantamount, in modern society, to class rule and political power. As long as there exist in society large groups of people with different positions in the process of production and different social and material positions, parliament or any other national system of representation will sanction the rule of that class which actually controls the activity of labor and the division of the product in the decisive sectors of the economy. That is why abolishing the exploitation of the working class presupposes the assumption of state power by the working class. It is, therefore, sheer nonsense to charge workers' democracy with its class character. It can only be accused of being *working class*. It is a charge levelled from the position of another class, one contending for power.

We are not acquainted with any "modern society" which our adversaries oppose to workers' democracy. Since such a society is neither a bureaucratic dictatorship nor neocapitalist, they probably mean a technocracy. We do not see why, in that kind of system, the role of the intelligentsia would be larger than in a workers' democracy. As long as exploitation exists there must also be the means to protect it (political police, propaganda, etc.) as well as an apologetic function for scholarship and culture. Each system based on an enslaved working class also deprives intellectuals, one way or another, of their freedom. Only the liberation of the working class will change this state of affairs. In its very nature, workers' democracy must provide much greater freedom for the intelligentsia than exists in any parliamentary bourgeois democracy or in the most modern managerial kingdom.

The sharpest attacks were directed at our practical proposals ("What Is To Be Done?") concerning strike action and the organization of workers' circles, nuclei of the future party. Distorting our analysis and hardly mentioning our program, the official reporters quoted profusely from our last section in order to provoke an indignant reaction to our attempts to violate the criminal laws. Since this relieves us of the need to report the details of that chapter, we shall limit ourselves to restating our position and refuting the objections.

We believe that the economic and social crisis must lead inevitably to revolution. Bureaucratic rule today does not rest on social support but only on its capacity to disorganize the social forces violently by atomizing a working class that is deprived of a party and a program.

Revolution is necessary for social progress, but its course and results would depend on the degree of preparation of the working class. Preparation could serve to limit the confusion associated with revolution and permit its peaceful course with minimum costs for society. If deprived of its own party and its program the working class could not play the leading role in the revolution; if it had neither party nor program, the working class would only bring to power a new oppressor.

For the sake of the whole society, then, the working class must become "a class for itself," conscious of its goals and politically organized. This can be achieved only by *conscious activity* which we consider the political and moral duty of all who want to fight in the interest of the working class. This activity should aim primarily at heightening the political consciousness of the working class and systematizing its interests into a program. This calls for programmatic discussions and involving factory workers in the struggle for their immediate interests by strike action culminating in the organization of workers' parties and unions.

It has been pointed out, indignantly, that all this is illegal, against the laws of the country. Let us be candid about it. Neither strikes nor the discussion of political programs is prohibited by law. It is true, however, that the present criminal code, created or maintained by the bureaucracy, allows for police persecution for such activities. We have in our country the Criminal Code of 1932, a tool of the semifascist "Sanacja" dictatorship and the Small Criminal Code, the tool of the Stalinist dictatorship. Both these Codes, the Small one particularly, are so vague and elastic that, in practice, repressive measures can be applied at will. Therefore, we can see strike organizers punished by law, although strikes are not forbidden, or the participant in a discussion arrested, although discussions are permitted, or the writer of a private letter held, although everybody writes letters.

In talking about legality, it should be mentioned that the basic legal document is the Constitution. But the criminal law (especially the MKK) is in flagrant contradiction to the Constitution. Preventive censorship is unconstitutional, as are all steps taken against freedom of speech, assembly, publication. The very power of the bureaucracy is unconstitutional as well. From the constitutional point of view, strikes, political discussions and organizing workers are not against the law, but against the prevailing lawlessness.

Our motive was not to defend the Constitution, but to commit ourselves to the struggle for the liberation of the working class and of society. Since we are charged, however, with actions which are contrary to the law, we had to demonstrate that the law is interpreted by the powers-that-be and by their defenders in an arbitrary way: what is convenient is mandatory. In reality, therefore, we are charged not with acting against the law, but against the arbitrary prohibitions used by the bureaucratic state power. This kind of morality, which allows one to do only that which the government allows, raises obedience to the rank of the highest virtue and is alien to us in view of our commitment and our traditions. Despite bourgeois prohibitions the KPP (Communist Party of Poland) worked illegally underground; despite prohibitions by the bureaucratic state power, the Communist Left Opposition was active in the USSR and fought the evolving totalitarian Stalinist dictatorship. All groups and parties which fought antipopular dictatorships for the emancipation of the working class acted in this way. People who are not interested in the class struggle and who consider Marxist analysis to be anachronistic in the modern world but who, at the same time, attacked us for offenses against Party censorship and, today, for offenses against the discipline imposed by the power of the state, have gone through quite a reversal in their thinking. Brought up under dogmatic Marxism, they have rejected Marxism but retained the dogma; they doubt the value of the Marxist theory of classes, but they have no doubt that there can be no factions in the Party and that the powers-that-be must be obeyed.

We are of the opinion that the present letter will contribute toward overcoming any misinformation about our paper and that it will enable Party members and members of the SYU at the university to have an honest discussion of our theses. We would also like to believe that this time the University Committee of the SYU, being in possession of their own copies of the open letter, will allow those it is really addressed to — i.e., all interested members of both organizations — to acquaint themselves with its text.

We do not know, of course, whether the authorities will decide, as a result of this letter, to apply repressive administrative measures to us or to try us in court. We consider, however, that we have *every right* to address ourselves to the political organizations which removed us from their ranks with the present open letter, which explains to the membership at large of both organizations our views and the motives for our actions.

March 1967

Disorder in Warsaw

Witold Jedlicki

There are two aspects to the March 1968 student revolt in
Poland: one is what actually happened and the other is what
the Polish regime says happened. One is the story of a tough,
desperate struggle; the other is an updating of the Protocols
of the Elders of Zion. There is little relationship between the
two, but neither story can be dismissed lightly.

The Polish government tried hard enough to link its story
to the events themselves. So hard, in fact, that the arrested
students were asked during their interrogation: "Why do you
allow the kikes to dupe you?" (It is interesting to observe
that the official claim of fighting "Zionists" instead of Jews—
the Jews are just loved—gets lost soon as the multisyllable
words of the official ideology get translated into the plain
talk of policemen.) And the government went so far as to
expel Richard Davy, the correspondent of the London *Times*,
for failing to preceive a link between the rioting students and
the "Zionist conspirators."

In the West, the government's campaign of Jew-baiting
has tended to overshadow the story of the student struggle.
And that is unfortunate, for the student struggle had nothing
to do with any Jewish question. Those students who were
Jews acted not as Jews but as students; they fought for

students' rights just as students in this country have done, and not in defense of Judaism. But with the government's anti-Semitism against them, the Polish students are in danger of respectability in the West, of being acclaimed nice anti-Communist fellows, at a time when respectable gentlemen in the West are becoming hostile to student rebellions everywhere else. The young Poles should be defended against such a respectable image.

The young Polish rebels face similar problems as their American counterparts, only from the opposite side, sort of upside down. Because the American Establishment calls itself democratic, student rebels, in order to fight it are forced either to call themselves antidemocratic, Eastern-style, or to say that they are better democrats than LBJ. But the Polish government calls itself Communist, so Polish students opposing it are compelled either to be anti-Communist, Western-style, or say that they are better Communists than Gomulka.

The evidence indicates that the young Poles have chosen the latter alternative. In a recent editorial (March 24), the Warsaw *Kultura* (not to be confused with the Paris-based magazine bearing the same name) attacked and deplored the heavy influence exercised upon students by what it called a "silly" piece of writing advocating (and here the reader is treated to the notion of a real horror) that the Polish army be dissolved and replaced by the "duty hours of workers serving the missile rockets." Of course the "silly" piece of writing that exercised so heavy an influence on the students was the Kuron-Modzelewski "Open Letter," published elsewhere in this volume. Similarly, an article in the daily newspaper, *Trybuna Ludu*, refers to a "not numerous but very mobile group of students around Modzelewski and Kuron." What such articles reveal is that the students were guided not by Western anti-communist slogans but by an ardently anticapitalist, Third Camp socialist ideological statement.

Not that all the resolutions, statements and programmatic documents produced by the students are very radical; some are surprisingly meek, such as the Zambrowski document, published in English in the London *Times* (March 22), which is reminiscent of those noble outpourings in our mildly "left wing" journals, which praise dissent and civil liberty and fair trials but express disgust with violence and illegality. But even so, the Zambrowski document, whose author has been accused of being a "ringleader" of the demonstrations, leaves no doubt that it has nothing in common with the Western Establishment's anti-Communism. And although Gomulka, in his speech of March 19, quoted some leaflet with slogans such as "down with Communism," the immense majority of pamphlets and resolutions published by the students stress devotion to Communism, to *true* Communism.

Like the rebelling American students, the Polish students press a demand for sensible, meaniful academic discourse, for scientific research unperverted by the vested interests of power-holders, for due process, for freedom of speech and freedom of association. Their methods of struggle are similar, most notably the sit-in. And like American students they even tend to yell "Gestapo" at the police and to adopt formal resolutions about the students' lack of personal access to his professor. These Polish students are quite plainly the allies and comrades of the New Left, not of the Polish emigres or of the United States troops fighting in Vietnam.

And they are allies of the Polish workers. By and large, the Polish working class stayed away from these recent demonstrations (in contrast to the struggles of 1956-1957). And the students, in their resolutions, made hardly any demands of direct concern to workers. But it is worth noting that the students received messages of solidarity from the crews of the two biggest industrial complexes in Poland: Nowa Huta near Cracow and Pafawag in Breslau. In the Danzig shipyard there was a solidarity demonstration. Moreover, some statistics provided by Gomulka in his speech of March 19 indicate that a substantial number of workers took part in the student demonstrations.

Gomulka's figures are as follows:

	Total	Students	Nonstudents
Persons arrested	1208	367	841
Released for lack of evidence	687	194	493
Still under investigation	521	173	348

Mind you, there are very few idle people in Poland, and very few businessmen. Those who do not study, work; and the arrest statistics link students with those who work.

There is another statistic, one which tries to lump workers with the police: it is the casualty list. There exists in the Ministry of the Interior a department cynically entitled the Department of People's Wrath. It recruits thugs, pays them, arms them, teaches them to pose as workers and dispatches them to strikes and demonstrations. The thugs are of two kinds: those who receive some police training and those who receive none, or very little. The former are called "volunteer reservists of the citizens' militia" and the latter are called "working-class activists." (Neither are to be confused with American vigilante groups: they are simply police agents with no particular ideology.) Combining casualties from all three categories — the professional cops, the "reservists" and the "activists" — Gomulka tells us that 146 were injured during the disturbances. One hundred forty-six injured cops, "reservists" and plain thugs. It gives a notion of how tough the fight was.

There were widely reported factory meetings and demonstrations protesting against the students. These, of course, are not hard to arrange. It simply means assembling a factory crew on a square, giving them signs and ordering them to look indignant. It is surprising, however, when more than half the crew resists intimidation and goes home instead of joining the show. And that was precisely what is reported to have happened.

But perhaps most impressive about the response of non-students to the demonstrations is the total absence of any important name from any statement attacking the students. This writer has reviewed the Polish newspapers for the entire period of the student rebellion. There have been hundreds of letters, speeches and statements against the students. But there is not one that is signed by any known scholar or artist or writer — not even by any known sportsman. Not one faculty member in all of Poland appears to have come out against the students. With amazing clumsiness the press attempted to disguise that fact; an example is the following item: "The protest demonstration [against the students] took place in the school of cinematography famous for the fact that among its faculty are Messrs. so-and-so, such-and-such, etc." Not one of the persons mentioned was said to have signed his name to any antistudent statement.

It is not difficult to discover who "incited" the riots and the unrest leading up to them. Plainly, the students were "incited" to collect their 3,145 signatures protesting the ban against Mickiewicz's classic play, *Dziady*, written in 1832 and cherished as a treasury of Polish poetry and national freedom, by the ban itself. When the government demanded that the Writers' Association condemn the unruly behavior of onlookers in the theatre, as a means of justifying the ban, it only "incited" the writers to vote by a large majority a resolution condemning the ban and approving the subsequent demonstrations. The expulsion of Adam Michnik and Henryk Schleifer from the University for their role in collecting the 3,145 signatures undoubtedly incited the students to stage their demonstration of March 8, in which they protested against the expulsion of the two popular student leaders.

We have several interesting reports on the March 8 demonstration. The *New York Times* reports that the tear gas used against the demonstrators did not stop them but merely incited them against the police. The students, red-eyed and wet-eyed, with blurred vision, remained or re-emerged and continued to taunt the police. The *Christian Science Monitor* reports that the brutalization of female students by the police had an inciting effect. Gomulka himself admitted that rumors to the effect that two girls, one a student, and other a nonstudent, had been killed by the police had an inciting effect. He denied the rumor vehemently, and the student was put on TV to announce "Here I am, alive." But the nonstudent did not appear on TV, so we have only Gomulka's word as proof that she is alive.

But there was more incitement at the later stage of the riots. A Cracow newspaper reports, for example, that 112 people were admitted to the hospital, most of them bitten by dogs. Several days later the same newspaper apologized for "creating the wrong impression that the dogs were police dogs" — without the inciting effect of those dogs the apology would never have been necessary. Almost a month after the riots began, the University incited the students by ousting seven popular faculty members, including the world-famous philosopher, Leszek Kolakowski, for "spiritual instigation," and for advocating in their classes ideas which "stand in glaring discrepancy with the dominant developmental tendencies of the country and of the nation." These seven faculty members had committed an unforgivable sin: each of them had a long and honorable record of defending individual students victimized by the authorities, and these actions were cited along with "spiritual instigation" and discrepant ideas as a third reason for their ouster. And more recently, the scuttling of the University of Warsaw — surely the right word for the closing of eight of its departments — must necessarily have had an inciting effect.

A reading of the Polish press gives a good idea of the regime's awareness of the inciting effects of its own actions. The official press endlessly and incessantly tries to convince the reader that whatever action the regime had taken was not responsible for further troubles. The ban against the play? A mere pretext for collecting signatures. The expulsion of Michnik and Schleifer? A mere pretext for staging the March 8 demonstration. And so on; the demonstrators, we are told, did not care about the play or about Michnik and Schleifer. This is said not once or twice or three times, but countless numbers of times, with stubborn obstinacy clumsily covering the incredibility of the government's argument.

But in a totalitarian country a newspaper article has the quality of law. The article may appear to state facts but, in reality, it spells out a rule under which anybody holding views contrary to those published becomes an "enemy of socialism." That is why the Polish students repeatedly demanded that the newspapers recant their slanderous accounts of demonstrations and street fighting; unlike the lies told in American papers about the FSM in Berkeley and the student strike at Columbia, the stories stridently repeated in the Polish newspapers have a normative force marking them as obligatory truths.

EXPLANATIONS IN THE POLISH PRESS

The Polish press offers three explanations for the disturbances: it blames them on the Stalinists, the intellectuals and the Zionists.

The Stalinists and the students? The only evidence offered for that is the undeniable fact that many of the student leaders come from families in the Communist elite; they are sons or daughters of men who occupy high party and governmental posts. But that is all that the Polish press offers as evidence of Stalinist incitement: a guilt-by-association theory pure and simple.

Apparently the theory was needed for some account-settling within the Communist party leadership. We read in the Polish press how Mr. So-and-so oppressed the peasants in 1951 or how Mr. Such-and-such fraudulently pretended to be a liberal in 1956. The stories are true, but they are merely individual scapegoating intended to cover over the fact of the regime's *collective* responsibility for the crimes of the Stalin era. Interestingly enough, these press attacks are aimed at losers — at those who lost their power and their positions five or ten years ago. It is reminiscent of the Moscow trials, held eight years after their defendants lost all power, or of the 1961 campaign against an "anti-Party group" four years after that group was demoted to obscurity. Such scapegoating offers an outlet for daydreaming by winners about the absolute humiliation and annihilation of yesterday's foe.

With the intellectuals the matter is not so simple. They fall into two categories: writers and scholars. We are told that the writers are more guilty because they took a public stand in their speeches and in their Association's resolution. Stefan Kisielewski, one of the writers, described the Polish regime in his speech as a dictatorship of ignoramuses. This provoked "the wrath of the Polish working class" against Mr. Kisielewski: the night after his speech he was badly beaten up in the darkness of a secluded street by three unidentified wrathful "workers." It is undeniable that the writers cooperated with the student leaders and resisted the government together with them.

By comparison with such accused writers as Pawel Jasie-

nica or Antoni Slonimski, the seven ousted faculty members
accused of "spiritual instigation" are rather moderate. The
writer knows six of them personally, five fairly well; not
one was a fighter for a revolutionary cause. They were cautious men trying to protect scientific research from the government's political pressure, so far as possible — fine men
and fair scholars, but without the temperament of revolutionaries. By antagonizing them, the government left itself
short of people in a position to mediate between the authorities and the students.

Thus we are left with the Zionists. The campaign against
them began with an article in the "progressive" Catholic
daily, *Slowa Powszechne*, charging that Zionists had provoked the riots "in order to avenge Comrade Gomulka's correct appraisal of Israel's aggression against the Arab states
last June." *Slowo Powszechne* is published by *Pax*, a Catholic
association headed by Boleslaw Piasecki, that has existed for
over 30 years with substantially the same leadership. Before
World War II its name was *Falanga*, in admiration for the
movement of the same name in Spain. Its chief activity then
was anti-Semitic propaganda and anti-Semitic violence;
the actual extent of its activity is difficult to determine because its press claimed credit for every act of anti-Semitic
violence that occurred. During the war it offered to form an
auxiliary police force to help the Nazis fight "subversives,"
but the Nazis turned down the offer and the group turned
against them. After the war, Piasecki was sentenced to death
by the NKVD but made some deals with them and returned
triumphantly to Warsaw, where he rallied his old followers
and founded the new "progressive Catholic" movement. In
1956 he allied himself with the Natolin faction, which opposed
any liberalizing change. Since then his association has proclaimed numerous moral-rearmament campaigns, none of
which succeeded in morally shaking the nation. While Poland
was still maintaining reasonably friendly relations with
Israel, from 1953 to 1967, and the Polish press avoided anti-
Zionism, Piasecki's press was busy warning about Zionist
agents and Zionist infiltration. So now his group can claim to
be the forerunner of the present policy.

As soon as the riots subsided, Piasecki was again in the news, providing ideological leadership for a purge of Jewish officials that had now stepped down from the top level to that of factory directors and the like. It is important to remember that the purge is not yet over.

Gomulka entered the scene with his speech of March 19, which the Western press incorrectly treated as an attack on anti-Semitism. His speech did differ from the line advanced by the Polish press in that (a) he was evidently opposed to the scapegoating of former Stalinists at that particular time and (b) he did not believe that Zionism constituted a real threat to the very existence of Poland. (Interestingly enough, when he said that in his speech, Gomulka was interrupted by voices shouting that Zionism does constitute such a threat. And there were cries of "Long live Gierek," referring to Gomulka's chief rival on the Politbureau, who had promised to "break the bones" of the students.)

But his speech contained its own version of anti-Semitism. Consider the following passage: "In the apartment of Jacek Kuron, a group of young men, mostly of Jewish descent, convened a meeting. . . ." Twice in his speech he mentioned a certain Irena Lasota as a perpetrator of two major acts of sedition; he referred to her as Irena Lasota-Hirszowicz. Is Hirszowicz the name of her husband? No, she is not married. Hirszowicz is the former name of her father, who long ago changed it to Lasota. This is the familiar Soviet technique of indicating a person's Jewishness through a patronymic or some other bit of information which, to put it mildly, is non-essential. And here is how Gomulka handled the story of Pawel Jasienica, the actual leader of the oppositionist intellectuals. "His real name," said Gomulka, "is not Jasienica. It is Leon Lech Bejnar." That is true enough; Jasienica is actually a pen-name. The name "Benjar" is evidently non-Polish and, since Jasienica was the first to publicly condemn official anti-Semitism ("perfidiously," the Polish press said), the reader is likely to assume that it is a Jewish name. (After all, Lasota is only half-Jewish. . . .) The truth is that the name "Bejnar" is Tartar or Samogitian.

Gomulka's speech, of course, set the new pattern for the

Polish press. As a result, one can now read, in an article dealing with a case of embezzlement involving a person with a
familiar Polish name, some "subtle" hint like this: "His
descent is irrelevant because, as everybody knows, embezzle-
ments are committed by persons of all nationalities." The new
style of the press is to distinguish "good" Jews from "bad"
ones. A "good" Jew is one who considers Poland his homeland, is attached to Polish language and culture, is grateful to
the Poles for his rescue during the war, loves the Communist
party and government, and publicly condemns Israel. Any
other Jew is a "bad" one. "Bad" Jews are Zionists, cosmopoli-
tans, traitors, a "new fifth column," etc. Until recently, the
Jewish danger was covered by a "cowardly silence," but now
the press is "bravely" refusing to be intimidated by accusations of anti-Semitism.

"I am no anti-Semite," declares a certain Mr. Pietrzak,
"because my father rescued five Jews during World War II."
(Some of his father's best friends. . . .) Nobody is anti-Semitic.
Not even Mr. Piasecki and his subordinates in *Pax*. Never.
Anti-Semitism just disappeared, vanished; what is more, it
never existed. There are only bad Jews.

ANTI-SEMITISM AND CULTURAL CONFLICT

There is not enough data to explain or account for all this
anti-Semitic hullabaloo. It may be explained as reflecting a
conflict between political factions within the Communist party hierarchy. More likely, however, it reflects conflict not over
issues but between cultures, in particular between the Party
doctrinaires with a background in the intelligentsia and the
apparatchiki from the lower classes. Life in the top leadership of the Communist party is one of constant paranoia
concerning adversaries and rivals, and that paranoia begets
corresponding delusions. The now-official Polish anti-Semitism seems to express the stereotyped view that *apparatchiki*
hold of the intelligentsia. When the *apparatchiki* become
dominant their delusions find public outlet; this is why we
have recurrent waves of official anti-Semitism in Eastern
Europe — now here, now there. It all depends upon the vicis-
situdes of never-ending struggles for posts, for succession,
for power.

That the present wave of anti-Semitism in Poland should be so intense is, of course, related to events elsewhere in Eastern Europe, for whenever a dictator in any of the Eastern countries dies or is removed, and his death or removal gives rise to a struggle for his succession, the resulting popular excitement is apt to give rise to demands for democratization not only in that country but in surrounding countries as well. This is not true in those instances where the entire ruling clique stands together in opposition to the Russians and, at the same time, in opposition to their own people, as has happened in Yugoslavia, Rumania, Albania and China. But when a fight between rivals at the top breaks out, the rivals may start fighting each other openly and, in order to mobilize popular opinion, grant or at least promise some degree of democratization. This happened in Poland after the death of Bierut in 1956, in Hungary after the removal of Rakosi in July 1956, and in Czechoslovakia after the removal of Novotny. This may mean the opening of a genuine process of democratization — genuine, because the masses, thus encouraged, demand more and more democracy and, to get it, put pressure on the leadership. Eventually they have to be stopped, either by Russian tanks or by such complicated and tricky deals as took place in Poland in 1956-1957, or by a combination of the two as is now being practiced with regard to Czechoslovakia. But before they are stopped, their accomplishments provoke intense envy in the neighboring countries. Envy prompts the neighbors to act, even though such efforts are as a rule abortive — as was the case with Wolfgang Harich in East Germany in 1956.

That is why the recent Czechoslovak events pose a danger to the Polish regime — and why the Polish students shouted and displayed signs saying "Long live Czechoslovakia" and "We want a Polish Dubcek!" It is why two Czechoslovak correspondents were expelled from Poland for taking the students' side in their reports. Mere nationalist opposition to the Russians — or opposition on the part of a unified Communist party hierarchy, such as the leadership of Ceausescu in Rumania — raises no threat to the established order in neighboring countries. The substitution of the fist of Ceausescu for the fist of Brezhnev gives people in neighboring countries no reason for envy because it offers little or nothing in the way of democratization. Not even China's strenuous efforts to undermine Soviet might in Eastern Europe, by supporting underground groups of hard-core Stalinists, has caused any real disturbance. Gomulka has nothing to fear from Mao or Ceausescu, but he has a great deal to fear from Dubcek. The democratic turbulence next door in Czechoslovakia gives him reason to fear the Polish people.

June 1968

The Trial of Polish Dissidents

Jerzy Giedroyc

The Warsaw trial of five young intellectuals (February 9-24, 1970) was described in the Polish Communist press as a trial of the monthly magazine *Kultura,* which we have been publishing in Paris for nearly 25 years. The formal charges by the public prosecutor merely consist of a complaint that the accused had maintained contact with us: documents and writings originating in Poland had been sent our way by various means, and our magazine and publications had been secretly peddled in Poland. This trial, typical of a totalitarian regime, was aimed at opinions and ideas. It had no legal justification or any basis in current Polish laws. The attitude taken by one the the the accused, Karpinski, as assistant professor of sociology at Warsaw University, was the only logical one in the circumstances. He refused to answer the questions put by the prosecutor and the defense. His behavior constituted an accusation in itself; moreover, in a short statement, the young sociologist emphasized the groundlessness of the charges.

The extreme severity of the sentences (from three to 4½ years of hard labor) was possibly due to the angry reaction of the authorities who found that the trial had not achieved its originally intended aims. There were two such aims: first, to

discredit *Kultura* in the eyes of Western public opinion,
particularly in France where it is published (it is well known
that this attempt was accompanied by parallel and ridicu-
lously clumsy efforts in Warsaw, where an attempt was
made, during Franco-Polish negotiations, to pressure the
French into promising to shut down, or at least curtail, the
activities of our magazine in Paris); second, to compromise
Kultura in the eyes of Polish public opinion by giving the
impression that our magazine was carrying on "espionage
activities" under cover of an ideological and political struggle
aimed at establishing socialism with a human face in Poland.

Total failure is the only term that can be used to describe
the outcome of this dual purpose enterprise. Practically all
the reports and comments published in the Western press
omitted the insinuations concocted by the organizers of the
trial; even the Italian newspaper *L'Unita* was unable to conceal a certain amount of embarrassment in speaking of the
event. If our interest in the construction of the Oder-Danube
canal or in the atmosphere prevailing in the Soviet garrisons
stationed in Czechoslovakia is to be regarded as evidence of
our "espionage activities," then any free journalist taking a
serious interest in Eastern Europe and its political and economic problems is a spy. For *Kultura*, which is a politically
committed Polish journal and therefore obliged to appear
outside Poland, such curiosity is not just a legitimate right
but an elementary duty. The accusations made in the course
of the trial in an attempt to make us admit that we were
"American agents" are no less absurd. If *Kultura* is an independent magazine and in a position to send some thousand
copies of each issue clandestinely to Poland, it is because it
has 5,000 subscribers among Polish emigrants, scattered
throughout the world.

In its attempt to influence opinion in Poland, the trial also
met with failure in all probability — suffice it to recall the
article by the *Le Monde* correspondent in Warsaw — its end
result was the opposite of that intended. *Kultura*, which was
best known among Polish intellectuals, became, as the trial
wore on, an open topic of conversation among thousands of
Poles who had hitherto been unaware of its existence. Press

reports on the trial in Czechoslovakia, Hungary, Bulgaria and especially in the USSR show this to be the case (the article on the subject in *Literaturnaya Gazeta* is typical).

One may well wonder why the Polish authorities decided to draw attention so ostentatiously to a magazine published by emigres in Paris — a magazine which only manages with difficulty to reach intellectuals in Poland and has a very scanty readership in the other countries of the Soviet bloc. The London *Times* writes:

> The Warsaw trial no doubt has its origins in the efforts to neutralize the effects of the Polish students' revolt in March 1968 and the influence of the Czechoslovak reform movement. At a time when they are trying to improve relations with Western Europe the Polish authorities fear that the ideas of the radical left in the West will be received with increasing favor in Poland.

This analysis was fully confirmed at the trial by the statement of the principal defendant, the young archeologist and journalist Kozlowski and, to some extent, by those of the biochemist Szymborski, as well as by the evidence given by some students who are now in prison (further trials are in preparation) and who appeared as witnesses. The demonstrations in March 1968 and the events in Czechoslovakia were stimuli which prodded the young Polish socialists, recruited from the intellectual scene, into action. The wave of brutal repression then forced some of these young people, who had originally decided to confine their activities to Poland, to seek assistance abroad. They decided on *Kultura.* The decision was not, needless to say, fortuitous. It was made because of the political line followed by our magazine. The publishers of *Kultura* were and still are convinced (in spite of the defeat suffered by the "new trend" in Czechoslovakia) that the fight for socialism with a human face in Eastern Europe and the USSR will have its ups and downs, will assume various guises, will at times be more intense and at others less forceful, but will continue. It seems that Moscow shares this opinion because it has just convened a conference of representatives of the parties to consider "the danger of revisionism."

The five defendants at the Warsaw trial have been convicted of "having damaged Poland's reputation" by their activities. *Le Monde's* Warsaw correspondent writes that "it is now time to consider whether the damage done to Poland's reputation by trials of this kind is not greater." It so happened that on the day that the Warsaw court announced its verdict, Prague published a decree whereby four eminent representatives of the Czech reform movement now abroad, Sik, Svitak, Pelikan and Rambusek, were deprived of their nationality. Was it really a coincidence? The Warsaw trial and the Prague decree show that political emigration is a factor of growing importance in the fight that is being waged. It was in anticipation of such a situation that *Kultura* was founded almost a quarter of a century ago.

March 1970

The Genius and the Apparatus

Ivan Svitak

*Master Chuang once dreamt that he was a butterfly, fluttering
hither and thither. The butterfly felt like a butterfly, and
lacked for nothing — it did not know that it was Chuang!
Suddenly Chuang awoke and was amazed — he is Chuang!
And he does not know if Chuang dreamt that he was a butter-
fly or if the butterfly is now dreaming that it is Chuang.
Chuang or butterfly — surely there must be some difference!
And that is what is called the transformability of phenonema.*

Chuang-Tse, old Chinese philosopher

THE TRUTH OF PARADOX

If Marx came to life and wished to define himself in relation
to the image of Marx that has been built up since his death,
he would find himself in Chuang's situation. Like the Chinese
philosopher 200 years ago, Marx, too, would master the problem of the truth of paradox. He would do so through the
antinomies and paradoxes of reality, for his genius is the
highly developed, clear and precise consciousness of the self
in the world and the world in the self; it is the transparent
reflection of contemporary society in the consciousness of
the individual. The more universal genius is, the more it
unites within itself scientific truth, the message of freedom
and authority for weaklings.

299

Marx the scholar is the Copernicus of social sciences; he brought about a transformation of the sciences dealing with man similar to that which marked the move from astrology to astronomy. In speaking of Marx as the Copernicus of social sciences, we are not implying that the founder of modern astronomy was infallible. It was Galileo who discovered that the orbit of planets around the sun is elliptical and not circular, as Copernicus himself believed. Similarly, modern social science reinterprets the functioning of man in the modern world but Marx's anthropocentric standpoint still holds true.

Marx was not, is not and will never be the discoverer and theoretician of totalitarian dictatorship that he appears today, when the original meaning of his work — true humanism — has been given a thoroughly Byzantine and Asian twist. Marx strove for a wider humanism than that of the bourgeois democracies that he knew and for wider civil rights, not for the setting up of the dictatorship of one class and one political party. What is today thought to be the Marxist theory of the state and Marxist social science is simply an ideological forgery, a false, contemporary conception as wrong as the idea that the orbits of heavenly bodies are circular.

To understand Marx truly we must be aware how much he was conditioned by his time, determine his theoretical place, and not confuse his thought with the later interpretations by Lenin, Stalin and Mao. A true picture of Marx depends on an awareness of his historicity, while the ideological conceptions of "Marxism," "Marxism-Leninism" or "Maoism" are functional ideological tools used by apparatuses to manipulate the masses, not objective, truthful and historically valid interpretations. Just as it was necessary to separate Stalin from Lenin, so Lenin must be separated from Marx, not in order to oppose one against the other but so that both may be understood as real historical personalities.

If we approach the writings of Marx and Lenin in this historical, truthful and objective manner, then we must distinguish Marx's great thought about the liberating role of the working class in modern history from Lenin's specifically Russian thought about the leading role of the Communist party. Broadly speaking, Marx defended the leading role of the *working class;* he defended its historical mission and workers' activity, but he never imagined that this class itself might be dominated by a political party — and especially by the apparatus of this party. According to him, the dictatorship of the proletariat was to be the *temporary* rule of the *majority* over the minority, not the *permanent* terror of a *minority* against the people.

Marx relies on man, on the working class, on the people as the motive force of history, not on the manipulation of people. For him, man is the subject of the historical process, not an object to be manipulated by apparatuses. Lenin's concept of the Bolshevik party is fundamentally different. This is due to the basic realities of Czarist Russia — an ocean of illiteracy with a numerically weak working class. However, that does not make any less valid the criticism of Lenin's conception that was made by Plekhanov, by Rosa Luxemburg and by Trotsky.

Putting Leninism into effect in Russia led to the political success of the working class, to a victorious revolution and to the founding of a socialist state. Putting the same pattern into effect in Czechoslovakia, where the literate working class was already the strongest political force at the time the Communist party came into being, and where it represented the majority of the population even at the very beginning of the building of socialism, has led to clear failure. It was, and is, just as inappropriate that the party should dominate the working class as that the party apparatus should dominate the state. And it is so not because we are against Marx or Lenin, but precisely because we are for Marx and for an understanding of the historical context in which Lenin specifically adapted Marx's heritage to Russia — not to Europe.

If we think of Marx the scholar historically, bearing in mind the time in which he lived, the question of the timeless truth of his individual statements and attitudes does not arise, and we can appreciate the real worth of Marx's valid and still applicable methodology; moreover, we can turn it against his apparent disciples — the ideologists. To see how right this approach is, one has only to notice how violently the very people who claim to be Marxists hate the ruthless search for truth which is their master's methodology. The power apparatus has won all along the line against the real Marx, but in this it has only paradoxically confirmed the genius' paradoxical truth that institutions are stronger than people, a truth the genius had already arrived at in his high-school essay, whereas it took the apparatus a whole century to get there.

Because of its mass diffusion, the false image of Marx, as forged by ideologists of all shades in order to justify totalitarian dictatorship, cannot be changed all at once. At the moment it is enough to say that the present process of democratization is being hampered not by Marx but by much more concrete individuals with much smaller intellectual capacities. We can hope that we shall defeat them, because reason alone can overcome power permanently.

The ideological caricature of Marx can perhaps be adequately conveyed by the absurdly surrealistic metaphor of one sociologist for whom Marx, perverted and deformed in the consciousness of society, is a monster with two heads which are trying to shout each other down, one with Soviet and one with Chinese slogans. By contrast, the faithful, historical, picture of the real Marx shows the scholar, the European, the democrat, the socialist, the tribune of the people, the humanist, the revolutionary, the internationalist, the giant personality and the messenger of freedom. This true picture of the man Marx really was has been transformed by the apparatuses of the movement and by history itself into an absolute labyrinth of contradictions.

THE MESSAGE OF FREEDOM

Marx was a scholar of genius. But scientific knowledge continues to develop. Insofar as this means that the limits of knowledge are constantly expanding, Marx's scholarship is being outstripped by the evolution of the very social science that he founded. In discovering a valid methodology of social science, Marx discovered a weapon against himself as a fetish-idol, against ideological authority and against the perversion of his own message of freedom.

Marx was an earnest European, with deep roots in the European culture based on antiquity, Christianity, the Renaissance and the Enlightenment. But his teaching was taken over in the east of Europe and in Asia, where there was not only no Enlightenment but also no Renaissance. The core of Marx's discoveries — his criticism — had to be transformed into a bigoted orthodox faith in the unity of church and state, which took the shape of a monopoly of power, irreconcilable with European cultural tradition, with criticism and with science.

Marx was one of the greatest democrats of history. He stood for human and civil rights as the basis of political life. But the rise of the giant bureaucratic apparatuses of the modern state, of industrial societies and of political machines, as well as the practical impossibility of following democratic procedures in Czarist Russia and then in a land of semi-literacy, have obstructed the development of those features of democracy which Marx took for granted, convinced as he was that "one form of freedom depends upon another. . . . Whenever a specific freedom is questioned, freedom itself becomes questionable."

Marx was a socialist; he worked to change production relations to emancipate the working class, humanity and man as an individual. But the narrow interpretation of his program in purely economic terms, as a program of future prosperity, has led to the technocratic effort to create a consumer society. The *means* to the emancipation of mankind have become an end, contrary to Marx's original intentions; for him, economic demands were only a means of emancipating man, not an end in themselves.

Marx was a tribune of the workers' movement in which he saw a guarantee that mankind would be emancipated. But eventually organizations, apparatuses and even state apparatuses acquired power over the movement itself and stifled every spontaneous expression of the workers' will as treason against Marx. The greatest treason against Marx, however, is the very existence of these power apparatuses dominating the political movement of the working class.

Marx was a humanist, for whom the meaning of human

life lay in creation, in the development of man as a many-sided personality, in people's participation in the historical process and in the growth of human freedom. But these original aims, through which Marx hoped to achieve a revolutionary transformation have, in the apparatus version of Marxism, been completely subordinated to the functional conception of man as a mere object to be manipulated. In the vocabulary of the apparatus, his central postulate, the freedom of man, has become a reactionary slogan; this is the most brutal castration that Marx has had to suffer.

Marx was a revolutionary fully aware of his goal. Being a radical humanist in the middle of the 19th century meant trying to bring about revolutionary change in the political and economic structure of society. But the transformation of the industrial countries of Europe that was brought about by the organized strength of the workers' movement set in motion processes which changed the social position of the working class, its opinions, its political goals and even the very character of the revolution. The original conception that the proletarian revolution is a means of winning power is being changed by the radical transformation of science and technology; this is the true revolution, which is bringing mankind, and the working class, much closer to freedom than any fighting in the barricades.

Marx was an internationalist, for whom national frontiers were barriers to understanding between nations and between the working classes. But the doctrine of socialism in one country, which is incompatible with Marx's appeal to the workers of the world, has created a nationalistic pattern of cooperation between unequal nations. The ploughed-up stretches of land and the barbed wire between European countries are the most flagrant violation of the idea of internationalism. It is *against this idea* that the armed units stand on guard along the frontiers of socialist countries.

Marx was a great and many-sided personality. But be became the refuge of nonentities who knew, and know, that they cannot hope to turn the zeros that they are into a number except by hiding behind his great figure. We need only compare the personality of Marx with that of today's leaders to become convinced that history has a sense of comedy as cruel as it is malicious.

Marx was a messenger of the freedom of man. That is why he attracted the hatred of apparatuses of all colors. And inasmuch as progress is the growth of human freedom, the living Marx will go on attracting their hatred, just as the embalmed corpse of the ideology connected with his name will go on and on being exhumed in the solemn discourses of the official spokesmen of the apparatuses, who shower their decorations upon the dead genius only because he does not have the strength to throw the medals back in their face in the name of the very working class whom they would like to use as an alibi before the judgement of history.

THE LIE OF SALVATION

The ideological conception of Marx is a perversion of the real Marx, which is being used to justify the domination of apparatuses over the workers' movement. Marx is at the same time turned into a myth, an irrational authority, into the guarantor of the faith in the messianic role of the working class in modern history, into the focal point of the prophetically foretold workings of the laws of history. But Marx is not a savior.

As the social function of his teaching has changed, Marx has been made a prophet, a visionary and a messiah; this was the outcome of the historical process in which, after his death, Marx's various scientific views became norms of behavior with absolute validity for the workers' movement. In this way, scientific analysis of capitalism gradually grew to be a stereotype of ideological formulae; for quite a long time these could reflect the reality of capitalism, but nevertheless they lost their scientific character. Marx is not an earthly messiah.

As the discrepancies between Marx's analysis — perfectly accurate in regard to the capitalism of his own time — and the reality at the turn of the century, and then in the period between the wars, grew, so the giant of critical thought had to be smothered in thicker and thicker clouds of the incense of faith and turned into the impotent dummy of May Day parades. The gap between dogma and reality can be bridged

only by faith — by faith in a leader, in the secular god of a
mass movement, or by faith in the institution, in the secular
church, which guarantees salvation to man. But Marx cannot
be the object of faith, he is not a secular god.

As soon as the lie of salvation, that is, faith in the revolutionary, liberating mission of the Communist party, was substituted as a principle for the discipline of truth, the problem
of faith and of the decline of faith emerged as the central
issue. There came the break with the intellectuals who were
unwilling to lay down their own intellect on the altar of the
party, of the nation or of the movement. The famous statement "Believe the Party, comrades"* and the endless discussions on whether the Party is always right revealed the total
bankruptcy of critical though, which was all the more absurd
for being brought about in the name of Marx.

At the same time, the absurd statement about the Party
being the guarantor of truth and the focus of faith reflects
the deep crisis in the consciousness of the left-wing intellectuals of the 1950s. It reflects the tragic confusion in thought
and in practice, which accompanied not only the trials but also the establishment, in the heart of Europe, of a measure of
barbarity such as Czechs and Slovaks had hitherto experienced only at the hands of foreign invaders, but never at the
hands of representatives of their own nations. To this day,
textbooks quote, as a warning example to schoolchildren of
the inhumanity of a system based on slavery, the killing,
2,000 years ago, of the woman mathematician Hypatia by the
mob of Alexandria, whom history holds fully responsible for
the murder. Yet the present apparatuses are just as fully
responsible for an act which is a unique performance in
modern world history — the execution of a woman, Milada
Horakova, for her political activity in time of peace. It is to be
hoped at least that she will not be covered with the filth of
rehabilitation by alibi-seekers, but rather that she will be

---

*   Translator's note: after the executions that followed the Slanksy trial,
Czechoslovak President and Party boss Klement Gottwald said in a
speech that many comrades were asking, if so many party leaders had
been traitors, whom were they to believe, and he answered, "Believe the
party, comrades."

revealed in her true character to the same schoolchildren, whose mental hygiene is so dear to those concerned with the political education of youth and, at college level, with the so-called social sciences.

Faith in the party was a defense against the appalling absurdities of life, which appeared totally incomprehensible and incompatible with the humanist goal that the ideology proclaimed in words and destroyed in practice. The psychological mechanisms, both individual and collective, of faith and despair, frustration and salvation, explain why, in a situation in which critical thought had totally ceased to function, attitudes toward the trials, toward the USSR or toward Stalin became the "touchstone." Once the premises according to which the discipline of truth about reality is subordinated to party discipline and to faith in salvation through the party accepted, all that remained was to believe — to believe even beyond the grave, like those imprisoned Communists who died with Stalin's name on their lips. It is precisely those who provoke the deepest disgust.

The problem of faith — in the trials, in the party, and in Stalin — also reflected the central issue, that is, the conviction that one has be accept guilt in order to save the meaning of one's former commitment to the cause of socialism, the meaning of the fight against fascism, the meaning of the building of socialism. The greater the doubts that arose, the higher did the flame of faith have to rise, the showier did the *auto da fé* have to be. And the readier was the average man to accept the stereotyped resolution of his doubts, presenting them *before his own conscience* as some kind of unessential, narrow considerations, insignificant in comparison with the cheering crowds, with the building of new plants and with the undoubtedly noble aim of helping the people, which was constantly put forward by the agile ideology as a reality, though in practice it did not exist.

Neither Marx nor the working class accept the ghastly game of pinning medals on the breasts of corpses in the name of their murderers. Neither Marx nor the working class, nor indeed history, recognizes the rehabilitation of corpses, for, unlike the alibi-seekers of the apparatuses, they know very well what justice is. The working class, as Marx's heir, has a clean slate, it did not murder and persecute freedom, so it does not need the alibi and the farce of the sinister ceremonies in which decorations are solemnly returned to corpses which gave thanks for their executions, accepting the appalling sacrifice as a logical service to the same apparatuses which executed them and to which, during their lives, they had themselves belonged. The working class, like the intellectuals, looks with horror upon this senseless performance which is meant to exculpate the apparatus in the eyes of history; it can only see it as a provocation by the apparatus against common sense, especially if these acts are performed in the name of the process of rebirth, on workers' day, on May 1st, 1968.

The baser the goals that are aimed at, the nobler must be the ideology that is used to justify them; for people do not normally have the courage to do evil, to hurt others, or to spread suffering, unless the institutions of salvation, the Church or the Party, offer them sedatives to calm their conscience. Man cannot save himself through faith in a leader, in an ideology or an institution; he cannot, through his emotions, win heaven, or reason, or happiness, which is a more civilian term for salvation. But he can understand himself as a free, active, responsible being, with his own reason and feelings: then he will not be deaf to the heritage of the genius, whose last will and testament, translated into the language of today, might sound something like this:

YES	*NO*
Internationalism	Nationalism
Europe	Asia and America
Sovereign Czechoslovakia	Neocolonialism
Socialism	State capitalism
Direct democracy	Dictatorship
Parliamentarianism	Monopoly of power
Culture	Apparatuses
Humanism	Manipulation
Critical attitude	Authorities
The people	The masses
The individual	The elite
Freedom	Anarchy

Yes to open society. No to totalitarian mechanism. People of the world unite against the rats of the world. Marx is dead. Long live Marx.

August 1968

Revolution in Czechoslovakia

Paul Barton

At the time of writing — May 10, 1968 — one can only wonder whether Czechoslovakia is on the road to historic achievement or on the brink of tragedy. Yesterday, for the second time in little more than a month, Moscow used the threat of military aggression against Czechoslovakia by moving troops close to its borders.

Nothing of this sort happened when the Rumanian Communists started curbing Russian domination of their country. The difference in treatment is all too logical. In their move toward greater independence, the Rumanians maintained their totalitarian regime intact; their defiance meant a certain loss for the Russian empire but hardly threatened Communist rule in Russia itself. By contrast, the reappearance of freedom in Czechoslovakia is only too likely to prove contagious. It is bound to encourage the deeply rooted desire for freedom, democracy and progress felt by people throughout the Communist world, in the Soviet Union as well as in the satellite countries. Whereas Rumanian defiance is a centrifugal action, what is happening in Czechoslovakia is the beginning of an antitotalitarian revolution which, by its very nature, is centripetal. Its success would threaten the center of power itself.

At this stage, no one knows the extent to which the Moscow leadership is prepared to disrupt peace in Central and Eastern Europe in order to stop this revolution. Perhaps there will be only repeated military threats within the limits of psychological warfare. But it is also possible that such threats are being used to test world reaction and to tame it before an actual invasion of Czechoslovakia.

The most remarkable feature of the revolution that has begun in Czechoslovakia is its peaceful and orderly conduct. The tragic Hungarian experience, which discouraged hopes and dimmed prospects for significant democratic change in the entire Soviet empire, has finally been absorbed and understood. People gradually moved from despair to patient, daily resistance, slowly eroding the entire totalitarian apparatus without attempting to crush it in one big blow.

HISTORY OF THE REVOLUTION

Today, the self-control exercised by the population is not particularly surprising given the fact that progress toward freedom is rapid and highly visible. What is surprising and new is that the breakdown of the Party leadership and apparatus, which took place around the turn of the year, was brought about without any major outburst of violence. This objective, which was attained briefly in Hungary only through a heroic uprising, and which even uprisings failed to attain in Czechoslovakia and East Germany in June 1953 and in Poznan three years later, was accomplished by the Czechs and Slovaks in such a way that nobody but themselves even noticed.

World opinion began to take developments in Czechoslovakia seriously when Antonin Novotny was replaced by Alexander Dubcek as first secretary of the Communist party. That event, however important it may have been as the beginning of a new period, was not the cause but the result of the breakdown of the Party leadership. Supported by Moscow up to the end, and with his own people in all the key positions, Novotny could not be eliminated so long as the apparatus remained intact. When the apparatus began to crack, however, Novotny's men suddenly felt insecure under his protection. Wherever they looked they met only hostility. As a result, they began to feel that they were on the losing side. One by one, they shifted over to the side of Novotny's opponents. When it was time to count heads, Novotny was reduced to such a tiny minority in the Party leadership that not even Brezhnev could help him. His last hope was an army coup which resulted merely in his trusted general fleeing to the United States.

The extent to which the Dubcek leadership asserts its authority depends entirely on its recognition of the breakdown of the Party apparatus. By tolerating disregard of censorship, stating that the Party will no longer interfere with the management of the factories, proclaiming that the unions' task is to defend workers' interests, promising a speedy investigation and review of political trials — the new leadership more or less creates the illusion that it is busy dismantling the totalitarian power apparatus. What it is really doing is publicly accepting the consequences of its breakdown.

Today's revolution in Czechoslovakia is the fruit of the Hungarian uprising in still another sense. It will be remembered that during the eventful autumn of 1956 the whole world was surprised by the lack of reaction on the part of the Czechs and Slovaks, before, during and after the Hungarian revolt. Contrary to what outside observers believed at the time, Czechoslovakia was far from calm and quiet during those weeks, but the fact remains that there was only minor and sporadic unrest. This meek reaction was to a large extent due to the people's own experience. Early in June 1953, they were the first in the whole satellite world to try to crush the Communist system through an uprising: what the Western press reported as a local affair — an uprising in the industrial city of Pilsen — was in reality a widespread urban workers' revolt, which broke out in a great number of industrial centers and mining areas throughout the country. Nevertheless, the revolt was promptly defeated; it was crushed before the rural population even learned what was going on in the cities, which were immediately encircled by the army and the police. The population drew the disheartening conclusion that this was not a viable means of doing away with a totalitarian dictatorship. It seems, however, that many people regretted, and still regret, the meekness of their own reaction to the Hungarian uprising. In their present courage there appears to be an element of remorse for having abandoned the Hungarians to their fate at the hands of the Russian army.

On the other hand, the relative passivity of the Czechs and Slovaks in 1956 was the result of the clever tactics of the Communist leadership. When pressure started mounting in Poland and Hungary, the Party there tried to tame it through concessions. By the same token, the old conflicts, disagreements and intrigues among the Communist leaders grew worse and became public. This naturally encouraged the revolt. In Czechoslovakia, the official reaction was exactly the opposite. Although the Czechoslovak Party leadership had been particularly ridden by infighting, it closed its ranks and began to operate, at least toward the population, as a monolith. Concessions were also made, but they were strictly controlled. As soon as any section of the population tried to extend such concessions by increasing its demands — such was, for instance, the case of the writers' congress in 1956 — the Party cracked down on it without hesitation. No major reforms were contemplated. At the same time, the Communist leadership avoided any new initiatives which might have upset the existing pattern of power, production, social relationships, cultural activities, etc. In other words, it adopted the same tactics which had been employed some seven years earlier by weak governments in France and which the French call *immobilisme*.

In this way, the Prague regime prevented the opening of any cracks in which the seeds of revolt would take root. However, *immobilisme* is something which a totalitarian system cannot really afford.

The economy of the country fell into a protracted depression. Notwithstanding the art of the official statisticians in producing optimistic figures, the authorities had to admit that in 1962 the national income had increased by a mere 1.4%, that in 1963 it actually decreased by 2.2%, that in 1964 it grew by 0.7% and in 1965, thanks to a 3.6% rise, it was only 2% higher than three years before. Under the burden of this depression, the determination of the Party leaders to avoid any major reforms began to collapse. They had to cede ground to reform-minded younger Communist economists—of these, Ota Sik has become the best known—who keenly devised an entire set of far-reaching changes in planning and management. Some of these changes were already introduced in January 1966, and more in January 1967.

Quite a few among the reform-minded economists were former *apparatchiki;* Ota Sik himself started his career in 1945 as a secretary of the head of the organization department in the Party Secretariat. However, at the time they raised their voices, they were no longer in the Party apparatus and occupied no political positions at the top. Therefore, the unwilling acceptance of their proposals did not cause the Party leadership to lose its monolithic face. But it did cause it to lose face.

The protracted economic slump naturally affected the situation of the workers. According to the official statistics themselves, the average nominal wage increased by 3% in 1960, by 2.5% in 1961, by 0.7% in 1962, decreased by 0.1% in 1963, increased again by 2.9% in 1964 and by 2.3% in 1965. This is pitiful enough. But if it were possible to calculate the real wages, the picture would be still worse. For instance, prices went up in 1962 and 1963, and the quality of the goods available for the same price constantly deteriorated throughout the period.

The growing bitterness of the workers was by no means soothed by the government's acceptance of the proposed reform measures. In fact, these measures clearly tend to make their situation worse. It is quite typical that the Communist economists, as reform-minded as they may be, can imagine only such reforms as would make the worker pay for the mismanagement of the national economy by the *apparatchiki.* These economists are still victims of the Party propaganda, by which they were bred, even when they criticize the Party leadership and press for reforms. They firmly believe that America and affluence mean the free play of market forces and prices. Whatever they may read about built-in stabilizers, redundancy arrangements, retraining facilities, etc., appears to them as capitalist propaganda, not as the conquests of organized labor. This is true not only of Ota Sik and his friends in Czechoslovakia but also of Liberman in Russia and the reformers in other Communist countries. Therefore, when they devise changes in planning and management, they are so keen on the free play of market forces that any injury they may cause to the workers is considered regrettable but necessary. In Czechoslovakia, the main features of the economic reform, as far as its effects on workers are concerned, are unemployment, pressure on wages and rise in salaries for people in the management, speed-up in work and no guaranteed earnings — the level of a worker's earnings is to depend on the profits of the company.

The passive resistance of the workers, which had never ceased during the 20 years since the Communist takeover, and which was resumed again after the defeat of the 1953 uprising, has tremendously increased over the last year or so, partly because the monolithic regime was losing face, partly because of the additional hardship brought about by the economic reform. As a result, the moral pressure which the factory workers bring to bear, day in, day out, on the local officers of the official pseudo-unions increased to such an extent that in many plants the workers managed to get these officers on their side. After twenty years of siding with the management, the locals began, in many places, to defend the interests of the workers. Yet these locals are intertwined with local Party organizations. That is where the power apparatus began to crumble and fall to pieces.

Many observers missed these developments, since by their very nature they are inconspicuous and mainly silent; that applies not only to observers abroad but also to those inside the country who are out of touch with the life of the factories—and under a totalitarian rule society is very much compartmented. As a result, it seemed to them that the Novotny leadership succumbed to the fire of criticism from writers, professors and intellectuals in general. This is not a new illusion. It was already widespread in the cases of Poland and Hungary in 1956: those who have the means of expressing their opinion publicly and in writing appear as the real force

that defeats the dictatorship. In reality, the writers and intellectuals were able to fan the fire only because the leadership's authority was undermined by the economic slump and
since its will was weakened and the possibility of using terror
was lessened by the unrest in the factories.

The great merit of the intellectuals was that they exploited
the situation fully and brought the feeling of insecurity into
higher levels of the apparatus, which could not be reached
directly from the bottom, by the factory workers. In this way
they demolished the monolithic features of the leadership, so
carefully maintained since the Hungarian uprising. Indeed,
by the time the leadership was getting ready to crack down
on the intellectuals last fall, it suddenly discovered that it
was itself divided. Men like Alexander Dubcek, who was to
replace Novotny at the top of the Party, Joseph Smrkovsky,
the former political prisoner who was to become the President
of the National Assembly, and a few surviving Communist
oldtimers, who recognized in the rebellious voices of young
writers an unmistakable echo of the ideals of their own past
youth, were already telling Novotny that the game was up.

FAILURES OF THE NEW LEADERSHIP

The Dubcek leadership has thus far failed to take positive
measures which might further consolidate this emancipating
process. Foreign correspondents in Prague write humorous
reports about newspaper, radio and television censors who
play cards in the office because they have nothing to do.
What this really means is that the censorship apparatus is
being artificially maintained, long after people working in
the information media have ceased to accept it. It is difficult
to imagine that drafting a law abolishing censorship is such
a time-consuming business.

It is certainly an improvement that a defense lawyer has
been made Procurator General, the key position in the law
enforcement system; still better, the new man dismissed two
Deputy Procurators General and replaced them with a former
defense lawyer and a university lecturer. However, the mon-
strous totalitarian institution of General Procuracy, which
combines the functions of public prosecution with final
supervisory power over the execution of the law by ministries,

courts, police, enterprises, public servants and all citizens, remains in force. Although it sounds like a bad joke, a special department of this very institution is now in charge of reviewing political trials and rehabilitating their victims.

Another example of the failure of the new leadership to do away with totalitarian institutions which cannot function at present is the following from the March 15 issue of the Prague Daily, *Zemedelske Listy,* which shows how the tools of police oppression remain while tremendous pressure from the population (even an association of former political prisoners has recently been founded) has forced a review of all political trials:

> Yesterday the presidium of the National Assembly examined a report by the General Procuracy on the methods, progress and present state of the review of political trials. . . . The report says that past illegal measures were encouraged by the way Security was organized at that time. They were encouraged by the fact that investigation organs, pre-trial detention and, in addition, the execution of the sentence and the prisons were all under the jurisdiction of Security and were not subject to thorough review by the Procuracy. And what is the present situation? The investigative apparatus is part of the Ministry of the Interior, pre-trial detention is under the jurisdiction of the Ministry of the Interior, the prisons are administered by the Ministry of Interior, as well. Once these facts are established, we are beset by a number of questions. Thanks to the fact that the press is no longer subject to political censorship, we shall pay careful attention to the possible consequences of organizing Security in this manner. We shall be particularly satisfied if — as is also being proposed in the report of the special department of the General Procuracy, headed by Dr. Jan Adamec — the security system is completely reorganized, the independence of the investigative organs and their complete separation from the Ministry of the Interior are guaranteed and the administration of prisons is taken out of the jurisdiction of the Ministry of Interior. This is far from all that is needed for a complete transformation of the work of security and justice. Difficult as it is to believe, we have learned from a trustworthy source that our lawyers must carry out the rehabilitation of innocent victims of the trials only partially on the basis of the original material, since the results of investigations by previous commissions must also be taken into account.

The structure of the Party apparatus also remains unchanged. The policy of preserving enfeebled institutions is dramatically illustrated in the trade union field. The leadership of the official pseudo-unions has been crippled by the events of the past several months. The president has been replaced by a former minister, selected by the Party presidium, but his election by the Central Council of Trade Unions has not been accepted by the membership. The works committees (officers of the locals) continue to protest his election. A Slovak vice president, added to the central set-up has already come into conflict with the controversial president on the vital issue of consolidating the leadership. This occurred at a public plenary meeting of the Central Council of Trade Unions. Of the six secretaries of the Central Council, five are out and the sixth will go as soon as new secretaries are elected. Yet, more than a month after the dismissal of the former president and the resignation of all the secretaries, the Central Council refused to elect new secretaries until Council members are given an evaluation of the work of every single member of the secretariat and of the presidium of the Council. As a result, the central apparatus must run a lame duck operation at a time when it is being flooded by resolutions, petitions and delegations presenting the workers' demands and when sporadic attempts are being made to build new unions outside the framework of the official Revolutionary Trade Union Movement.

The Dubcek leadership has thus far resisted the temptation to take the simple, basic step that could reshape the trade union structure, i.e., to give back to the Ministry of Labor and Social Welfare its functions and prerogatives that had been transferred to the Central Council of Trade Unions, its presidium and secretariat. So long as its secretariat drafts laws, issues decrees, administers health insurance, carries out factory inspections, etc., the Central Council of Trade Unions cannot simply be the executive body of the organization and cannot reform itself in response to mounting demands from the membership.

The apparent insensitivity of the Dubcek leadership to the growing need to dismantle the apparatus and to start building or permit the building of democratic institutions is undoubtedly one of its characteristic features.

DUBCEK'S OBJECTIVES

Everyone is speculating about the real objectives of Dubcek and his allies but no one seems to know the answer. Dubcek's biography is one of the perfect *apparatchik*. Brought up in the Soviet Union, he returned there for extensive party schooling in the 1950s. On the other hand, he was the Party boss in Slovakia from 1962 on, throughout the period when the disillusioned and liberal minded survivors of the Stalinist purges were raising their critical voices, while cleverly asserting their authority as Communist oldtimers. This was one of the processes that eventually led to the breakdown of the Party leadership.

The composition of Dubcek's team is hardly more conclusive as evidence of his aims. Among his allies are some who spent years in jail and many others who reached high positions during the same period. In any case, given the mystique of Party membership and the enormous gap between Party propaganda and reality, a Communist's past does not necessarily determine his attitude in this kind of crisis.

There are many signs that the new leadership is divided between those who, like Dubcek, are trying to convert the revolution into a cautious process of reform, and those who are determined to draw all the lessons of the Stalinist disaster. Voices in favor of freedom for opposition parties to organize and recruit have been heard within Dubcek's innermost circle. These divisions may help to explain the ambiguities of the new leadership.

What about the objective of those favoring cautious reforms? They may be trying to gain time to avoid Russian armed aggression or, on the contrary, to gain time to deprive the population of the fruit of its long, patient resistance to totalitarian rule. Their apparent insensitivity to the growing need to dismantle the disintegrating apparatus may be based on a speculation: if the pace of the revolution were to be decelerated and eventually brought to a halt by Russian military threats, the apparatus could be made to work again, under the new leadership.

Between these two extreme interpretations, which are the only rational ones, many others are possible. They are more or less irrational but, then, there is much that is absurd in the reasoning of Communist party members. It is even possible that Dubcek and his closest associates fought Novotny to save the Party from ruin. They might well be sincere in their attempts to persuade Moscow that they are reinvigorating the Communist regime.

In this connection, what is happening in the rebellious writers' union is indicative. For a long time, that organization, whose leadership is almost entirely composed of Party members, defied Novotny and his apparatus. The writers' union even had a fund to finance those victimized writers who were deprived of a livelihood because publication of their work was prohibited. The president of the writers' union is an oldtime Communist, formerly president of the Communist student organization before World War II, who spent years in jail under Communist rule. Now that freedom has exploded in all spheres of life, it has become increasingly evident that these Communist writers believe in the Party mystique. While their bitter opposition to the soulless dictatorship of the Party apparatus induces them to respect non-Communist writers and publish their books and even their political comments, they make certain that these non-Communist writers are kept from positions of real leadership of the writers' union.

So far as the intentions and objectives of the Dubcek leadership are concerned, the picture remains extremely confused. It may well be that even within the leadership there is uncertainty about the real roles played by individuals. Until recently, after all, they were all saying things they did not mean and now they all speak an ambiguous language. For the moment, however, these ambiguities do not seriously hamper the revolution. This is not a revolution from above. Therefore, people are not too concerned about the objectives of the men at the top. Their own objectives are perfectly clear.

Professor Ivan Svitak, an old-time socialist, put it most clearly when he declared that what people wanted was not democratization but democracy. What matters to the people is that, up to now, the new leadership has not prevented them from pursuing their revolution in that peaceful, orderly way that would make Russian military intervention as unlikely as possible. However, no matter how the people proceed, the possibility of such intervention remains terribly real.

May 1968

The Czechoslovak Revolution: Background, Forces and Objectives

Vitezslav Pravda

The last day of March 1968 witnessed the birth of an organization unique in the entire East European bloc: an association of thousands of former political prisoners of the present regime, known as "K 231" ("K" for club, "231" for the law under which political enemies used to be sentenced to harsh penalties).

At about the same time, an association calling itself the "Club of Committed Non-Party Members" was founded for the purposes of uniting people who were not members of any of the existing political parties.

The Ministry of the Interior, responsible for authorizing new organizations, refused to issue licenses for these associations. The Czechoslovak Communist Party refused to recognize any political groupings other than the already-existing ones. But the debates on that question divided Party members.

Young students and workers flocked to public gatherings at which high-ranking Party officials answered questions that only a few months earlier had been frowned upon or prohibited altogether. There was a feeling of the birth of democracy. On March 4, the Communist party presidium repealed the 1964 resolution that had introduced harsher censorship measures: for the next few months Czechoslovakia had practically no censorship although the formal abolition of censorship was not approved by the National Assembly until June.

This freedom, this period of "letting a hundred flowers blossom," became a thorn in the sides of Polish, Soviet and East German Communists. But despite repeated attacks from those Party quarters that were controlled by higher officials of the apparatus, no restrictions were reimposed. Any regulation or Party resolution containing restrictive measures, any official pronouncement that failed to respect newly won freedoms, came under attack in the press and/or radio. Television was suddenly discovered to be of immense power if any personality or idea were to get a wide hearing. Thus politics were "democratized" anew after 20 years.

This first act of the democratization process drew slowly to a close without exerting any real impact on life in Czechoslovakia . All the changes seemed to be merely at the top. But at the beginning of April, the Central Committee presidium had been newly elected; the National Front — comprising every existing political party and "social organization" — got a new chairman, Frantisek Kriegel, who seemed to bring some fresh ideas about cooperation between Communists and non-Communists; a new government was formed; the National Assembly chose a new chairman; the Supreme Court had a new president. Although these were only surface changes, they did seem to give people the assurance that the ruling party was ridding itself of old methods and the people associated with those methods. Dubcek and many minor officials took every opportunity to stress the merits of the lower level officials.

What could be seen clearly enough through the maze of speeches was the concern of the apparatus for keeping itself intact against the assults of men like the philosopher, Ivan Svitak, and the signers of manifestos like the "Two Thousand Words." The "Two Thousand Words" met with a chorus of criticism from the Czechoslovak Communist Party and with quite vicious attacks from the leaderships of the Russian, East German and Polish Communist parties, which were

beginning to issue ominous warnings to the effect that "counterrevolutionary" elements were threatening "the social
achievements." What aroused their ire were these words: "We
can assure the government that we will back it, if necessary,
even with weapons, as long as the government does what we
gave it the mandate to do." In the case of Ivan Svitak, a
lecturer in philosophy at Charles University attempting to
establish relations not only with rebellious students but also
with miners, what angered them was his description of the
Czechoslovak system as a "totalitarian dictatorship."

The greatest achievement of the Czechoslovak experiment
in democratization, however, is the fact that for the first
time in 20 years (actually, 40 years if you consider the theoretical void since the death of Lenin) Marxists are debating the
fundamental questions openly. Here is how Professor Svitak
expressed it:

> Workers and intellectuals have a common enemy — bureau-
> cratic dictatorship of the apparatus. . . . And it is for this reason
> that in the interests of socialist democracy we have to strengthen
> the unity of those working with their hands and those working
> with their brains against the apparatus of the elite which has
> been, is, and remains the main obstacle to the unique experiment
> of our nation with socialist democracy.

PRELUDE TO SPRING

The prelude to the Spring events actually occurred last
year. Economic conditions were very grave and there was all
sorts of talk in ruling circles about the need for "economic
reform." Then, in June 1967, there was a cry for freedom from
the writers' congress. Its action reflected the restlessness in
the country among all strata of the population. Finally, in
Fall 1967, the student demonstrations occurred and the attacks on them brought home to every citizen an accurate
awareness of the Stalinist tinge of the Novotny clique. The
scene was set for the meeting of the Party Central Committee, in October 1967, to consider "the position and the role of
the Party." The economic and social crisis deeply affected the
Party as well. The widespread passivity of its rank and file
had been a long-standing concern, often mentioned in Party
newspapers. An undercurrent of dissatisfaction and criticism
of the discrepancy between reality and the hollow claptrap
of Party officials was growing increasingly stronger.

At first sight, the outcome of the October session seemed limited to one more lengthy document reaffirming the leading role of the Party. However, it was at this session that a question arose that helps to illuminate the internal crisis of the Communist party: Alexander Dubcek — who was (in January 1968) to become the First Secretary of the Party, the first Slovak to hold this crucial post — had come forward with sharp criticism of the Party "solution" of the national question, which Lenin had considered critical. The clash of Dubcek and Novotny, the previous and long-time first Secretary of the Party, was not altogether clear at first, especially since the Central Committee session was adjourned so that Novotny could go to Moscow to celebrate the anniversary of the October Revolution. However, Novotny promised to allow the work of the "central authorities, above all of the government," to be analyzed at the December session.

The Central Committee presidium that had to prepare the plenary session was not convened until December 11, just before the session was to begin. The clash with Novotny continued, the presidium being unable to unite on a proposal to be presented at the plenum. Some members pressed for a separation of the functions of the president of the republic from those of the Party's first secretary. (Novotny held both posts.)

At the plenary session, Novotny's report on a new division of governmental responsibilities was rejected. This was something unheard of: it had never happened before and was a clear sign of mistrust of the most powerful man in Party and State.

After stormy debates, some echo of which reached a wider public, individual members of the presidium as well as Central Committee secretaries were called upon to give their personal views. This quite unusual procedure made it impossible for them to hide behind a collectively accepted "resolution" and to ponder over their views. The discussions dragged on too long for the sessions to end before Christmas, as a result of which everyone was happy to agree to a woman member's proposal to adjourn and reconvene at the beginning of January 1968.

The December plenum decided to create a consultative

group to propose to the January session — in agreement with
the presidium — a solution to the "cumulation of the highest
functions" and, if need be, to propose an alternative proposal
for first secretary. Two problems arose at this point. The
first one, of course, the economic crisis. The second was the
national question.

The authoritarian regime had proved incapable of dealing
with the economic crisis that had occurred as far back as
1963, when national production had decreased and economic
growth stagnated. A few figures will illustrate: One crown of
national income was produced between 1956-1960 for every
2½ crowns of investment; during 1960-1965 the proportion
rose to 1:9.50. In 1938, an apartment could be built in 1392
work hours; in 1964, in 1720 hours. While agricultural production in Western Europe increased roughly by half between
1961 and 1963, Czechoslovak agriculture reached only its pre-
war level in that period. Some half-hearted attempts were
made at "industrial reorganization," but they were insufficient to stop the downward trend of the economy. By 1967
the clash between the economists' demands for decentralization and the extreme political centralization exploded into the
open. Still, some members of the presidium hesitated to stand
up against Novotny. Few of them were linked to him by years
of their "common" rule, but none had a clear concept of what
to do if Novotny were to be overthrown. The older ones, who
had been Party members since before the war, had spent
their lives serving the idea of Stalinism. They could not
develop any new idea: they might have sensed the need for a
change, even for a profound change, especially in the economy
— but as subsequent events were to demonstrate they simply
could not keep up with the January developments once the
latter quickened their pace.

No doubt, Novotny had his own thoughts about the proposed changes. During the days of the January session,
People's Militia — special armed workers' units consisting
entirely of Communists, with a tradition of dogmatic loyalty
to the Party — held maneuvers in Prague and around the
capital, where some extra police units were concentrated as
well. Also, Novotny's most loyal follower in the army command, General Sejna, tried to persuade a group of officers of

their duty to oppose the prospective change in the person of the first secretary — but the letter they sent came just one hour after the election had taken place. Nor was there any consolation for Novotny in the visit of Brezhnev, whom he invited as early as December 1967. The Russian may have subsequently regretted his non-intervention, but by then the situation had changed more than any of them, Brezhnev, Novotny and Dubcek, could have foreseen.

The second sequel to the December session began on January 3. After three days of heated debates, with a great many of the Central Committee members hesitating and remaining undecided for a long time, a majority of the Central Committee not only supported the proposal of the presidium to separate the functions of the first secretary and head of state but also elected four new members of the presidium, at least three of whom were among those who had criticized Novotny since Autumn 1967.

The resolution approved on January 5 and published together with a short communique on January 6, still linked Novotny's "personality" with important successes of socialist construction. But the attempt to paper over the differences between the "economic reformers" and the majority of the Central Committee could not hide the clash between Dubcek and Novotny on the national question, which had become one of the central issues in dispute between the two Communist leaders. In order to understand fully what was involved, we must here roll back the film of history to the period between the end of the second world war and the Communist takeover in Czechoslovakia in 1948. (For space considerations we must omit the question of other national minorities such as the Ukrainians, Hungarians and Germans.)

A SHORT HISTORY — 1944-1948

The Slovaks, for centuries oppressed and exploited by the Hungarian gentry, remained the last part of the Czechoslovak Republic (established in 1918) to be developed. What made things still worse was the theory of a single "Czechoslovak" nation. In spite of all evidence to the contrary, the "theory" stubbornly denied that the Czechs and the Slovaks were two different nations.

What may seem a play on words is, unfortunately, for

Czechoslovakia and its working class, a vital question: denying the Slovaks their own nationality meant denying their
self-determination. The depression hit Slovakia in the thirties
far harder than the rest of the country, giving rise to a strong
nationalist movement there. It entered into agreement with
Hitler, thus helping to destroy Czechoslovakia in 1938. While
the western parts of Czechoslovakia became a German "pro-
tectorate," Slovakia emerged as a "free state" allied with
Germany.

Though prospering relatively, the majority of the Slovaks
detested the Nazis and, after Hitler's assault on Soviet Russia, when the Slovak government sent its troops to help the
Germans on the eastern front, anti-German feeling came to a
head. In collaboration with other national anti-German elements, the Slovak Communist party organized a broad political union on the eve of 1943 and, counting on Soviet help and
cooperation once the Red Army stood on Slovak borders,
prepared an armed uprising. Let's note that most of the Slovak troops that were sent to fight along with the Germans
crossed over to the Soviets and became part of the Czechoslovak armed units fighting with the Red Army.

The uprising broke out in August 1944. The Red Army
helped as little as possible, for the Soviets had their own
military plans. Thus the uprising, in spite of heroic battles,
was crushed. It is against this tragic background that one
must also view the heroism of the Prague uprising in May
1945.

Few in the world outside of Czechoslovakia know of either
uprising and fewer still understand them. There are those
who are all too ready to speak about the ease with which the
Communists are able to take over in 1948, claiming that it
proves the "passivity" of the working class in accepting Communist leadership in Slovakia in 1945 and in Prague in 1948.
What they forget is that it was the Nazis, not the Communists, who held state power during the war; that the six years
of Nazi occupation and terror had been preceded by a disastrous depression, caused by private capitalism, not by Communism; and that the Communists, once the Nazis invaded
Soviet Russia, became the most militant resistance fighters.

It is true that, despite the fact that workers played the leading role in the 1945 uprising, they let control slip from their hands and that the trade union organizations as well as the political ones came under the rule of the *apparatchiki* and were at no time subject to control from below. Moreover, the Communists promptly created an amalgam of bureaucracies. State capitalism, or what the Communists were pleased to call "a mixed economy," was established, and established from above.

One important outcome of the 1944 uprising was the decision of the Slovak political parties to unite with the Czechs and to build a common state again as soon as Germany was defeated. The only condition was to be autonomy for Slovakia. This was solemnly promised in the first Czechoslovak postwar government declaration issued in the East Slovakian town of Kosice in April 1945. Though it met with some resistance from the adherents of the idea of a "Czechoslovak" nation, the agreement was carried out.

The political system of Czechoslovakia between 1945 and 1948 was that of a bourgeois democracy with civil liberties rather strictly observed and political parties united in a National Front. The Communists smashed it as soon as they took over: they made other parties mere puppets, first by purging them of "reactionary" elements, and then by severely restricting their membership. The Social Democratic party, the only party which could have become a contender against the Communists for the working class vote, was led into fusion with the Communist party in June 1948 by the same leadership that had closely cooperated with the Communists long before 1948 — indeed just as soon as the Communists showed they could control state power. After the fusion, the only political organizations allowed to exist in factories and in offices were the Communist cells. The trade unions that united in the Revolutionary Trade Union Movement in 1945 were then made a tool of the Party. As a consequence of this monolithic domination, it became impossible for any genuine workers' leader to appear during 20 years of the Communist reign.

Needless to say, the behavior of the Communists was a

perversion of Marxism, both in the political field and in the establishment of its command in the economy. It was not the means of production that were expropriated from the bourgeoisie in 1945, but only the so-called "key industries." The bourgeoisie that collapsed was not removed but was driven into the position of a petty bourgeoisie. The power and positions of the latter rose accordingly. The petty bourgeoisie was increased also by the recolonization of the border districts from which the Germans had been expelled by the land reform that gave the rural proletariat land ownership, and by price increases on goods in stock that gave a sudden addition to the shopkeepers' wealth. Between 1945 and 1948 the reins of economic power which the bourgeoisie had lost fell to the civil service apparatus.

AFTER 1948

After the February coup of 1948, the civil service bureaucracy, soon "purged" by the Party and refilled from the Party ranks, fused with the Communist party apparatus. This amalgamation became the backbone of the Communist regime. Earlier, in the short period between 1945 and 1948, the Communists had based their public appeal on the record of their resistance to the Nazis, their large intellectual following and their friendship with the Russian liberators. Gottwald, the chairman of the Communist party summed up his Party's policy in the immediate postwar period with the slogan "No Soviets, no socialization." Naturally, this could easily be agreed to by other, even nonsocialist, parties. A mixed economy was established and a kind of planning introduced. Full employment, achieved soon after the economy recovered from the worst war losses, prevented misery on a massive scale.

In this mixed economy the biggest trusts — in spite of their nationalization — retained their significant role in the making of economic policy. After the Communist takeover, this tendency gained strength since Communist planning put an ever-increasing emphasis on the production of the means of production. One argument put forward at the time — quite plausible at first sight — was that the stepping up of the cold war and the embargo on goods for Czechoslovakia and the socialist bloc made this necessary, and made closer relations with the USSR necessary as well. Stalin's pressure for shipments of finished products, above all from the engineering industry, met the "needs" of the Czechoslovak iron and steel industry and heavy engineering. The beginnings of the vicious circle of the Czechoslovak economy can be found here. Besides, these tendencies were intensified after 1952 by a planning system copied from the Soviet example. An advanced industrial country, Czechoslovakia was gradually falling behind both in industry and agriculture as it increased production for the sake of production.

For the first few years the immense waves of investment seemed to bring increased well-being. Social security, so dear to the generation which remembered the dreadful years of unemployment, was assured. Living standards partly rose — not because of higher wages, however, which rose far less than in the neighboring capitalist states of Austria and Western Germany, but because more members of the same family were employed.

Under the surface, economic problems and contradictions accumulated and moral disintegration set in. Czechoslovak society as it had emerged from the war had a strong sense of national values since solidarity had been a weapon against the Nazis. Soon after the February coup, however, leading Communists in Prague, helped by some Slovak Communists who were planted in the offices of the Slovak party branch, ousted the resistance leaders, accusing them of "bourgeois nationalism." The constitution of 1960 then sealed the fate of Slovakia, making it a mere province of the central government whatever the outward signs of autonomy. Novotny made things worse by openly offending the Slovaks during his visits to Slovakia as head of state.

The Communists pretended to give the working class a leading role and systematically denigrated all other social groups. Pompous words, the oft-repeated but never fulfilled promises and the contradiction between the rosy picture of would-be socialism and the drab, ever-worsening reality of day-to-day life led to a deep-seated skepticism and distrust of "intellectuals." The trials played a special role in the corrosion of moral values.

The first of these trials took place at the beginning of June 1950. In the dock stood the woman socialist and former M. P., Horakova, with 12 codefendants. Horakova and three others were sentenced to death. One of the victims was B. Nalandra, an eminent Marxist, whose actual "guilt" was that he had strongly opposed the Moscow frame-up trials. The biggest of these frame-up trials — prepared with the assistance of Soviet "specialists" — was that of Rudolf Slansky (former Communist party Secretary General) in November 1952. Eleven of the 14 accused were executed.

Recent research discloses that in the two-month period between January 1 and March 1, 1951, there were 391 public trials in Bohemia alone. 14.8% of these cases concerned charges of "anti-State" activities and 27% "economic criminal offenses." Workers represented 39.1% of the defendants.

At the same time, the Party forced tens of thousands of "white-collar" workers — artisans, shop keepers and what were called "bourgeois elements" — to go into production. A single campaign in 1951 was organized under the slogan of "77,000"; it drove that many into the plants. The pretense that the Slansky trials were needed to stop "the nationalistic road to socialism" was belied, not only by the frame-up character of the trials against the leaders, but above all by the fact that they victimized thousands of workers. It was all part and parcel of what has since become known, during de-Stalinization, as "the crimes of Stalin." Fraudulent lies and vulgar insults spread wildly, accompanied by hate campaigns with a strong pogromist flavor. Far from clearing the road, as the officials then claimed, for "history-making social layers" — resistance members, soldiers who had fought abroad during the war, the proletariat — the distinctly anti-Semitic line pursued in connection with Slansky's trial and the terror in the country reached their height for that period, threatening all layers of the population.

POINT, COUNTERPOINT: BACK TO THE MAIN DRAMA

The irony of the situation of 1967-1968, as the "economic reformers" and those who were fighting for a degree of self-determination for Slovakia continued their behind-the-scenes struggle, is that the political crisis was triggered by the anti-Semitism which flowed from the Communist position during the Arab-Israeli War. The rebelliousness at the Writers' Congress in June 1967 and the totally different debate in the Central Committee of the Party in October, which was climaxed by the replacement of Novotny by Dubcek, seemed to spring from much more than a mere personality fight between top Communists. People rightly felt that this held special importance for everyone. Somehow, everyone felt that the change in personalities did signify a change in the operation of the system itself. Quite surprisingly, a change in the composition of the presidium placed emphasis on the concept of "democratization."

The lack of information was strongly criticized later. Continuing the old policy of not telling the membership the whole truth, the inauguration of a new policy of democratization seemed rather ominous. It was as much convincing proof of the power of the conservatives, as the men around Novotny came to be known, as it was proof of the same attitude toward "lower" levels of membership both on the part of the old clique and new guard. It was a first confirmation that the January changes were no experiment — as deeply as they might cut — but simply a change within the system.

But the one important new phenomenon emerging in consequence was the creation of a real public opinion. Press, radio and television seized the opportunity offered by the dismissal of their enemy Novotny and began to pound at particular features of the "previous" system. It took some time before the new leadership grasped the significance of these allies. For it was only with the assistance of the mass communications that the crack that had opened in January widened into a real breach. Their newly won freedom to report, their "daring" attitudes toward controversial aspects of domestic policy, served to stimulate a public mood of impatient expectancy and sustained an atmosphere of dissatisfaction with the old methods and ways. Gradually, citizens began to understand that the change at the top might really mean more this time. Not until the end of the month, however, did one of the new men who had been instrumental in the fall of Novotny, Josef Smrkovsky, publish a lead article in the trade union paper, called "What Is at Stake Today?" which stressed democratic principles as the basis of decisions.

At the end of January, Dubcek, up to then also first secretary of the Slovak branch of the Communist party, ceded that post to Vasil Bilak. The latter had no clear "democratic" record and his advance was taken as a sign that in Slovakia the "democratization process" was not even to become as "radical" as in the western parts of the state. Only two or three of the most prominent representatives of the Novotny regime were changed in the Slovak capital. Not only were new men emerging in command posts there very slowly, but some of the newcomers soon proved to have attitudes only barely distinguishable from those of their predecessors, merely shielding themselves with the magic word "federalization," i.e., federal status for autonomous Slovakia.

Indeed, at the congress of agricultural cooperatives that met on February 1, Dubcek stressed the limitations of the changes. "We do not change the general line, neither in domestic nor foreign policy. The starting base of a more rapid socialist development lies in the field of politics. In the development of socialist democracy . . . we have to make more room for the activities of all social groups in our society."

Nevertheless, further personnel changes began to indicate some new developments: Mamula, the almighty head of the Eighth Department of the Communist party Central Committee (to which army, security forces and intelligence services were subordinated) and one of the most faithful followers of Novotny who was hardly more evil than he, was replaced by the head of the army's political administration, Lt. General Prchlik. The second strong man pushed out of his post was Jiri Hendrych, for years ruler of the ideological section of the Party, regimenting arts and literature. His furious attack on the rebellious writers at their 1967 congress brought him into special disrepute at that time.

In the presence of the Communist leaders of the neighboring "socialist" countries, assembled for the twentieth anniversary of the February 1948 coup, Dubcek stressed the desire of workers and peasants "by decisive action indeed [to] radically change the state of affairs." "The discussion during our drawn-out sessions in December and January, for which we hardly could find any similarity in the last 20-30 years," he continued, "touched on every essential issue of our Party's policy."

At this time the hopeful trend seemed to be in full swing. Letters poured into newspaper offices as well as to radio and television stations, as the public reached out for genuine democracy. At about the same time the president of the Union of Fighters Against Fascism, which united resistance members and survivors of Nazi concentration camps, put out the winged word, "rehabilitation." As far as resistance fighters alone were concerned Dubcek estimated that 40,000 to 50,000 people had been unjustly sentenced during the fifties. He asked for an act rehabilitating them and other victims of discrimination and repression.

The popular rage, roused every day by some fresh revelation of the crimes perpetrated in Nazi-like style during the Novotny era was climaxed in the first days of March by the Sejna affair.[1] Since Sejna had been a close friend of the president's son — and an intimate of the head of state himself, Novotny was rightly seen as embodying all the evils of the preceding period. Sejna had belonged to the top hierarchy since 1951. As early as March 8, Communists from the Army GHQ demanded that all accomplices and protectors of Sejna, including the president of the republic and Mamula, be called to account. To the surprise of the Central Committee, the campaign against Novotny was so strong throughout the country that it led to his resignation on March 21 and to the election of General Svoboda as president on March 30.[2]

The manner of the elections was, however, fresh proof that the old practices were continuing. Although a majority of the public approved of the election results, the candidate

1. This general was secretary of the party's leading committee at the Ministry of Defense — as such independent of the Minister himself and subordinated to the Eighth Department of the Central Committee — and head of the Minister's secretariat. He was involved in a swindle. But, due to the connivance of civil and military investigating officers as well as members of the presidium of the national assembly, he was able to flee with his son and mistress. The details of the affair known so far remind one of "the good times" of any bourgeois society.

was imposed on the country, since no other was put forward and the electoral preparations and procedures were carried through in a single week.

The dramatic March developments could not be stilled by this concession. The demand that the representatives of the old order leave the scene became so loud and was supported by mass communications to such an extent that heads began to fall at last: on March 12 the chairman of the TUC resigned, the National Assembly gave a vote of no confidence both to the Minister of Interior and to the Prosecutor-General. Throughout February and March pressure for postponing the general election due to take place in May grew and found some support in the Party district conferences, so that the presidium of the Communist party Central Committee "recommended" at the end of March the postponement of the election to the end of June.

On April 5, the first day of its session, the Central Committee of the Communist party accepted an Action Program. On 27 closely printed pages — in chapters called: "Czechoslovakia's road to Socialism"; "For the development of Socialist Democracy"; "For a new system of political management of society"; "National economy and living standards"; "Development of science, education and culture" — it presents a program such as the Communist party had not known for many decades. The program proclaims: "The party can not enforce its authority, but has to obtain it anew by its deeds. It cannot enforce its line by ordering, but by the work of its members, by the veracity of its ideals."

As we have seen, the Communist party has no intention of resigning its "leading role" — all it wants is to change the form in which it will carry on with its leadership. It is, however, changing its methods of operation; it is even proposing the establishment of "workers' councils." A careful reading

2. Svoboda had organized the Czechoslovak army in exile in the USSR and has been something of a popular hero ever since his victorious return in 1945. As Minister of Defense, his support of the Communist coup in 1948 was one of the major reasons for its success. Dismissed soon afterward, he was sent to an agricultural cooperative as accountant clerk and was in other ways also a victim of the regime.

of the "Development of Socialist Democracy" will show, however, that what it means by workers' councils is not workers' control, but workers' discipline. Here is how the program reads:

> The economic reform will more and more force the entire labor force of socialist enterprises to face a situation in which they will directly perceive the consequences of either good or bad management of the enterprises. The Party considers it, therefore, inevitable for the whole labor collective that bears the consequences also to influence the management of the enterprise. A need arises for democratic authorities in the enterprises which would have limited competence in regard to management. It is to these authorities that the directors and leading officials of the enterprises would be responsible and they would be appointed to their functions by these authorities. These authorities must be an immediate part of the managing mechanism of enterprises; they cannot be a social organization (for this reason they cannot be identified with trade unions). These authorities would be formed partly by election of representatives of the labor collective, partly by representation of some organizations from outside of the enterprise that would assure an influence of the interests of the entire society at an expert, qualified decision level; it is necessary for the representation of these organizations to be also subject to democratic forms of control.

Further discussion showed that the proposed formula might be interpreted in several ways; one would emphasize the need for "managerial experts" because of the economic misery to be overcome, another would stress the necessity for workers to decide as much as possible on what they have to produce and how their product is to be distributed. For the present, it seems that the more "practical" point of view prevails, and the composition of the workers' councils will only partly represent the workers: a third of the council will probably be elected directly by the workers; a third might be nominated or elected from among "outside experts"; the last third may be chosen otherwise.

We see that there are plenty of loopholes to permit the same ordering from above which killed the trade unions as independent organs of the working class. At best, they point the way to the Yugoslav example of Workers' Councils, which bear little resemblance to factory committees controlled by the workers themselves. And behind it all there is the ubiquitous Communist party. Yet, to the extent that it is breaking away from the Russian model, and is resisting Russian, Polish and East German pressures to return to the old methods of Novotny, it has the popular support of the overwhelming majority of the people of Czechoslovakia.

The first phase of what is called "democratization" may be assumed to have ended by the end of April. The Communist party tried very hard at this time not only to take the lead (high officials kept repeating that the Party would not renounce its leading role) but emphasized their wish to "enlarge and deepen" democracy and to offer "real partnership" to other political parties in the National Front. The Party therefore had to turn — no matter how hesitantly — against its most conservative wing. Thus, at the end of April, when the first leaflets appeared denouncing the new leadership as "revisionist" and slandering the more progressive elements, the Dubcek leadership had to rely on public opinion. Ironically, the authors of these leaflets make their appeal to the workers, asking them to defend "their achievements" — in spite of the obvious facts, known to everybody, and in spite, too, of what the press is now revealing. These revelations concern not only the old guard's bureaucratic methods, but show also that the standard of living of the working class in the neighboring capitalist states (which had to start from scratch after World War II) is far higher than that in "socialist" Czechoslovakia.

There has been much talk throughout the years about a "workers' policy" and this slogan has appeared again during the past few months. Yet those who have used it most often have been, in practice, the workers' worst enemies. We have seen where they have brought the working class: not only is the level of working and living conditions, wages, living standards and basic freedoms below that of the capitalist countries; in addition, as we have shown, the whole economy has been stagnating since 1963.

Yet, the old-guard leaflets with the brand-new slogans have intensified their campaign. These leaflets appear at every railway station, are released by time bombs, scattered by planes in the surroundings of the capital and so forth. Moreover, this has been done without any apparent effort on the part of the police to identify the offenders. All this points to the continuing strength of the Novotny wing of the Party, and follows the line set by the Russian, East German and Polish press attacks upon the democratization in Czechoslovakia. Obviously, the joint "ideological struggle" has been backed up by the Soviet troops remaining in the country after the maneuvers of the Warsaw Pact nations were over. At the same time, a campaign has been unleashed in *Pravda* about "counterrevolutionary elements," not stopping even at Stalin-type amalgams, such as the suggestion that the democratization movement is infiltrated by "CIA agents." Finally they demanded a confrontation between the Czech leadership and the Russian Politburo, as well as with the Warsaw Pact nations. In this they succeeded, after a compromise with the Dubcek leadership, that these be held not in Russia but on Czech soil.

Even before this, the Communist party Central Committee, between May 29 and June 1, struck a compromise between the "progressives" and "conservatives." All that the progressives achieved was a temporary expulsion of Novotny and those of his worst companions who had taken part in the organization of the political trials during the fifties (all of them have been expelled "until final results of the inquiry commission are known").

The same session decided to call the extraordinary Party congress for September 9th. A real battle preceded this decision, since the progressives called for it against the resistance of Dubcek himself (who, at the moment, is very popular among the population despite the evidence of his being rather a middle-of-the-road man). But, as the conservatives had become an acute danger because of the positions of power they retained, Dubcek understood that his own position, and that of the progressives, could be held only if a Party congress gave its consent.

Basic freedoms are guaranteed for the time being: freedom of speech, freedom of the press. With the free flow of ideas, the Communist spell is being broken. There are difficult struggles ahead which the workers will have to fight. There may be two fronts on which particular dangers loom: one is contained in the words of a high official, a member of the Ministry of Economic Planning, to a French journalist: "Full employment is a fiction we have created, to which we are accustomed and which has become an obstacle today for a solution of our problems." [3] The second front is the danger to freedom that is just now intensely demonstrated by the Soviets and their allies.

The maneuvers announced as "command and headquarters maneuvers" might, indeed, have been planned months before. But although Premier Cernik told the public that all foreign troops would be gone on June 30th, they did not do so. Contradictory explanations by the Minister of Defense and his speakers could not calm public opinion. Gradually the public learned the facts of the situation; that the High Command of the Warsaw Pact consisted exclusively of Soviet officers, and that commanders of other bloc countries were mere liaison officers, so that the Czechoslovak army command had no power to tell the Soviets when to leave. When the troops did begin to move they did so in a curious manner: some of the units that had crossed into Czechoslovakia from East Germany were now to move east, across the whole of the country, to cross into the Soviet Union.

The troops were still in the country when the "Warsaw letter" of the five Communist parties arrived in Prague. The Bulgarian, East German, Hungarian, Polish and Soviet Communists told the Czechoslovak Communist party that "hostile forces" were "threatening to break Czechoslovakia away from the socialist community." "A situation has arisen that is absolutely unacceptable to the socialist countries," the letter declared, and it issued an ultimatum to Czechoslovak Communists: either follow our line or we will unleash a campaign about "counterrevolutionary forces."

All these threats had an effect opposite to that intended. The overwhelming majority of the Czechoslovak people came out in support of the leadership in its resistance to the

3. *L'Express*, No. 881.

Russian threats. At the same time, the West European Communist parties, as opposed to those from East Europe, rallied behind the Czechoslovak Communist party, because they saw the intransigent Soviet gesture as a threat to any Communist party outside the Soviet or Chinese blocs. If the Soviets feel so imperilled by these modest changes — and, indeed, what they keep stressing is the fear that the Communist party might lose its dominant role — then they make it clear to everyone that Russian Communists are the worst enemies of freedom. They have demonstrated this more than once.

The case of Czechoslovakia underlines this lesson. There was, after all, no armed uprising here. The Czechoslovak experiment, therefore, is merely testing the Russian willingness to allow its most obedient disciple to make a few variations in the Russian type of Communism. Why, then, should Russia feel that Communism is doomed? Why should the Polish regime fear that it means the disintegration of Communism? Why should the East German regime, seemingly the most stable, feel itself endangered, as if it meant the breakup of the whole East European system?

What the Czech and Slovak Communists are trying to do is, after all, only to make a change *within* the system. Let's have no illusions on that score. Whatever freedom the "democratization" movement may have brought about, no basic structure has, so far, been changed. There has been no fundamental change in the life or role of the producers — the working class.

WHAT NOW?

As these lines are being written, it would seem that only the first act has ended. The second act has hardly begun, and the third act is not yet in sight. We are told very little about the compromise worked out with the Russians and the East European hard-liners at their confrontation. Supposedly, the latter will not interfere in the "internal affairs" of Czechoslovakia. But will that great new force, public opinion, be allowed to develop without interference? The mass media — radio and TV — are thus far keeping up even more than the press itself their criticisms of individual politicians, discussing each one's share in the crimes of the past, and dissecting the present windy rhetoric. The non-Communist newspapers of the Czech Socialist party and the People's party — *Svobodne Slovo* and *Lidova Demokracie*, respectively — have published letters from their readers pointing out the guilt of the Communist party, not only of its individual members.

We have found our tongue, none more so than the youth. Two student weeklies, *Student* in Prague and *Echo* in the Slovak capitol of Bratislava, appear to be the most consistent critics of the regime. They offer their pages most readily to Rudi Dutschke or Ivan Svitak and go far in their criticism of the Soviet Union.

The most crucial issue, however, remains: the condition of the working class and its role in production. The workers themselves complain that they have been depoliticized: though it is constantly hammered into their heads that they are "the masters" of the country, only their self-styled "representatives" speak for them. It has not been possible for a non-Communist to become anything like a leader, whatever his capacities. Genuine workers' organizations have been destroyed; the trade union movement has been changed into a government-supporting body whose only function has been to whip up and intensify labor efficiency. Workers' and employees' interests have been neglected entirely. Only Communist party cells were allowed to exist in plants and offices.

Yet there are those who now give the Communist party credit for initiating the process of change, as if it did so from the goodness of its heart rather than because it was forced to do so by the economic crisis, the restlessness in all strata of the population, as well as by the rebellions the world over. Some workers, no doubt, had been corrupted by their inclusion in the State or Party apparatus. And, no doubt, there is "apathy" among the workers regarding the "workers' councils." Some see in this lack of enthusiasm for the councils only apathy, and not a justified distrust, because the councils were initiated by the very forces that have kept the lid down on workers' initiative. Indeed, the Communists themselves almost admit as much. Thus, Vaclav Velek from the Modrany Engineering Works said in a group interview with the trade union paper *Prace:* "I think self-government will fulfill what we expect from it: as regards production democracy, self government seems to put it at the right place and make it effective. It will no doubt be useful for the workers to have a maximum of influence on who will manage the plant and who will guide the work at their place."

That is the whole point. The working class is yet to have its say. This drama will not be completed until it does.

POSTSCRIPT

The leading men in the Czech crises — Dubcek, Smrkovsky, Svoboda, Cernik — are still trusted. They may deserve this trust but it is difficult to believe their repeated assurances that the "post-January line" of the Party remains largely intact. Censorship of the mass communications grows more and more severe daily. Economic policy, seemingly the same, will be affected by the Russian insistence of "deeper" cooperation with the Soviets, thus preventing the much-needed modernization of Czechoslovak industry.

Strict observance of "public order" does not allow any public gathering organized by the existing parties, and no new political grouping can emerge legally. Thus, basic liberties — the very core of Czechoslovakian developments during the last year — are very much restricted.

Also, in the name of "national unity" (this slogan has great emotional appeal and played an important role during the first days of the crisis), even the small workers' movement for workers' councils and greater workers' self-government in the factories may be brought to a standstill.

What the leaders are to be blamed for is their insufficient reliance on the people. That is the old "sin" for the Communists. Since they are not revolutionaries they cannot be expected to propose, even less to carry out, any radical measure. Had they relied more on the people in Spring, had they responded to the then general desire to remove the old guard from its positions, they would have convened the party congress in the summer and the Russians either could not have occupied Czechoslovakia or would have done it under much different circumstances. Seen in this way, these leading men bear a share of the responsibility, though naturally this is no excuse for the invasion.

As far as the present course is concerned, these leaders

may be right in stressing the necessity for the Czechoslovak people to fulfill the Moscow agreements. Yet, for the moment, no one is able to say where fulfillment ends and "collaboration" (in the sense given to it in Hitler's Europe) begins. (Some of the inside information I have received from newspaper and state radio editorial offices indicates instances of the latter.)

A few of the men, I suspect, are now going so far as to attempt to convince the people that in practice there are no great differences between the line to be pursued now and the proper one before the occupation. (The Slovak leader, Husak, I would count among such men.) This is the gravest political error. It underestimates the Russian aim to suppress Czechoslovakian freedoms and it lulls the popular vigilance of its own government's responses. Here again, the contradictions of a Communist government can be seen clearly.

In this hour of actual danger for the nation as a whole — and the menacing posture of the Russians during the Moscow negotiations was directed at the entire nation — working class interests recede into the background. This adds to the difficulties encountered by the working class during the "democratization process." Although the working class gave proof that it was the backbone of the nation during the invasion and remains so these most difficult days of occupation, there is no guarantee that its interests will be heeded now, any more than they were previously.

July 1968

The Gordian Knot: Intellectuals and Workers in Czechoslovak Democratization

Ivan Svitak

The relationship between the intellectuals and the workers was one of the most important issues in the process of democratization in Czechoslovakia. It was also one of its greatest weaknesses. The so-called progressive Communists persistently tried to keep the drive for reform under the control of the Party apparatus and did not wish to do more than make certain concessions to the broad movement for democratic rights and civil liberties. At the same time, among the radical spokesmen of the students and the intellectuals, there were some who saw the driving force outside the Party apparatuses and the trade union organizations and who put their faith in the working class and its spontaneous will to reconquer the workers' basic rights and its own organizations. They tried to speak directly to the working class — or rather to the workers in the factories — and their belief that that is where the greatest potential strength of the opposition to totalitarian dictatorship, both old and new, lies, was proved to be right.

The Communist party apparatus strove for a long time to preserve the idea that the workers have great reservations about the economic reforms and that they were keeping very much aloof from the new leadership of Alexander Dubcek. As late as March 1968, for instance, several of the officials elected at the district Party conferences, which were manipulated, as always, by the apparatus, were men who supported the conservative wing loudly and aggressively, who did not mince their words in expressing disagreement with the new leadership and who went so far as to threaten their opponents with the weapons of the People's Militia (the armed Party groups in the plants). In Northern Moravia (the most important industrial region of Czechoslovakia), there arose the so-called Ostrava faction, led by Drahomir Kolder, who subsequently became a Soviet collaborator. This faction tried to form, inside the Central Committee of the Communist Party, a kind of middle-of-the-road element, the so-called center or centrist group, whose principal spokesmen were Drahomir Kolder himself, Alois Indra, Oldrich Svestka and later Vasil Bilak. It looked in summer as if this group would manage to get power into its own hands and force Dubcek to give up the support he had among the radical reformers, writers and students.

THE MAIN PROBLEM OF DEMOCRATIZATION — THE WORKERS

For Marxists with a theoretical training it was clear from the beginning that one set of elite cadres had taken the place of another and that a much more radical kind of action than the vilification of the out-going president was required if the renaissance were not to degenerate very quickly. While the well-known intellectuals in the Congress Palace were trying to outdo one another in their witticisms about Antonin Novotny's political downfall, a program of democratization, later published under the title "Head Against the Wall," was being propounded before a small group of philosophy students at Charles University. It needs to be said out loud that this program — together with several other articles of a programmatic nature — proved unacceptable to the intellectuals of the writers' club, and that the *Literarni Listy* refused to print it, and refused all other articles which then appeared in *Student*.

The Writers' Union was incapable of formulating any politically relevant program and left all the decisive political initiative to the Communist party. But outside the frame-

work of the writers' club several important attempts were
made to stimulate those democratic tendencies which alone
could further the democratization. In this connection, new
political organizations of non-Party members were founded,
the ground was prepared for the renewed activity of socialist
democracy and an effort was made to win over the key sector
of the population — the workers — to the program of democratization. These attempts were surprisingly successful
and in every case where the intellectuals and the radical
youth grasped the fact that they were facing a common enemy, the labor organizations and especially the newly elected
union committees became firm supporters of the democratization.

When judging the relations between workers and intellectuals, it is important to bear in mind three basic facts which
Western observers tend to overlook. First of all, the democratization was a movement, a process which shaped itself
as time went on and passed through four stages, taking on a
significantly different form in each. Secondly, the official
democratization program of the Communist party, which was
managed in the spirit of the apparatus' totalitarian monopoly of power, must be distinguished from the really democratic movement which constantly overstepped the limits conceded by the Communists. Finally, it is this democratic movement for human rights and civil liberties which has constantly put pressure on the Communist party to make it go beyond
its own program and which has not allowed it to put an end to
the democratization, although the great majority of the leading politicians of the Communist party — including some of
the national heroes — have done their best at every step to
check and curb the people's movement and to preserve the
elitist character of the state and the technocratic character of
the economic reforms.

Today, after the occupation of Czechoslovakia, we can see
quite clearly that the elitist-technocratic group of Communist reformers had gone as far as its nature would allow. Its
fear of the people, of the workers and intellectuals, made it
incapable of creating an alliance for the common cause between those who work with their heads and those who work

with their hands. Such an alliance was diametrically opposed to the elite's group interests, because it challenged its privileges and called in question not only its policy but its very existence. Only radical democrats, humanists and Marxist socialists were able and willing to form this decisive alliance as the basis for future political action. It was only these people, whom simple-minded editors ridiculed as extremists, who heard the rumbling of the tanks in the distance and tried to make the sole move which, in the spring of 1968, might have saved the democratization — *the mobilization of the working class for the defense of its own interests*. This attempt had such far-reaching implications that it fully deserved the hatred it received from all the apparatuses; even among the well-known progressives there was nobody who understood and supported this program.

The isolated efforts made by individual intellectuals in the factories could not change the fact that the representatives of the progressive movement did not manage to win as unequivocal and open an endorsement in the factories as among the middle classes and the intelligentsia. But this meant that there was a rift between the aims of the liberal intelligentsia and those of the labor organizations. Here is one of those Gordian knots which is very obvious today but which was probably impossible to untie in the spring of 1968. After 20 years of the policy of distrust which was deliberately cultivated by the Communist party apparatus, it was very difficult for the intellectuals and the workers to find a common language and to bridge the apparent abyss over which hung the bureaucratic dictatorship's mighty apparatus. The myth of the worker as the new man repelled the humanist intelligentsia by its falseness, while the worker who thought realistically regarded the technical intelligentsia of his plant as the accomplices of the oppressive machine which was forcing him to produce more for less pay. Both these ideological illusions, carefully fostered by the ruling ideology, were a real force which prevented the two basic social groups from coming to an understanding, until they realized that they were both victims manipulated by the power and ideology of the political apparatus.

So the liberal intellectuals put forward a program which reflected only their particular group demands, with emphasis on civil liberties; this allowed the program of the Communist party to appear as the more general one, embracing the whole nation and representing the specific interests of the workers. The liberal intelligentsia took as its goal the implementation of democratic freedoms, especially the freedom of the press and the freedom of association, and elections by secret ballot in which independent candidates could stand — in short the democratization of political life. But this had no effect upon life in the factories, because the reestablishment of civil liberties did not give any real new opportunities for action to the labor organizations, and especially to the trade unions, while for the workers the economic reforms represented a real and tangible danger in that they called for the closing of uneconomic enterprises. The middle classes and their intellectual spokesmen had reason to be enthusiastic about the new dimensions which creative activity took on in hitherto forbidden spheres. But what reason did the workers have for such enthusiasm? None. The conservative groups in the Party apparatus, in the unions and in the militia in the plants cleverly turned these facts to their own use and made it appear that there was no support for the democratization program in the factories. That was not true, and it soon became apparent that the local geurillas of the militia did not even have the backing of those Communists who were militia members and that Novotny was as discredited in the eyes of the average worker as he was for every other sector of the population.

In spirit the aims of the intelligentsia were confined to matters of particular interest for the middle classes; they were tolerated by the new leadership of the Communist party, which dared not forfeit the support of the intellectuals because it was directly threatened by the conservatives. But the objectives of the democratic intelligentsia — if we can use this term to cover both the Communist and the non-Party intellectuals — were not homogeneous; we have only to compare the *Literarni Listy* and *Student* to see the sharp differences between them. The *Literarni Listy* was dominated by a group of Communists who showed great indulgence to non-Party members but who consistently tried to keep the changes within the bounds set by the Communist party program. *Student*, on the other hand, gave uncensored expression to the attitudes of the young intellectuals, students and youth, and threw open for debate issues which were unacceptable to the Communists, even to the reformers among them — the revision of the political trials of the representatives of the political parties of the past, the creation of a second political party, totalitarian dictatorship, refugees, foreign policy. Behind the immediate community of interests among the intelligentsia as a whole, there was in fact a considerable degree of diversity.

The intelligentsia of the democratic tendency was internally divided especially according to whether the people concerned were members of the Communist party or not and whether they were Czechs or Slovaks and according to the generation to which they belonged. The basic position expressing the common denominator of the various political currents was formulated by the Communist writers, and it is a fact that during 1968 there were no substantive political differences between Communists and non-Communists within the unions of artists; the Communists' line was completely in accordance with the non-Party members' interests. The radical students did occasionally go beyond the generally accepted framework, but the fact remains that a common policy brought together the hitherto strictly divided groups of Party members and non-Party members. At first, there was indeed a considerable difference between the two, but it gradually faded away as spring went on and as politics grew progressively more radical, with the result that the program of democratization more and more became the real program of the Party members themselves. The non-Communist intelligentsia founded its own factional groups within the artists' unions but here, too, both sides easily reached agreement. Only in Slovakia did a group of older Communist intellectuals come out against the general trend and try to defend the conservative nationalist positions.

In the heat of the summer there came an important

turning point. The manifesto of the "Two Thousand Words" formulated the particular group interests of the intelligentsia together with the general national and popular interests of a free, sovereign and socialist Czechoslovakia. The clear threat to the State, the endless maneuvers and the criticism contained in the Warsaw letter created a situation favorable to a temporary national unity, to an alliance of workers and intellectuals for a common cause and to mass support for the Communist party. The idea of socialist democracy and Marxist humanism came nearer to victory in the months preceding the Russian occupation than ever before. Then the Soviet tanks arrived to cement the alliance of workers and intellectuals which had been impossible in the spring, to produce the remarkable and unparalleled conjunction of interests and to create, perhaps for the first time in history, the political configuration of the real forces of society which is alone capable of surpassing the limitations of state capitalism which have proved incompatible with freedom and socialism.

TOWARD A COMMUNITY OF INTERESTS

The leadership of the Communist party — and here both factions in the Central Committee were in complete agreement — did not want to allow the real political decision-making to become more democratic, to reach wider layers of the populations and to provide scope for the activity of the people. The program of the alliance of intellectuals and workers endangered the Communists' power monopoly in its very principles; it tended to limit the potential power even of the victorious party faction and threatened the progressives and the conservatives alike. Therefore it had to be nipped in the bud, in April and May, so that the apparently "realistic" conception of successive compromises inside the Communist party could again hold the field. The elitist conception of politics, which is closely connected with the Communist party's monopoly, again became the basis of the ruling group's political practice while the radical currents were being crushed wherever they appeared and attacked as extremism — not only by the old bosses of the party apparatus but also by the smart editors of the *Literarni Listy* and the bright radio and television commentators.

At the beginning of spring the intellectuals and the workers went their different ways; in fact, as regards the aims of their programs, they had never come together. The leading Communist intellectuals were so dominated by their feeling of solidarity with the new leadership that they tried only to expand the freedom of the press and to popularize the program of political rehabilitations. Though this program was good in itself and opened up many political possibilities for the future, it meant nothing to the average worker because the slogans of the *Literarni Listy* did not express the basic interests and needs of the factories. The absence of enthusiasm and the distrust with which the workers awaited the outcome of the reforms then in preparation were just as well-founded and far-sighted as the reservations of the skeptical intellectuals who saw behind the scenes and realized that, apart from a change of elite, almost nothing could be expected from the Communists. The class character of the state did not allow the State elite to do anything about its monopoly of power. The intellectuals' program therefore cut itself off from the people, because the leading Communists insisted on the leading role of the Party, made no attempt to formulate any goals and contented themselves with supporting the progressive faction. So political life went on in the form of mere backroom quarrels with no mass involvement and no support among the population.

Only at the end of June did the Communist intellectuals realize how critically lacking in perspective their policy was and they came out — perhaps too late — with a unique document, the "Two Thousand Words." It was only now that they obtained majority support for democratization, when they proposed that it should be based on the activity of the people themselves, and thus *went beyond the framework of the elitist policy.* In this way they put the facts into the only proper perspective: what had hitherto been the Communists' reform faction now appeared in its true light — as a group openly opposed to the rule of the people. It unanimously rejected the manifesto. The publication of the "Two Thousand Words" was preceded by three months of intensive activity in the newly founded groups of non-Party members inside the artists' unions, by the forming of the Union of Scientific Workers and by a shift in the political leadership of the intellectuals from the Writers' Union to groups of a more radical tendency. The manifesto of "Two Thousand Words" represented *the first formulation of the intellectuals' and workers' community of interests;* this alliance for the common cause grew steadily closer in the course of the next two months, as the slogans of socialism, sovereignty and freedom became matters of vital concern to every citizen. But there was then a clear-cut opposition between the common interests of the workers and intellectuals on the one hand and, on the other, the various factions of the Communist elite, both conservative and progressive.

Looking back, we may wonder if the intellectuals' attempt to accelerate the internal democratization of the regime — especially as it was expressed in the "Two Thousand Words" — was right, or if a more moderate course of action might have prevented the Warsaw Pact's military action. But history does not care for the conditional in the pluperfect. History is a series of changing situations, each of which opens up many alternatives; but it is irreversible. At every step only one course can be chosen and this eliminates all the other possible alternatives of the given situation. Historians toying with these possible alternatives can find an answer to their "ifs" only if they regard the historical process, wrongly, as a play of eventualities that would have run a different course if only. . . . In the Marxist conception of history, this apparently unlimited possibility of choice is considerably narrowed down by the idea that social evolution follows certain laws; therefore though it may seem that the number of permutations in the course that history could take are infinite, this in fact applies only to the secondary aspects. The general current of history, of the laws of social evolution and of the system's own logic goes on with the irresistible dynamism of an elemental process of nature.

Perhaps from this point of view we can say that the only possibility of resistance to the armed intervention lay in a much more intensive pursuit of internal democratization. The Soviet generals would not have risked a war in Europe.

But unfortunately they were never put in a position where they had to take this risk into account. Thanks to the Czechoslovak Communists, the only decision they ever faced was whether or not to occupy a defenseless country which no one was ready to help. Instead of reacting to the repeated army maneuvers and to the Warsaw letter by a partial mobilization and taking the risk of conflict, the Communist leaders accepted a compromise in Bratislava and signed the death-warrant of their democratization. They were incapable, both for personal reasons and because of the class character of Czechoslovakia's state-capitalist structure, of choosing the only alternative that could have saved them — a popular movement. This was the alternative advocated by some individuals in March and by the intellectuals as a class in June. It finally came into existence at the end of August, in the form of an absurd and heroic resistance; but then, in spite of its enormous potential strength, the movement was as tragically helpless as it was admirable.

A more cautious course of action might have deferred the intervention, but it was the very essence of the social changes in Czechoslovakia which was unacceptable to the Soviet leadership. The reaction to the continual readiness of Dubcek's group to compromise proved that compromise led nowhere; the Soviet side regarded it as proof of weakness and not of a desire for a certain degree of democracy in the relations between nations and states. The group's moderate approach meant that the Soviet generals were repeatedly invited into the country whose government so readily proclaimed its fidelity to the military interests of the Warsaw Pact. So, finally, the generals were quite sure they were on safe ground and they decided to stay in the country, together with several divisons. A still more restrained course of action might have managed to postpone the crisis by a few months, but insofar as the Czechoslovak movement really was a democratizing and popular one and insofar as it tended to break up the mechanism of the totalitarian dictatorship, there was absolutely no way of preventing the Soviet intervention except by accepting the risk of war, of open conflict.

Consequently, if today we seek the hypothetical alterna-

tive which could have prevented the intervention, we shall
certainly not find it in greater moderation of the intellectuals' policy but, on the contrary, in more radicalism in the
struggle for socialist democracy, in a more radical readiness
to defend one's own country by force of arms. If the Communists had prepared the country for the possibility of armed
conflict, they might have prevented the intervention, because
the Soviet leadership would have had to deal with a much
more complicated politico-military problem then the occupation itself represented. The risks connected with war in the
heart of Europe were so great, especially in view of the
proximity of Germany, that the need to decide whether to
risk outright war would have strengthened the more moderate group in the Soviet Politburo. The knowledge that we
have to deal with a man of courage affects the way we behave; in the same way, awareness of the risk of conflict
would have affected the strategy of the measures taken
against Czechoslovakia. If Finland could defend itself, if
Rumania and Yugoslavia are ready to fight for their national
independence, there is no reason to doubt that the policy
which ruled out armed struggle against the aggressor was
fatally wrong. In dismissing General Prchlik, the Prague
leadership made a grave mistake, because by the same token
it ruled out the possibility that the country would defend
itself and neutralized the only real force which was, in fact,
both able and willing to fight — the Czechoslovak army.

No shots were fired when the invasion came, because by
then it was too late. There is no doubt, as a glance at the map
will show, that any armed resistance could have lasted only a
matter of hours or, at best, of days. At the same time, however, it must be said that the state could and should have
defended itself, because the final outcome of a war is never
certain. For what is at issue is not only the actual occupation
of the country but also what can be done in the country once
it has been occupied. The American experience in Vietnam
shows clearly enough that though the five countries might
have conquered within a few hours, their military victory
would have proved a radical defeat if during the crucial night
the leading statesmen had had the courage to do their duty

and defend the country's sovereignty by force of arms. What are armies for, if not to fight when their country is attacked by an enemy?

Finally, from the point of view of political strategy, we may wonder if the intellectuals' and politicians' big mistake was not to overestimate the danger of the conservatives at home and to underestimate the threat represented by the Soviet tanks. Perhaps a moderate internal democratization coupled with a more intensive effort to get out of the sphere of the USSR's power-play would have been successful; the case of Rumania suggests that it might have been. This hypothetical question is as speculative as every kind of playing about with possible alternatives after a battle has been lost. But it must be recognized that the political leaders, the skeptical intellectuals and the radical students were none of them ready to face the possibility of the USSR's repeating its performance of Hungary 1956. This outcome seemed improbable until the Cierna conference. Why? Because the brutality of the Soviet foreign policy is beyond anything central Europe and the Western world could imagine.

The more absurd the picture the imagination paints, the nearer it will bring us to the truth about the nature of the Soviet State and its imperialist ambitions. History is a play of eventualities, but the politician must always bear in mind the fact that, whatever action he happens to choose, it will be irreversible and that a wrong move or political apathy will lose the game long before the tank columns arrive to impose their will on history and on nations.

Recent developments in Czechoslovakia have proved once more that the community of interest between intellectuals and workers is the most productive political idea for a future socialist movement. What appeared to be the utopian idea of isolated intellectuals in the spring of 1968 became a reality in the months that followed and plays the most important role in current political developments. The student strike in November of 1968 was supported by workers, and during the campaign in support of Smrkovsky against the "realist" Husak, the unity of workers and intellectuals again proved to be the most important political force in the country. These experiences are proof that the conditions for a new type of political alliance exist in modern industrial society but only if intellectuals formulate a Marxist-humanist program which appeals to the working class — the majority of the population. If intellectuals are incapable of achieving this end, the living torches announce the tragedy. In the poet's words: "Where man ends, the living torch begins."

Translated from the Czech by Jarmila Veltrusky
December 1968

Appeal and Declaration by a Group of Delegates to the Fourteenth Congress of the Czechoslovak Communist Party

Eduard Goldstucker
Zdenek Hejzlar
Jiri Pelikan
Joseph Pokstefl
Ota Sik

APPEAL

The undersigned, delegates to the Fourteenth Congress of the Czechoslovak Communist party, democratically elected in 1968, declare, in their own names and in the names of their comrades who cannot speak freely:

That they regard the only legal Fourteenth Party Congress as that which took place on August 22, 1968, at Prague-Vysocany;

That the meeting taking place on May 25, 1971, is not a Congress of the whole Communist party of Czechoslovakia, but solely of the "normalized" Party after the expulsion of half a million members. This Congress will thus make decisions only according to the will of the minority that, since April 1969, has seized control of the Party through an internal coup d'etat imposed by foreign intervention. This Congress will be propped up by an artificial, falsified and essentially reactionary interpretation of the development of Czechoslovak society.

The signers consequently deny the legitimacy of this Congress, which will take place in an atmosphere of political and juridical persecutions, in the presence of foreign armed forces, the objective of which is to legalize the military intervention and the violation of sovereignty and to impose on the Party and the State a direction contrary to the will of the Communists and the people as a whole.

The signers reaffirm that, in the present circumstances, the democratic and socialist development of Czechoslovakia requires the following preconditions: the withdrawal of all foreign troops from Czechoslovak territory; the restoration of democratic and civil liberties; an end to political persecutions, to trials and confinement of dissidents, to attacks on the means of living and to all other forms of political repression; and freedom for scientific research and for artistic creation.

The signers appeal to the Communist and Workers parties invited to attend this Congress, that they state plainly their disagreement with the military intervention of August 21, 1968, and its consequences, in the interest of the common cause of socialism.

The signers appeal to progressive and democratic opinion to support the just struggle of the Czech and Slovak peoples for a free, democratic, and socialist Czechoslovakia. They hope that world opinion will not stay silent at the spectacle of "normalization" and persecution, and that the voices of protest and solidarity will be powerfully raised.

DECLARATION

In May 1971, a Congress of the Czechoslovak Communist party was convened and presented as the Fourteenth Party Congress. We feel that it is necessary to remind Czechoslovak and world opinion that the only valid Fourteenth Congress was that which met on August 22, 1968, at Prague-Vysocany, which consisted of democratically elected delegates.

The annulment of the decisions of the legal Fourteenth Party Congress, the exclusion from the Party of the majority of its participants, along with half a million other Communists, have been imposed by a *diktat* from Moscow, under the threat of terror and military reprisals. The present leading committees of the Czechoslovak Communist party as well as of the state, have been installed by the will of the

foreign occupying power and against the will of the Czechoslovak people.

The Congress which is now being organized will be forced
to endorse the "normalization," of which the principal aim
has been to deprive the Czechoslovak people of the possibility
of deciding their own social development and their own destiny. The purges which have been carried out in the Czechoslovak Communist party and in the other political parties
that formally exist, in the trade unions, in the youth organizations, as well as in the governmental and ideological institutions, have been aimed at eliminating and depriving of all
political influence those who support the democratization and
humanization of socialist society.

This regime, which claims to represent the working class,
has crushed the seeds of a system of self-direction and workers' councils. Just as in the period of the Moscow Trials,
every activity that tends to promote progressive and democratic reforms is called "counterrevolutionary," without the
slightest proof. Every key position in the country has been
filled by the most conservative and reactionary elements of
the Czechoslovak Communist party. Thanks to a corrupt and
bureaucratic apparatus, backed by the constant menace of
reprisals and by the total ideological monopolization of
communications and education, this little group holds the
entire population under its fist.

The bureaucratic-centralist system, with all its insidious
consequences for the country's development as a modern
industrial state, has been reinstated. The basic civil rights
and civil liberties have been trodden underfoot. Anyone who
expresses dissatisfaction with the foreign occupation exposes
himself to brutal economic and political reprisals.

Thousands of the most talented and courageous citizens
have been driven from their jobs. The most capable intellectuals have been denied the chance to continue their work in
science, education, journalism, the arts and all the other
activities in which they formerly participated. The purge has
also been widely extended in the ranks of the army. Whoever
dares to protest and to speak the truth is tried and sentenced
by rigged courts. Censorship, manipulated news and lying

propaganda have reached dimensions that recall the decade of the fifites. All worthwhile artistic works — books, films, plays, etc. — are once again under the censor's thumb. Even national and world classics are censored and mutilated according to current political needs.

The economy is again dominated by the old system of centralized planning which has already proven its inability to carry on modern, efficient and competitive production able to meet the needs of the people. The losses that spring from wasted investments and materials, from abnormally long lags in construction, from the great number of useless goods manufactured, from the lack of promotion of foreign trade, from the inadequate services and commercial outlets at home, from the aging transportation system and from a grossly inflated administrative apparatus, lower the standard of living of the whole population.

Economic relations between the USSR and Czechoslovakia are not based on equality and mutual benefit. The economy of Czechoslovakia is more and more chained to that of the USSR and subordinated to its needs and objectives. Contrary to official propaganda, which presents the situation as advantageous to Czechoslovakia, a constantly increasing portion of Czechoslovak labor is thus drained off, in the form of merchandise shipments and long-term investments, into the Soviet Union, without obtaining the necessary quantities of consumer goods, housing and services. The result is a constant growth in hidden inflation.

Czechoslovakia is a developed industrial country whose people, by their capacity, their talent and their professional qualifications, are able to rival those of the advanced industrial countries. However, because of the inadequate economic and political system that has been imposed on the country, this state remains behind in technical development, in productivity and in the standard of living.

These "normalized" conditions, imposed by the foreign occupation, are in the first place symptoms of a limitation of the sovereignty of the Czechoslovak state. One of the fundamental preconditions for change is the departure of the foreign army from Czechoslovak soil and the end of all foreign meddling in the internal affairs of the country. The leaders of the present regime, who not only conceal the loss of national sovereignty but even give thanks for the deed, do not represent the interests of the Czechoslovak people.

The Congress which is about to meet would like to give the impression — before world public opinion, and especially before the Communist parties of the world — that the Communists and the people of Czechoslovakia accept the present situation. At the same time, this Congress is bound to direct the Party toward even closer collaboration with the Great Power politics of the USSR. The fact that all the delegates to this Congress were chosen by the Party apparatus, the careful tailoring given all the speeches, resolutions and elections by the apparatus, make of this Congress a fraud and a swindle of the highest order. The only purpose of the Congress, and of the elections that will follow it, is to legitimize the status quo.

A regime which has deprived the people of its fundamental democratic liberties, which robs citizens of their work and persecutes them for their political opinions, which destroys every initiative of the people, which makes the standard of living depend on the whims of bureaucrats — such a regime must remain alien and hostile, and can maintain itself in power only by brute force. It is a mockery of all the great humanitarian ideals of socialism. The Czech and Slovak peoples will never be reconciled with this regime. They will fight to change it and will discover the appropriate forms for the struggle, which is waged in the interests of the peoples of all the socialist countries, including the Soviet Union.

As delegates to the Fourteenth Party Congress of the Czechoslovak Communist Party who are still able to express our opinions freely, we refuse to recognize the legality of either the Congress now being organized or the present regime. We see the only solution to the present crisis as the institution of fundamental democratic reforms that will open the way for our citizens to participate in the decisions that affect our society and to establish the democratic socialism toward which the "Prague Spring" of 1968 was leading. We shall continue, together will all democrats and all who espouse the ideals of socialism in Czechoslovakia and throughout the world, to struggle for these aims.

May 1971

CONTRIBUTORS

Paul Barton has written several books on labor problems in Communist countries and is the AFL-CIO representative to Europe.

Zbigniew Byrski joined the Polish Communist Party in 1935. From 1947 to 1951 he was Polish Vice-Consul in Chicago. After that he worked for Polish radio and television and became their correspondent in Africa. He came to the United States in 1969.

Jacob S. Dreyer is a student of Soviet affairs whose articles have appeared in a number of political and scholarly journals.

Maurice Friedberg is professor of Slavic languages and literature at Indiana University, Bloomington, Indiana. He was formerly director of the Russian and East European Institute there.

Jerzy Giedroyc is the Editor of *Kultura* which is published in Paris.

Julius Jacobson is the editor of *New Politics*. Among his books is *The Negro and the American Labor Movement*.

Witold Jedlicki was graduated from the University of Warsaw in 1953 and taught in Poland from 1957-1962. One of the leading members of the Crooked Circle Club, he wrote a history of that group. He is a citizen of Israel.

Walter Kendal is the author of a history of the British Communist Party and an active trade unionist who edits *The Voice of the Unions*. He is presently teaching at Nuffield College, Oxford University.

Jacek Kuron was a lecturer at Warsaw University in 1964 when he was expelled from the Polish United Workers Party. Tried *in camera* in 1965, he was sentenced to three years in prison.

Wolfgang Leonhard is the author of a number of books on the Stalinist system, including the well known *Child of the Revolution*. He is currently teaching history at Yale University.

Karol Modzelewski was expelled from the Polish United Workers Party in 1964, when he was a lecturer at Warsaw University. Tried *in camera* in 1965 for writing a document calling for workers' democracy, he was sentenced to three and a half years in prison.

Vitezslav Pravda is the pseudonym of a Czech socialist participant in the 1968 events.

Ivan Svitak taught philosophy at Charles University in Prague until the Russian invasion. He was a leader of those intellectuals and students who fought most vigorously for socialist democracy. He has been deprived of his Czech citizenship by the Husak regime and now lives in California where he teaches at Chico State. His latest book is *The Czechoslovakian Experiment* published by Columbia University Press.